The Creative Thinker's Toolkit

Gerard Puccio, Ph.D.

PUBLISHED BY:

THE GREAT COURSES
Corporate Headquarters
4840 Westfields Boulevard, Suite 500
Chantilly, Virginia 20151-2299
Phone: 1-800-832-2412
Fax: 703-378-3819
www.thegreatcourses.com

Printed in the United States of America

Gerard Puccio, Ph.D.

Department Chair and Professor,
International Center for Studies in Creativity
Buffalo State—The State University
of New York

Professor Gerard Puccio is Department Chair and Professor at Buffalo State's International Center for Studies in Creativity, a unique academic department that offers the world's first and leading master of science degree in creativity. Professor Puccio holds a Ph.D. in Organizational Psychology from The University of Manchester in England.

Professor Puccio has written more than 50 articles, chapters, and books. He has coauthored three recent books—*The Innovative Team: Unleashing Creative Potential for Breakthrough Results*; *Creativity Rising: Creative Thinking and Creative Problem Solving in the 21st Century*; and *Creative Leadership: Skills That Drive Change*—and is under contract to write a new book on preparing students to join the innovation economy.

In recognition of his outstanding work as a scholar, Professor Puccio received The State University of New York's Research and Scholarship Award in 2004 and the Buffalo State President's Award for Excellence in Research, Scholarship, and Creativity in 2007.

Professor Puccio is an accomplished speaker and consultant; he has worked with major corporations, universities, and numerous school districts to deliver training programs and keynote speeches. Some of his clients include the British Broadcasting Corporation (BBC), Fisher-Price brands, Sun Life Financial, Blue Cross and Blue Shield, Kraft Foods, Coca-Cola, Rochester Institute of Technology, and Oklahoma State University. Recently, Professor Puccio was a featured speaker at TEDxGramercy on the topic of creative thinking as a life skill. He has delivered creativity workshops and presentations in such countries as France, England, Spain, Italy, Tanzania, Hong Kong, Singapore, the Dominican Republic, and Canada.

Professor Puccio's research interests include the identification of creative thinking preferences, person-environment fit, and the efficacy of creativity training. He is currently working on an impact study of a creative leadership training program at the BBC. ■

Table of Contents

INTRODUCTION

LECTURE GUIDES

Table of Contents

Table of Contents

The Creative Thinker's Toolkit

Scope:

The highest level of human thought is creativity. Rather than being a skill that is exclusive to a rare gifted few, it is a way of thinking and behaving that can be achieved by all. However, many see creativity as mysterious, intuitive, or strictly innate. To the contrary, creative thinking is a skill that can be examined, practiced, and deliberately developed.

Scientific study demonstrates that, like other skills, creative thinking can be enhanced. This course draws on the more than 60 years of research and practice in the field of creativity studies and creativity education. Research and practice has highlighted the programs, approaches, and tools that are most effective in moving creativity from a chance occurrence to a more predictable outcome. Additionally, lectures throughout this course make direct connections between deliberate creative methods used by great creators—such as Mozart, Spielberg, Picasso, Jobs, Angelou, Wright, Rowling, Edison—and learnable tools that can be applied to a range of creative challenges, from everyday to grand. By the end of this course, you will have acquired a toolkit of creative methods usable in a variety of contexts, from professional to personal, and across all disciplines, from more artistic endeavors to business applications.

The course follows the waves of research associated with the scientific study of creativity. The first three lectures explore what it means to be a creative person. The first lecture examines the importance of play, passion, and purpose as the necessary fuel to individual creativity. In this lecture, you are encouraged to apply your first tool, "yes and," in place of the more commonly used "yes but" reaction to new ideas. The second lecture examines how creativity is a natural human phenomenon, drawing on information from evolution that highlights the fact that our ability to creatively solve problems provides the human species with a necessary competitive advantage. The ability to think in lateral ways, being flexible in thought—as opposed to vertical thinking, which is digging deeper into the same line of reasoning—is essential to the generation of breakthrough ideas.

The third lecture takes a contemporary look at the creative person, shifting from identifying characteristics of highly creative people to looking at the different ways in which people express their creativity.

The next wave of investigation in the field of creativity explored whether creative thinking was teachable and trainable. The fourth lecture lays the foundation for the fundamental thinking skills that unleash imagination, known as divergent thinking, and those skills that help to improve the retention and development of the most promising options, referred to as convergent thinking. The effective balance between divergent thinking and convergent thinking is the heartbeat of the creative process. Lectures 5 and 6 delve deeply into these two skill areas, providing specific principles proven to enhance divergent and convergent thinking abilities.

The seventh lecture introduces the complete creative process and explores how individuals report different degrees of preference for the thinking associated with the four areas found in the universal creative process: clarify, ideate, develop, and implement. Lectures 8 through 19 move you sequentially through the stages of the creative process, adding a large set of tools designed to improve problem clarification, idea generation, solution development, and implementation planning. A range of tools, from basic to advanced, are provided for each step—tools that can be applied immediately, either when working alone or to help improve creative thinking in groups.

Creativity involves both the head and the heart. In Lecture 20, the emotional side of creativity is explored; without the right emotional attitude, the cognitive tools become rather limited. Emotions can be thought of as the internal climate for creativity. The next lecture identifies aspects of the external environment, both physical and psychological, that promote creative thinking. Whether a manager, parent, teacher, or someone who decides to exert influence, creative thinking is now considered a core leadership competence, and effective leadership, in turn, fosters an environment conducive for creative thinking (see Lecture 22).

Life is fraught with challenges, and thus, many consider creative thinking to be a life skill. As such, the ways in which you can apply the material from this course is limited only by your imagination. Lecture 23 provides strategies to overcome blocks that creative thinking learners might face in the future. The final lecture lays out six universal principles for making creative thinking a way of life. Many report that developing their creativity is a life-changing experience; the principles and tools taught in this course have the power to be transformative. ■

The Creative Person—Practice and Passion

Lecture 1

Creativity is not just about innate talent—what you come into the world with. In fact, research shows that innate talent is a weak predictor of creativity. Instead, creativity is a teachable and learnable skill that can be enhanced through practice and hard work. This course is about sharpening your creative thinking skills by giving you more tools and enhancing the mindset that acts as a lubricant for your creative thinking. Learning without application achieves the same end as ignorance, so you are encouraged to practice your creativity, and as a result, you will raise your creative ability.

Creativity Is a Skill

- Creativity is a skill like all other skills, and as such, it's something that we can practice and something that we can learn. What's slightly different about creativity is that it's a life skill. It's a skill that cuts across all areas of our lives.

- We're surrounded by creativity. Our world was constructed on human imagination. What we see, what we touch, what we interact with in our world were once ideas. They were once in someone's imagination. The buildings that surround us, the books we read, the music we listen to, the products we purchase, the services we use all came from human creativity. However, although we're surrounded by creativity, sometimes we really aren't very clear in terms of understanding how creativity happens.

- Perhaps the first to explore the meaning of creativity were the Greeks, who attributed their creativity to a muse. They felt that creativity must come from some outside source—that a breakthrough brilliant idea couldn't come from a human being. It must have come from the gods, and therefore, they believed creativity started at Mount Olympus.

- Creativity is an interesting area of research. It's been primarily undertaken by psychologists, and it had an interesting beginning. In fact, some of the scientific foundation for looking at creativity had its start during World War II, when psychologists studied Air Force pilots and their survival skills. Additionally, psychologists worked with spies at the Office of Strategic Services, looking at the kinds of skills that would predict survival out in the field.

- Psychologist J. P. Guilford discovered that when looking at these kinds of survival skills, it wasn't IQ that predicted survival; it was creativity, especially divergent thinking—the ability to see many options, to be able to create alternatives for yourself. This promoted survival and good problem-solving skills.

Misconceptions of Creativity

- **Fiction: Creativity results from innate talent.** The belief that creativity comes to a few special people is incorrect. The fact is that creativity is the result of hard work.

- The 10,000-hour rule—popularized by Malcolm Gladwell in his book *Outliers*, based on research by Benjamin Bloom and Anders Ericsson—states that it takes 10,000 hours in order to achieve mastery of a domain or task. It takes even more time to be creative.

- Harvard's Howard Gardner studied seven great creators—Freud, Einstein, Picasso, Stravinsky, Eliot, Graham, and Gandhi—and he observed a consistent pattern that, on average, it took 10 years before they came to their first major creative breakthrough, and it wasn't just practice that happened during this 10-year period. They experimented and explored; they failed and learned from their failure. They borrowed ideas, cross-fertilized, and revised their thinking.

- Benjamin Franklin was an inventor, businessman, and Founding Father. We could assume that he was born to be creative, but this is not so. Benjamin Franklin is an exemplar of how to deliberately develop one's creativity.

- To develop his creative writing skills, Benjamin Franklin began by studying his favorite articles in a popular British publication called *The Spectator*. Days later, he reconstructed the article in his own words, and then he compared his work to the original piece and corrected his faults. But he didn't stop there. He translated these favorite articles into rhyme and then from rhyme back to essay in his own words.

Benjamin Franklin (1706–1790), one of the Founding Fathers, is still recognized for his elegant writing.

- Geoffrey Colvin's book *Talent Is Overrated* gives a wonderful description of deliberate practice. The following is a description of some of the components of deliberate practice.

- The first attribute of deliberate practice is that it involves lots of repetition—and not things that are already comfortable to you, but always going a little further and trying something new. However, it's important not to do this during the performance because it's not effective.

- The next attribute of deliberate practice is to get a coach or a mentor—someone who knows that domain well, who can share strategies with you and provide details in terms of best practices that work.

- In addition, when dealing with deliberate practice, we need to have feedback continuously available to us so that we can correct what we're doing wrong, so that we're not practicing bad habits. This is crucial to deliberate practice.

- In his book *Creativity and Problem Solving at Work*, Tudor Rickards introduces a tool that can be used to deliberately practice creativity. When people are presented with a new idea, often the immediate reaction—especially when it's a novel, original idea—is "yes but …". This indicates that there's something terminally wrong with the idea.

- Instead, Rickards recommends using "yes and …". This helps to prevent premature judgment. When we say "yes and," we're suggesting that there's something good about the idea and that it can be improved.

- "Yes and" promotes more creative thinking. It encourages creative thinking to be applied to the idea to further refine and enhance it. It keeps creative momentum going forward.

- To apply this tool, you'll first have to become self-aware, recognizing when that reflexive "yes but" is coming up. Notice if and how often you use it; then, when you find that phrase coming up, redirect your thinking from "yes but" to "yes and" and then seek feedback. See how others respond to it. Empathize with them. See how they react differently to you when you say "yes and" versus "yes but."

- **Fiction: Creativity is about being different.** When someone says the phrase "Oh, that's creative" usually what is meant is "Wow, that's bizarre." The fact is that creativity is the ability to produce ideas that are both original and valuable. It's not about just being different; it's both. It's the union of what may feel like two opposites—novelty that has value.

- Creativity needs to be rooted in reality; it is not merely bizarre. When we develop ideas that are both new and useful, original and valuable, they can come in tangible forms and intangible forms. They can also occur at different levels. We might create for ourselves, solve our own problems, developing interesting things that are new and valuable for us, and that's perfectly fine.

- Sometimes we share our creativity with others and affect some group, such as our family. Sometimes our creativity impacts our organizations: We create new and valuable ideas that are adopted in our organizations. Then, some of us create new and valuable ideas that are adopted into society and impact all of humankind.

What Makes People Creative?

- In the field of creativity, there happens to be a lot of consensus on what makes people creative. Teresa Amabile from Harvard has a model that gets at the essence of what's required for someone to be creative.

- In her model, creative people have three overlapping attributes. Picture a Venn diagram. One of the circles—one of the components in this Venn diagram—she refers to as domain-relevant skills. This involves practice and expertise; we have to master our domain.

- However, if you've mastered your domain, you've been able to know what everyone else knows—to think like everyone else. How do you go beyond that? That's the second component. Amabile refers to this as creativity-relevant skills. This allows us to add to our domain, to create new knowledge.

- In creativity-relevant skills, we have cognitive skills—thinking skills—and attitudes that put us in a better position to challenge our domain and contribute to it in new ways. Throughout this course, we will practice using tools to enhance skills specific to thinking creatively.

- The third component is motivation. Amabile and others have discovered that there's a particular kind of motivation that predicts creativity: intrinsic motivation. This is the kind of motivation that comes from the inside. It's engaging in a task for the love of that task, for the reward that you get from merely doing the task itself.

- How do you know when you're intrinsically motivated? There are three indicators, known as the three Ps: play, passion, and purpose.
  - In your life, where do you play? Where do you show a childlike wonder? Where do you get lost in your curiosity? Where do you have fun?
  - What are you passionate about? What drives you? What gives you energy and gets you excited?
  - What is your purpose? What gives you meaning? What's your mission? What's your legacy? You could have more than one purpose.
- When you experience play, passion, and purpose, you get to that flow state—the optimal psychological experience where your creativity pours out of you and you lose the sense of time. There are no boundaries on your imagination. That's when you're going to be most creative.
- Creativity is like all other abilities, which implies that we all possess it to varying degrees. Research shows that whatever your level of ability is, it can be enhanced.

Suggested Reading

Brown, *Play*.

Colvin, *Talent Is Overrated.*

Rickards, *Creativity and Problem Solving at Work.*

Activities

Activity 1: "Yes And" Thinking

Recall that when faced with a less-than-perfect solution, it is helpful to use "yes and" thinking. This requires that you be self-aware, use empathy, and redirect your thinking.

How might you use "yes and" thinking in the following scenarios?

- You are planning an elaborate dinner on a strict budget. When the caterer suggests some delicious appetizers that would put you over budget, you say ....

- You and your coworkers have spent hours waiting for tech support to solve a problem, and you are about to miss an important deadline. One coworker says, "Let's ask for more time." You say ....

Think of a recent situation where you said "yes but ...". Now imagine that you replied using "yes and" thinking instead. What might have been your response, and how might that have changed the direction of the conversation?

Activity 2: Intrinsic Motivation

Take some time to respond thoughtfully to these questions from the closing of Lecture 1 about play, passion, and purpose. It might be helpful to fill in the diagram below with your responses.

- In my life, right now, where do I play?

- What am I passionate about?

- What is my purpose? (It's fine to have more than one.)

- Are there any commonalities among these areas? If so, what does that tell you about where your intrinsic motivation lies?

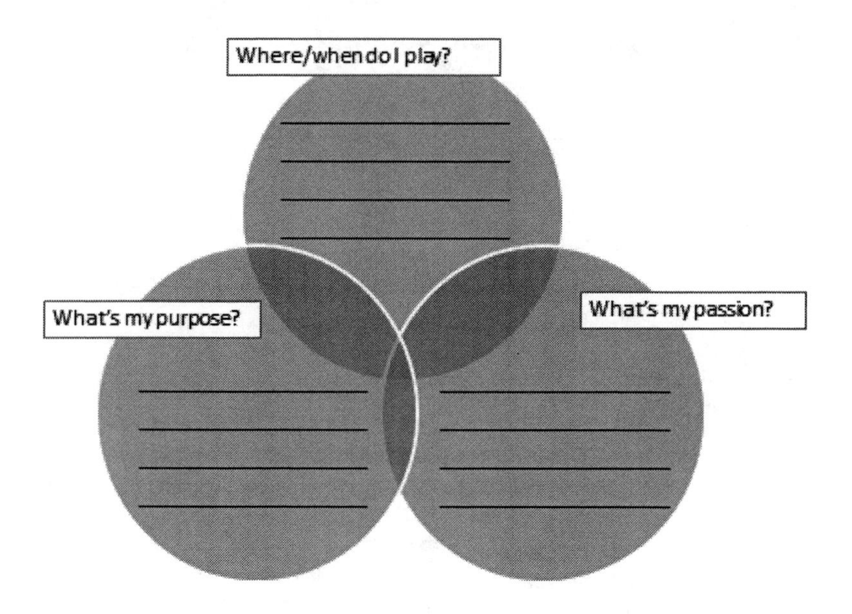
Where/when do I play?
What's my purpose?
What's my passion?

The Creative Person—Practice and Passion
Lecture 1—Transcript

Wolfgang Amadeus Mozart. Mozart. The quintessential creative genius. Born to be creative, right? Wrong. Let's begin by looking at Mozart's famous resume. He began composing music at age five, incredibly impressive. Public performances on violin and piano started at age eight. At 17, still a teenager, he was appointed court musician in Salzburg. Over his career, he produced more than 600 compositions, and to add to his legend, he died mysteriously at the age of 35, a child prodigy; someone born to create; gifted with some rare, special, innate talent. As radio host, Paul Harvey would say, "and here's the rest of the story."

You see, Mozart had a domineering father, Leopold Mozart, who wrote the book on violin instruction. It was published, in fact, the same year Wolfgang was born. In a way, Leopold had a learning laboratory, his son. And he was able to test his theories on instruction with his young son. In fact, he began Wolfgang at the age of three on an intensive training program. When you examine Wolfgang's early work, they're not considered to be terribly monumental. And when you look closely at this early work, as scholars have, you see that Leopold had a heavy hand in revising young Mozart's earliest compositions. Many consider his first masterpiece to be the Piano Concerto #9, written when he was 21. Young, to be sure, but this was already his 271st composition. So his first breakthrough came roughly 40% of the way into his lifetime output of some 600 compositions. His best work, according to critics, was produced while in Vienna, just before his premature death at the age of 35.

Why did I share this story with you? I want to suggest that creativity is not just about innate talent—what you come into the world with. In fact, research shows that innate talent is a weak predictor of creativity. Instead, creativity is a teachable and learnable skill that can be enhanced through practice and through hard work. I don't believe this view diminishes Mozart's stature at all as a creative genius. In fact, in some ways I think it makes it even more impressive, even more special to recognize that it just didn't come automatically to him because he had some gift that he brought with him into the world, but that it came through dedication, and hard work, and through years of practice.

This course is about proven techniques. It draws from 60 years of practice, proven through research and examination of high creatives. Let me ask you a question; let me pause to have you reflect about your own experiences. Have you ever played a musical instrument? Or, perhaps, you still do. Have you been dedicated to a sport or a hobby? In these areas, how do you develop mastery? Think back to your past experience. How did you develop proficiency in these areas? When I posed this question to audiences I work with, almost always the first response I hear is practice, practice, practice. Beyond that, we also need to engage in learning. We look to instructors to give us strategies, to give us tips so that we can be more proficient in that particular area. And then, also, audiences often say "Well, we also need feedback." We need feedback from others to help us to know what's working, what's not working.

Here's the point; creativity is a skill. Creativity is a skill like all other skills, and as such, it's something that we can practice and something that we can learn. Now, what's slightly different about creativity is that it's a life skill; it's a skill that cuts across all areas of our lives. Benjamin Franklin said it well when he said, "To cease to think creatively is but little different from ceasing to live."

What you'll learn in this course will be applicable, both in your professional life, as well your personal life. And in terms of your professional life, creativity cuts across all disciplines, all interests, all careers—managers, engineers, scientists, artists, lawyers, nurses, doctors. In our professions we're often called on to solve problems that have no easy answer, no immediate answer that we can grab a hold of, and we're forced to discover answers, to discover solutions. In such situations, we need to rely on our creative thinking.

But, what is creativity? Let's take a closer look. We're literally surrounded by creativity. Our world was constructed on human imagination. What we see, what we touch, what we interact with in our world were once ideas. They were once in someone's imagination. The buildings that surround us, the books that we read, the music we listen to, the products we purchase, the services we use all came from human creativity. But although we're surrounded by creativity, sometimes we really aren't very clear in terms of understanding how creativity happens.

Perhaps the first to explore the meaning of creativity were the Greeks. The Greeks attributed our creativity to a muse. They felt that creativity must come from some outside source, that a breakthrough brilliant idea couldn't come from a human being; it must have come from the gods, and therefore, they believed creativity started at Mount Olympus, outside of us. In some ways, this still shows up today—that bolt of lightning. Lightning strikes, and then we're creative. It comes from some outside source or force. But how do you encourage lightning to strike you, not just once, but every day? This course aims to put lightning in a bottle, to move creativity from a chance occurrence to something that we can do on demand. This course is based on the explicit study of all aspects of creativity, from beginning steps to finished achievements.

Creativity is an interesting area of research. It's been primarily undertaken by psychologists, and it had an interesting beginning. In fact, some of the scientific foundations for looking at creativity had its start during World War II, when psychologists studied Air Force pilots and their survival skills, and psychologists worked with spies at the Office of Strategic Services and looked at the kinds of skills that would predict survival out in the field. Psychologists like J.P. Guilford, who discovered that when they looked at these kinds of survival skills, it wasn't IQ that predicted survival, but it was creativity, especially divergent thinking. The ability to see many options, to be able to create alternatives for yourself. This promoted survival, and it promoted good problem solving skills.

This course draws on this more than 60 years of scientific research, and not just from psychology, but we'll also draw from business and education as well. So we know some things about creativity, and we know that the science often challenges popular conceptions, or perhaps better said, misconceptions, of creativity. Let's review some of these and distinguish fiction from fact. Fiction: Creativity results from innate talent. The Mozart story I shared with you—the rest of the story—challenges this belief that creativity comes to a few special people. The fact is, creativity is the result of hard work. Perhaps you've heard of the 10,000 hour rule, that it takes 10,000 hours in order to achieve mastery of a domain or an activity.

This was popularized by Malcolm Gladwell in his book *Outliers*, based on research by Benjamin Bloom and Anders Ericsson. Well, get this. It takes 10,000 hours to master a domain, a practice, or a task. It takes even more time to be creative. Howard Gardner, from Harvard, studied seven great creators—Freud, Einstein, Picasso, Stravinsky, Eliot, Graham, and Gandhi—and what he observed was a consistent pattern that, on average, it took 10 years before they came to their first major creative breakthrough. And it wasn't just practice that happened during this 10-year period. No, they experimented, and they explored. They failed, and they learned from their failure. They borrowed ideas, and they cross-fertilized, and they revised their thinking. This is true for Mozart as well. It took him, in fact, more than 10 years. Remember, he began composing at age 5, and his first breakthrough came at age 21.

So, what does it look like to develop your creativity? Let's return to Benjamin Franklin; I quoted Benjamin Franklin earlier. Inventor, business man, founding father, we could assume someone, again, who was born to be creative, but not so. I think Benjamin Franklin is an exemplar of how to deliberately develop one's creativity. Let me give you an example. This is the process he would go through to develop his creative writing skills. He began by studying his favorite articles in a popular British publication called *The Spectator*. Days later, he reconstructed the article in his own words, and then he compared his work to the original piece and corrected his faults. But he didn't stop there. He took these favorite articles, and he translated them into rhyme, and then from rhyme back to essay in his own words. I think it was this kind of practice that was the origin of catchy sayings like "Early to bed and early to rise makes a man healthy, wealthy, and wise."

So what does deliberate practice mean? Let's talk about deliberate practice; picture three concentric circles, a small circle in the center. We'll call this our comfort zone. The next ring out is the learning zone, and then, the third ring, the furthest ring out is the panic zone. Now, Steve Jobs delivered one of the most eloquent business speeches ever when he introduced the iPhone. He did this without PowerPoint or notes. He seemed completely at ease. This is a great example of what it looks like when someone is in the comfort zone.

But what is it like when you get outside of your comfort zone? How does that look? How does that feel? Let's try this out. Do this with me, if you can. Fold your arms in front of you as you would naturally, and note which forearm you have on top. I have my left forearm on top. Now, take them apart and fold them together with the opposite forearm on top. Now, let's do that again. The first time I had you fold your arms the natural way, you probably didn't have to think about it. It was comfortable. It was natural. It took little energy to consider how your arms were going to go together. That's what it feels like when you're in your comfort zone. In some ways, it's so comfortable it's unconscious. Now the second time, when you switched your arms from the first position to the second position, how did that feel? It felt a little uncomfortable. Perhaps you had to think about it. This is what most audiences tell me. That's what it's like when you go from the comfort zone to the learning zone. It feels a little awkward; it stretches us; we sort of become more aware of what we're doing.

How about the panic zone? What does that feel like? Well generally, when we're in the panic zone, we know it because we're having a strong physical reaction, such as butterflies in your stomach. Now, guess what. We can go back to Steve Jobs to find an example of what it looks like when someone is in the panic zone. In one of his first television interviews, before the interview, when he's getting prepared, as he's talking to the stage crew, he asks for where the nearest bathroom is, and they thought he was joking, and he said "No, seriously. I may get sick." He was visibly anxious, so much so he was on the verge of being sick. How did Steve Jobs move from being in the panic zone to his iPhone speech—the comfort zone? My guess is deliberate practice.

So, what is deliberate practice? What are the components of deliberate practice? Geoffrey Colvin's book, *Talent is Overrated*, gives a wonderful description of this. I recommend the book. Here are some of the components of deliberate practice. First of all, it involves lots of repetition. Repeating, over and over again, and not things that are already comfortable to you, but always going a little further. Trying something new. Pushing the envelope.

And when you engage in repetitious practice, it's important not to do this during the performance. I love to golf, and because I love to golf, I enjoy playing a round of golf. But when I'm playing a round of golf, that's not the best time to practice. I can't drop 30 balls in the sand trap and stop and hit them out; I can only do that on the golf range. That's where you can engage in practice over and over and over again. It's not effective to try to practice in the midst of a performance. That's the first attribute of deliberate practice.

The next is to get a coach or a mentor, someone who knows that domain well, who can share with you, can share strategies, can provide details in terms of best practices that work. Also, in terms of deliberate practice, we need to have feedback continuously available to us so that we can correct what we're doing wrong, so we're not practicing bad habits. This is crucial to deliberate practice. But how do you deliberately practice creativity; how will we do that in this course? Let's try a tool, a creativity tool. This was a tool introduced to me by Tudor Rickards, one of my mentors. When people are presented with a new idea, often the immediate reaction, especially when it's a novel idea, it's a bit original, is "Yes, but…" Have you had that experience? Have you been on the receiving end of a "Yes, but…"? What "Yes, but…" indicates is that there's something terminally wrong with the idea. Instead, Rickards recommends using "Yes, and…" this helps to prevent premature judgment. When we say "Yes, and…" we're suggesting there's something good about the idea and that it can be improved.

Here's an example Tudor gives in his book. Have you ever gone on a long trip and had a fly trapped in the car? If you have, then you know how annoying this could be. So, someone generates a new idea. Flypaper in a car. What's the response? Well, generally, because this is such a novel idea, the response would be "Yes, but…" "Yes, but…it will stick to passengers." Let's change that around; let's replace that with "Yes, and…" "Yes, and…if there were a way to design it so passengers never get stuck to the paper, it's even better."

Now, what's the difference here? "Yes, and…" promotes more creative thinking. It encourages creative thinking to be applied to the idea to further refine it an enhance it. It keeps creative momentum going forward. I want to encourage you to apply this tool. In order to do this, you'll first have to become self-aware. Recognize when that reflexive "Yes, but…" is coming up. Notice if and how often you use it, and then, when you find that phrase coming up, redirect. Redirect your thinking from the "Yes, but…" to the "Yes, and…," and then seek feedback. See how that works with others, how others respond to it. Empathize with them. See how they react differently to you when you say "Yes, and…" versus "Yes, but…"

Let's move to the next misconception of creativity. Fiction. Creativity is about being different. Have you heard the phrase, "Oh, that's creative." When you hear it said like that, usually what someone is trying to communicate is, "Wow, that's bizarre." The fact is, creativity is the ability to produce ideas that are both original and valuable. It's not about just being different; It's both. It's the union of what may feel like two opposites—novelty that has value. You see, creativity needs to be rooted in reality, not merely bizarre. When it's rooted in reality, when we develop ideas that are both new and useful, original and valuable, they can come in tangible forms, and they can come in intangible forms. They can also occur at different levels. We might create for ourselves, solve our own problems, developing interesting things that are new and valuable for us, and that's perfectly fine. Sometimes we share our creativity with others. we affect some group, like our family. Sometimes our creativity impacts our organizations. We create new and valuable ideas that are adopted in our organizations. And then some of us create new and valuable ideas that are adopted into society and impact all of humankind.

But how does this happen? What makes people creative? There happens to be a lot of consensus on this in the field of creativity. Teresa Amabile from Harvard has a model that does a very nice job in getting at the essence of what's required for someone to be creative. In her model, creative people have three overlapping attributes; I'm going to describe these. Think about how they apply to you. Picture a Venn diagram. One of the circles, one of the components in this Venn diagram, she refers to as domain-relevant skills. We've talked about practice and expertise and how we have to master our domain, and what it takes to master our domain. But, if you've mastered your domain, what you've been able to do is to know what everyone else knows, to be able to think like everyone else. How do you go beyond that? That's the second component. Amabile refers to this as creativity-relevant skills. This allows us to add to our domain, to create new knowledge.

In creativity-relevant skills, we have cognitive skills—thinking skills—and attitudes that put us in a better position to challenge our domain and contribute to it in new ways. Throughout this course, we will practice using tools to enhance skills specific to thinking creatively. That's the main subject of this course. And as we go through tools in this course, I ask you to practice a creative attitude, an open-mindedness. You will see a range of tools. From those, there are some that are simple, easy to deploy. Others will be more complex. They all have value. I want to give you lots of choices, and after all the choices, then you can look and see which ones you want to add to your tool kit. You see, having choices is crucial to the creative process. Try them out; practice with them; and decide which ones you wish to retain. In the initial lectures, we'll present some basic tools. And from Lecture 8 onward, you can see more complex tools coming in the form of a universal creative process. You can skip around in these lectures, focusing on whichever aspects of creative problem solving and this universal creative process you find most immediately helpful to you.

So we've looked at domain skills, that's one component of a creative person, and creativity skills, like the skills you'll learn in this course. There's a third component—motivation. Amabile and others have discovered that there's a particular kind of motivation that predicts creativity. Intrinsic motivation. This is the kind of motivation that comes from the inside. It's engaging in a task for the love of that task, for the reward that you get from merely doing the task itself, the self-reward that you get.

How do you know when you're intrinsically motivated? There are three indicators, the three Ps—play, passion, and purpose. Let me describe these to you in a way that gets you to think about these three Ps relative to your own life. Play, in your life right now, where do you play? Where do you show a childlike wonder? Where do you get lost in your curiosity? Where do you have fun? How about passion? What are you passionate about? What drives you? What gives you energy and gets you excited? And finally, purpose, what is your purpose? What gives you meaning? What's your mission? What's your legacy? And you could have more than one purpose. You see, when you experience play, passion, and purpose, you get to that flow state, the optimal psychological experience, where your creativity pours out of you, and you lose the sense of time. There are no boundaries on your imagination. That's when you're going to be most creative.

Let me share a story with you. This is a story I enjoy sharing for a number of reasons; one is, it really captures well these three Ps. Now, the other reason is I have a personal connection to the story. It takes place in Manchester, England, where I did my Ph.D., and the opening scene in the story takes place in the railway station in the city center of Manchester, where I often took the train from Manchester to London to visit my friends.

So, J.K. Rowling was in Manchester in 1990. She was about to take the train from Manchester to London, but the train was delayed, so she had an hour to stand on the platform, and she allowed her imagination to roam. And what came to her mind was the story of a wizardry school and a character, Harry Potter. She continued to think about that story. When the train arrived and she boarded it, she discovered, after she sat down, that she had no pen or pencil to capture her ideas. Now, J.K. Rowling is wickedly shy, so shy that she wouldn't ask anyone to borrow a pen or a pencil, so she used the next three to four hours on that train to allow her imagination to explore this story, to elaborate on it. When she returned to London that day, she raced home, and she had that flow experience. The story poured out of her; she got lost in time; she got lost in the story.

You might say, that's the end of the story, but it's not. It took seven more years before that first book came out, and despite setbacks, she persisted. Her mother's death, divorce, the fact that she was a single mother living on welfare, she persisted through this. And I would suggest it was the three Ps that ensured her success through these difficult times. And as a result, it led to one of the best-selling book series of all time, more than 400 million sales worldwide. But I would also suggest it took practice. The other P we talked about. You see, she began writing as a child; this wasn't the first story she had written. She had written many stories beforehand.

So here's what I want you to remember. Creativity is like all other abilities, which implies we all possess it to varying degrees, and whatever your level of ability is, it can be enhanced; there's research that shows that.

Let me close with a story from Stephen Covey, a story about two lumberjacks who are in a competition. It's the finals. Two very different lumberjacks. One is a young, strapping lumberjack. The other one is a veteran. In the competition, in the finals, they have to cut wood to see who could cut the most. During the competition, the young lumberjack occasionally looks over at the older lumberjack and he sees him sitting, and he thinks "Oh, I must be beating him. Look at this poor old man. He's tired." At the end of the competition, they count up the wood that had been cut, and it turns out that the older, veteran lumberjack had won. The young lumberjack runs to him and says, "How could this be? Every time I looked over, you seemed tired. You were sitting down. You were hunched over." And he said, "No, you're mistaken. I wasn't resting. When you happened to look at me, I was taking a break to sharpen my saw and to lubricate it so I could be more effective."

This course is about sharpening your creative thinking skills, your saw, if you will, by giving you more tools. Tools like, "Yes, and…," and enhancing the mindset that acts as a lubricant for your creative thinking. Learning without application achieves the same end as ignorance. I'll be asking you to practice your creativity, and I'm confident—I know—that, as a result, you will raise your creative ability.

Lateral Thinking Is a Survival Skill

Lecture 2

Humans have evolved by getting creative and by communicating and working together. In general, working together trumps individual creativity. As you will learn in this lecture, provocation encourages us to find a new pathway. It encourages playful thinking. When we force our minds to take a new neural path, we discover new connections. This path leads to creativity. There are many lateral-thinking tools that can help you start on this path to creativity.

Conformity and Creativity

- There are several benefits to conformity.
  - First, conformity lends to collaboration—solving problems together. You have a woolly mammoth and you need to take it down. Get some buddies.
  - Second, it aids in learning. We observe others; we watch what they do. We pick up what works for them, and then we use it ourselves.
  - Third, it forms culture, as in accepted norms, practices, morals, and rituals.
  - Finally, it saves us energy. When we're conforming, we're in our comfort zone, so we save energy. We don't have to think about what we're doing. We simply continue to do what we're already comfortable with.
- However, there's a downside to conformity: If that were all we ever did, there'd be no change and little growth. Conformity and creativity, a necessary paradox in our evolution, had to work together.

- Evolutionary psychologists say that we all have this internal tension between conformity and creativity and that people will vary in terms of the strength of their conformity bias.

- Those who are less likely to conform are more sensitive to the changing conditions of their environment, and as a result, they can spot opportunities. They're more likely to develop new solutions, adaptive responses to a changing environment.

- That's hugely valuable, but so is conformity, because as others see these new ideas, they learn. They replicate. They repeat. They imitate. In this way, these creative ideas get spread. A new paradigm is created. And then, the process repeats itself.

- Creativity was an important partner, alongside conformity, in human evolution. If we look back through history, even to prehumans, we can see problem solving. Prehumans found objects, such as sticks, that they used for tools.

- The first *Homo* species, *Homo habilis*, about 2.5 million years ago, had the first manufactured tool—the first purpose-built tool, called the flake tool. *Homo habilis* had a brain size that was roughly 50 percent that of modern humans.

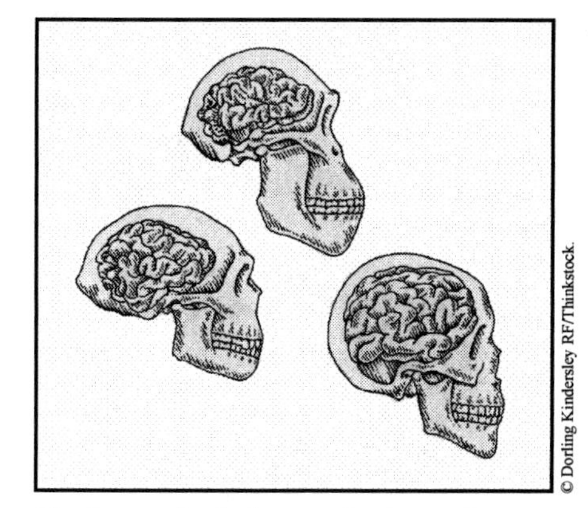

The human brain has evolved over time, developing the capacity for creativity.

- *Homo erectus* appeared about 1.8 million years ago, with a brain size that was roughly 75 percent that of modern human brains. They developed the hand axe, which took greater skill to create, manually and mentally.

- About 150,000 years ago, *Homo sapiens*, the modern human, appeared. Creativity continued to expand slowly with the appearance of *Homo sapiens*, and then about 40,000 years ago, something remarkable happened. There was a creative explosion. Suddenly, there were throwing weapons, body decorations and cave paintings, burial rituals, clothing, shelter, and so forth.

- Creative thinking is a survival skill. Some call it creative problem solving, and it helped early humans in a very functional way to survive in hostile environments. However, once we had the skill known as imagination, as it grew, as humans evolved, that imagination grew to be applied in other ways. We went from functional to aesthetic—from allowing us to survive to creating such things as art. And perhaps art depicting large animals contributed in some way to our survival as well.

- Brain size and development correlated with creativity. As our brains developed, we were able to generate more complex products as our brains got larger. However, humans don't have the biggest brains—elephants and some whales do—so it's not just size that makes a difference. It's greater information-processing capacity. Creativity is associated with mental flexibility and novel solutions.

- It's not just cognition, or thinking, that led to the creative explosion. We also needed the right attitude. We had the cognitive skills in place about 100,000 years ago, but we needed something else to enhance these thinking skills. And here we can look at play.

- The offspring of all mammals engage in some type of play. When you look at human play, young children engage in pretend play. It's supposition. This is crucial in our evolution. This developed an important attitude—the attitude of being able to suspend judgment. This allowed our imagination to roam freely.

Why People Say They're Not Creative

- It appears that humans were born to be creative. But many say, "I'm not creative." There seem to be two reasons why people say that. First, we mix up a distinction that's made in the literature of creativity between two different kinds of creativity: special talent versus self-actualized creativity, which is creativity in daily life. Sometimes it's referred to as "big-C" versus "little-c" creativity, or eminent superstar creativity versus everyday creativity.

- Everyday creativity is about reaching your creative potential. Creative problem solving is used to address everyday life. When people say, "I'm not creative," it's often because they're comparing themselves to the superstar eminent creators. But here's the truth: The same thought process that we use for everyday creativity is what's used in big-C creativity.

- The second reason why people say they're not creative is that we lose our imagination over time as we grow from children to adults, but it's something we can relearn, and we can turn to people like Edward de Bono.

- Some refer to Edward de Bono as "the father of creativity." He has written many books on the subject, especially around and focused on applied creativity. He makes a distinction between vertical thinking and lateral thinking. Vertical thinking is when you follow one line of thought. Lateral thinking is when you move in a different direction with your thinking; you're looking for a solution to a problem. Lateral thinking is the movement away from a pattern.

- De Bono created a tool whimsically called PO, which stands for provocative operation. Our brain creates patterns. We build neural networks. This increases the speed of our thinking, which can make us very efficient thinkers, except when it comes to creativity. Creativity requires, in a way, slowing down our thinking, looking at unexplored pathways.

- PO is a made-up word, like "suppose," but it's deliberately silly and playful sounding. It indicates movement—a shift, the backing off of judgment. The way it works is you create a provocative statement. It can be even illogical. POs are created by exaggeration, wishful thinking. It can even be outrageous.

- For example, consider the following statement: "PO schools had no teachers." You create a PO, and then you capture new ideas—new lines of thought that come from that provocation. What might this statement suggest? Well, the kids could be responsible for their own learning. Teachers might be replaced by project managers. You could have computer-assisted learning only.

Creativity Testing

- In the 21st century, many educational and business leaders put creativity, creative thinking, and creative problem solving at the top of the skills necessary for success, but do schools promote this kind of thinking, or do they focus mainly on vertical thinking, helping you to learn to think like everyone else?

- Some would suggest that schools are undermining creativity. Creativity is a crucial skill. We're born with it. But there seems to be a creativity crisis in America.

- A measure of creativity called the Torrance Test of Creative Thinking (TTCT) was used on nearly 300,000 students over a long period of time, between 1974 and 2008, and across all grade levels from kindergarten through grade 12, and it clearly showed a creativity loss over time.

- This creativity measure possesses open-ended tasks such as product improvement. You're presented with a product and you're asked to think of other ways that this product might be made more interesting or fun to play with. There's also a visual format in which you're presented with figures and you have to complete figures in an interesting way.

- The TTCT is focused on divergent thinking, which includes such skills as fluency, which is the ability to generate many responses when you're faced with a challenge; flexibility, which is the ability to generate different kinds of responses; originality, which is the ability to generate a response that's infrequent and novel; and elaboration, which is the ability to expound on one's thinking.

- When researchers looked at students over grade levels, they found that they increased in their ability to think fluently until third grade, and then it continuously dropped dramatically after fifth grade. When we look at the divergent thinking ability of originality, it increased up to about fifth grade, and then it suddenly dropped significantly thereafter. Creative attitudes such as curiosity and open-mindedness followed the same path.

- Creative thinking is considered a 21st-century skill and is seen as being crucial to be able to survive and be productive in times with rampant change, but perhaps education undermines it. Conformity pressures help to dilute it as well, and kids have less free time. While divergent thinking is a skill that's highly touted, it's rarely taught in schools.

- The TTCT is a predictor of adult success. People who score higher on the TTCT are more likely to be entrepreneurs, inventors, college presidents, authors, doctors, and so on. Childhood creativity measures like the TTCT are three times stronger predictors of lifetime creative achievement than childhood IQ.

- To reinvigorate your imagination, the first thing you can do is identify what you find intrinsically interesting—what intrinsically motivates you—and then pursue it. Encourage divergent thinking and idea generation. Don't worry about whether answers are right or wrong. Ask yourself open-ended questions, and use tools to encourage lateral thinking.

- Edward de Bono created many lateral-thinking tools. The one that he says is the easiest to apply is random word, which involves using a random word to shift your thinking to solve a problem. It's important that the word be randomly selected. It forces new thinking, because it kind of creates a provocation. Injecting a random word into your thinking requires thoughts to take a new neural pathway.

Suggested Reading

Amabile, *Growing Up Creative.*

Wagner, *Creating Innovators.*

———, *The Global Achievement Gap.*

Activities

Activity 1: Random Words
Use the random word provided to generate unusual ideas for the situation.

- Random word: tire — Situation: studying for an exam
- Random word: stove — Situation: planting a garden
- Random word: pillow — Situation: debugging a computer
- Random word: shampoo — Situation: planning for retirement
- Random word: necklace — Situation: preventing an asteroid from hitting the Earth

Activity 2: PO Statements
Use PO to provoke your childlike ability to pretend. For example, "PO people can fly." You could think of PO as a part of the word "supPOse," as in "Suppose things were different." Try creating five or more statements starting with PO. Choose one and expand on what new insights or ideas you get from that provocative statement.

Lateral Thinking is a Survival Skill

Lecture 2—Transcript

Imagine, imagine a tiger; create in your mind the image of a tiger, and try to see it in as much detail as you can. Let me help you out. On average, tigers grow to about 11 feet. They weigh roughly 600 pounds. Of the felines on planet Earth, they have the longest canine teeth, growing between 2½ and 3 inches in length. They have stripes for camouflage. Now imagine you've just come face-to-face with a very unhappy tiger. Well, this is the challenge. Most of us don't have tigers around in daily life, so we tend to fall back on instincts—fight, flight, or freeze. Not great options. We're too slow to run away, not strong enough to fight, and probably not going to blend in enough to prevent the tiger from seeing us.

So why did I pick a tiger? Humans emerged on Earth roughly 2½ million years ago. The first Homo-species, that is. Tigers arrived about two million years ago. How did we survive with such predators around us, with such threats in our environment? We're pretty frail in comparison to a tiger and other kinds of predators, so what competitive advantage allowed us to evolve?

But let's suppose you live near a tiger. The tiger is no longer a surprise. Now you can decide what the problem is and what to do. Now you have time to get creative, and you can work with others. You can plan. You can build walls, create traps, weapons, and whatever happens, the tiger no longer has the advantage. You have the advantage. You see, this is what humans have always done. And notice there are two things going on here. We get creative, and we communicate and work together. And working together generally trumps individual creativity. Any shared plan about the tiger is better than no plan.

So, one of the reasons why we were successful in evolving was conformity. Let's look at conformity. Here's the classic study by Solomon Asch. Now, imagine you are in this study. I'll describe it as if you're a participant. So, a group of students are brought into a room. The researcher presents them with four lines. We'll label those lines A, B, C, and D. You're asked a very simple question. Which of the lines is the shortest? Each person is asked to report out loud the line he or she believes is the shortest. Now, you look at these lines, and it's obvious to you that Line C is the shortest, and in fact, it is the shortest. But what you don't know is that every other person in that room is working with the researcher. So, as they respond to the researcher, before they get to you, each person before you says "Line A." Now, what do you do? Everyone else has said "A," but you know Line C is the shortest. Well, if you're like most people, in fact, 75% of the participants in this research study, you're likely to say "Line A."

So how is this an advantage, giving the wrong answer, going along with the crowd? There are benefits to conformity. Number one, conformity lends to collaboration—solving problems together. You have a woolly mammoth and you need to take it down? Get some buddies. Second, it aids in learning. We observe others; we watch what they do; we pick up what works for them, and then we use it ourselves. Third, it forms culture, as in accepted norms, practices, morals, and rituals. And finally, it saves us energy. Remember folding your arms? When we're conforming, we're in our comfort zone, so we save energy; we don't have to think about what we're doing. We simply continue to do what we're already comfortable with.

But we know there's a down side to conformity, that if that's all we ever did, there'd be no change and little growth. So I would suggest that conformity and creativity, a necessary paradox, if you will, a necessary paradox in our evolution, that they had to work together. Let's examine this.

Evolutionary psychologists say that we all have this internal tension between conformity and creativity, and that people will vary in terms of the strength of their conformity bias. For some, it's stronger. For others, less so. For those who are less likely to conform, they're more sensitive to the changing conditions of their environment, and as a result, they can spot opportunities. They're more likely to develop new solutions, adaptive responses, to a changing environment. Now that's hugely valuable, but so is conformity, because as others see these new ideas, they learn; they replicate; they repeat; they imitate. And in this way, the ideas, these creative ideas, get spread. A new paradigm is created. And then guess what, the process repeats itself.

So I believe creativity was an important partner, alongside conformity, in human evolution. Let's examine the case for this. If we look back through history, even to pre-humans, we can see problem solving. Pre-humans found objects, such as sticks, that they used for tools. Now, with the first Homo-species, Homo habilis, about 2.5 million years ago, we had the first manufactured tool. The first purpose-built tool called the flake tool. Homo habilis had the brain size roughly 50% that of modern humans. This tool, this flake tool, created by Homo habilis, had a product life cycle of about one million years. Now, we're going to skip a few human species and go to Homo erectus. They appeared about 1.8 million years ago, with the brain size roughly 75% of modern humans. They developed the hand axe. The hand axe took greater skill to create, manually and mentally, and the product life cycle for the hand axe was roughly a million years also.

Flash forward, about 150,000 years ago, Homo sapiens appeared, the modern human. Creativity continued to expand slowly with the appearance of Homo sapiens, and then about 40,000 years ago, something remarkable happened. There was a creative explosion. Suddenly, there were throwing weapons, body decorations, and cave paintings, and burial rituals, and clothing, and shelter, and so forth. And as you can imagine, the product life cycle of these creative products was a lot shorter than the hand axe and the flake tool.

So what conclusions can we draw from this quick review of evolution? First, I would suggest that creative thinking is a survival skill. Some call it creative problem solving, and that creative problem solving helped early humans in a very functional way to survive in hostile environments. But, once we had that skill, once we had imagination, and as it grew, as humans evolved, that imagination grew to be applied in other ways, so we went from functional to aesthetic; from allowing us to survive, to creating such things as art. And, who knows, perhaps it's possible that art depicting large animals contributed in some way to our survival as well.

Second conclusion from this review of evolution, brain size and development correlated with creativity. As our brains developed, we were able to generate more complex products as our brains got larger. But humans don't have the biggest brains. That goes to elephants and some whales. So it's not just size that makes a difference; it's greater information processing capacity. You see, our brains have a high cell density in the cortex, plus higher conduction velocity and relatively smaller distances between neurons. That means we process information extremely efficiently, and it is this structure and analysis of the evolution of our brain that led Roth and Dicke to conclude that humans are the most intelligent animal on our planet. Now, what's interesting is how they define intelligence. They define intelligence as the degree of mental or behavioral flexibility resulting in novel solutions, sounds a lot like creativity to me—mental flexibility, novel solutions.

Here's the third conclusion from reviewing evolution. It's not just cognition, not just thinking that led to the creative explosion. We needed something else. We needed the right attitude. You see, we had the cognitive skills in place about 100,000 years ago, but we needed something else to enhance these thinking skills, and here we can look at play. When you look at the play of all mammals, their offspring engage in some form of play. This is true of all mammals. When you look at cats, for example, they stalk, and they pounce, and they wrestle, and this kind of play prepares them for survival later, and it's argued it's the same for humans. And when you look at human play, what kind of play do young children engage in? It's pretend play. It's supposition. This is crucial in our evolution. This developed an important attitude, the attitude of being able to suspend judgment, to believe that a banana could be a telephone. This allowed our imagination to roam freely.

So I say you were born to be creative. But many say, "I'm not creative." When I tell people I teach creativity, I'm a professor of creativity, I study the science of creativity, often the immediate response is, "I'm not creative." I think there are two reasons why people say that. First, we mix up a distinction that's made in the literature of creativity between two different kinds of creativity—special talent versus self-actualized creativity, or creativity in daily life. Sometimes it's referred to as Big-C versus Little-C creativity, or eminent superstar creativity versus everyday creativity.

Everyday creativity is about reaching your creative potential, creative problem solving used to address everyday life, such as an example from when I was raising my children when they were young. My youngest son, Anthony, had a difficult time staying in bed. When he was a toddler, we would put him to bed, and he would get out of bed and come downstairs, or he'd call out to us, and it really broke up our evening. It was fairly stressful. So I began to use my imagination. I began to actively, creatively solve this problem, and this is the solution that I came up with. It involved three pennies. I presented Anthony with three pennies, and I said, "Anthony, it's fine. You can call us back into your room, but every time you do that, you have to give us a penny. You have to spend a penny. And when you've used up all three pennies, Mom and Dad can't come back anymore." Well, it worked like a charm. We put him to bed, I would give him his three pennies, and within a few minutes he'd call out, "I have a penny!" And I'd come in and I'd spend a minute with him; that was part of the rule as well. Afterwards, after a minute, I would take the penny and I'd go away. And almost every night, after that first penny, he'd fall asleep. You see, he didn't want to spend the other two pennies. He wanted to keep them in reserve.

You see, when people say, "I'm not creative," it's often because they're comparing themselves to the superstar eminent creators, but here's the truth, the same thought process that we use for everyday creativity is what's used in Big-C creativity.

Here's the second reason why I think people say they're not creative. We lose our imagination over time as we grow from children to adults, but it's something we can relearn. And we can turn to people like Edward de Bono. Some refer to Edward de Bono as the father of creativity. He's written many books on the subject, especially around and focused on applied creativity. He makes a distinction between vertical thinking and lateral thinking. Vertical thinking is when you dig the hole deeper. You follow one line of thought. Lateral thinking is when you move in a different direction. You go laterally. You dig different holes. So, you're hunting for treasure. You're looking for a solution to a problem. One way to go about it is to dig the hole deeper, and deeper, and deeper, hoping that you find the treasure or your solution. The other way to go about this is to think laterally. You dig one hole; you don't find the treasure; you don't find your solution; you dig a second hole. And then you move laterally again, and again, and again until you find the treasure or you find your solution.

Jokes work because of lateral thinking. When someone's telling a joke, they're moving you along a vertical line of thought, and when they get to the punch line, suddenly there's a lateral shift. So, lateral thinking is the movement away from a pattern, like the major shifts in tools from flake tools, to hand axe, to the creative explosion. De Bono created a tool whimsically called PO, which stands for Provocative Operation. You see, our brain creates patterns. We build neural networks. This increases the speed of our thinking, which can make us very efficient thinkers, except when it comes to creativity. Creativity requires, in a way, slowing our thinking down, looking at unexplored pathways. In fact, highly divergent thinkers are more flexible in terms of how they use their neural pathways; they're less dense and less rigid. It allows them to meander, for their thoughts to cast a very wide net.

Provocation encourages us to find a new pathway. It encourages playful thinking. Here's an analogy. If you were forced to take a different route from home to work, there's a detour; you're likely to discover new things because you're going on a new path, places that you hadn't seen before, restaurants that you hadn't seen. The mind works the same way. When we force our minds to take a new neural path, we discover new connections. So PO, this tool developed by de Bono, it's a made-up word, like "suppose," but it's deliberately silly and playful sounding. It indicates movement, a shift, the backing off of judgment. According to de Bono, he was inspired by the words "hypothesis," "possible," "poetry," and "suppose."

So, the way it works is you create a provocative statement; it can be even illogical. POs are created by exaggeration, wishful thinking. It can even be outrageous. Here are some examples of some PO statements. PO cups were made from ice. PO cars had square wheels. PO planes landed upside down. You create a PO, and then you capture new ideas, new lines of thought that come from that provocation. PO planes land upside down. What might that suggest? Well, it might suggest moving the pilot. Here's an example from de Bono. They were working on an issue related to water pollution, and the PO that was created was, PO the factory was downstream from itself. Well, that led to a new idea. The discharge from the plant would be upstream, intake downstream. This would lead to less pollution in that the plant wouldn't want to take in its own waste.

Here's another PO. PO schools had no teachers. Hmm, what might that suggest? Well, the kids could be responsible for their own learning. Teachers might be replaced by project managers. You could have computer-assisted learning only. I want to encourage you to practice provocation. Try this PO tool. It will help you to get back to that playful, childlike way of thinking. Start with yourself, then try it out with the family and friends, and then perhaps try it at work.

In the 21st century, many educational and business leaders put creativity, creative thinking, and creative problem solving at the top of the skills necessary for success. But do schools promote this kind of thinking, or do they focus mainly on vertical thinking, helping you to learn to think like everyone else? Some would suggest that the schools are undermining creativity. It's a crucial skill. We're born with it. But, there seems to be a creativity crisis in America. And there was study done that provides some evidence to support this, a study using a measure of creativity. In fact, there are some 200-plus measures of creativity out in the field of creativity. This measure is called the Torrance Test of Creative Thinking, and it was used on nearly 300,000 students. And it was used over a long period of time, between 1974 and 2008, and across all grade levels from K to 12, and what it clearly showed was a creativity loss over time.

Now, let's look at the TTCT, just briefly. How does this creativity measure work? Well, it possesses open-ended tasks such as a product improvement. You're presented with a product and you're asked to think of other ways that this product might be made more interesting or fun to play with. There's also a visual format in which you're presented with figures, and you have to complete figures in an interesting way. Now, the TTCT is focused on divergent thinking. It's trying to measure divergence. Remember the predictor of survival for pilots and spies? Divergent thinking includes such skills as fluency, which is the ability to generate many responses when you're faced with a challenge. Flexibility, which is the ability to generate different kinds of responses, not just one single thought or many thoughts along one single track, but a diverse array of thoughts. Then you have originality, which is the ability to generate a response that's infrequent, that's novel, that others hadn't thought of. And then, also, elaboration, which is the ability to expound on one's thinking, to expand and describe a concept.

Let's try it out. Pick an object in your environment. Look around and see how many different uses you can imagine for that object. Let me give you an example, a paper clip. A paper clip can hold papers, or it might be used as jewelry, an emergency clothes fastener, a tool to restart electronics, a temporary keychain, a lock pick, a scraping tool, to create sculptures, to teach math, etcetera. That's a divergent thinking task, and the better you are at responding in numerous ways, in flexible ways, in original ways, and being able to elaborate on your ideas, the greater your skill at divergent thinking. Hopefully you get the idea. For fun, you might want to try that out with a partner.

Let's go back to the study. Fluency on tasks like this, when they looked at students over grade levels, they found that they increased in their ability to think fluently until third grade, and then it continuously dropped dramatically after fifth grade. When we look at the divergent thinking ability of originality, it, too, increased up to about fifth grade, and then suddenly dropped significantly thereafter. Creative attitudes, such as curiosity and open-mindedness, followed the exact same path. I think this creates kind of a perfect storm. Creative thinking is considered a 21st-century skill, seen as being crucial to be able to survive and be productive in times with rampant change, but perhaps education undermines it. Conformity pressures help to dilute it as well, and kids have less free time. In schools, Mark Runco, who is a researcher at the University of Georgia working at the Torrance Center for Creative Thinking, says that schools primarily focus on convergent thinking and pay much less attention to divergent thinking. Again, I think this creates kind of a perfect storm. While this is a skill that's highly touted, it's rarely taught in schools.

You might say "So what?" "Who cares?" What's the big deal?" Well, obviously if you have children in schools, this might be a concern, or if you know children in schools. You see, the TTCT, the Torrance Test of Creative Thinking, is a predictor of adult success. People who score higher on the TTCT are more likely to be entrepreneurs, inventors, college presidents, authors, doctors, software developers. And get this, childhood creativity measured by measures like the Torrance Test of Creative Thinking are three times stronger predictors of lifetime creative achievement than childhood IQ.

So what can you do to reinvigorate your imagination, or your children's, or your grandchildren's? The first thing you can do is identify what you, or your child, or your grandchild finds intrinsically interesting, what intrinsically motivates you or them, and then pursue it. Encourage divergent thinking and idea generation. Don't worry about whether answers are right or wrong. When they're doing art, whether it's good or bad, when they're playing music, whether it's being played well or not, if they're experimenting, especially, ask a child, ask yourself open-ended questions. What would you do? How might you? What else might you do? And use tools to encourage lateral thinking.

Here's a creative thinking tool that promotes lateral thinking and can be used by adults and children. Edward de Bono created many lateral thinking tools. The one that he says is the easiest to apply is random word. It's literally using a random word to shift our thinking to solve a problem. It's important that the word be randomly selected. It forces new thinking, because it kind of creates a provocation. Injecting a random word into our thinking requires thoughts to take a new neural pathway. Again, you must select the word randomly, as remote as possible to the challenge that you're working on. How? Well, you can use a dictionary or randomly select a word from a dictionary, looking for a noun or a verb. There are random word generators on the web, and books like *Thinker Toys* also provide lists of random words. Here's an example, de Bono was working in a country that had a teacher shortage. They thought of the word "tadpole," randomly selecting the word. That led to an image of teachers with tails. That suggested that each teacher have two apprentices to follow him or her around, taking on greater responsibility over time. In this way, they could relieve the pressure to find more teachers.

I'd like you to practice lateral thinking. Develop this skill. In your guide book, there are exercises on PO and random word. Use these tools to force your brain to go down unexplored neural pathways. And remember, learning without application achieves the same end as ignorance. Try it out, and I'll see you next time.

Creative Styles—Adaptors and Innovators

Lecture 3

When applying the adaptor-innovator theory, you must first understand yourself. You also need to be flexible; use the thinking necessary for that situation. And make sure you're in the right circumstance: If you need adaptive thinking, think like an adaptor. If you need innovative thinking, think like an innovator. The six hats tool, which helps people shift their thinking, is a simple and effective tool that can be used to minimize egos and to create a solution-oriented discussion among differing perspectives.

The Adaptor-Innovator Theory

- There are two views in terms of examining creativity in people. The classic way, the traditional way, is to think about one's level of creativity—how much creativity someone possesses. In fact, this is where the early research focused, on identifying highly creative people, examining them closely to determine what traits they had that distinguished them from less creative counterparts.

- From this, we learned that creativity is normally distributed along a bell curve, where most people fall in the middle; some are at the extreme high end, and a few others are at the extreme low end. When we talk about level, we're answering the question, "How creative are you?"

- But there's another way to think about creativity. More recently, researchers have begun to ask, "How do people express their creativity in different ways?" This is called the style approach.

- In theory, style is unrelated to level. Your style does not determine how far you can go in terms of being creative. A theory in the field of creativity, called adaptors and innovators, specifically examines this. Developed by British researcher Michael Kirton, this theory suggests that all people fall along a style continuum. At one end, we have a more adaptive approach to creativity; at the other end, we have a more innovative approach. Wherever you are along this continuum does not determine how creative you are.

- The origins of Kirton's theory were the result of his observations in organizations. He found that some managers were much more comfortable with introducing change that perfected, improved, and extended current operations and systems. By contrast, there was another kind of manager—a manager who tended to generate more radical change, change that threatened the existing operations.

- Kirton called the kind of manager who generated ideas that improved current systems the "adapter." This is a more evolutionary style of creativity. The manager who tended to generate more radical change he called an "innovator," a more revolutionary kind of creativity.

- Adaptors are described as focusing on the details. They are precise. They are reliable. They are predictable. They can be original. They can engage in original thinking. Their kind of originality is applied to finding new ways to improve traditional ways of working.

- Innovators, by contrast, are described as focusing on novelty. They approach problems from unsuspected angles. They challenge assumptions. They are irreverent of consensual views. They're original, just like adaptors are, but in a different kind of way. Their originality comes in paradigm-breaking forms.

- According to Kirton, all people fall on this adaptor-innovator continuum, and he has a measure that people respond to that identifies their preferences. Kirton suggests that both styles, or anywhere you fall along this continuum, can be highly creative. It's just two different ways of being creative.

- People can be high-creative innovators. You can also have low-creative innovators. You can have people who are highly creative that have an adaptive orientation. You can have people who are low creative who have an adaptive orientation. It doesn't matter where you fall on the style continuum; in theory, it's not related to your level.

- However, we might have subjective preferences for the kind of style of creativity we appreciate. The risk is not so much having a preference—it's when those preferences for what you like become pejorative labels, when you start to label a style of creativity in a negative way, because it's a style of creativity that you don't appreciate. When it becomes particularly problematic is when people with a certain preference along this continuum judge those on the other end of the continuum.

- For example, adaptors might see innovators as "those crazy dreamers." Innovators may see adaptors as rigid and being stuck in the rut. And it might just be that our culture has an overall bias, at least in terms of how we think about high creators. That is, it seems that we have a preference as a culture to assuming that innovators, not adaptors, are highly creative.

- The consequence is that sometimes we may underappreciate the adaptive style and, as a consequence, erode the confidence of adaptors. The reality is we need both adaptors and innovators, especially in organizations. Adaptors improve practices, and innovators change practices. They complement one another.

- The adaptor-innovator theory challenges us to expand our view of creativity beyond just level and to recognize that there are different styles. It might also help to highlight and help us to recognize and appreciate both styles, and perhaps to understand our style of creativity.

- You should play to your style. In fact, you might even find someone who creates in a way that's similar to your way of creating. Find a paragon. But be cautious. You may need to adopt different ways of thinking, as necessary.

- Kirton's theory also tells us about when communication breaks down between people. In fact, on his continuum, when you find people are more than a standard deviation apart from each other, he suggests that you'll see communication break down between adaptors and innovators.

- He has also suggested that in organizations we create certain cognitive climates—when you get a group of people together, their preferences may slide one way or another on the scale.

- For example, engineering and accounting tend to be more adaptive. R & D and marketing tend to be more innovative. As a consequence, if someone is in that kind of environment, that kind of cognitive climate, and his or her preferences are different than the prevailing cognitive climate, that might create a little stress for him or her.

- Kirton also talks about teams and how it's natural that in certain areas, you may slide in one direction or the other because of the responsibilities that you have.

- This makes sense in terms of accounting. Accountants tend to be more adaptive. And in R & D, where they're looking to the future and often trying to break the paradigm, there's a more innovative bias.

- In terms of a personal implication to consider, Kirton talks about coping skills, and he suggests that when we're in a situation that requires us to adopt a style of thinking that's foreign to us, we have to move our adaptor or innovator preference that, over the short term, might cause a little tension. But if you're caught in a situation over a long term, where you have to adopt a different way of thinking, that will result in stress.

The Six Hats

- A tool called the six hats, developed by Edward de Bono, helps us shift our thinking. It's designed to help, especially in groups, to get parallel thinking to occur from different perspectives.

- Each hat, which has a different color, represents a different way of thinking. The six hats are white, red, black, yellow, green, and blue.
  - The white hat is objective—facts and figures.
  - The red hat is for emotions—bringing emotions into the discussion. It's fiery.
  - Black is for evaluation—critical thinking. It's careful and cautious. It's the devil's advocate.
  - Yellow is sunny—positive outlook.
  - The green hat—green for growth—is for creativity and new ideas.
  - The blue hat is a special hat. The blue hat is like the sky; it stands above the others. It's the organizing hat. It's the hat that helps you determine which hat should be worn.

- The hats can be used individually, or they can be used in teams. Using the six hats helps, especially, groups to have more productive conversations. It creates parallel thinking.

The six-hats tool is used to engage people in discussions.

- In meetings, discussions break down because often people are using a different way of thinking. Meetings have different kinds of thinking happening at the same time, and that can create frustration and argument. One person is talking about facts; he or she has the white hat on. Another is talking about feelings; he or she is coming from an emotional perspective, wearing the red hat. A third is generating possibilities; he or she is using a green hat. How could you ever get to consensus when you have people thinking in very different ways?

- The six-hats tool creates a more focused and orderly discussion, and it's useful to appoint someone to wear the blue hat, who determines and controls the sequence—helps to keep people focused. In other words, this person facilitates the meeting.

Suggested Reading

de Bono, *Serious Creativity*.

———, *Six Thinking Hats*.

Kirton, *Adaptors and Innovators*.

Activities

Activity 1: Innovative versus Adaptive Creativity
Identify someone you know who appears to have an innovative creativity style and someone who appears to have an adaptive creative style. In what ways are both people able to be creative?

How does knowledge of creativity styles affect your implicit understanding of who is creative and how people express their creativity?

Activity 2: Six Thinking Hats
Think about a problem you want to solve. Write down some steps you would normally take. Do any of the steps correspond to one of the six types of thinking (below)? Which types might be missing? Deliberately use each type of thinking at least once (meaning, try wearing all of the hats, but not at the same time) and make a note of the result. Use the blue hat to think through the order of the different thinking hats that will work best for you.

- Blue (sky, above everything else, organizing hat)

- White (objective, facts and figures)

- Red (emotional view)

- Green (growth, creativity, new ideas)

- Black (careful, cautious, devil's advocate)

- Yellow (sunny, positive)

When you are done, consider how the six types of thinking worked together to help solve the problem. What are the advantages of this approach?

Creative Styles—Adaptors and Innovators

Lecture 3—Transcript

Edison. Gates. Picasso. Rockwell. What does it mean to be a creative person? What are the traits, skills, and attributes of a creative person? Let's examine what it means to be creative. I'm going to describe two very different people to you. I'm going to ask you to tell me who you believe is more creative. We'll use this as a way to explore the traits, skills, and attributes of a creative person. I'm not going to give them names. I'm simply going to call them person A and person B. So, here's person A. Person A is precise, reliable, predictable, and disciplined. Person A seeks solutions to problems in tried and understood ways. They seek to improve, working within the box. They're seen as sound, conforming, safe, dependable. Let's turn to person B, Person B is undisciplined, thinking tangentially, approaching tasks from unusual angles. Person B challenges assumptions; they manipulate the problem. Person B serves as a catalyst for settled groups, irreverent of their consensual views. And person B is seen as unsound, impractical, and shocks others.

So, make a choice. Who's more creative? Who would you predict over time would show higher levels of creativity? I'm going to guess you chose person B. How do I know this? Well, we did the study. A former graduate student and I, Melanie Chimento, provided 200 lay people with these same descriptions; 200 people who weren't familiar with the scientific study of creativity. Then we presented them with two scales. We didn't ask them to choose one over the other, as I did with you. Instead, they rated each, person A and person B, on a 10-point scale, from not at all creative to exceptionally creative. What our analysis showed us, overwhelmingly, people chose person B as being much more creative.

In this study, we compared implicit beliefs, those are the beliefs that are formed in a subjective way about a topic; they're sort of folk theories. We compared implicit beliefs to an explicit theory of creativity. Explicit theories are based on research and analysis. They're objective. It's an objective understanding of some psychological concept. We wanted to test whether people's implicit views, their general conceptions of creativity, corresponded with an explicit theory. This lecture is based on that theory.

When we look at creativity in people, it can be broadly defined and examined in two ways. There are two views in terms of examining creativity in people. The classic way, the traditional way, is to think about level of creativity. How much creativity someone possesses—the amount, the degree. And in fact, this is where the early research focused, on identifying highly creative people, examining them closely to determine what traits they had that distinguished them from less creative counterparts. Well, what did we learn? We learned that creativity is normally distributed along a bell curve, where most people fall in the middle, some are at the extreme high end, and a few others are at the extreme low end.

When we talk about level, we're answering the question "How creative are you?" But there's another way to think about creativity, another dimension. More recently, researchers have begun to ask, "How do people express their creativity in different ways?" From how much creativity do you have, to how are you creative. This is called the style approach. Now, you, in your own experience, may have observed, as you've interacted with others in creative work, that your way of engaging in creativity might be different from others'.

Many years ago, in fact, when I was a young assistant professor, just new, starting out, I was collaborating with a colleague to write a chapter. Her name was Mary Murdock; she was a senior faculty member in my department, and we got together to have our first writing meeting. When I showed up to the meeting, I began by saying "Okay, Mary, we're going to be writing this chapter together. Let's create an outline." And she looked at me and she said "Well, I've already started writing." And I said, "Well, okay. Do you have the outline, then?" She said, "No, I just started writing." And I said "Well, where did you start writing?" And she said "Well, I kind of jumped in the middle and just started writing the chapter." I was shocked. I said, "How could you write a chapter from the middle, and without an outline?" You see, this is the only way I've ever written, in a sequential way, having a framework to guide me.

Kurt Vonnegut says that there are two kinds of writers, bashers and swoopers. Bashers are methodical. They write from the start. They're sequential. They're structured. One idea must precede the next; they write in a building fashion. That's me. Then there are swoopers. They're more intuitive. They're random. They can leap around. That's what Mary was like. So here we were, doing creative work together, and we were displaying our creativity styles in very evident ways, and they were very different from each other.

In theory, style is unrelated to level. Your style does not determine how far you can go in terms of being creative. There's a theory, specifically, that examines this. It's not about bashers and swoopers. It's called Adaptors and Innovators, an explicit theory in the field of creativity, developed by a British researcher, Michael Kirton. His theory suggests that all people fall along a style continuum. At one end, we have a more adaptive approach to creativity. At the other end, we have a more innovative approach. And wherever you are along this continuum does not determine how creative you are.

Here's an example. Let's go to the world of art. I'm going to share with you two of my favorite artists. Now, in terms of the level dimension of creativity, they're both highly creative. But I'm going to suggest that although they're both highly creative, they show their creativity in two very different ways. So, they were born 13 years apart. They had a similar longevity to their careers. They both passed away in the 1970s. Both were incredibly prolific, producing many creative products. But, their approach, that is, their process, and the products they created, I would suggest, are substantially different, giving us some evidence of two very different styles, and I think one was more adaptive, while the other was more innovative.

Let's start with the first artist, Norman Rockwell. Some call his work realism. Others call it idealism. He said, "I paint life as I would like it to be." He filled his canvases with details and nuances of everyday life. Steven Spielberg is a collector. Spielberg said, "I had a great deal of respect for how he could tell stories in a single frozen image—entire stories." One critic observed that Rockwell gave uncommon detail to imaginary subjects. His paintings are in demand today, not only collected by Spielberg, but also George Lucas. And today they sell for millions of dollars. For example, a canvas was recently found in a false wall in a Vermont home. Later, it sold at auction for 15.4 million dollars.

So, those were his products. Let's look at his process. How did he go about creating? He would stage very elaborate scenes in his studio. He claimed he couldn't draw from his imagination. If he wanted to paint a train set, he had to have it there in front of him. In fact, he actually borrowed a train set from the Santa Fe Railway Company, and then he mailed it back to them when he was done. Rockwell even said, "I couldn't paint a pair of woolen socks unless they were there in front of me." To be able to scrutinize his scenes later, he had professional photographers come in and capture the scenes that he had staged so that he could make sure he got the details right.

Let's shift to Picasso. We're going to focus on cubism, an art form most identified with Picasso, along with Braque, who are credited with originating this particular style of art. What's interesting about Picasso is that he first mastered representational art, and then he broke away; he broke away from that traditional approach. You see, he wanted to show what artists knew, not just what they saw. He wanted to challenge the constraints of the flat canvas, that is, the single point of view and the illusion of depth. Instead, Picasso wanted to show the object from multiple points of view and from different perspectives independently. He didn't want to merely copy nature. Instead, he wanted the art to stand alone as its own form of creativity. Cubism dissects the subject and reconstructs it to focus on the essence rather than the appearance. Geometric facets create recognizable, yet abstract depictions of the subject.

Now, when you look at his process, you look across his career, he moved from one style to another. In fact, some describe his career as a patchwork of different styles, different periods. The blue, the rose, the African influence, the analytic cubism, synthetic cubism, neo-classic. He borrowed and synthesized as he moved across these different periods. For example, African art was an early inspiration for cubism. And he didn't just work in one medium. He had paintings and collages, sculpture, common household objects, and ceramics.

So, why this story? Again, the traditional view of creativity is level. How creative are you? And yes, Rockwell and Picasso were highly creative. They were eminent. They were superstar creators. I also told you this story to draw a distinction between different ways of expressing creativity and to introduce you to another dimension in terms of looking at creativity in people, their style. Person A and person B that I described earlier are reflective of Kirton's adaptor/innovator theory. Person A, predictable, reliable, focuses on the details, is the example of a more adaptive orientation. Person B is an example of the more innovative orientation. So, let's think about these artists. Let's not talk about person A and person B.

Did you get a sense from my description of these two artists, whether one showed a more adaptive preference for creativity, versus another who showed a more innovative orientation? I would suggest that Rockwell was more adaptive, was more like person A, focused on the details. Highly creative, to be sure, but was methodical in his approach to how he created, working in a very traditional way. Picasso, I would suggest, was more innovative, more like person B, challenged the paradigm, created an entire new movement, Cubism.

Now, this doesn't apply only to artists and individuals. We could think about organizations in this way too. Here are some creative organizations: Boeing, American Express, General Motors, Nokia. They're all creative. In some cases, organizations lean a little more towards the adaptive orientation. We can look at airplane manufacturing, for example—Boeing. I would suggest that Boeing is a highly adaptive creative organization; a highly creative organization, but adaptive in its nature. They engage in mainly incremental improvements, and this is hugely valuable. This is an excellent example of important kinds of creativity. As you look at the models of their planes, moving from the 747 to other planes, with each plane, they make improvements. If you're not sure about the value of this kind of creativity, ask yourself, would you rather cross the Atlantic in a World War I biplane or use Boeing's 747?

Let's look at an innovative example of a corporation. Let's take American Express. Now, we know American Express mainly as a financial company. William Fargo was one of its founders. When it was founded, it was a regional freight express company. Later, the executive, J.C. Fargo, was on a trip to Europe in the late 1800s, carrying letters of credit, which ended up being useless. He couldn't convert them into the local currency. When he came back from this European trip, because of the frustration that he had with that experience, he challenged those inside the company to come up with a solution. That led to the American Express traveler's check. The result was a new international currency, a paradigm shift, and this permanently shifted that company towards being a financial company.

Let's go back to Kirton's theory, and let's explore it a little more deeply. Michael Kirton developed his theory, the origins of his theory, in fact, were the result of his observations in organizations. What he found was that some managers were much more comfortable with introducing change that perfected, improved, extended current operations and systems. By contrast, you recognize another kind of manager. A manager who tended to generate more radical change, change that threatened the existing operations. He called the kind of manager who generated ideas that improved current systems the adapter. This is a more evolutionary style of creativity. The manager who tended to generate more radical change he called an innovator, a more revolutionary kind of creativity.

Adaptors, let's look at them a little more closely. As I describe this theory, as I go into it in more detail, think about yourself and your preferences, your way of expressing creativity. Adaptors are described as focusing on the details. They are precise. They are reliable. They are predictable. They can be original. They can engage in original thinking. Their kind of originality is applied to finding new ways to improve traditional ways of working. Innovators, by contrast, are described as focusing on novelty. They approach problems from unsuspected angles. They challenge assumptions. They are irreverent of consensual views. They're original too, just like adaptors are, but in a different kind of way. Their originality comes in paradigm-breaking forms. According to Kirton, all people fall on this AI continuum, and he has a measure, which people respond to, that identifies their preferences. Do you have a sense where you might fall on this continuum?

Let's look at some implications of this theory. Kirton suggests that both styles, or anywhere you fall along this continuum can be highly creative. It's just two different ways of being creative, and people can be low-creative, as well. You can have high-creative innovators. You can have low-creative innovators. You can have people who are highly creative that have an adaptive orientation. You can have people who are low creative who have an adaptive orientation. It doesn't matter where you fall on the style continuum. In theory, it's not related to your level.

However, we might have subjective preferences for the kind of style of creativity we appreciate. Maybe when we're looking at the art of Norman Rockwell or Pablo Picasso. The risk is not so much having a preference, it's when those preferences for what you like become pejorative labels, when you start to label a style of creativity in a negative way, because it's a style of creativity that you don't appreciate. And when it becomes particularly problematic is when you have people have a certain preference along this continuum who judge those on the other end of the continuum.

For example, adaptors might see innovators as "those crazy dreamers." Innovators may see adaptors as rigid and being stuck in the rut. And it might just be that our culture has an overall bias, at least in terms of how we think about high creators. That is, I have a sense that we have a preference as a culture to assuming that innovators, not adaptors, are highly creative. The earlier study that I talked about with person A and person B and the fact that person B, the innovators, were statistically significantly ranked as being more creative, might give us some evidence about this bias. And we can see this in our everyday language. How often do you hear the expression "Think outside the box," as if that's the only way to be creative, which is an innovative bias. What about building a better box? That's just as important.

The consequence is that sometimes we may under appreciate the adaptive style and, as a consequence, erode the confidence of adaptors. Normal Rockwell, perhaps, illustrated this in a comment he made late in his life. He said, "If I were young and starting out again, I would try to be an abstract artist." Well, he said this during the period of the 1960s with the counter-culture movement, the beatnik movement, this very innovative way of being creative, breaking away from the cultural norms. Perhaps he felt a little guilty about being more traditional and adaptive. The reality is we need both, especially in organizations. Adaptors improve practices, and innovators change practices. They complement one another.

Let's look at what we can learn from the AI theory—Adaptor-Innovator theory. First of all, it challenges us to expand our view of creativity beyond just level and to recognize that there are different styles. It might also help to highlight and help us to recognize and appreciate both styles, and perhaps to understand our style of creativity. You should play to your style. In fact, you might even find someone who creates in a way that's similar to your way of creating. Find a paragon. But be cautious. You may need to adopt different ways of thinking, as necessary.

Kirton's theory also tells us about when communication breaks down between people. In fact, on his continuum, when you find people are more than a standard deviation apart from each other, he suggests you'll see communication breakdown between adaptors and innovators. He has also suggested that in organizations we create certain cognitive climates; when you get a group of people together that their preferences may slide one way or another on the scale. For example, engineering and accounting tend to be more adaptive. R&D and marketing tend to be more innovative. So, as a consequence, if someone is in that kind of environment, that kind of cognitive climate, and their preferences are different than the prevailing cognitive climate, that might create a little stress for them.

Kirton also talks about teams and how it's natural that in certain areas that you may slide in one direction or the other because of the responsibilities that you have. Makes sense, then, in accounting—accountants tend to be more adaptive—and in R&D, where they're looking to the future and often trying to break the paradigm, that there's a more innovative bias. So you might want to think about your team, if you're on a team, and is the right mix of adaptors and innovators on that team?

In terms of a personal implication to consider, Kirton talks about coping skills. And then he suggests that when we're in a situation that requires us to adopt a style of thinking that's foreign to us, that we have to move our adaptor or innovator preference, that over the short term, that might cause a little tension. But if you're caught in a situation over a long term, where you have to adopt a different way of thinking, that that will result in stress. So, here's a take-away. Understand yourself. Be flexible. Use the thinking necessary for that situation. Make sure you're in the right circumstance. If you need adaptive thinking, think like an adaptor. If you need innovative thinking, think like an innovator.

Here's a tool that helps us to shift our thinking. It's called The Six Hats. This was developed by Edward de Bono. It's designed to help, especially in groups, to get parallel thinking to occur. You might remember the parable of the blind men and the elephant, and they each described the elephant a different way based on how they come into contact with the elephant. One holds the tail and says the elephant is very much like a rope. Another puts his arms around the leg and says the elephant is very much like a tree trunk. That's not parallel thinking, and that often happens in meetings. So each hat, which has a different color, represents a different way of thinking, a way of shifting the blind men from different perspectives to all thinking in parallel ways.

Here are the six hats, white, red, black, yellow, green, and blue. So what's the kind of thinking that goes along with each one? The white hat is for objective, facts and figures. The red hat is for emotions, bringing emotions into the discussion; red, it's fiery. Black is for evaluation, critical thinking; it's careful and cautious, the devil's advocate. Yellow is sunny, positive outlook; let's look for what's good. The green hat—green for growth—is for creativity and new ideas. Now, the blue hat, the blue hat is a special hat; the blue hat is like the sky. It stands above the others. It's the organizing hat. It's the hat that helps you determine what hat should be worn.

Now, these can be used individually, or they could be used in teams. Let me give you an example of a team application. Actually, my family. You see, we're very concerned about the boys. They were spending a lot of time with electronic games as they were growing older. And we wanted to have a discussion. But we wanted to have a productive discussion, not a fight, not a conflict. So, I put the blue hat on. Not literally, but hypothetically. I put the blue hat on, and I decided which hats we would follow in this discussion. I had to think through what order made the most sense, and this is the order that we followed.

We began with the white hat. We began looking at facts. We were kind of keeping track of how much time they were spending in front of screens playing games. We talked about the impact of this, looking at some facts that we were able to get through the internet. Then we moved to the red hat—feelings. How do you guys feel about this? And we allowed them to open up and share their feelings about reducing gaming, and the issue that we were raising to their attention. Then, once we moved through that, we went to the green hat. So what ideas? Now, collectively, what new ideas do we have for reducing the amount of gaming in the house?

After the ideas were generated wearing the green hat, we then went to the yellow hat, and we looked at which ideas seemed to be most promising. Let's look at this in a positive way. Which ideas of the ones we generated seemed workable? Then we needed to evaluate those promising ideas, and we put the black hat on, and we played devil's advocate, and looked at the shortcomings of those most promising ideas. And then, finally, we returned to the green hat, so that we could generate ideas to improve those solutions based on the shortcomings that we saw. And ultimately, we created a plan. A plan that everyone bought into. We decided to have time limits. We would play more board games as a family. The kids insisted that the adults participate in gaming more, that we would get involved with the kids. And the adults asked the kids if, over meals, that we could discuss what they were learning from gaming.

So how do adults learn best? Well, we learn best from hands-on experience. I want to encourage you to experiment with the six hats. Try it individually, then try it with your family or friends, then at work. Using the six hats helps, especially, groups to have more productive conversations. Again, it creates parallel thinking. Have you ever noticed in meetings how discussions break down? They break down because often people are using a different way of thinking. Meetings literally have different kinds of thinking happening at the same time, and that can create frustration and argument. One person is talking about facts, they have the white hat on. Another is talking about feelings; they're coming from an emotional perspective. They have the red hat on. A third is generating possibilities, a green hat. How could you ever get to consensus when you have people thinking in very different ways?

The six hats creates a more focused and orderly discussion, and it's useful to appoint someone to wear the blue hat, who determines and controls the sequence, helps to keep people focused. In other words, they facilitate the meeting. Perhaps this is a role you might want to play in these discussions. As de Bono says, a discussion should be a genuine attempt to explore a subject, rather than a battle between competing egos. The six hats is a simple and effective way to minimize egos and to create a solution-oriented discussion. I encourage you to try it out. And remember, there's more than one way to be creative.

Combining Opposites—Diverge, Then Converge

Lecture 4

In this lecture, you will learn about the importance of striking a balance between divergent and convergent thinking—two forms of thinking that often seem to be at contrast with one another. The focus of this lecture is on the nature of creative thinking and ways of improving it. In terms of the creative process, there are multiple right answers, and the more shots you take, there is a greater chance of a breakthrough.

Bloom's Taxonomy

- Not all thinking is the same. Bloom's taxonomy provides us an excellent description of different levels of thought. It's an organization of thinking along a hierarchy from the least complex forms of thinking to more complex forms of thinking.

- At the lowest level, we have remembering, which is simple recall—being able to list facts. At the next level, we have understanding, which is an ability to explain, to make meaning. The next level up, we have applying, which is an ability to implement, to use procedures. Then, we have analyzing, which is an ability to differentiate, organize, and categorize. The next level up, we have evaluating, which is the ability to critique and make recommendations. Then, at the highest level of human thought, we have creating, which is an ability to generate something new.

- What can we learn from Bloom's taxonomy? What does it tell us about thinking? First of all, there are different forms of thinking. Not all thinking is the same, and thinking has a range. When we look at different forms of thinking, they vary in terms of the amount of complexity.

- The next point is that in 2001, when Bloom's taxonomy was updated, the creative thinking component was moved to the highest level of thought. Before this revision, it was at the second level, and evaluating was considered to be the most complex form of thinking.

- Evaluating is reacting to something that already exists whereas creating is more proactive—it's producing something that hadn't existed before. This is in keeping with talk about the necessity for creative thinking as a professional and personal skill in the 21st century.

- If creative thinking is the most complex form of thinking, then shouldn't our goal always be to get people to the highest level of thinking—whether it's in schools, in businesses, in organizations, or in our own family?

- There is one more thing we can learn from Bloom's taxonomy. As we look at these higher-order thinking skills—more complex thinking skills—what we realize is that more complex kinds of thinking must be made up of subskills: There must be lower-order skills that, when added together, create a higher-order thinking skill. This is true for creativity.

Bad versus Good Thinking Habits

- Typically, when we generate ideas, the first set of ideas that we think of are already familiar to us. They travel along neural pathways that are already well developed. They're not terribly novel. This is within an area of what we call familiarity. It's only until we exhaust what is familiar to us that we start to really generate novel and unusual options. This is known in the literature as the extended effort principle.

- Research has shown that if you take a list of ideas generated by a person or by a group and break it into the first third, the second third, and the third third and then evaluate those three blocks for novelty, the most novel ideas generally come in the last third, and the least original come in the first third.

- This is because when we are initially responding to a problem, we sort of go through a brain dump. We generate first what we've already thought of. Many people stop thinking there. Rather, that's when you need to continue to push your thinking into new areas of discovery.

- Another mistake that people often make is to mix divergent and convergent thinking. They might generate an idea and then immediately critique and evaluate it. In some cases, the idea is dismissed.

- A better thinking habit is to separate these two forms of thinking. We're all born to be able to engage in these two forms of thinking and to shift between them—to be able to engage in divergent thinking and then to engage in convergent thinking. However, although we've come into the world already wired to be able to engage in divergent and convergent thinking, we often don't apply it to the best of our ability.

- The ability to shift our thinking and to direct our thinking is called contextual focus. We can vary our cognitive receptive field. We can cast a wide or narrow net. We can defocus or focus our attention.

© iStockphoto/Thinkstock.

The creative thinking process evolves from divergent to convergent thinking.

- Stuck? Start searching for a solution. We begin by defocusing. We activate a broad region of our memory. This allows us to remotely search for original connections. Then, we shift our thinking from defocused to focused attention. We've struck on an insight. We see a possibility that has some value. We restrict our attention then. We engage in logical mental operations, and we isolate aspects of it, and we evaluate the aspects of that concept to see if it's workable.

- This is how we move from divergent to convergent thinking. It's fundamental to the creative process. Divergent thinking is making new connections. Convergent thinking is selecting and developing the most promising connections.

- Peter Carruthers, who has looked at evaluation and creativity, says that this is the universal cognitive underpinning of normal, everyday human creativity. It's kind of like evolution, in fact. Evolution has a marriage between novel variation, the search for and the generation of variation, and then the selective retention of those novel variations that are most adaptable.

- Gabora and Kaufman talk about contextual focus as a breakthrough in human evolution. They say that the fruits of one mode of thought provide the ingredients for another. And it's not just applicable for individuals; we see this in businesses as well.

- Successful companies try a lot of stuff and keep what works; they experiment and accept failure. Organizations have to experiment all the time, testing new ideas. The conditions in our environment are always changing, and companies need to vary. Otherwise, they run the risk of extinction.

Combinations of Convergence and Divergence

- Let's explore the ways that thinking can go wrong. The following seven different combinations of divergence help us to examine the consequences of divergent and convergent thinking and when the balance isn't there. We'll look at the result and the risk associated with each of these combinations.

- In the first scenario, there is no divergent thinking—no exploration of novelty. The result of this is status quo; you're in the same place you were before. The risk of this is stagnation and extinction.
- In the next scenario, you've diverged—you've explored novelty. But no convergent thinking, no systematic convergence, has occurred, and the idea was blindly accepted. If that idea proves to be ineffective, that's reckless novelty. The risk is disastrous change.
- In the next scenario, you've generated novelty, but once again, there is no systematic convergence. The novelty was blindly accepted. Let's say it ended up being effective. We call this blind creativity. In other words, you were just lucky. The risk with this is overconfidence.
- In our next example, we have a combination of divergence. Someone has decided to intentionally stretch and come up with a novel idea. We've gone through a systematic evaluation process, so we used convergent thinking, and as a result, the idea was rejected. If it turns out that the new idea was ineffective, then this is actually a positive scenario. We call this noncreativity. You didn't make things worse. The risk with this is complacency.
- In the next scenario, we've engaged in divergent thinking, and we've also been systematic in evaluating the idea. Let's say that the idea is rejected, but it turns out that the new idea would have been effective. We call this stifled creativity. In other words, you missed a great opportunity. The risk is a lost chance.
- In the next scenario, you've engaged in divergent thinking and convergent thinking. You were systematic in exploring novelty. The idea is accepted, but if it turns out that the new idea is ineffective, we call this mistaken creativity. When at first you fail, try, try again. The risk is loss of confidence.
- In our next scenario, we've generated ideas; we've deliberately diverged. We've gone through a systematic convergent process. The

idea is accepted. This is the ideal scenario. If it turns that out the idea is effective, we've been creative. We've produced something new that works. It sounds wonderful, and it is, but there's also a risk of falling in love with what you've created and not challenging yourself to generate new ideas in the future.

- Separating divergent and convergent thinking can immediately make you a better thinker. It can immediately make meetings more effective. We're born with an ability to shift our thinking and direct it, but often we're not very effective at this. We might shift prematurely.

- We can improve this by separating these two forms of thinking, first beginning with divergent thinking, and then knowing when it's time to shift. We can improve by learning the right mindset for divergent and convergent thinking, so we can learn to shift these two forms of thinking. We can also enhance the abilities to engage in divergent and convergent thinking.

Suggested Reading

Collins and Porras, *Built to Last.*

Gabora and Kaufman, "Evolutionary Approaches to Creativity."

Sawyer, *Zig Zag.*

Activities

Activity 1: Diverging and Converging
Think of a scenario at work or elsewhere in which you saw real creative potential, but the most creative solution was not accepted. Consider the following areas and how they played a role in determining the final outcome.

- Divergent thinking: Were many options generated?

- Convergent thinking: Were new and unusual options considered?

- Were good ideas produced that were ultimately rejected?

- Was a good idea selected but poorly executed?

Activity 2: Writing Challenge

Write a funny, clever, or intriguing sentence that uses these three words: blue, square, sweet. First, take the time to apply divergent thinking by coming up with 20 or more complete sentences. Then, use a deliberate process to converge so that you choose the three best sentences. How did using explicit—and separate—divergent and convergent thinking phases assist your creative thinking?

Combining Opposites—Diverge, Then Converge

Lecture 4—Transcript

Smart, yet naïve; a great deal of physical energy, but often quiet and at rest; a combination of playfulness and discipline; an alternation between imagination and a rooted sense of reality; extroversion and introversion; humble and proud; masculine and feminine; famously creative people are often combinations of opposites. The examples of contrast in traits I just gave you were compiled by the pioneering psychologist of flow, Mihaly Csikszentmihalyi. In this lecture, we look at a combination of divergent and convergent thinking, two forms of thinking that often seem to be at contrast with one another. In the first three lectures we focused mainly on understanding the creative person. The historical waves of research have focused, first, on person, and then, secondly, on process. The first wave looked at "How do we identify the creative person?" The second wave then asked the question "How do we enhance creativity in people?"

In this lecture, we focus on the nature of creative thinking, ways of improving creative thinking. Let's start by looking at thinking. Not all thinking is the same. Bloom's taxonomy provides us an excellent description of different levels of thought. It's an organization of thinking along a hierarchy from the least complex forms of thinking to more complex forms of thinking. Let me take you through that hierarchy. At the lowest level, we have remembering, which is simple recall, being able to list facts. At the next level, we have understanding, which is an ability to explain, to make meaning. The next level up, we have applying, which is an ability to implement, to use procedures. Then we have analyzing, which is an ability to differentiate, to organize, and to categorize. Next level up, we have evaluating, which is the ability to critique and make recommendations. And then, at the highest level of human thought we have creating, which is an ability to generate something new.

Let's put this into a context. Imagine we're working with an engine. At the lowest level, remembering is an ability to list the parts of an engine. The next level up, understanding, is an ability to explain the function of each part. Next level up, we have applying, which is the ability to follow up procedure, to replace a part. Then we have analyzing, which is an ability to illustrate the relationships and interactions among the parts of the engine. Then evaluating, which is an ability to look and critique the engine and identify areas for improvement. And then, finally, at the highest level, we have creating, which is an ability to generate a new kind of engine or new parts within the engine. What can we learn from Bloom's taxonomy? What does it tell us about thinking? Well, we can take away at least three things. First of all, there are different forms of thinking, again, not all thinking is the same; and that thinking has a range. When we look at different forms of thinking, they vary in terms of the amount of complexity.

The next point, in 2001, when Bloom's taxonomy was updated, the creative-thinking component was moved to the highest level of thought. Before this revision, it was at the second level, and evaluating was considered to be the most complex form of thinking. I think, with the revision, they got it right. Evaluating is reacting to something that already exists, whereas creating is more proactive. It's producing something that hadn't existed before, and I think this is in keeping with the 21st century skills and the talk about the necessity for creative thinking as a professional and personal skill in the 21st century. So, if creative thinking is the most complex form of thinking, shouldn't our goal always be to get people to the highest level of thinking, whether it's in schools or in businesses, in organizations, in our own family?

The third thing that we can learn from Bloom's taxonomy is that as we look at these higher-order thinking skills and the more complex thinking skills, what this suggests is that the more complex the kind of thinking, then it must be made up of sub skills, that there must be lower order skills that, when added together, create a higher-order thinking skill, and this is true for creativity.

Let's examine your creative thinking. Let's move from theory to application. I'm going to ask you to involve yourself in an exercise, and here's the exercise. The goal of this exercise is for you to write the three most creative sentences that you can think of. The three most creative sentences possible. If you're in a place where you can't record these sentences, then be like J.K. Rowling on that train from Manchester to London and record this in your mind. Now, I'm going to give you some constraints. I'm going to challenge you to be creative, and the constraint is this. In each sentence that you write, use these three words: Yellow, round, and sour. So each sentence must contain those three words. Let me give you an example. The little round boy had a sour expression on his face when he bit into the yellow lemon. Now, I hope that makes sense. Let me repeat the goal. The goal is to write the three most creative sentences you can think of. Go ahead and try it and come back to the lecture when you're ready. So, did you achieve the goal? Did you come up with the three most creative sentences you can think of? I hope that you did, but here's the real goal behind this exercise. The real goal was to explore your creative thinking, to identify the subskills related to creative thinking. Recall I said earlier that because creative thinking is a higher order thinking skill, it must be made up of subskills, and we're going to explore those subskills as they relate to your own experience.

We use a diamond shape to represent these two forms of thinking. Where the diamond begins at a point and spreads out, we refer to this as divergent thinking, because it's opening up; it's branching out. Divergent thinking is associative thought. It's intuitive; it's diverse; it's the production of many varied and original thoughts. Where the diamond begins to close down, when it comes to a single point, we refer to this as convergent thinking, which is analytical, logical, and controlled. It's the selection, evaluation, and development of the most promising thoughts.

So let's see how you used these skills. How did these skills work in this exercise for you? When I do this exercise with groups of audiences that I'm training, often it reveals for them a number of poor thinking habits. Here's the first one that often is apparent through this exercise. Most people stop after three sentences. Remember the goal. The goal was to write the three most creative sentences you can think of. Often what people do is they write three sentences and stop. Even if I give them 10, 15, 20 minutes, they'll sit there, patiently waiting for others to finish while they look at the first three sentences that they've written. If that's the case, then my question for you or for those individuals is, how do you know the first three sentences you wrote are the most creative sentences you could think of?

Here's a better thinking habit. In the creativity literature it's called the Extended Effort Principle. Here's the notion behind the Extended Effort Principle. Typically, when we generate options, when we generate ideas, the first set of ideas that we think of are already familiar to us. They travel along neural pathways that are already well developed. They're not terribly novel. This is within an area of what we call familiarity. It's only after we exhaust what is familiar to us that we start to really generate novel and unusual options. In the research, if you take a list of ideas generated by a person or by a group—and this has been examined—and you take that list of ideas and you break it into the first third, the second third, and the third third, and then evaluate those three blocks for novelty, the most original ideas, the most novel ideas generally come in the last third, and the least original come in the first third. Why is this? Because when we are initially responding to a problem, we sort of go through a brain dump. We generate, first, what we've already thought of. Many people stop thinking there. Rather, I would suggest that that's when you need to continue to push your thinking into new areas of discovery.

Poor thinking habit number two. This exercise often reveals to folks that they mix two forms of thinking, the divergent and convergent thinking. They might generate an idea, might think of a sentence, and then immediately critique and evaluate their sentence. And in some cases, the sentence is dismissed. The classic example of this occurs in meetings. Have you ever been in a meeting where the boss calls everyone together and says "Right, we have a difficult challenge. We need some ideas. This is a serious problem. Anyone have any ideas?" And someone raises their hand and shares an idea. Often, the next comment that's made is a criticism. What happens to the momentum in that meeting? You've been there. What happens to the thinking? What happens to the divergence? Typically, it's lost. This kind of start-and-stop thinking, where we diverge, generate a novel thought, and immediately evaluate it is not terribly efficient.

Here's a better thinking habit. Separate these two forms of thinking. We're all born to be able to engage in these two forms of thinking and to shift between them, to be able to engage in divergent thinking, and then to engage in convergent thinking. But although we've come into the world already wired to be able to engage in divergent and convergent thinking, often we don't apply it to the best of our ability. In Lecture 2, we discussed human evolution, and I suggested that a competitive advantage for humans, in order to be able to survive the test of time, was creative thinking and creative problem solving, and we explored how, initially, our creative thinking was, perhaps, applied to issues of survival, and that later, this ability to imagine then led to the creative explosion. You may recall the creative explosion was about 40,000 years ago. Homo sapiens arrived about 150,000 years ago. In between that time, our brains continued to develop. Our brains chemically developed in a way that allowed us to shift our thinking and to direct our thinking. This is called contextual focus.

So, we can vary our cognitive receptive field. We can cast a wide or narrow net. We can de-focus or focus our attention. Stuck? Start searching for a solution. We begin by de-focusing. We activate a broad region of our memory. This allows us to remotely search for original connections. Then we shift our thinking from de-focused to focused attention. We've struck on an insight. We see a possibility that has some value. We restrict our attention then. We engage in logical mental operations, and we isolate aspects of it, and we evaluate the aspects of that concept to see if it's workable. This is how we move from divergent to convergent thinking. It's fundamental to the creative process. Divergent thinking is making new connections. Convergent thinking is selecting and developing the most promising connections.

Peter Carruthers, who has looked at evaluation and creativity, says that this is the universal cognitive underpinnings of normal, everyday human creativity. It's kind of like evolution, in fact. Evolution has a marriage between novel variation, the search for and the generation of variation, and then the selective retention of those novel variations that are most adaptable. Gabora and Kaufman talk about contextual focus as a breakthrough in human evolution. They say that the fruits of one mode of thought provide the ingredients for another. And it's not just applicable for individuals. We see this in businesses as well. Collins and Porras wrote a book called *Built to Last*, where they analyzed successful companies that stood the test of time, and they identified habits that these companies had that allowed them to be successful, to navigate through difficult times, through change. One of the habits that they talk about is the habit to try a lot of stuff and keep what works, to experiment and to accept failure.

Here's an example, the Walmart greeter, we all know about the Walmart greeter, but do you know how the Walmart greeter got started? This wasn't some grand strategy that came from a strategic plan out of the corporation. It was a little idea, a little idea that was tested in a store in Louisiana. You see, the manager of this store noticed that shoplifting was on the increase, and he wanted to find some way to resolve this issue. So, he thought if he put an older gentleman by the door to greet people as they came in that it might help solve this problem, and it did. As customers came in, if they were honest, they enjoyed being welcomed. But if you came in with the intention to shoplift, then you were put on warning. It had a positive result. It decreased shoplifting significantly. The rest of Walmart saw how successful this was, this experiment, and then they adopted that throughout the organization. Organizations have to experiment all the time, testing new ideas. You see, the conditions in our environment are always changing, and companies need to vary. Otherwise, they run the risk of extinction.

Let's go back to the writing task. Remember what happened, and for most people, they diverged and converged; they mixed these two forms of thinking. Let me give you an analogy. Alex Osborn, who invented the tool "brainstorming" talked about divergent and convergent thinking sort of being like the two pedals in your car—the accelerator and the brake. Divergent thinking is like the accelerator. You're getting the most out of your horsepower and your engine. Convergent thinking is like the brake. We apply judgment to evaluate. We apply the brake to slow down so we don't overshoot our goal. Convergent thinking is the same way. And just like driving while jumping back and forth between these two pedals isn't very effective, the same thing is true for thinking.

Let me give you an example. I enjoy photography, and when I began taking photographs, it was in a period of film photography. We were limited by the canister of film that you had. You had 12 exposures, 24, 36 at most. Because we were limited, because I was limited in the number of photographs I could take, it forced me to evaluate while I was trying to diverge, trying to take photographs. Is this the right angle? Is it the right lighting? This made taking photographs much more complicated, especially when you compare it to digital photography. What a gift digital photography is. We don't have to converge while we're trying to diverge on photographs and scenes to take pictures of. Instead, we can shoot away. We're able to hit the accelerator without having to worry about the brake. We can take 100, 200,

300 photographs, 400 photographs, and then later evaluate. We can postpone converging. You think that photography is instructive in terms of this diverge/converge balance. Well, we can look to professional photographers to learn even more about the creative process.

There's a professional photographer I came across in preparing for this course by the name of Dewitt Jones. He's a renowned professional photographer. He has taken photographs for National Geographic, and now he's a speaker on creative thinking, and he says there are some important lessons that can be learned from photography relative to the creative process, much like I just described in terms of moving from film photography to digital photography. Here are two points that he makes that I think are very instructive in terms of the creative process. First of all, there are multiple right answers. When we're taking photographs, we need to experiment, and there are multiple right photos to be able to take, and the same thing is true for creativity. And the second key principle that he suggests photography can teach us about the creative process is, the more shots you take, the greater chance of a breakthrough.

When I was growing up, one of my favorite comedians was Bob Hope. I'm going to tell you a little bit of the backstory behind how Bob Hope was so creative and humorous. You see, Bob Hope had a team of writers that worked for him; they were called the Double Cross and Circle Club. The team would diverge on jokes. They would write 2 to 500 jokes for his monologues, and then Hope would go through the converging process. Again, the team diverged, Hope converged. And here's how he converged; he would read through the list of jokes. He would put an X next to those jokes that made him laugh, and then he would take a second pass through, reading only the jokes that made him laugh the first time—the jokes with one X, and he'd place a second X, another cross, next to the jokes that made him laugh a second time. And then third, he would go through the jokes looking at only those that had two Xs, the double cross, and circle those that made him laugh a third time. Hope and his writing team got it right in terms of this balance between divergent and convergent thinking.

Let's explore the ways that it can go wrong. I'm going to review seven different combinations of divergence and examine the consequences of divergent and convergent thinking and when the balance isn't there. We'll look at the result and the risk associated with each of these combinations. Here's the first scenario. No divergent thinking, no attempt to generate novelty, no exploration of novelty, the result of this is status quo. You're in the same place you were before. The risk of this is stagnation and extinction. An example of this is Blockbuster, the ubiquitous video-rental store now is bankrupt. Why? Once innovative for its distribution systems, they didn't keep up, and they were surpassed by Netflix and Redbox.

Here's the next scenario. You've diverged. You've explored novelty. That's great. But no convergent thinking has occurred, no systematic convergence, and the idea was blindly accepted. If that idea proves to be ineffective, that's reckless novelty. That's the result. Guess you should have thought about that before you tried it out. The risk is disastrous change. The classic example of this is New Coke. Many, many years ago, there was a decision to change the formula. This shocked the customers. There was a revolt, and New Coke was rejected.

Next scenario. You've generated novelty. That's nice. But once again, no systematic convergence, like Hope did. The novelty was blindly accepted. Let's say you got it right and it ended up being effective. We call this blind creativity. In other words, you were just lucky. Now, the risk with this is overconfidence. Many examples of this. Think of one-hit wonders.

In our next example, we have a combination of divergence, so someone has decided to intentionally stretch and come up with a novel idea. We've gone through a systematic evaluation process like Hope, so we used convergent thinking, and as a result the idea was rejected. If it turns out that that new idea was ineffective, well, this is actually a positive scenario. We call this non creativity. Hey, good decision. You didn't make things worse. Now, the risk with this is complacency.

In the next scenario, we've engaged in divergent thinking, we've also been systematic, like Bob Hope, in evaluating the idea. Let's say the idea is rejected, but it turns out that that new idea would have been effective. We call this stifled creativity. In other words, damn, you missed a great opportunity. The risk is a lost chance. Kodak is a good example of this.

We were talking about film photography earlier. Kodak built their business around the chemical processing of photographs. They were the developers of digital photography. They had the idea, but it didn't fit their paradigm; they rejected it. Now Kodak is a shadow of the company that it was at one time.

Next scenario. You've engaged in divergent thinking. You've engaged in convergent thinking. You were systematic in exploring novelty. The idea is accepted, but if it turns out that that new idea is ineffective, we call this mistaken creativity. When at first you fail, try, try again. The risk here is loss of confidence. J.K. Rowling, we talked about in an earlier lecture, how successful the Harry Potter series was. Well, the next book that she released was much less successful, *The Casual Vacancy*. This might, as a consequence, undermine her creative confidence.

In our next scenario, we've generated ideas. We've deliberately diverged. We've gone through a systematic convergent process. The idea is accepted. This is the ideal scenario. If it turns out the idea is effective, we've been creative. We've produced something new that works. Sounds wonderful, and it is, but there's also a risk of falling in love with what you've created and not challenge yourself to generate new ideas in the future.

Separating divergent and convergent thinking can immediately make you a better thinker. It can immediately make meetings more effective. We're born with an ability to shift our thinking and direct it, but often we're not very effective at this. We might shift prematurely. We can improve this by separating these two forms of thinking, first, beginning with divergent thinking, and then knowing when it's time to shift. We can improve by learning the right mindset for divergent and convergent thinking, so we can learn to shift these two forms of thinking, but we can enhance the abilities to engage in divergent and convergent thinking, and in fact, this is what the next two lectures will be looking at—how to develop the mindset to enhance these skills.

Let's look at how we can apply what you've learned in today's lecture. I want to challenge you to make your thinking more effective by learning how to balance divergent and convergent thinking; make this a habit. Replace the older bad habits. I suggest practicing divergent and convergent thinking. It's foundational to the creative process we'll be going through in Lectures 5 through 18. You see, in every step of the process we'll be learning, we'll be applying these two fundamental thinking skills.

Explore and see if you can enhance your ability to engage in divergent thinking and convergent thinking. I want you to try the writing exercise again, now with the learning from this lecture in place. Just as you did before, when you used the three words—round, yellow, and sour—but this time let's replace those three words with three new words. It would be too easy to use the old words. Let's use red, circle, and salty. But this time, change your process. Deliberately balance divergent and convergent thinking. Extend your effort. Don't stop your thinking short. Get beyond what's familiar to you. Push yourself to generate many options. And then, when you're satisfied that you've exhausted the possibilities, and only then, shift to convergent thinking. And when you shift to convergent thinking, be like Bob Hope. Pass through your list, culling it down until you get to the three that you believe are the most creative.

Remember the saying that I shared in an earlier lecture; learning without application achieves the same end as ignorance. Compare the outcome the second time you went through this creative writing task, the second time in which you formally used divergent and convergent thinking, and compare it to the first time through. My guess is you'll see that the outcomes are much more creative. When you balance divergent and convergent thinking, it seems like opposing thinking skills, but really, they're quite complimentary ways of thinking and your creative output will be much greater as a result. And I'll see you next time.

Principles for Unleashing Your Imagination

Lecture 5

We can deliberately enhance our ability to think divergently. The principles that you will learn about in this lecture are sort of the lubricant to enhance our ability to engage in divergent thinking, creating more fluidity in our thinking. Make these principles a way of life—or use them as guidelines in a formal meeting where you're looking to generate options. The goal is to remove your creativity from chance to on demand, and as with evolution, by following these principles, you can breed greater levels of creativity.

Mindset and Creativity

- Ruth Noller, a founding faculty member at Buffalo State, developed a mathematical formula that helps us to understand how attitude—mindset—engages with other variables to predict high levels of creativity. She suggested that creativity is a function of attitude as well as knowledge, imagination, and evaluation.

- The three main elements of this formula are knowledge, imagination, and evaluation. Children are naturally strong in imagination and weaker in knowledge and evaluation; for adults, it's the opposite. Part of what this formula suggests to us is that it's tricky getting the balance right. We need equal amounts of knowledge, imagination, and evaluation.

- The second point behind this model is that creativity is a function of knowledge, imagination, and evaluation—and attitude. Without the right attitude, we can't capitalize on our knowledge, imagination, and evaluation.

- Evolution can occur naturally, and evolution can be sped up through breeding. Creativity is the same way. Creativity occurs naturally, and creativity can be directed.

- Creativity is like breathing. No one has to teach us how to breathe. We come into the world knowing how to breathe. It is natural. But there are times when we want to be more deliberate about our breathing. If we're playing a musical instrument or we're involved in sports, it's important and valuable to us to be more conscious about our breathing and to learn strategies to be more deliberate.

- With creativity, we want to move it from natural to deliberate, just like with breathing. Why leave our creativity up to chance? There are times when we want to be creative on demand.

- To move creativity from chance to on demand, we begin by looking at the fundamental skill of divergent thinking. We'll examine four proven principles for improving divergent thinking, ways to improve your mindset. These come from eminent creators and have been supported by research. It turns out that creativity training has been demonstrated to have a profound impact on our divergent thinking skills.

Principles for Divergent Thinking: Defer Judgment

- The key principle for divergent thinking is to defer judgment, which means to temporarily suspend one's evaluation. This is the key principle because it's required for all the others. You've got to get this one right or it's very difficult to be able to adhere to the other principles and guidelines.

- Neuroscience gives us some insight into how deferring judgment works. We're most creative when our prefrontal lobe, the self-monitoring part of our brain, is less active.

- There is research that has demonstrated the profound positive effects of deferred judgment. In fact, one of the earliest studies of the creative process was conducted by another founding faculty member at Buffalo State, Sid Parnes, who conducted a simple yet elegant study.

- Parnes had two groups of students. They were given a real-life challenge to solve and were asked to generate ideas, but the two sets of students were given different instructions. One set was told to suspend judgment—not to evaluate their ideas as they were generating them. The second group was told to come up with good ideas—to generate good ideas. "Good ideas" suggested the need to evaluate.

- When they evaluated the sets of ideas generated by these students, the researchers found that those who deferred judgment, who followed that principle, ended up generating twice as many good ideas as those who were told to generate good ideas.

- Judgment kills momentum. When we use judgment prematurely as an individual or in meetings, after judgment occurs, all the creative momentum is lost in a meeting. Meetings are often conducted in the following way: Someone asks for ideas, an idea is shared, and then it's immediately met with a criticism. What happens then? The momentum dies because as those individuals sit in that meeting and see that idea being judged, often harshly and critically, they stop their thinking.

Principles for Divergent Thinking: Go for Quantity

- The second principle for divergent thinking is called go for quantity. Nobel Laureate Linus Pauling perhaps said it best when he said, "The best way to have a good idea is to have a lot of ideas." The notion is that quantity will lead to quality. We want to leverage probability: The more options you have, the more probable you are to have a breakthrough.

- This has been demonstrated through creativity researcher Dean Simonton's research. He has studied eminently creative individuals, and he has found that the number of creative breakthroughs they generate is directly related to the amount of work they produce.

- For example, Nobel Prize scientists published twice as many papers as nonwinners. Einstein had 248 publications. Edison had

1,093 patents. Mozart had over 600 compositions. J. S. Bach had 1,000 compositions. Picasso completed more than 20,000 works in his life.

- This doesn't just apply to individuals; this is also true for businesses. When it comes to a successful product, innovation, or service—one that got to the marketplace and was adopted—a recent study showed that, on average, it took 3,000 initial ideas to get to that one successful new product or service.

- IDEO is a well-known design company in California. They have a toy unit, and in one year, this toy unit generated 4,000 new ideas—230 of which were deemed to be promising and went to the prototype stage. Of those 230, eventually 12 were deemed to have commercial potential and were sold to clients.

- What are some of the benefits of this go-for-quantity principle? First of all, when you go for quantity, you're exercising one of the fundamental abilities of divergent thinking—fluency, which is the ability to generate many options when faced with a challenge.

- Another benefit is that you create more choices, and when you create more choices, you make yourself more powerful in terms of reaching your goal.

- Finally, more choices equate to more originality. The more we stretch our thinking, the more we get outside of that narrow area of familiarity, and the more we get into those areas of new discovery.

Principles for Divergent Thinking: Make Connections

- The next principle for divergent thinking is making connections. Our minds are wired to make associations. Our minds link ideas together, and this is a powerful source for creativity. Hearing a song brings back a memory if you had an experience referenced, or as you look around and see something, it reminds you of something that you have to do. This occurs all the time.

- New ideas don't come from thin air. If there is a muse to creativity, the muse is past ideas. The mobile phone, the car, and the Internet are all clearly creative ideas. But they didn't pop up in full and complete and perfect form. They built off of past ideas. They came from ideas that were borrowed and synthesized.

- There are many examples of real-life people—superstar creators—who made connections. Salvador Dali's painting, *Persistence of Memory*, in which a number of clock faces appear to be melting, came from a dream he had about runny Camembert cheese. George Lucas was inspired by mythology and his love for westerns when he created *Star Wars*. Think of Han Solo as sort of a cowboy in a sci-fi movie.

- How might you make connections in your life? How might you make it a habit? Look at something you normally avoid or overlook. Flip through a magazine. What ideas do you get by looking at the photographs? Save those photographs that are most striking to you and return to them later and see what ideas it stimulates. Attend conferences, both within your field and outside of your field. Travel widely. Meet different people.

© Stockbyte/Thinkstock.

You can stimulate ideas simply by looking at pictures in a magazine.

Principles for Divergent Thinking: Seek Novelty

- The fourth principle for divergent thinking is seeking novelty, which is about having dreams. It's blue-sky thinking. It's going big. It's trying out new things.

- Alex Osborn, who created these four principles for divergent thinking, said, "It's easier to tame down a wild idea than it is to invigorate a weak idea."

- What seems impractical today can be reality tomorrow. Science fiction is full of examples. Think of *Star Trek* in the 1960s and their then-futuristic communicators. Today, we have mobile phones.

Applying the Four Principles

- The first way that you can apply the four principles for divergent thinking is to manage your own thinking—to make them rules to follow. So when you're explicitly engaging in divergent thinking, use these to guide your thinking.

- The second way to apply these principles is to apply them as general principles as you go through your life. Make them habits. Defer judgment on your ideas and others, just naturally. Learn to be less critical, less self-critical. When challenged, generate many options. When you're confronted with an obstacle, ask yourself, "What else might I do?" Force your mind to make connections. Expose yourself to lots of stimuli. Intentionally look outside of your area to stimulate new thinking.

Suggested Reading

Carruthers, "Human Creativity."

Dunbar, et al., *Evolutionary Psychology*.

Mithen, *The Singing Neanderthals*.

Parnes, *Source Book for Creative Problem Solving*.

Activities

Activity 1: Applying Divergent Thinking

In what areas of your life might you deliberately practice using the principles of divergent thinking (defer judgment, go for quantity, make connections, seek novelty)? Choose one of the areas below and stretch yourself by generating a list of at least 50 ideas. When you get stuck, review the principles of divergent thinking and actively apply them.

- A theme for a party
- A list of places to go on a vacation
- Ideas for a new business venture
- A new hobby
- Personal or professional goals
- Improvements for a product you use
- Ideas for solving a particular problem

Activity 2: Making Connections

Develop your ability to make connections so that you can find fresh ideas when you need them. First, choose one of the areas above and write it down. Then, deliberately seek new stimulation. You can simply try looking around in your current environment, taking a walk, having a conversation with someone, or looking at images. Ask yourself, what new ideas do I get from this challenge by forcing a connection with _______? Add the ideas to your list.

Principles for Unleashing Your Imagination

Lecture 5—Transcript

Imagine a man who loves and collects art. His nephew comes to him, excited to share his art. The man looks at it and says, "It's not very good," and throws it away. How does this scene strike you? Does it surprise you? Does it bother you? When we have intentionally decided to be creative, we've made a conscious decision to go after novelty, to entertain something new. Therefore, we have to be careful when we explore novelty to recognize that raw ideas, at first, are fragile, and we need to be cautious in terms of how we respond to those ideas. We have to learn to manage our attitude in order to unleash our imagination and to preserve novelty.

This course is aimed at developing creative thinking skills. These skills are enhanced through tools, but we need to pay attention to our mindset. Our mindset serves as a ceiling, or a lid for or skills. We can't maximize our skills or use the tools to their fullest potential without the right mindset. In this lecture, we look at that cognitive mindset, the mindset for creative thinking. In a later lecture, in Lecture 22, we'll explore more broadly emotions and their relationship to creativity.

In the last lecture, we discussed the development of the modern brain and how it developed a capacity to shift from divergent to convergent thinking. The brain reached its present size about 150,000 years ago, and then later it developed contextual focusing skills. This is a term for that ability to shift from divergent to convergent thinking. Language came about 100,000 years ago. So, at this point, Homo sapiens had the thinking skills and the language. Is that all we needed to be creative? Right? Well, not quite. Remember, the creative explosion didn't occur until about 40,000 years ago, so there was about a 60,000-year gap. What happened during this gap? What was missing? Well, what was missing was the mindset that unshackled our imagination.

There's a formula, a mathematical formula, that was developed by one of our founding faculty members at Buffalo State. Her name was Ruth Noller. She was a mathematician. In fact, she helped to build the first computer in the U.S. As a mathematician, she provided a formula that helps us to understand how attitude, mindset, engages with other variables to predict high levels of creativity, and this is her mathematical formula. She suggested that creativity is a function of attitude, small a, as well as knowledge, imagination, and evaluation.

Let's start with the three main elements of this formula—knowledge, imagination, and evaluation, and let me ask you a question. Where are children naturally strong in terms of these three elements? When asked this question to audiences, the immediate response is, "Well, imagination." Where do children need some help? The response that I get there is "Knowledge and evaluation." Now, let's consider adults. Where are adults naturally strong? The response I often get is "Knowledge and evaluation." But where do adults need some help? Typical response, "Imagination."

Part of what this formula suggests to us is that it's tricky getting the balance right. We need equal amounts of knowledge, imagination, and evaluation. But the second point behind this model is that little a, that creativity is a function of knowledge, imagination, and evaluation, and attitude. You see, without the right attitude, we can't capitalize on our knowledge, imagination, and evaluation. In this lecture, we look at attitude. We look at the mindset. The mindset towards thinking that supports imagination. In this lecture, we're moving from natural creativity to deliberate creativity. In the last lecture, we talked about how it's natural for us to be able to engage in divergent and convergent thinking.

So, you see, evolution can occur naturally and evolution can be sped up through breeding. Creativity is the same way. Creativity occurs naturally, and creativity can be directed. It's like breathing. I'll use breathing as an analogy. No one has to teach us how to breathe. We come into the world knowing how to breathe. This is natural. But there are times we want to be more deliberate about our breathing. If we're playing a musical instrument or we're involved in sports, it's important and valuable to us to be more conscious about our breathing and to learn strategies to be more deliberate. In fact, Tom Watson, the famous golfer, said he didn't learn how to win until he learned how to breathe. We're going to do the same thing with creativity. We're going to move it from natural to deliberate. Why leave our creativity up to chance? There are times when we want to be creative on demand. We can take lessons from those eminent creators, and in fact, we'll look at Hemingway.

Hemingway didn't leave his creativity up to chance, he had a deliberate creative process. When he was writing from home, this was his typical routine. He would begin at six in the morning, when it was cool and there was little to distract him. He stood at his desk in his bedroom, and he worked from left to right, starting with handwriting at first, using hardly any punctuation so that he could build momentum, and then, when he felt he had enough material to work with, then he moved to his typewriter. He stopped around noon, while he still, as he said, "had some juice." At the end of the day, he would chart the number of words that he had written, and then he would take his daily half-mile swim. The next morning, he would reread and revise, and then he would repeat the same process. This was Hemingway's deliberate creative process. This is how he moved creativity from chance to on demand. You can do the same.

We'll begin by looking at divergent thinking, this fundamental skill, and we'll examine four proven principles for improving divergent thinking, ways to improve your mindset, your attitude. And when I say these are proven, I mean that these come from eminent creators—people like Hemingway—and have been supported by research. And it turns out that creativity training has been demonstrated to have a profound impact on our divergent thinking skills. Here are four principles we're going to go through. Defer judgment. Go for quantity. Make connections. Seek novelty. As I go through each of these four principles, or guidelines, I'll give examples of how Hemingway reflected these same principles.

The key principle is to defer judgment. Defer judgment means to temporarily suspend one's evaluation. Now, I said this is the key principle. The reason why I suggested this is the key principle is that it's required for all the others. You've got to get this one right, or it's very difficult to be able to adhere to the other principles and guidelines. Neuroscience gives us some insight into how deferring judgment works. You see, we're creative, we're most creative when our prefrontal lobe, the self-monitoring part of our brain, is less active.

Hemingway displayed this when he got up in the morning and began writing with pencil. He worked furiously to capture his ideas. He didn't let punctuation get in his way. He captured half sentences and half thoughts in order to build his momentum, to have enough material to work with. In fact, he said that writing should be free from excessive scrutiny. Remember in our last lecture, the analogy I gave between the accelerator and the brake and how divergent thinking is like the accelerator. And convergent thinking is the brake; it's applying evaluation. You see, Hemingway began every morning by stepping on the accelerator, getting the most out of his imagination. When you start a trip, you always begin with the accelerator first.

There is research that has demonstrated the profound positive effects of deferred judgment. In fact, one of the earliest studies of the creative process conducted by another one of our founding faculty members, Sid Parnes. He conducted a simple, yet elegant study. He had two groups of students. They were given a challenge, a real-life challenge, to solve and asked to generate ideas, but the two sets of students were given different instructions. One set was told to suspend judgment, not to evaluate their ideas as they were generating them. The second group was told to come up with good ideas, to generate good ideas, And by suggesting good ideas, this communicates the need to evaluate. What they found at the end of the study when they evaluated the sets of ideas generated by these students is that those who defer judgment, who follow that principle, ended up generating twice as many good ideas as those who were told to generate good ideas.

You see, judgment kills momentum. When we use judgment prematurely as an individual or in meetings, after judgment occurs, all the creative momentum is lost in a meeting. In our last lecture, we talked about how meetings are often conducted, and someone asks for ideas, an idea is shared, then it's immediately met with a criticism. What happens then? Well, the momentum dies, because as those individuals sit in that meeting, and they see that idea being judged, often harshly and critically, they stop their thinking. They literally stop their thinking. Who's going to suggest an idea after the initial idea in that meeting was met with such harsh criticism?

We'll move to the second principle of divergent thinking. It's called Go for Quantity." Nobel Laureate Linus Pauling perhaps said it best. He said, "The best way to have a good idea is to have a lot of ideas." See, the notion here is that quantity will lead to quality. We want to leverage probability; the more options you have, the more probable you are to have a breakthrough. And this has been demonstrated through Dean Simonton's research—Dean Simonton, a well-known current creativity researcher. He's looked at eminently creative individuals, and he's found that the number of creative breakthroughs they generate is directly related to the amount of work they produce.

Here are some examples. Nobel Prize scientists published twice as many papers as non-winners. Einstein himself had 248 publications. Edison had 1,093 patents. As we learned earlier, Mozart had over 600 compositions. J.S. Bach had 1,000 compositions. And Picasso, boy, could he Go for Quantity; Picasso completed more than 20,000 works in his life.

This doesn't just apply to individuals. This is also true for businesses. When you look at a successful product, innovation, or a service, one that got to the marketplace and was adopted, on average, a recent study showed that it took 3,000 initial ideas to get to that one successful new product or service. IDEO is a well-known design company out in the bay area in California. They have a toy unit, and in one year this toy unit generated 4,000 new ideas; 230 of those ideas were deemed to be promising, and they went to the prototype stage. And of those 230, eventually 12 were deemed to have commercial potential and were sold to clients—from 4,000 to 12.

So how did Hemingway model the Go for Quantity? And in an interview, when asked how he comes up with the titles for his books, Hemingway said this: "I make a list of titles after I finish the story or the book, sometimes as many as a hundred. Then I start eliminating them. Sometimes all of them." Here are some alternative titles he came up with for his book *A Farewell to Arms*: Love and War; World Enough and Time; Every Night and All. The Enchantment.

For this well-known book, he also displayed the Go for Quantity principle when he generated the endings for this book. He had, in fact, written 47 different endings for *A Farewell to Arms*. The number-one ending was called "The Nada Ending." Hemingway wrote the following: "This is all there is to the story. Catherine died, and you will die, and I will die, and that is all I can promise you." There was the "Live Baby" ending, which was listed as number seven, which concludes, "There is no end except death, and birth is the only beginning." His friend, Fitzgerald, suggested an ending; it was number 34. Hemingway wrote the following based on F. Scott Fitzgerald's suggestion: "The world breaks everyone, and those it does not break, it kills. It kills the very good and the very gentle and the very brave impartially," he wrote. "If you are none of these, you can be sure it will kill you too, but there will be no special hurry." I'm not going to reveal the end to this book if you've not read it, but it's very different from the ones I just described—terse in the way you might expect from Hemingway, but also more rooted in the story itself.

So, what can we learn from this principle of Go for Quantity? What are some of the benefits? First of all, when you Go for Quantity, you're exercising one of the fundamental abilities of divergent thinking—fluency, which is the ability to generate many options when faced with a challenge. Another benefit is that you create more choices, and when you create more choices, you make yourself more powerful in terms of reaching your goal, whether it's solving a problem or some other goal, such as my goal when I was looking for a doctoral program. When I had graduated with my Bachelor's degree, I knew I wanted to go on for a Ph.D., but I made a mistake. I applied to one university, and I wasn't accepted.

Now, don't feel too badly for me. When I wasn't accepted into this doctoral program, I decided to go get a Master's degree in creativity, and that was the decision that created the trajectory of my life and put me into this particular field. But the next time I applied for a doctoral program, you can be assured I didn't apply just to one program. The next time, I applied to nine and was accepted by three, which put me in a position to make a choice, to choose the option that was best suited for me. Finally, more choices means more originality. Remember the Extended Effort principle. The more we stretch our thinking, the more we get outside of that narrow area of familiarity, the more we get into those areas of new discovery. That's Go for Quantity.

Let's look at the next principle. Let's start off by playing a little word association. I'm going to say a word, you think of the first word that comes to mind. Salt. Table. Up. Our minds are wired to make associations. In fact, it's predictable, probably, the words that came to mind when I said salt, table, and up. You probably said "pepper" when I said "salt." You said "chair" when I said "table." You thought of "down" when I said "up." It's natural. Hearing a song brings back a memory if you had that experience, or as you look around and you see something, it reminds you of something that you have to do. This occurs all the time. Our mind links ideas together, and this is a powerful source for creativity. You see, new ideas don't come from thin air. If there is a muse to creativity, the muse is past ideas. The mobile phone, the car, the internet; clearly creative. They didn't pop full and complete and perfect form. They built off of past ideas. They came from ideas that were borrowed and synthesized.

This third principle of divergent thinking we call Make Connections. Let me give you some examples of real-life people who made connections, those superstar creators. Salvador Dali's painting, *Persistence of Memory*, in which a number of clock faces appear to be melting, came from a dream he had about runny camembert cheese. George Lucas was inspired by mythology and love for westerns when he created Star Wars. Think of Han Solo as sort of a cowboy in a sci-fi movie. And mark Zuckerberg built Facebook, in part, off of dormitory facebooks that Harvard provided to students to identify one another, later as an online study tool and, at first, as a "hot-or-not" site that Harvard promptly shut down.

So how did Hemingway—let's return to Hemingway and his deliberate process—how did he borrow ideas, did he make connections? In fact, this is what Hemingway said: "It was no new thing to me to learn from everyone I could, living or dead." In an interview, he said it would take a day, in fact, to list everyone he borrowed ideas from. Some he did cite were Twain and Tolstoy, Shakespeare, Kipling, Bach, Cézanne, Mozart, and Dante. In fact, Hemingway said, "I learn as much from painters about how to write as I do from writers." And he not only learned from other famous, eminent creators, but he learned from ordinary people. His short story, "Hills Like White Elephants," in which a young American couple are discussing a simple operation, was drafted in an afternoon after a conversation with a girl. Hemingway put it as follows, "I met a girl in a Parisian restaurant, where I'd gone to eat oysters before lunch. I knew she had an abortion. I went over and we talked—not about that, but on the way home I thought of the story. I skipped lunch and spent the afternoon writing."

How might you make connections in your life? How might you make it a habit? Well, look around. Look at something you normally avoid or overlook. Flip through a magazine. What ideas do you get by looking at the photographs? Save those photographs that are most striking to you and return to them later, and see what ideas it stimulates. Attend conferences, both within your field and outside of your field. Travel widely. Meet different people.

In a later lecture, we'll learn deliberate tools that are really based on this principle of Make Connections. This is an important and valuable principle, and we'll dedicate time specifically to this, and tools related to this tool later.

Let's move to the fourth principle. It's called "Seek Novelty." Seeking novelty is about having dreams. It's blue-sky thinking. It's going big. It's trying out new things. Alex Osborn, who created these four principles for divergent thinking, said "It's easier to tame down a wild idea than it is to invigorate a weak idea." What seems impractical today can be reality tomorrow. Science fiction is full of examples. Think of Star Trek in the 1960s and their communicators, and today we have mobile phones.

Hemingway demonstrated this 'Seek Novelty' principle. He's well-known for having an adventurous lifestyle, and he believed that novel experiences were the spark to write. So strong was he in this opinion, when asked "What advice would you give to young writers?" he said "Get experience. And if you have no experience, hang yourself. And if you're lucky enough to survive, well, at least you can write about that." Some examples of his novel experiences that led to stories, a harrowing 10-week trip in Africa in 1933 in which he became very seriously ill led to the novel *The Green Hills of Africa*. A platonic love affair in Venice inspired the novel *Across the River and Into the Trees*.

In this lecture, we're looking at the cognitive mindset for creativity, the attitude that enables divergent thinking to really be free. Let's review these four principles. Defer judgment, Go for Quantity, Make Connections, and Seek Novelty. How might you apply these principles? I'm going to suggest that you apply them in at least two ways. I refer to these using two terms, guidelines and principles, and I refer to those as if they were interchangeable. Let me be very clear; the first way that you can apply these guidelines is to manage your own thinking, to make them rules, if you will, to follow. So when you're explicitly engaging in divergent thinking, use these to guide your thinking.

When you decide to explicitly use divergent thinking, let's say, alone, it would be good to refresh your mind; revisit these four guidelines; keep them in place as you're engaging in divergent thinking. And if you're engaging in divergent thinking with a group, it would be good to explain these guidelines so that you can create a team mindset, a shared mindset. In fact, you might even want to display these guidelines if they're being used with a group. And be sure they know the goal of divergent thinking, because most people haven't been exposed to divergent thinking. Inform them that the goal is to come up with many varied and original options. And when using it as a team, it's particularly useful to have someone there to enforce the guidelines, make sure that everyone is adhering to those rules.

I encourage you to try it out. Try it out on problems that are open-ended, that have multiple right answers. For example, you might try generating ideas for a theme for a party, solving a problem at work, places to go on vacation, generating ideas for a new business venture, maybe even thinking about new hobbies. Force yourself to come up with, maybe, 47 new hobbies that you might try out. Remember, creativity is like all other skill areas. It takes practice. I suggest that when you practice this, that you stop and evaluate your performance. Remember, in deliberate practice we have to examine our performance and seek feedback, so evaluate your performance, both individually and as a group, and see if you were able to adhere to these guidelines.

I also recommend, as a second way to apply these principles, is to make them part of your life. Make them principles for living. So the second way to use them is to apply as a general principle as you go through your life. Make them habits. Defer judgment on your ideas and others, just naturally. Learn to be less critical, less self-critical. When challenged, generate many options. When you're confronted with an obstacle, ask yourself "What else might I do?" and "What else might I do?" Force your mind to make connections. Expose yourself to lots of stimuli. Intentionally look outside of your area to stimulate new thinking.

In terms of the fourth principle, think in highly novel ways. Be adventurous. Be like Hemingway. Intentionally try new experiences. Be provocative in your thinking. Remember the tool we learned earlier from Edward de Bono, the Po tool, where we generate these exaggerated statements to provoke our thinking and to provoke the thinking of others.

To conclude, we can deliberately enhance our ability to think divergently. The principles that we went through in this lecture are sort of the lubricant for that skill, the lubricant to enhance our ability to engage in divergent thinking. It's going to create more fluidity in our thinking. Make these principles a way of life, or guidelines in a formal meeting where you're looking to generate options. Remember, our goal here is to move our creativity from chance to on demand, and as with evolution, by following these principles, you can literally breed greater levels of creativity. You can breed your own creativity. And I'll see you next time.

Principles for Converging on the Best Ideas

Lecture 6

In this lecture, you will learn about the mindset for convergence—the attitudes that enhance convergent thinking. In divergent thinking, the key principle is deferring judgment, which is learning to suspend evaluation. When we converge, we bring judgment back in. We get real. We introduce judgment, but in a productive way. When faced with an original idea, generally, the most immediate response is to judge it in terms of what's wrong with it. This kind of critical thinking kills novelty. The principles for convergent thinking that you will learn about in this lecture create the mindset for effective convergence within a creative process.

Principles for Convergent Thinking: Use Affirmative Judgment

- Like deferring judgment for divergence, the key principle for convergent thinking is to use affirmative judgment. Research shows that when given too early, negative feedback hinders scientific creativity.

- Premature criticism results in creative people withdrawing their ideas, especially when ideas are in the formative stage. And neuroscience shows us that we're more creative when we're in a good mood. We're more open to new connections.

- We need to take a balanced approach to evaluation. When we're done diverging, it's not time to come in and rip out all the novel ideas. Rather, we need to take an affirmative, open-minded approach, first looking for the positives and then looking for the shortcomings.

- We resist the all-too-often tendency to prematurely criticize an original idea. Shortcomings are viewed as ways to improve. Remember the tool "yes and" and how that focuses on improving the idea.

Principles for Convergent Thinking: Keep Novelty Alive

- The second principle for convergent thinking—the second attitude that helps us to converge effectively in a creative process—is to keep novelty alive, not to ignore original concepts and immediately move to the safe and not terribly risky solutions. Instead, it's staying open. After all, in divergent thinking, we've left that zone of familiarity. We went into the zone of new discovery.

- What happens when you engage in divergent thinking but you never select the novel options in convergent thinking is that you teach people that there's no point in dreaming, that there's no point engaging in divergent thinking—no point in pursuing new thoughts—and this is risky because without variation, without novelty, there can be no evolution, no growth.

- Keeping novelty alive also refers to staying open to unexpected experiences, and exploring the value of that unexpected experience. Microwave ovens are everywhere. But the discovery of the microwave oven was an accident. It was an unexpected incident that was not ignored.

- The magnetron was invented during World War II in England. A magnetron tube, which emits microwaves, was installed in the radar system, and this was useful in spotting German warplanes. A few years later, while working with magnetron tubes, a scientist named Percy LeBaron Spencer found a melted chocolate bar in his pocket. He didn't ignore that. This was a novel surprise. He got curious, and he deduced that the microwaves were the cause of this. Further investigation showed that microwaves cooked faster than conventional ovens.

Principles for Convergent Thinking: Check Your Objectives

- The next principle for convergent thinking is called check your objectives. During divergent thinking, we're escaping from reality, ignoring the constraints of reality. When we begin to converge, however, we have to bring ideas and our options back into reality. We need to be conscious of reality.

- Creativity is the production of original ideas that are made useful or have value. To ensure that ideas are useful, we need to evaluate potential solutions against success criteria. What will make it work in reality?

- While intuition can bring insight, ultimately novel ideas must work in reality. In order to stick, they must meet the needs of that reality. Sometimes our objectives to screen these promising options are subjective; sometimes our objectives can be more concrete, taking money, cost, time, space, and resources into account.

Principles for Convergent Thinking: Stay Focused

- The fourth principle for convergent thinking is to stay focused. Divergent thinking is playful. It's fun. There's lots of energy. Convergent thinking has a different feel to it. It requires close scrutiny and persistence. Creative ideas rarely come complete and well formed. We need to evaluate and use critical thinking to test and refine them.

- Creativity is hard work. Having an idea sometimes is easy. The hard work is making an interesting, novel idea a great solution. Staying focused helps us to ensure that the best alternatives are selected and developed.

- The poet William Wordsworth spent 40 years revising and rewriting *The Prelude*. The lines about nature in this poem were eloquent, so much so that it seems they must have been natural for him to pen—but they weren't. It really came through brute force. In fact, one critic observed that this naturalism was not achieved by simple spontaneity. It required a great deal of deliberate knowing, self-criticism, and revision.

William Wordsworth (1770–1850) was an English poet.

- There's a misconception about creativity that's popular and often embraced by many individuals—that all we need is that aha moment. We need that bolt of lightning to hit us, and we're creative. The reality is that the aha moment, in order for creativity to really happen, must be followed by hard work.

Tools for Convergent Thinking

- There are three tools that move our convergent process from a more intuitive process to a more deliberate, systematic process. The first tool is called hits. We review our divergent list, identifying the most promising options, and we mark those options that are most appealing to us. We mark the ones that we think will be successful—the ones that hold the greatest value. This tool can be used as a group and individually.

- Hits can also be used as a tool to help teams converge. Naturally, when you're using it as a team, it's more complicated, and it will take more time. A recommendation is if you use hits to evaluate a list of divergent ideas, marking the ones that seem most promising, you might want to limit the number of hits that you give members of the team. The general rule of thumb is the 10-percent rule: If you've generated 100 options, you take 10 percent and give each individual 10 votes, or 10 hits.

- When you do this, be careful of groupthink. We want to avoid people selecting options because someone else has selected that option, so you might first want to allow people to review the options, the list of ideas that were generated through divergent thinking, and to make their choices independently, and then later show them publicly.

- Hits can be expanded to a second tool: clustering. We begin by identifying our hits, and sometimes when we identify our hits, we notice that there are some themes that emerge—that there are options that naturally relate to one another—and we can categorize them, or put them into clusters. To ensure that these clusters really hang together, put labels on the cluster. Identify what the theme is and give some descriptive theme to that cluster.

- When you use this clustering tool, be sure that the clusters remain independent. They shouldn't overlap. Also, be sure that all of the items in that cluster really belong to that cluster. That's the importance of having the theme. We don't want to force all of our options or all of our ideas into clusters, and if there's one that's unique, we lose the uniqueness if we force it into a group. It's OK to leave unique items alone.

- The third tool is called blue-sky voting, in which we use codes to help us to understand our reaction to our hits. We use coding labels or electronic bullets. We use two colors: green and blue. When we go through and identify our hits, we use these two colors to represent two different reactions to these options that we're evaluating.

- For some hits, we use green dots or green bullets—green meaning that we're green-lighting that idea or option. It's fairly straightforward, and we're excited about it. It's easy to implement; we can just do it. Then, in the spirit of staying open to novelty, we reserve some of our hits for those blue-sky ideas, and we use blue dots or blue bullets. These are options that are highly novel. We're excited about these options, but we're not sure how to implement them. But if we could, they would be dynamite.

- We split our hits between these two sets. When we do this, if we're giving 10 hits to group members, we might want to give more dots to the green-lighted ideas (for example, seven) and less for the blue-sky ideas (for example, three). In fact, you can do the same thing yourself, and in this way, you're intentionally staying open to those novel options.

- There are some further things to be thinking about in terms of divergent and convergent thinking. A common question is: "How do you balance? How do you split your time between divergent and convergent thinking?" There's no right answer to this, but it's a common mistake to spend too much time on divergent thinking. After all, it's fun and people enjoy it, and they get lost in the divergent thinking, and suddenly they realize that they need to come to a decision, and they will often make a quick convergent decision.

Suggested Reading

Arnold, *The Art of Decision Making*.

Cropley, "In Praise of Convergent Thinking."

Proctor, *Creative Problem Solving for Managers*.

Activities

Activity 1: Using Affirmative Judgment
Recall a time when you or someone else in a group responded to a new idea by saying, "That will never work." Formulate an alternative response to the idea, making sure to apply affirmative judgment by first finding something positive to say about the idea.

Activity 2: Individual and Group Practice

- Find a challenge you want to work on (work or personal). Use divergent thinking; then, afterward, apply one of the convergent tools (hits, cluster, blue-sky voting).

- Find a challenge that you can solve in a group (family, friends, coworkers). First, identify a challenge, such as what to do this weekend, where to go on vacation, some goals for next year, etc. Use divergent thinking, and then apply one of the convergent tools (hits, highlighting, blue-sky voting).

Principles for Converging on the Best Ideas
Lecture 6—Transcript

Let's start by looking at three novel ideas that got rejected. This is from an internal memo written by Western Union in 1876. It said, "This telephone has too many shortcomings to be seriously considered as a means of communication. The device is inherently of no value." Next, a Yale University professor critiquing Fred Smith's paper proposing an overnight delivery service. As you probably know, Smith later founded FedEx. The feedback said this: "The concept is interesting and well formed, but in order to earn a grade of C or better, the idea must be feasible." And finally, our third example, "Guitar groups are on the way out." This was from Decca Recording Company rejecting the Beatles in 1962.

In our last lecture, we looked at divergent thinking, which is generating novelty. In convergent thinking, which we use to balance off divergent thinking, we're applying evaluation. We're examining and exploring novelty. Convergent thinking is about selective retention, finding the novelty that's going to be most adaptable. When we diverge, we are generating lots of novelty. Effective convergence is about exploring and extracting value from novelty. The quotes I just shared with you reflect pure, outright rejection of novelty.

You may recall the car analogy in that divergent thinking is like using the accelerator. We've enhanced and worked on the mindset for improving divergent thinking. We've, in a way, enhanced the horse power of your mental engine, your creative thinking skill related to divergent thinking. Now we shift to convergent thinking. Convergent thinking is the braking system, and in this lecture, we work on improving the braking system. If you have a more powerful engine, you need an equally powerful braking system.

So, in this lecture we look at the mindset for convergence, the attitudes that enhance convergent thinking. In divergent thinking, I suggested that deferring judgment was the key principle, which is learning to suspend evaluation, putting it off temporarily. When we converge, we bring judgment back in. We get real. We introduce judgment, but, in a productive way. When faced with an original idea, generally, the way we respond, the most immediate response is to judge it in terms of what's wrong with it. Have you heard the expressions "That won't work," "It's impossible," "We can't afford that," or "We've tried that before already"? This kind of critical thinking kills novelty.

So, the key principle, like deferring judgment for divergence, the key principle for convergent thinking is to use affirmative judgment. Here's what research tells us about criticism. When given too early, negative feedback hinders scientific creativity. Premature criticism resulted in creative people withdrawing their ideas, especially when ideas are in the formative stage. And neuroscience shows us that we're more creative when we're in a good mood. We're more open to new connections.

Let me share with you a real story about lack of affirmative judgment. Aviation celebrated its 100th anniversary in terms of controlled, powered flight a short while ago. However, early on, there were staunch opponents to the use of planes in the military, and this came primarily from military leaders in the established branches, the Navy and Army. They believed airplanes had no real advantage. They lacked that mindset to affirmatively explore novelty. There was one visionary by the name of Billy Mitchell; he was the first American to fly over enemy positions during World War I, and he saw many benefits. When he flew over the trenches, he realized that there was a stalemate that cost many lives, and he believed that adding a third dimension to warfare would, in fact, save lives.

After World War I, he returned to the U.S. with the rank of General. He spoke out about airplanes and their role in future warfare and their importance, but he was viewed as a heretic. He was a threat to the establishment. In fact, he was ordered to tone it down. Instead, he got louder. It came to a head in July of 1921. He was challenged to a test. Here was the challenge, to attack a captured German battleship, a massive battleship believed to be unsinkable. December 19, the day of the test, a fleet of small Martin bombers appeared on the horizon, tiny in comparison to this behemoth of a battleship. Twenty minutes later, the battleship disappeared; it had been successfully sunk.

General John Pershing, even after this test, who was the General of the armies at that time, still wrote a report suggesting that battleships would remain the backbone of the Navy. Despite intense criticism, Billy Mitchell continued to speak out. In response, the military sent Mitchell on an extended inspection tour of Hawaii, the Philippines, China, India, and Japan. The exile did not dampen his enthusiasm. In fact, it had the opposite effect. It made him more convinced that, in the future, that they would need to control the skies in order to win the war.

In the mid-1920s, he predicted war with Japan and hypothesized a surprise attack from the air. This was the last straw. Mitchell was court-martialed for insubordination. He was found guilty and sentenced to five years without pay. This was unacceptable to him. He resigned, and he continued to speak out. On February 19 of 1936, at age 57, Billy Mitchell passed away. Some suggest that he passed away prematurely because of the stress that he endured. Less than six years later, Japan attacked Pearl Harbor from the air. At the outset of the war, President Roosevelt met with his advisors to look at how they might ramp up for war. They recommended to build up the traditional military. But Roosevelt remembered Mitchell and his vision, and he diverted money to military aircraft. You see, before World War II, in a two-year period, only 800 planes had been built in the U.S., and Roosevelt now demanded that 2,000 planes be built each year.

This story illustrates the rejection of a novel idea, a lack of affirmative judgment. We need to take a balanced approach to evaluation. When we're done diverging, it's not time to come in and slaughter and rip out all the novel ideas. Rather, we need to take an affirmative, open-minded approach, first looking for the positives, and then looking for the shortcomings. We resist the all-too-often tendency to prematurely criticize an original idea. Shortcomings are viewed as ways to improve; remember the tool "yes, and" and how that focuses on improving the idea.

I had a funny reaction several years ago in a training program when I had completed training a group in divergent thinking and brainstorming, and after we had gone through some brainstorming exercises, one of the participants in the group immediately said, "You know, we do brainstorming all the time in our organization. We have lots of brainstorming meetings, and they never work." And so I inquired, I said to this person, "Well, in brainstorming, our goal is to generate lots of ideas. When you do brainstorming in your organization, do you get lots of ideas?" And the person said, "Oh, yeah,

yeah, yeah, I get lots of ideas." "OK, well, when you brainstorm, the goal is to come up with original ideas. We're engaging in divergent thinking, and our goal is to come up with some novel perspectives and options. Do you have that kind of novelty?" And this person said, "Yeah, yeah. We get novel options." I'm perplexed. I'm confused now. "When you say brainstorming doesn't work, it sounds to me like you are effectively engaging in divergent thinking. What do you mean it doesn't work?" And this is when the person told me that when they brainstorm, sure, they come up with lots of ideas and they're novel, but when they go to select the ideas and options that are going to carry forward, they only select the safe ideas.

You see, brainstorming worked. They generated many options, and they had novel options, but when they converged, their braking system, if you will, couldn't keep up with their engine, the horsepower that they were using for divergent thinking. So, the second principle of convergent thinking, the second attitude that helps us to converge effectively in a creative process, is to keep novelty alive, not to ignore original concepts and immediately move to the safe and not terribly risky solutions. Instead, it's staying open. After all, in divergent thinking we've left that zone of familiarity. We went into the zone of new discovery.

What happens when you engage in divergent thinking but you never select the novel options in convergent thinking is that you teach people that there's no point in dreaming, that there's no point engaging in divergent thinking, no point in pursuing new thoughts, and this is risky, because without variation, without novelty, there can be no evolution; there can be no growth.

Keeping novelty alive also refers to staying open to unexpected experiences, exploring the value of that unexpected experience. Microwave ovens, they're everywhere. But the discovery of the microwave oven was an accident. It was an unexpected incident that was not ignored. The magnetron was invented during World War II in England. A magnetron tube, which emits microwaves, is installed in the radar system, and this is useful, or was useful in spotting German warplanes. A few years later, while working with magnetron tubes, a scientist named Percy LeBaron Spencer, found a melted chocolate bar in his pocket. He didn't ignore that. This was a novel surprise. He got curious, and he deduced that the microwaves were the cause of this. Further investigation showed that microwaves cooked faster than conventional ovens.

Let me give you another example. Pfizer, multinational pharmaceutical company, didn't start out searching for a drug to address penile dysfunction, but thanks to a sharp-eyed clinician, that is what they found. Originally known as Compound UK 92,480, which was originally created as an antihypertensive drug, and later for angina, they discovered that during clinical trials there was an interesting side effect, penile erection. Now, despite prevailing belief that penile dysfunction was psychological, the team explored this novel outcome. They investigated it, and the net result led to Viagra. In summary, to keep novelty alive refers to doing at least two things; eliminating premature judgment, not ignoring novel ideas. It also refers to staying curious about unexpected experiences and outcomes, as we heard in our two stories about the microwave and Viagra.

Let's look at the next principle for convergent thinking, the next attitude. Check your objectives. During divergent thinking, we're escaping from reality. We're ignoring the constraints of reality. When we begin to converge, however, we have to bring ideas and our options back into reality. We need to be conscious of reality. Remember, creativity is the production of original ideas that are made useful, or have value. To ensure ideas are useful, we need to evaluate potential solutions against success criteria. What will make it work in reality? So, this third principle we call Check Your Objectives.

While intuition can bring insight, ultimately novel ideas must work in reality. In order to stick, they must meet the needs of that reality. Bob Hope did this. We discussed Bob Hope earlier in terms of how he went through a process of evaluating jokes that were generated by his team of writers, The Double Cross and Circle Club. He had specific objectives. Well, he had a specific objective in mind; jokes had to make him laugh, and not just once, they had to make him laugh three times. Hope was clear. We can be explicit just like Bob Hope. Sometimes our objectives to screen these promising options are subjective, like "Does it make me laugh?" Sometimes our objectives can be more concrete, like money, cost, time, space, resources. Later, we'll learn some specific tools that will help us to apply these as criteria, these objectives.

Let's move on to the fourth principle in convergent thinking. Edison said that genius is one percent inspiration and 99 percent perspiration. Accordingly, a genius is often merely a talented person who's done all of his or her homework. Divergent thinking is playful. It's fun. There's lots of energy. Convergent thinking has a different feel to it. It does require close scrutiny and persistence. Creative ideas rarely come complete and well-formed. We need to evaluate and use critical thinking to test and refine them. Creativity is hard work. Having an idea sometimes is easy. The hard work is making an interesting, novel idea a great solution. So, this fourth principle we formally call Stay Focused. This helps us to ensure that the best alternatives are selected and developed.

At the beginning of the lecture, I mentioned the Beatles and how they were rejected in 1962 by Decca Records. I believe the Beatles are a shining example of this principle—staying focused. Here's a specific example from the Beatles. One of their all-time greatest hits, "Yesterday," was originally titled "Scrambled Eggs." Paul McCartney woke up one morning with a tune in his head, and he worked on it for months. At first, he only had the melody. As he said, "I didn't have any words at first, so I blocked it out with 'Scrambled eggs, oh, my baby, how I love your legs, diddle diddle, I believe in scrambled eggs.'"

McCartney spent weeks playing with the song without lyrics. In fact, some of the other Beatles were beginning to get annoyed and told him he needed to move on. When the words finally came, he spent about two weeks finalizing the song. Stay Focused, I believe, clearly, is a characteristic of the Beatles, where they refined and refined, and it's also evident in their recording process. Let's look at three songs: "Blackbird," "Lucy in the Sky with Diamonds," and "Something." "Blackbird," Paul McCartney recorded 32 takes in one day before selecting the eventual version that would appear in the *White* album. In terms of "Lucy in the Sky with Diamonds," the Beatles spent eight hours rehearsing, and reworking, and reworking that song, while the crew sat around waiting for them to finish it. And when they finally recorded it, it took only seven takes. "Something," which was originally recorded on April 16th, 1969, there were three takes of the basic track. On May 2nd, they remade the song, recording 36 takes, and they decided the 36th was the best. In August, they added an orchestra. Later, they cut two minutes of instrumental and released the final form on September 26th.

The Beatles reflect, I think, that 1 percent inspiration and 99 percent perspiration. But I think the prize for staying focused goes to poet William Wordsworth. You see, he spent 40 years revising and rewriting "The Prelude." The lines about nature in this poem were beautiful and eloquent, so much so that they must have been natural for him, natural for him to pen. But no, they really came through brute force. In fact, one critic observed that this naturalism was not achieved by simple spontaneity. It required a great deal of deliberate knowing, self-criticism, and revision. Here's the lesson. There's a misconception about creativity that's popular and often embraced by many individuals that all we need is that aha moment; we need that bolt of lightning to hit us, and we're creative. The reality is that that aha moment, in order for creativity to really happen, must be followed by hard work. So, the principles for effective convergence, those principles that create the mindset for effective convergence within a creative process are, to apply affirmative judgment, to keep novelty alive, to check your objectives to make sure that your options meet the needs of reality, and stay focused.

Let's look at three tools, three deliberate tools, that move our convergent process from a more intuitive process to a more deliberate, systematic process. The first tool we call Hits. It's much like what Bob Hope did when he was converging on jokes. We review our divergent list, identifying the most promising options, and we mark those options that are most appealing to us. The ones that we think will be successful, the ones that hold the greatest value. This tool can be used as a group, so it can be done individually, as Bob Hope probably worked.

Hits can also be used as a tool to help teams to converge. Now, naturally, when you're using it as a team, it's more complicated, and it will take more time. So, a recommendation that I have is, if you use Hits to evaluate a list of divergent ideas, to mark the ones that seem most promising, you might want to limit the number of hits that you give members of the team. The general rule of thumb we use is the 10 percent rule. So, if you've generated 100 options, you take 10 percent and give each individual 10 votes, 10 hits. Now, when you do this, be careful of group-think. We want to avoid people selecting options because someone else has selected that option, so you might first want to allow people to review the options, the list of ideas that were generated through divergent thinking, and to make their choices independently, and then later show them publicly.

Hits can be expanded to a second tool, Clustering. So we begin by identifying our hits, and sometimes when we identify our hits, we notice that there are some themes that emerge, that there are options that naturally relate to one another, and can categorize them; we can put them into clusters. To ensure that these clusters really hang together, we suggest that you put labels on the cluster, you identify what the theme is, and you give some descriptive theme to that cluster. When you use this tool and you cluster, be sure that the clusters remain independent. They shouldn't overlap. Also, be sure that all of the items in that cluster really belong to that cluster. That's the importance of having the theme. We don't want to force all of our options, or all of our ideas, into clusters, and if there's one that's unique, we lose the uniqueness if we force it into a group. It's okay to leave unique items alone.

The third tool is called Blue Sky Voting. Here, we use codes to help us to understand our reaction to our hits. We use coding labels, or electronic bullets. We use two colors, green and blue. When we go through and we identify our hits, we use these two colors to represent two different reactions to these options that we're evaluating. Some hits, we use green dots or green bullets, green meaning we're green-lighting that idea or that option. It's fairly straightforward. We're excited about it. It's easy to implement. We can just do it. Then we reserve, in the spirit of staying open to novelty, we reserve some of our hits for those blue sky ideas, and we use blue dots, or blue bullets. These are options that are out there, that are highly novel. We're excited about these options but, gosh, we're not sure how to implement them. But, if we could, wow, they would be dynamite.

So, we split our hits between these two sets. And now, when we do this, let's go back to the example of doing this in a group, if we're giving 10 hits to group members, what we might want to do is to give more dots to the green-lighted ideas, let's say seven, and three for the blue-sky ideas. In fact, you can do the same thing yourself, and in this way you're intentionally staying open to those novel options.

In fact, this blue sky voting is my preferred way of going through convergence. I use this very often when I'm working with groups, because it does help to keep novelty alive, and it helps to sort options into those that are easier to pursue versus those that will require more thought. And it's also interesting in a group application, because you begin to see different perceptions and is there consensus and excitement building around those blue sky options?

So, there are some further things to be thinking about in terms of divergent and convergent thinking, and a common question that I'm asked when I work with groups is, "How do you balance? How do you split your time between divergent and convergent thinking?" Well, there's no right answer to this, but I can tell you it's a common mistake to spend too much time on divergent thinking. After all, it's fun, and people enjoy it, and they get lost in the divergent thinking, and suddenly they realize, "Oh, gosh. We need to come to a decision," and they will often make a quick, convergent decision. As a very loose general rule, I recommend that you spend about the same amount of time on convergent thinking as you do on divergent thinking. And because convergent thinking is a bit more complicated with groups where you have to discuss and move towards consensus, we might even want to dedicate slightly more time, perhaps 60 percent to convergent thinking and 40 percent to divergent thinking.

So let's apply what we've learned. I want to encourage you to practice these principles of convergent thinking individually. Find a challenge, either at work, or perhaps, a personal challenge. Start with some divergent thinking. And then, once you're satisfied that you've generated enough options, then shift to convergent thinking. Use one of the tools that you learned in this lecture. Try out doing hits, or clustering, where you do hits and then you group the options. Try out Blue Sky Voting.

Try this out with groups as well, first with groups that are safe, maybe families and friends and coworkers that you get along well with, who you can experiment with. Identify a challenge. If you're working with the family, perhaps what to do this weekend, or where to go on vacation. With work, maybe goals for next year. And again, begin by divergent thinking, and then apply convergent thinking. See what the difference is like when you apply these tools of Hits, Clustering, and Blue Sky Voting with groups.

It's important to master the skill of convergent thinking and the tools, because these tools will be used throughout the creative process, whether you're clarifying, or you're generating ideas, or you're thinking about ways to carry the idea forward, we'll be using these tools.

We used divergent and convergent thinking recently with our boys. We generated ideas for what to do over the weekend. So, we began by telling them the guidelines for divergent thinking, and we all generated ideas for what we might do for the weekend. And then we taught them Blue Sky Voting for convergence. We gave them green dots for just-do-its, and we gave them blue dots for their wishes, and, I have to be honest, I was surprised by their decision. They wanted to spend the night in a hotel in Buffalo, where we live. That was the green-light idea, but their blue-sky idea I wouldn't have predicted. These three boys wanted to go on a shopping spree, and then the next day they wanted to visit boutiques and artisan shops on a well-known street in Buffalo, Elmwood Avenue.

Follow the guidelines for convergent thinking. Try these tools with your family and friends, and you might just be surprised by the results, like I was. And I'll see you next time.

Stages of the Creative Process—and You

Lecture 7

This lecture examines a universal process known as creative problem solving, the steps and stages of thought that we move through to close the gap between what we have and what we want. Research shows that everyone goes through these steps, whether it's in regard to superstar creativity or everyday creativity. Graphic analysis of people who have created drawings of the process that they move through to solve problems in their professional and personal lives reflect these stages that you will be introduced to in this lecture.

Creative Problem Solving

- In the model known as creative problem solving, there are four steps that we move through. The first is called clarify, in which we're identifying the challenge or challenges that need to be worked on. The second step is called ideate, in which we begin to generate ideas. These are tentative solutions. In the third step of the process, called develop, we take those initial concepts and ideas, and we turn them from good, promising ideas into really great solutions. Finally, in the fourth step, called implement, we have to move our solutions from our own head into reality.

- Creative problem solving is intuitive and natural. It's not designed to replace our natural creative process; rather, it builds on this process.

- In addition, it's research based. The creative problem solving process has, perhaps, been the most widely researched deliberate creative process model, and it has been found to be one of the most effective methods used in creativity training. The most effective methods are cognitive models, models in which we're given thinking strategies or tools that help us to guide and direct our thinking.

Solving a problem is like solving a puzzle. It causes you to think about different pieces of the problem, which then come together into a solution.

- Furthermore, creative problem solving is highly generalizable. It can be used in all areas of life. Some creative process models are a bit more domain specific.

- Creative problem solving requires the use of different mental operations, and in this way, because creative thinking is a higher-order thinking skill that has subskills to it, we're taking those subskills and improving those skills in order to achieve this complex form of thinking.

- Because creative problem solving involves different ways of thinking, we can look at how people connect to that process. Psychologists call it cognitive style, a preference for how we process and organize information—how we engage in thinking.

- Research has shown that we don't all move through creative problem solving in the same way. While we all use creative problem solving and it's natural for us to be creative problem solvers, we may have a preference for some of the mental operations, or steps in the process, over others.

Preferences for Ways of Thinking

- Like handedness, we have different preferences for ways of thinking. There are areas within this creative process that will meet our preferences, just as most of us have a preference for the right hand over the left hand, and when we're using that way of thinking, it will flow. It will feel natural and comfortable.

- But you can use different preferences. You can switch your hands, and you can write with the other hand. It might feel a little uncomfortable because it's not preferred, but you can do it.

- The clarifier is the person in the meeting who's calling a halt to the discussion and saying, "Are we really solving the right problem?" Clarifiers tend not to be too quick to move to solutions. They enjoy doing research and gathering information. They attend to the details. They're methodical in making sure they do their homework. They tend to ask lots of questions because they need information.

- If you take any of these preferences to an extreme, there can be a liability, and the liability for a clarifier is analysis paralysis. They may overanalyze. Clarifiers annoy others by asking too many questions, being realistic to a fault, or overloading people with information.

- The next preference is the ideator, who looks at the big picture. Ideators dream of possibilities. They toy with ideas. They're highly fluent. You need an idea? Go to an ideator. They don't know where the stop button is. They stretch their imagination. They will offer out-of-the-box ideas. They take an intuitive approach to problem solving. They jump from A to Z. They can't tell you how they did that, but they often do that. They're adventurous, and they're dreamers.

- Take this to an extreme, and the potential liability for an ideator is that they may overlook the details. They might annoy others by drawing attention to themselves, by not being able to stick to one idea, by being abstract, or by offering ideas that are off the wall. Sometimes, in fact, they offer ideas that are off the wall just to get a reaction from other people.

- The third preference is the developer preference. A developer takes an idea and tinkers with it. Developers improve upon ideas. Developers put together workable solutions. They analyze and compare competing solutions, looking at the pros and the cons. They can get lost in a single idea, going very deeply into it. They craft and refine and perfect a single idea, working it up into a fantastic solution.

- The potential liability for developers is that they're perfectionists. They may get stuck developing the perfect solution. How they may annoy others is by being too nitpicky—finding flaws in others' ideas or getting locked into one approach.

- The fourth preference is the implementer. Implementers are individuals who are quick to action, always moving forward. They love to see ideas brought to fruition. They want to see things happen. They're decisive and determined.

- The potential liability for implementers is that they sometimes leap to action too quickly. They might annoy others by being too pushy, expressing their frustration readily when others do not move as quickly as they're moving, and overselling their ideas.

- There are some people who struggle to rank these four preferences—clarifier, ideator, developer, implementer—and they struggle in that they like all four stages of the creative process. Their energy is equally distributed across all four. There aren't peak preferences or low preferences in their profile. We call these individuals integrators.

- Integrators have some unique qualities. Something that's unique to the integrator when they work on teams is that they like to focus on harmony and relationships and collaboration and cooperation. They're excellent team members, because team chemistry is important to them. They easily relate to the other preferences.

The Value of Understanding Your Preferences

- Understanding where you flow and excel in the creative process and where you come up short can improve your creative performance. Where you don't have preferences, you might tend to skip those steps of thinking. If something doesn't come naturally to you, you can learn a tool.

- We have tools in the creative process and creative problem solving that make tasks easier. We have tools for clarify, tools for ideate, tools for develop, and tools for implement.

- There are also implications for teams. Sometimes when we're working with others who have a different preference from us, there's friction and conflict, and by understanding these differences, we can hopefully move to a place where we begin to appreciate the differences. Ultimately, strong teams have a mix of these preferences, and they're able to complement one another.

- One of the benefits of understanding your preferences is individual management—managing yourself and managing your development by learning tools that make up for your preferences. You can't use your low preferences as a shield.

- Consider doing this, and consider sharing your results with others, because there are individual implications—understanding ourselves and managing ourselves—but this also has massive implications for relationships. Compare your results. Identify differences and similarities. Discuss how this might impact your relationship.

- A main activity we do with others is to solve problems together, and by understanding these different preferences, or these similar preferences, it might help us to be more effective in terms of how we solve problems together.

- Finally, don't stop there. Share your individual results with others, as many as you can, so that they can better understand you. Knowing your preference will help you to maximize the benefit of these tools so that you can practice those areas that either complement what you already do naturally or to use tools that help to fill in areas that may not naturally come to you. Understanding your process preferences, along with someone else in your life, just might help you to have an even stronger relationship.

Suggested Reading

Grivas and Puccio, *The Innovative Team*.

Puccio, et al., *Creativity Rising*.

VanGundy, *Idea Power*.

Activities

Activity 1: Your Creative Thinking Preference
Based on the descriptions of the four creative thinking preferences—clarifier, ideator, developer, and implementer—for which area(s) do you have a preference? Or, if you took the FourSight measure, how have the results helped you to understand your creativity?

Activity 2: Comparing Preferences
Encourage others to reflect on their preferences within the creative problem solving process, or have them complete the FourSight measure. Share your results; then, discuss differences and similarities. Consider how they might impact your relationship.

Stages of the Creative Process—and You

Lecture 7—Transcript

Did you face a problem this week that didn't have an easy answer? A challenge that required you to search for a solution, to use your creative imagination? Perhaps professionally or personally. You probably did. J.P. Guilford, one of the pioneering researchers in the field of creativity, said that to live is to have problems, and to solve problems creatively is to grow. The bottom line is that we all face challenges; we all face problems. One definition of a problem is it's the gap between what we have and what we want, and often we need creative thinking when we don't know how to close that gap. In fact, that's when we especially need creative thinking, when the solution to help us close that gap is not there, ready for us to pick it up and to implement, and we have to search for that solution. We have to generate that solution ourselves.

Recall creativity is the production of novel solutions. These are novel solutions that help us to resolve open-ended problems, problems that have multiple directions that we can go in, that have multiple right answers, versus closed-ended problems. Closed-ended problems have a known solution, a single right answer. This lecture examines a universal process, the steps and stages of thought that we move through to close that gap between what we have and what we want. Research shows that everyone goes through these steps, whether it's superstar big creativity or everyday creativity. Graphic analysis of people who've created drawings of the process that they move through to solve problems in their professional and personal lives reflect these stages that we'll be introduced to in this lecture.

The past three lectures looked at two fundamental creative thinking skills—divergent and convergent thinking. We now put those two skills into a full and complete creative process, from the beginning of the process, where we identify the challenge that we want to work on, all the way through to the successful implementation of a new, useful solution. So, what is that universal process? In this course, we'll be looking at a model called creative problem solving. And in creative problem solving, there are four stages, four steps that we move through. The first is called clarify. In clarify, we're identifying the challenge, or challenges, that need to be worked on. In the second step, we call it ideate. We begin to generate ideas. These are tentative solutions. In the third step of the process, we take those tentative solutions, those initial concepts and ideas, and we turn them from good, promising ideas into really great solutions. And then, finally, in the fourth step, we have to put legs on our ideas. We have to move our solutions from our own head into reality. We call this step implement.

I refer to this process as creative problem solving, the creative problem solving process. Let me break down each word in this process. "Creative" means our goal is to look for novelty. By "problem" we mean we're attempting to close the gap between where we are and where we wish to be. And by "solving," we're meeting the needs of the situation. We're resolving the situation. The focus is on producing something useful and valuable. And finally, we call this a "process," because there are identifiable and deliberate steps and procedures in this process and tools. And because it's a process, it's a method that's learnable and repeatable.

So, why use creative problem solving in this course? Why use that as our creative model to organize our tools that we'll be learning and applying? Well, firstly, creative problem solving is intuitive, and it's natural. It's not designed to replace our natural creative process. Rather, it builds on this process. And the second reason is that it's research-based. The creative problem solving process has, perhaps, been the most widely researched deliberate creative process model. In fact, a meta-analytic study that went after the basic question, "Can creativity be trained?" evaluated some 70 different studies that looked at programs for creativity. It looked at these 70 different studies, and it concluded that creative problem solving was one of the most effective methods used in creativity training.

You see, the most effective methods are cognitive models, models in which we're given thinking strategies, thinking tools, that help us to guide and direct our thinking. Another reason why we're looking at creative problem solving and using that in this course is that it's highly generalizable. It can be used in all areas of life. Some creative process models are a bit more domain-specific. TRIZ, the inventive thinking process that originated in Russia, is designed mainly for engineers. The other reason why we've selected creative problem solving is that we know that it requires the use of different mental operations, and in this way, because creative thinking is a higher order thinking skill that has subskills to it, we're taking those subskills and we're improving upon those skills in order to achieve this complex form of thinking.

Now, because creative problem solving in these steps that I've just described to you, of clarify, ideate, develop, and implement involve different ways of thinking, we can look at how people connect to that process. Psychologists call it cognitive style; that's a preference for how we process and organize information, how we engage in thinking. And what we've discovered through research is that when you look at creative problem solving, we all don't move through creative problem solving in the same way. While we all use creative problem solving, and it's natural for us to be creative problem solvers, we may have a preference for some mental operations within this process. Some of the steps in the process over other steps in the process.

I'm going to invite you to test this out. Let's have an experience. Let's look and see what your connection is to creative problem solving. If you're in a place where you can record your responses, that would be helpful. If not, that's okay. You can be like J.K. Rowling and do this in your mind. So, what I'd like you to do is to record the numbers 1, 2, 3, and 4, just in a column, and I'd like you to think about these four steps of the creative problem solving process. I'm going to ask you to prioritize these four steps relative to yourself. No right or wrong answer, it's just your opinions about yourself. And let me help you out.

So, think about these four areas of the process. Let me review them again. Clarify is where you closely examine a situation to define the problem, to identify the challenges; you're closely examining the situation. Ideate is a more playful way of thinking; it's generating possibilities; it's brainstorming. The third step, develop, is taking an idea and perfecting it, improving upon it. And then, fourth, we have implement, which is taking action. Now, choose which one of those four steps comes most naturally to you. Which one do you prefer? Which one do you have the greatest energy for? Which one gives you great energy? And write that in next to number one.

Now, let's go to the opposite end. Let's think about number four. We've eliminated one. Three steps remain. Of the three steps that remain, which one of these three do you struggle with? You really have to concentrate. It takes energy for you to do it. It doesn't come naturally to you. And write that in next to number four. That will leave two steps. Next to number two, write in, of the two remaining steps, the one that you prefer, the one that comes most naturally to you. And obviously, that number three blank and it leaves one more step. That can get slotted in next to number three.

I do this with groups as a warm-up to get individuals to see how creative problem solving is, in a way, already inside of them. What we used this exercise for, in addition to that, is to have people then compare their results with someone else. And when they do this, they discover something interesting. They discover something that I call psychological diversity. We talk about diversity and the value of diversity. In fact, diversity has been shown to enhance and improve creativity. But we tend to think about diversity as the kind of diversity that you see, the kind of diversity related to ethnicity, race, gender, and age. Psychological diversity refers to the kind of diversity that's in our head, that relates to how we think and behave in different ways.

So what people often discover when they start to compare how they rank these four steps to someone else is, "Gosh, your rankings are completely different from mine. I have implement as my highest preference and, look, you have ideate, or clarify." So, in this way, we begin to discover that we have preferences for these steps of the creative process, some we'll be more comfortable with; others may be a little less comfortable for us.

Now, The Great Courses has provided two ways for you to complete the full measure. There's a psychological measure that's been around for some time, that's been shown to be reliable and valid, a more scientific way of examining these preferences; it's called FourSight. And if you look into your guide book, you can find instructions on how to complete this tool, this tool called FourSight.

When we take these four steps of the process and we personify them, we call them clarifier, ideator, developer, and implementer. So, someone who prefers clarify, we call them a clarifier; Someone who prefers ideate, we call them an ideator; develop, developer; implement, implementer. We're going to go into each of these preferences, and we'll explore the meaning behind these preferences. Notice that I'm referring to these as preferences. They're not abilities. If you have a high preference to ideate, you wrote that in next to number one, it doesn't necessarily mean you're a genius ideator. What it means is that that's where you have your energy; that's what comes naturally to you. You tend to think in ideational ways.

To drive this point home, I'm going to ask you to do something for me, and if you're in a place where you can do this, that's fine. You'll find this useful. But you can also do this in your mind as well, and I think you'll get the point behind the exercise rather quickly. So if you're somewhere where you can write, take a pen or a pencil and sign your name, as if you were signing a check or a contract. How did that go? It probably felt comfortable to you. It probably felt natural. It was easy. Now, take your pen and put it in your non-preferred hand. If you're right-handed, in your left hand, and vice-versa. Now sign your name a second time next to your first signature. How did that go? Probably took more time; probably felt a little awkward; probably really had to concentrate in order to do that.

So, this is an analogy. Like handedness, we have different preferences for ways of thinking. There are areas within this creative process that will meet our preferences, just like we have a preference for the right hand over the left hand, and when we're using that way of thinking, it will flow. It will feel natural. It will feel comfortable. But you can use different preferences. You can switch your hands, and you can write with the other hand. It might feel a little uncomfortable because it's not preferred, but you can do it.

So let's go into these preferences, now that we recognize that they're not necessarily about ability, and let's start with the clarifier. So, if you ranked this as your highest preference or you've had the opportunity to already complete the foresight measure, this is likely to describe you. The clarifier is the person in the meeting who's calling a halt to the discussion and is saying "Are we really solving the right problem?" They tend not to be too quick to move to solutions. They enjoy doing research and gathering information.

They attend to the details. They're methodical in making sure they do their homework. They tend to ask lots of questions because they need information.

Now, if you take any of these preferences to an extreme, there can be a liability, and the liability for a clarifier is analysis paralysis. They may over analyze. We can all be annoying. We can rub people the wrong way, and each of these preferences have their own unique way of doing this. Clarifiers annoy others by asking too many questions, being too realistic. Overloading people with information.

Now, for each preference, I'll give you an example of a person I consider to be a creative representation of that preference, and for the clarifier, I'm going to suggest that Irish journalist Veronica Guerin is an example of a creative clarifier. She's credited with bringing down organized crime in Dublin. There were many unsolved crimes at the time. Drug use was up, but no one knew why. She conducted deep investigation. She initially used her accountant's training and her business experience to take fraud reporting to an entirely new level of detail. She craved firsthand information, firsthand detail. She showed little regard for her personal safety in chasing down these stories and getting to the heart of the matter, to the truth. In a moment's notice, she would fly off and chase a lead, literally. She used a technique called doorstepping where she'd show up and pummel someone with questions. It was described that her work was "undiluted." She searched for truth in details, and ultimately it created change. It improved the situation. Sadly, she was assassinated in 1996.

Let's move to the next preference. We call this one ideator. If you ranked this as your highest area, ideate, in that ranking exercise we did earlier, this is likely to describe you, but, if it was your lowest ranking, it's important to understand that there are people like this. Ideators look at the big picture. They dream of possibilities. They toy with ideas. They're highly fluent. You need an idea? Go to an ideator. They don't know where the stop button is. They stretch their imagination. They will offer out-of-the-box ideas. They're intuitive. They take an intuitive approach to problem solving. They jump from A to Z. They can't tell you how they did that, but they often do that. They're adventurous, and they're dreamers. Take this to an extreme, and the potential liability for an ideator is that they may overlook the details.

How might they annoy others? Drawing attention to themselves. Not being able to stick to one idea. Being abstract. Offering ideas that are off the wall. Sometimes, in fact, they offer ideas that are off the wall just to get a reaction from other people.

Here's a quote from an ideator. "I was shocked at college to see 100 of my classmates in the library all reading copies of the same book. Instead of doing as they did, I went into the stacks and read the first book written by an author whose name began with 'Z'. I received the highest grade in the class. That convinced me that the institution was not being run correctly, and I left." This is a quote from John Cage. He's an influential 20th century American composer. His ideas were original, and sometimes even shocking.

Imagine this. You walk into the performance hall. The conductor comes out, and he stands in front of the orchestra, and he does nothing. He stands there for 4 minutes and 33 seconds. This was a piece written by John Cage. The purpose was to get the audience to tune into the sounds naturally occurring in their environment. Another revolutionary idea of John Cage was the prepared piano, where objects, like nuts and bolts, were placed into the piano to alter the sound. Originality and a diverse range of ideas independent in nature; seems to me that John Cage, though he never completed FourSight, exemplifies the ideator preference.

Let's look at the developer preference. Now, I'll be honest with you. This is where I get to be a little more comfortable, because this is one of my preferences. A developer takes an idea and tinkers with it. They improve upon it. In some ways, in an earlier lecture, with the Beatles, we looked at how they stayed focused in their studio work and refined and refined the songs that they were performing. Developers put together workable solutions. They analyze and compare competing solutions, looking at the pros and the cons. They can get lost in a single idea, going very deeply into it. They craft and refine and perfect a single idea, working it up into a fantastic solution. The potential liability for a developer is that they're perfectionists. They may get stuck developing the perfect solution. How they may annoy others is being too nitpicky, finding flaws in others' ideas, and getting locked into one approach.

Here's a newspaper quote of someone I think who displays a developer preference.

> "Because he's been on the top of the comic heap for so long, it is easy to assume that Mr. Rock can make the whole big room shake with the same convulsive laughter because he was born that way. Like Tiger Woods, Bill Clinton, or Tom Brady, he seems genetically predisposed to do precisely what he does."

Born to be funny? Innate talent? Maybe. Certainly, I think, hard work, and I think this reflects the developer tendency. Chris Rock may also be an ideator. In fact, you can have multiple preferences. If you use the foresight measure, you can see this in your profile. So it's likely that he may be an ideator as well, but I also think that his process shows developer qualities. You see, before a really big show, he begins by making appearances in small comedy clubs to test out his jokes. He shows up unannounced; there may be as few as 50 people in the audience. His ideas are sketched out on a yellow legal pad. He might perform for 45 minutes, and out of that, walk away with 5 to 10 good lines. Get this, he does this 40 to 50 times before he appears in a big show. That sounds like a developer.

The fourth area, the fourth preference, is called implementer. This is my highest preference. These are individuals who are quick to action, always moving forward. They love to see ideas brought to fruition. This is the person in the meeting who pounds the table and says "Alright, enough discussion. Let's make a decision and move forward." They want to see things happen. They take the Nike approach, if you remember the old Nike slogan, "Just do it." They're decisive and determined, and the potential liability—and I know I suffer from this—is they sometimes leap to action too quickly. They might annoy others by being too pushy, expressing their frustration readily when others do not move as quickly as they're moving, and overselling their ideas.

So, a creative implementer? I would suggest Dean Kamen as an example of a creative implementer. With more than 400 patents, you might think Dean Kamen is an ideator. With novel ideas like the Segway, it's certainly possible that he may have an ideator preference as well. But, Dean Kamen gets things done. Even from an early age, before he graduated from high school, he automated the Times Square ball drop for New Year's Eve. He built control systems for sound and light shows in his basement, and he had contracts with Hayden Planetarium, the Four Seasons, and the Museum of the City of New York.

In fact, before he graduated from high school—and this was in the 1960s—he was earning $60,000 a year, and he kept right on going. In 1976, at age 25, he founded his first company, AutoSyringe, and he sold it before age 30. Following the sale of AutoSyringe, he founded DEKA Research and Development Corporation.

So, there's another combination that I should mention to you, and some of you may have experienced this. I talked about clarifiers, and ideators, and developers and implementers independently. But there are some folks who struggle, and perhaps struggled with that activity that we did earlier, where you had to rank these four steps, and they struggle in that they like all four stages of the creative process. Their energy is equally distributed across all four. There aren't peak preferences or low preferences. No peaks or valleys in their profile. We call these individuals integrators, and integrators have some unique qualities. And something that's unique to the integrator, when they work on teams, is that they like to focus on harmony, and relationships, and collaboration, and cooperation. They're excellent team members, because team chemistry is important to them. They easily relate to the other preferences.

So we've talked about clarifiers, ideators, developers, implementers, and integrators. How is this valuable? What are the individual implications? Well, first of all, it can improve your creative performance, understanding where you, perhaps, flow and excel in the creative process and, perhaps, where you come up short in the creative process. And where you come up short, where you don't have preferences, you might tend to skip those stages, those steps of thinking. We can get around that by learning tools. If something doesn't come naturally to you, you can learn a tool. In fact, that's how I got into the field of creativity. You see, I'm a low ideator. That's my lowest preference.

When I was first introduced to the field of creativity, I was amazed by all these ideation tools that made this way of thinking easier for me. I can't put a screw in without a screwdriver, so someone invented a screwdriver. We have tools in the creative process and creative problem solving that, like the screwdriver, makes tasks easier. We have tools for clarify, tools for ideate, tools for develop, and tools for implement.

There are also implications for how we team. Sometimes when we're working with others who have a different preference from us, there's friction, there's conflict, and by understanding these differences, we can hopefully move to a place where we begin to appreciate the differences. And ultimately, strong teams have a mix of these preferences, and they're able to complement one another.

Here's a real life story. This is a story about a married couple, Carl and Gert Cori. The insights that they made into carbohydrate metabolism led to improved treatment for diabetes. In fact, because of this, they won the Nobel Prize in 1947 for chemistry. As biochemists, they insisted on collaborating in the laboratory. In fact, when they were offered university positions, they would turn down the position if they weren't permitted to work together in the laboratory. They were collaborative creators.

Here are three quotes. In these quotes, I think you'll begin to see how their foresight preferences made them a powerful team. This is a quote from a post-doc who worked in the lab with them. "They were a remarkable pair," he said. "Gerty would have flights of fancy. She'd come up with extraordinary ideas. Carl had the ability to put them into concrete questions to answer. And, therefore, as a team, they were extraordinary."

This is what their son had to say about his parents. "Mother had the ideas, then they would both go into the lab to execute the idea or disprove it." And here's a quote from Carl Cori, from the speech that he delivered at the Nobel banquet. He said, "Our efforts have been largely complementary, and one without the other would not have gone as far as in combination."

So, what's the value of understanding your preferences? Well, one is individual management. Managing yourself and managing your development, learning tools that make up for your preferences. You can't use your low preferences as a shield. I'm a low ideator. I can't say I'm sorry, I don't ideate. Don't ask me for ideas. Again, The Great Courses has provided you with ways to complete the measure if you choose to look at a scientific way of recognizing and examining your full profile. Consider doing this, and consider sharing your results with others, because, remember, I mentioned that we have individual implications, understanding ourselves and managing ourselves, but this also has massive implications for relationships. I encourage you to share your results with others, and perhaps get others to go through the warm-up exercise that we did, so you might see their preferences or make the foresight measure available to them. And compare your results. Identify differences and similarities. Discuss how this might impact your relationship. A main activity we do with others is to solve problems together, and by understanding these different preferences, or these similar preferences, it might help us to be more effective in terms of how we solve problems together.

And finally, don't stop there. Share your individual results with others, as many as you can, so that they can better understand you. Again, Lectures 8 through 19, we dive into each of the creative problem solving steps, learning tools. Knowing your preference will help you to maximize the benefit of these tools as we go through them, so that you can practice those areas that either complement what you already do naturally, or to use tools that help to fill in areas that may not naturally come to you. And understanding your process preferences, along with someone else in your life, just might help you to have an even stronger relationship. And I'll see you next time.

Clarifying the Challenge

Lecture 8

This lecture focuses on the role of problem clarification in creative thinking and the importance of how we see the problem and how that determines all of the thinking that occurs afterward. In this lecture, you will learn tools for clarification. To clarify, we generate wishes and goals. We start by diverging on goals, and then we converge. We explore the data by diverging and converging. We use our data to move us to identify challenge statements using statement starters.

Tools for Clarification

- There is a natural sequence that we move through as we go from the initial challenge through to implementation. We first begin by problem identification.

- In the clarify step, we do three things. We begin by defining our goal. What's our wish? Then, we gather data; we examine the situation. The third aspect is to formulate a challenge or challenges that we need to address in order to get to our goal.

- Each step of creative problem solving involves a different kind of thinking, and in clarify, we suggest that the kind of thinking that's being used is strategic thinking.

- Strategic thinking can be defined as the ability to sense the problem, to identify the key issues, and to see the paths that will move you toward your desired future.

- Robert Fritz created a model for creativity called the creative tension model, which states when we create a desired future, a goal or a wish, and we understand what our current reality is, it creates tension between where we want to go and where we are. In other words, we have a problem.

- There are two ways to reduce that tension. One way is to forget all about our desired future. That's probably not a productive way to resolve the tension. A more productive way to resolve that tension is to change our current reality—to move it toward our desired future, resolving those challenges. As we overcome those challenges that stop us from our wish, we turn our current reality into our future.

- In clarify, we're attempting to define where we want to go, creating an understanding of where we are, and then identifying in a strategic way of thinking those challenges that, if we could overcome them, we would be able to realize our vision. In creative problem solving, we diverge and converge in all of the steps and all of the major aspects within the steps of the process.

Influence, Imagination, Interest

- Generate a list of wishes by answering the following questions. What's been on your mind lately? What have you done lately that you wish you could do better? What challenges have been on your mind lately? What opportunities have you been thinking about? What are some goals that you would like to accomplish in the next six months? What are some goals that you would like to accomplish within a year? Finally, what are your big dreams? What are your wishes?

- Convergent thinking follows divergent thinking. We're going to use the tool known as hits. The three criteria that are most appropriate for creative problem solving for this activity are influence, imagination, and interest.

- Look over your list of wishes that you've generated, and identify first which ones you have influence over. Where are you the chief decision maker? You can execute any decision that you make. You can change the situation. You clearly have some influence. In reviewing your list, place an X or some other symbol next to those that you believe you have influence.

Writing down your goals once you set them is a great way for you to see the path to completing your goals that lies ahead of you.

- For only those wishes and goals that you have influence, forgetting the others, now examine those for imagination—meaning you need new thinking. The solution isn't apparent. You can't simply just look it up, find it in a book, or find it on the Internet. You need to apply your creative thinking in order to make this happen, and place a second X or other symbol next to those for which you have influence and you need imagination.

- Go through the wishes, only those for which you have two Xs already, and circle those for which you have interest—those that you're motivated to work on. It's important to you. Through this, hopefully you sorted your list down from a larger list to a shorter list, and these wishes and goals are the kinds of wishes and goals that really benefit from creative problem solving.

- In creative problem solving, we use specific language. Language guides thinking. How we phrase things influences how we think about things. Phrase your wish statements that have the two Xs and a circle in the following form: "I wish," or "It would be great if," and now it begins to open it up for possibilities.

The Five W's and the H

- Identifying the goal or wish is the first part of the clarify step. The second part is to look at the current reality—to gather data. Where does data come from? What are sources of data?

- One source of data is facts. What do we know? What do we know as truth, for certain, relative to this situation? Another source of data is observations. What do we see happening? Another source is feelings. How do we feel about the situation? What emotions are involved in the situation? What are our impressions and hunches about the situation? Finally, another source of data is to recognize what you don't know. What questions need to be answered? What are we uncertain about?

- To help us gather data, we use an old journalism tool called the five W's and the H: who, what, why, when, where, and how. Journalists use it to get at the details of a story.

- "Who" stands for individuals or groups that are involved in the situation. "What" stands for examining the history. What has occurred? What have you already thought of or tried? "Why" helps us to understand the reasons behind what's occurring. Why is this an issue for you? Why do you want to take care of it? Why is this important for you?

- When we think of "when," we're thinking of timing issues. Are there particular times when you might want to get started or times when this is more problematic than others? "Where" gets us to think about locations, either physical locations or a location within a process. "How" gets us to think about operations. How might this be resolved? How has this been dealt with in the past? How have others thought about this?

- We use the five W's and the H to provoke our thinking—to make sure that we cover a range of data. It's important that we diverge on data so that we don't miss any important data, and then we converge, using tools like hits and clustering and selecting the most important data.

Challenge Statements

- It's important to understand your current reality. The better we understand our current reality, the better we can go on to the next phase of clarify—to identify the pathways that will help us to move to our desired future. We call these challenge statements because they challenge us, and they challenge our thinking.

- Why identify challenge statements? Why not leap right into the massive goal and begin to generate ideas? You've already looked at the current situation. Isn't it time to get on to ideas? There's a limitation in that. It's impossible. It's too large. It's too vague and too abstract, so it's valuable to take that broad goal and break it into smaller parts that we're more easily able to address.

- What's the formula for a good challenge statement? We start with a statement starter, such as "how might …" We have an owner, for example, "I"; a verb, such as "obtain"; and an object, such as "funding for my idea." Put it all together, and the challenge statement is: "How might I obtain funding for my idea?"

- There are a variety of statement starters that you can use when creating challenge statements. "How to," "how might," "in what ways might," and "what might" are the ones that are recommended. There's power in language, and these statement starters invite multiple responses. When we phrase it in this way, we're assuming that there are multiple ways to attack the challenge.

Is Clarifying Important?

- A classic research study carried out by Jacob Getzels looked at artists' behavior. He had 31 fine artists draw a still life. He brought them into a room, and there were two tables. On one table, he had 27 different objects laid out. They were to select one or more objects and then move them to the second table to construct their still life scene.

- The artists were observed by psychologists, and they were rated on their problem clarification behavior. They were rated on the following variables: breadth, the number of objects that they examined; depth, the amount of time taken to explore the objects; and uniqueness, the extent to which they selected unusual objects.

- Their artwork was then displayed, and it was rated by expert art critics. The result was that the greater the problem clarification behavior, the more positively the art was judged. In fact, there was a rather large correlation.

- What's really interesting is that this was a longitudinal study. Seven years later, they looked at the professional success of these fine artists, and they still found significant relationships between those problem identification behaviors from when they were students and their real-life accomplishments as fine artists.

Suggested Reading

Kanji and Asher, *100 Methods for Total Quality Management.*

Weisberg, *Creativity*.

Activities

Activity 1: Writing Challenge Statements
Practice stating problems in good challenge statement form—for example, open-ended questions that begin with a statement starter (How to …, How might …, In what ways might …, What might be all the …) and include an owner, verb, and object.

Activity 2: Problem Clarification and Reflection

1. Generate 20 or more wish statements.

2. Use the three I's to determine where to invest your creative thinking efforts.

3. After selecting an area to focus on, use the five W's and H to gather data.

4. Use your data to help generate challenge statements that begin with statement starters.

5. Reflect: American educator and philosopher John Dewey said that a problem properly stated is already half solved. How did the clarify step of the creative process help you? What insights did it give you?

Clarifying the Challenge
Lecture 8—Transcript

In 1970, a dead sperm whale, 45 feet long, washed up on an Oregon beach. Beaches at that time were under the Oregon Highway Division, probably a good thing, because this was a big problem, a dead, decaying whale. Big problem, probably very well suited for the Oregon Highway Division. They were accustomed to dealing with big problems, at least, big boulders that came down the mountainside onto highways. They were accustomed to getting rid of these kinds of problems, so they transferred the same solution that they used for getting rid of boulders to taking care of this large whale. They took dynamite; they bore holes into this whale—now, remember, it was a dead whale; and they stuffed it full of dynamite. Picture the scene. A crowd gathered around. The supervisor for the demolition of this whale ushered people away and had them move back. They had this countdown, and then they set off the explosives. When you watch the video, at first there are cheers, and then the cheers quickly turn to screams. As you watch the video, the camera that's on the tripod is knocked over by flying whale, and you see feet scampering by, running for their lives. When the scene ends, the camera pans the parking lot, and there are cars in the parking lot that have been crushed by large chunks of whale. Unfortunately, the problem wasn't solved. The whale was mainly intact.

What can we learn from this story? What can we learn about process and creative problem solving? First of all, we have to be careful not to leap to action, not to immediately leap to a solution. The second thing that we can learn is how we see the problem determines the action steps we take. You see, the highway department is accustomed to big problems, working with big boulders, but not with whales, and they transferred the same solution. They used that frame of thinking to confine their thinking around how they might get rid of this whale.

This lecture focuses on the role of problem clarification in creative thinking and the importance of how we see the problem and how that determines all of the thinking that occurs afterwards. Let's locate the step within the creative problem-solving process. When you look at the natural sequence of the process, it's clarify, ideate, develop, and implement. Before we can come up with ideas, we have to first clarify the situation; we have to define the problem. Then we can ideate. Then develop follows. We don't immediately rush out and implement an idea. We have to refine an idea into a workable solution, then we can implement.

During this last week, when did you use clarify? Think back to your week. When did you have to gather information, do research, closely examine a situation? Did you ideate at all during this last week, where you had to generate novel ideas? How about develop? Did you develop at any time during this last week? Did you take an idea or a concept and improve upon it? And finally, did you implement at any point during the last week, where you took a decision or a solution or a proposed change and you brought it to fruition; you put it into action; you made it a reality? Remember our preferences for these different aspects of the creative problem-solving process. Some of us prefer some steps of this process over others.

I know I revealed to you that I'm a high implementer, and I may have mentioned to you that I'm also a low ideator. I don't think I've told you yet that I'm also a low clarifier. This is my second-lowest preference, and sometimes this is problematic for me, such as recently, when I showed up at the airport, and I suddenly recognized, or realized, that I didn't know what airline I was flying with. So I went from kiosk to kiosk inserting my credit card until one of the machines finally recognized me. I have lots of low clarifier stories like that. You see, these process preferences tell us about our mindset for the creative process. As we develop skills, we have to be mindful of these preferences. Let me give you an analogy. I used to play tennis, and I enjoyed playing tennis. When I first learned how to play tennis, I had a very good forehand, but I had an extremely unreliable backhand. So as a consequence, what did I do? Well, I ran around. I tried to make everything a forehand. I would go through great contortions to stay on the forehand side, not a very effective way to play tennis. In life, it's not a very effective way to go about problem solving either, or being creative, avoiding those steps of the process that might not come naturally to you. So what can we do about this? Well, we can learn tools. Eventually, someone taught me how to do a two-handed backhand, and that worked like a charm. I was much more reliable now, but I had to learn a strategy, a technique, a tool, if you will. In creative problem solving, we learn cognitive strategies that can make certain cognitive activities easier. They guide and direct and facilitate our thinking, just like having two hands on the backhand guided my backhand stroke.

In this lecture, we learn tools for clarification. CPS is a toolbox; creative problem solving is a toolbox that contains a set of tools. Picture a toolbox with four drawers, one drawer labeled clarify, one drawer labeled ideate, another drawer develop, and another drawer implement. You're at a place where you need to clarify? Well, you open up the clarify drawer. Need ideas? You open up the ideate drawer, and you pull out tools from that drawer. As we look at creative problem solving, I think it's important to point out that ideate, which is often synonymous with creativity. ideation, creativity is all about producing ideas, notice that ideate is only one quarter of the process. We'll be moving through each step of the process and we'll give you tools in each step to add to your toolbox. Again, why creative problem solving? Well, frankly, it works. It's been demonstrated through research that this is a highly effective process. Why start with clarify? As I mentioned earlier, there is a natural sequence that we move through as we go from the initial challenge through to implementation. We first begin by problem identification.

Einstein is evidence of that. Einstein was being interviewed by a journalist, and this journalist wanted to understand Einstein's creative process, so he posed a scenario, a fictitious scenario to Einstein. He said "Dr. Einstein, if you had one hour to resolve a problem that threatened all of humanity, how would you spend that time?" Einstein said immediately that "I would take the first 55 minutes to define the problem, and the last five minutes to come up with a solution." John Dewey, a famous American philosopher and educator, said that a problem properly stated is already half-solved.

In a meta-analytic study of creativity, where an in-depth analysis was done of 70 different studies that looked at training programs and whether they were effective in improving creative thinking, the authors, Scott, Leritz, and Mumford, did a detailed analysis of many aspects of these programs and these studies, and one of the things that they evaluated was the content used in these programs and evaluated, of the content, what made the greatest contribution to training effectiveness. Now you might think, idea generation, that had to be number one. But it wasn't. In fact, actually, what they found was that problem identification was the strongest predictor of program effectiveness, program effectiveness meaning that it significantly enhanced creative thinking skills. Seems counter intuitive, but it's not. You see, how we define the problem then channels and frames all of the thinking that occurs afterwards. In the study, they did find that idea generation was the second strongest predictor of effectiveness of creativity training.

So what happens in the clarify step? In the clarify step, we do three things. We begin by defining our goal. What's our wish? Then we gather data. We examine the situation. And then, the third aspect to clarify is to formulate a challenge, or the challenges that we need to address in order to get to our goal. Earlier I mentioned that each step of creative problem solving involves a different kind of thinking, and in clarify we suggest that the kind of thinking that's being used is strategic thinking. Strategic thinking can be defined as the ability to sense the problem, to identify the key issues, and to see the paths that will move you toward your desired future.

Here's another way to think about clarify. I'm going to borrow work done by Robert Fritz, who created a model for creativity called the Creative Tension Model, and in this model he talks about how we create our desired future, and using this rubber band, the desired future is represented by my top hand. When we create a desired future, we stretch ourselves into the future. My bottom hand represents the current reality. When we create a desired future, a goal or a wish, and we understand what our current reality is, it creates tension, tension between where we want to go and where we are. In other words, we have a problem. There are two ways to reduce that tension. One way to reduce that tension is to forget all about our desired future, to say, oh, that goal wasn't important anyhow. I would suggest that's probably not a productive way to resolve the tension. A more productive way to resolve that tension is to change our current reality, to take our current reality, which, again, is represented by my bottom hand, and to move it towards our desired future, resolving those challenges, and as we overcome those challenges that stop us from our wish, we turn our current reality into our future.

That's what we do in clarify. We're attempting to define where we want to go, create an image for where we are, an understanding of where we are, and then identifying in a strategic way of thinking those challenges that, gosh, if we could overcome them, we would be able to realize our vision. Now, in creative problem solving we diverge and converge in all of the steps, and all of the aspects, major aspects within the steps of the process. So, let's start. Let's have you engage in some creative thinking. We're going to use divergent thinking to do the first part of clarify; we're going to diverge on wishes. And I'm going to remind you that when we're engaged in divergent thinking, we're following the four guidelines. We're going to defer judgment; we're going to strive for quantity; we're going to make connections; and we're going to seek novelty.

I'm going to ask you some questions, questions designed to encourage your divergent thinking. I'd like you to record your responses. If I get ahead of you, you can pause the lecture. If you're not able to literally record your responses, then I'm going to ask you to act like J.K. Rowling on that train ride from Manchester to London. Record these thoughts in your mind. So, here are the questions. What's been on your mind lately? What have you done lately that you wish you could do better? What challenges have been on your mind lately? Let's look at a more positive question. What opportunities have you been thinking about? What are some goals that you would like to accomplish in the next six months? Let's look further out. What are some goals that you would like to accomplish within a year? And finally, what are your big dreams? What are your wishes?

So remembering that convergent thinking follows divergent thinking—remember our diamond shape, divergent thinking is branching out; convergent thinking is coming to a point; it's selecting. Let's engage in convergent thinking, and we're going to do Hits, a tool we were introduced to earlier, thinking like Bob Hope. In fact, we're going to mirror what Bob Hope did. I'm going to give you three criteria to choose a wish or a goal that's really most appropriate for creative problem solving.

So here are the three. I'll say them quickly, and then I'll take you through each one. influence, imagination, and interest. Look over your list of wishes that you've generated, and identify first which ones you have influence over. Where are you the chief decision-maker? You can execute any decision that you make. You can change the situation. You clearly have some influence. In reviewing your list, like Bob Hope, place an X across, or some other symbol next to those that you believe you have influence.

Let's move to the next I, imagination. Now, for only those items, those wishes and goals that you have influence, forgetting the others, now examine those for imagination; imagination meaning you need new thinking. The solution isn't apparent. You can't simply just look it up, find it in a book or find it on the internet. You need to apply your creative thinking in order to make this happen, and place a second X, or a cross, if you will, or another symbol next to those for which you have influence and you need imagination.

And the third I is interest. Let's go through the wishes, only those for which you have two Xs already. And let's circle for those for which you have interest; you're motivated to work on; it's important to you. Through this, hopefully we sorted our list down from a larger list to a shorter list, and these wishes and goals are the kinds of wishes and goals that really benefit from creative problem solving. We don't use creative problem solving on all problems. We use it on those where we have influence, we're looking for something new and we have interest.

In creative problem solving, we use specific language. Language guides thinking. How we phrase things influences how we think about things. I'd like you to phrase your wish statement, or wish statements, that have the two Xs and you've circled them. Phrase them in the following form: I wish, or, it would be great if. And now it begins to open it up for possibilities. You can set this aside. We'll use it in this lecture later, and in a future lecture, but make sure you do keep this list handy.

So, we've identified the goal or the wish. This is the first part of the clarify step. The second part is to look at the current reality, to gather data. Where does data come from? What are sources of data? Well, here are some. Facts, what do we know? What do we know as truth, for sure, for certain, relative to this situation? Observations, what do we see happening? Feelings, how do we feel about the situation? What emotions are involved in the situation? What are our impressions and our hunches about the situation? And finally, another source of data is to recognize what you don't know. What questions need to be answered? What are we uncertain about?

To help us gather data, here's a tool. It's an old journalist tool called the five Ws and the H. Journalists use it to get at the details of a story. I'll describe each of these to you, but we won't apply it right now. You can use this tool later. So here are the five Ws and the H: who, what, why, when, where, and how. Let's explore these a little more closely so you get a sense for how you can use them. Who stands for individuals, groups, people that are involved in the situation. What stands for examining the history. What's occurred? What have you already thought of or tried? Why helps us to understand the reasons behind what's occurring. Why is this an issue for you? Why do you want to take care of it? Why is this important for you? When we think of when, we're thinking of timing issues. Are there particular times when you might want to get started or times when this is more problematic than others? Where gets us to think about locations, either physical locations or a location within a process. And how gets us to think about operations. How might this be resolved? How has this been dealt with in the past? How have others thought about this?

So we use the five Ws and the H to provoke our thinking, to make sure that we cover a range of data, that we don't overlook. And it's important that we diverge on data, so then we don't miss any important data. Remember, in creative problem solving we diverge and converge in every step, and the major aspects in each step. So we diverge on our data, then we converge, using tools like hits, and clustering, and selecting the most important data.

It's important, remember, to understand your current reality, because when we understand our current reality, and the better we understand our current reality, we're in a better position to go on to the next phase of clarify. We're in a better position to identify the pathways that will help us to move to our desired future. We call these challenge statements because they challenge us, and they challenge our thinking.

Why identify challenge statements? Why not start with the massive, big goal? Why not leap right into that and begin to generate ideas? You've already looked at the current situation. Isn't it time to get on to ideas? Well, there's a limitation in that. When I did some consulting work for IBM in the 1980s, they called it boiling the ocean. It's impossible. It's too large. It's too vague and too abstract, so it's valuable to take that broad goal and break it into smaller parts that we're more easily able to address.

Let me give you an example, one familiar to me in my hometown, Buffalo. The Buffalo Bills, our National Football League team. As many of you may know, they lost four Super Bowls. They've never won the Super Bowl. So what might their goal be? Their goal might be, it would be great if we could win the Super Bowl. Now, we could leap right in and start generating ideas, but that's too broad. Where would we start? We'd be all over the place generating ideas. By examining the current reality, using five Ws and an H, it will help us to understand the data in the situation, then we can use that data, then, to pinpoint more specific challenges. So, specific challenges might be how to improve the offense, how to retain the best players, how to improve at the quarterback position, how to do better in the draft. So, by breaking the broad goal up into more specific challenge statements and then selecting the challenge statement to work on, we're a little closer to action.

Now, let's take some time to look at what it means to create a good challenge statement. I'll give you an example of what I consider to be a poor challenge statement. Imagine someone comes into a meeting with great enthusiasm, looking at his or her team, and says, "Hey, guys, can we improve our performance?" and the team says, "No." Well, all the problem-solving efforts are done. That's a poor challenge statement, or a poor way of phrasing a challenge, for at least two reasons. First of all, it's a yes/no; it's a closed-ended question. The team says, "no," creative thinking doesn't happen. It's also too vague. Improve performance in what ways?

Here's a better way to phrase that challenge. "In what ways might we enhance our team's performance on long-term projects?" We've done two things to modify that challenge. We've opened it up by using the statement "In what ways might we..." This encourages lots of ideas, and then we've been more specific in terms of the area for which we're looking at performance improvement.

Here's another poor challenge statement. "How to develop a new healthcare product that we can get to the market quickly and cost less to produce than our last venture." Wow. That's a mouthful. There's too much in that challenge statement, and in particular, there are criteria that will restrict our thinking. We'll be concerned about timing, getting to the market quickly, and we'll be concerned about cost. How could you generate ideas in a creative way if you're restricting your thinking by having criteria in the challenge statement? So a better way to phrase that challenge statement would be something like, "What might be some new product ideas within our healthcare line for seniors?" Again, we're opening it up by asking the question, "what might" and we've removed the criteria, so that we don't need to worry about the criteria. That comes later when you're screening the ideas.

So what's the formula for a good challenge statement? Well, we start with a statement starter, "how might…" We have an owner, for example, "I," a verb, like "obtain," and an object, "funding for my idea." Put it all together, and the challenge statement is, "How might I obtain funding for my idea?" There are a variety of statement starters that you can use when creating challenge statements. "How to," "how might," "in what ways might," "what might" are the ones that we recommend. There's power in language, and by using these statement starters—I don't mean to be pedantic—but by using these statement starters, we know that they invite multiple responses. When we phrase it in this way, we're assuming that there are multiple ways to attack the challenge.

Let's put it all together and look at an example. I'll share an example with you that's familiar to me. Let's say our department, as many businesses and academic units wish to do in the 21st century, wants to be more entrepreneurial. So, our wish is, "It would be great if our department could engage in entrepreneurial activities." We look at the data, and then we come up with challenge statements. For example, how to offer public programs. In what ways might we license our curriculum? How to develop non-credit certificate programs. How might we partner with other organizations to offer training services?

Now, in each of those examples, the "how to," the "in what ways might," or the "how might" statement starters ask for process answers. Now, notice in the next challenge statement what might be some merchandise that we can produce and sell. When we ask the question "what might," we're looking at things so you can sort your challenge statements and be careful in using these statement starters based on the kinds of ideas you wish to generate. Some more challenge statements we might generate: "expand our conference."

how to expand our conference. Another one. "how to attract more people to our conference."

So what's the value in doing this? Let's review. We've identified a goal, and we've looked at data. We've diverged on challenge statements, and then, at this point, we would converge on those challenge statements that we need to address in order to get to our goal. This can be challenging if you think about your mindset. If you have a mindset of a low clarifier, you might not have a lot of tolerance for this, but it's highly valuable. It's better to precisely define the challenge, the problem, before leaping to action. Speaking of action, this can also be frustrating for a high implementer who wants to get to action. But the value of clarifying will pay off many dividends later in the process. It's important. You can't get to the right answer if at first you don't have the right question, and that's what we're attempting to do in the clarify step.

So I've told you stories, and we've learned tools, but is clarifying really important? Let me share with you a classic research study carried out by Jacob Getzels. In the study, he looked at artists' behavior. It's an interesting study. What he did was he had 31 fine artists draw a still life. He brought them into a room, and there were two tables. On one table, he had 27 different objects laid out. They were to select one or more objects and then move them to the second table to construct their still-life scene, and the artists were observed by psychologists, and they were rated on their problem clarification behavior. They were rated on the following variables: breadth, the number of objects that they examined; depth, the amount of time taken to explore the objects; and uniqueness, the extent to which they selected unusual objects.

Their artwork was then displayed. It was exhibited, and it was rated by experts, expert art critics. The result? The greater the problem-clarification behavior, the more positively the art was judged. In fact, there was a rather large correlation here. Now, that's interesting, but what I really find interesting is that this was a longitudinal study. Seven years later, they looked at the professional success of these fine artists, and they still found significant relationships between those problem identification behaviors from when they were students and their real-life accomplishments as fine artists.

So let's review. What have we done in clarify? We've generated wishes and goals. We start by diverging on goals; then we converged. We explored the data by diverging and converging. We used our data to move us to identify challenge statements using statement starters. So now, you've identified some goals early on in this lecture. If you didn't, I encourage you to do this, and I want you to completely go through the aspects of this step of the process. Gather data. Use the five Ws and the H. Remember to diverge and converge. Then generate challenge statements, converging on challenge statements that will be most useful for you in terms of addressing and getting to your goal, closing that gap between your current reality and where you wish to be. It's important to practice these skills, and these tools that will help to sharpen your saw.

In the next lecture, we'll learn advanced clarify tools. You'll need your list of goals to practice these tools. And I'll see you next time.

Clarify Even More—Webbing and Storyboarding

Lecture 9

In this lecture, you will learn about a few advanced tools for clarifying. These are more structured approaches to problem clarification. They're helpful in moving us from the problem as given to really understanding the true nature of the problem that needs to be addressed. They will take more practice, but once learned, they're powerful. The two tools that you will learn about in this lecture are called webbing and storyboarding. By the end of the lecture, you should be able to apply them to your wishes or goals.

Advanced Tools for Clarifying: Webbing

- Webbing leverages two fundamental questions. The first question is why. When we ask this question, it forces us to think in more abstract terms—to broaden our perspective. The second basic question in webbing is what's stopping you. When you ask this question, it forces you to take a more concrete view. We use these two questions to fully scope out the problem space.

- Let's say our initial challenge is the fact that someone is not getting to work consistently on time. We ask, what's stopping you from being able to arrive on time? The response might be not leaving the house on time. What's stopping you from being able to leave your house on time? I have too many responsibilities in the morning. What's stopping you from finding ways to reduce those responsibilities? I do everything; I'm not able to delegate. What stops you from being able to delegate? I need to assign appropriate tasks to others. And what's stopping you from doing that? I just haven't made a checklist. Maybe I need to make a checklist for my family and review it to see who might be able to do which chore.

- By asking the question what's stopping you, we moved from our initial problem, which is not getting to work on time, to something very concrete—making a checklist. As we ask the question what's stopping you consecutively, we drive the response to a more concrete action-oriented frame.

- By asking these two questions, we've moved vertically, in a way. But Edward de Bono talks about lateral thinking and the ability to move sideways. In the webbing tool, we simply don't move up with the why question once without exploring, in a lateral fashion, nor do we do the same with the question what's stopping you—simply taking one line of thought and drilling down.

- The way to move sideways, or laterally, is to tag the word "else" onto these two basic questions: Why else is this important to you, or why else is this a problem? What else is stopping you? In this fashion, we begin to spread out, fully scoping out the problem space. The goal is to move from the problem as given, assuming that it is the issue that needs to be resolved, and to a problem as understood.

- In the webbing tool, we engage in divergent thinking. The questions help us respond, but we need to use that mindset of divergent thinking to fully explore all the alternative ways of looking at the problem—all of the alternative challenge statements that help us better understand our situation.

- We start with an initial problem statement, the problem as it's initially presented to us. Our goal is to branch out, to fully scope out the problem space by asking the following questions: Why? Why else? What's stopping you? What else is stopping you?

- One of the benefits of using this tool is that we're revealing the full breadth of challenges related to the problem. Another benefit is that it forces you to look at the problem from different angles and different perspectives. It may uncover the true problem.

- Sometimes, the initial problem really isn't the problem you are trying to solve. Sometimes, when you're webbing, a different challenge statement comes up. If you accept the new challenge

Webbing Worksheet

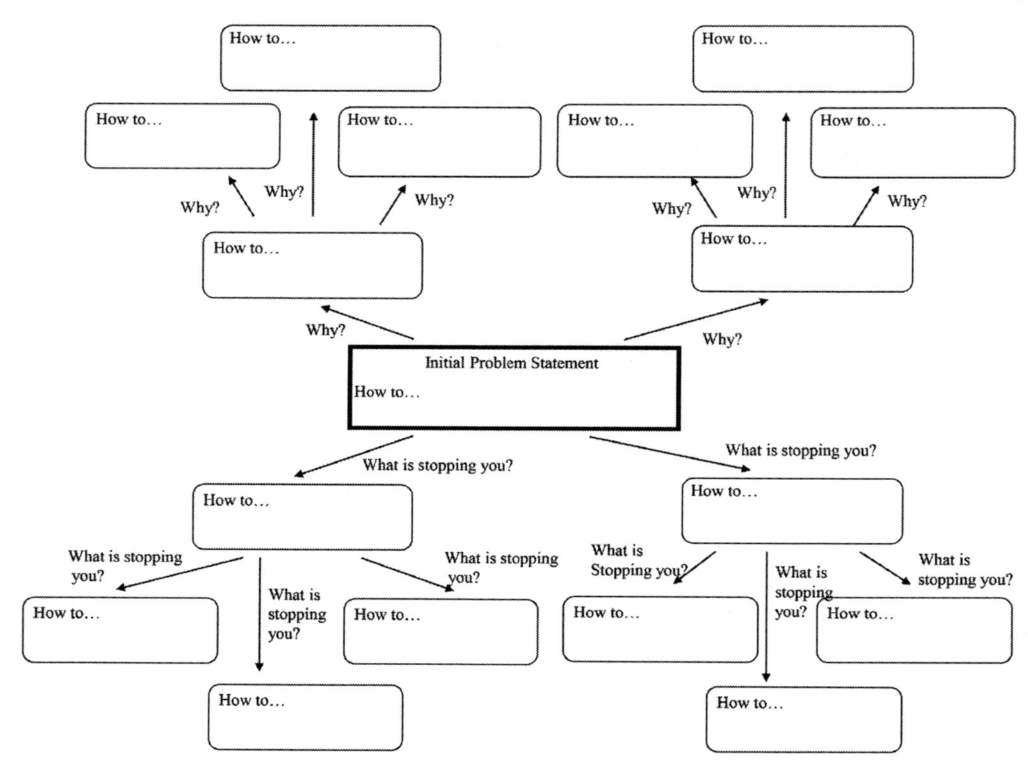

statement as the challenge statement to focus on, it opens up different possibilities and different solutions. It also gives you an order of attack.

- In order to resolve a complex problem, there are sometimes multiple challenges that need to be addressed, and by looking at the web, you can perhaps begin to identify a sequence. It also shows the relationships among the challenges, so if you tackle one challenge and resolve that challenge, it may have a positive, knock-on effect and solve other challenges.

- When we're using the webbing tool, in order for the webbing tool to work, we have to look at all the options. Therefore, when we first begin using the webbing tool, we're putting evaluation off to the side, suspending our judgment. We're striving for quantity, trying to generate many challenge statements. We're seeking novelty, so we're looking for unusual perspectives.

- The first phase in terms of using the webbing tool is to engage in divergent thinking. Then, when we think we've fully fleshed out the problem space, we move on to convergent thinking and, hopefully, by fully exploring this, move from the problem as initially given to a better understanding of the problem.

Advanced Tools for Clarifying: Storyboarding

- Storyboarding is a visual tool designed to tell a story in a visual sequence. Many credit Walt Disney with creating this tool, and certainly Disney used this tool, but he credits an animator, Webb Smith, who sketched scenes on separate pieces of paper and posted them on a bulletin board in a sequence. That's how it became known as a storyboard. When you think of a storyboard, think of a cartoon strip with panels.

- Others say that it started with silent movies and soon became the industry standard for previsualization to help create the scene in our minds before going to actual filming. *Gone with the Wind* was the first live-action film to be completely storyboarded.

- Storyboarding is still in use today. In fact, it's very popular. Pixar uses tens of thousands of storyboards when they create their films in order to be deliberately creative. They've had a terrific track record in producing wonderful animated films like *A Bug's Life*, *Finding Nemo*, *Ratatouille*, and *Wall-E*. They use storyboards to explore the possibilities, the characters, the plots, the scenes, and to identify unforeseen problems.

- We can use storyboarding to help us clarify in the creative problem solving step. To use storyboarding, you need at least six panels. You can have more, but start with six.

- In the last panel, you begin by telling the end of the story. This is a visual tool, so use images, not words. We're trying to see that which we wish to create, so we start with the sixth panel. This is our desired future—our goal, our wish. Your image for what it would look like if you accomplished that goal goes into the sixth panel.

- Then, we jump back to the first panel, in which we draw a picture of our current reality. Relative to this goal, where are we now? What does the current situation look like? Now we have our desired future, where we wish to go, and our current reality, where we are.

- In a way, this is like the Robert Fritz creative tension model. How do we resolve that tension? On one end is the desired future, our destiny, and on another is our current reality. We fill in the panels in between. We resolve the tension by identifying the challenges that we have to address in order to get to our goal.

- In the four panels in between the desired future and the current reality, in sequence, we draw images of the milestones we have to hit. In this way, we start to tell the story from the beginning, the middle, and the end.

Sample Storyboard Template

Project Name:		**Class:**
X	X	X
Narration:		Narration:
X	X	X
Narration:		Narration:

- This mirrors the clarify step of the process, because our desired future is our goal. The current reality exemplifies the data related to the current situation, and the four panels in between give us insight into the challenges that we have to address in order to get to our desired future.

- You can use storyboarding for personal goal setting. You can also use it for strategic planning with teams by having individuals draw their desired futures in terms of the organization or the unit that they're in. Individuals draw their current reality and the milestones that they have to hit in order to move from their current reality to the goals that they have for the team or their organization. Then, individuals compare storyboards and create one master storyboard by synthesizing the team members into one organizational storyboard. Then, this is converted into a strategic plan.

- Applications of storyboarding include planning a presentation or writing a book. In fact, it's becoming increasingly more popular among novelists to storyboard before they write a book. In addition, it can be used for planning a trip or laying out a project.

Applying These Tools

- Webbing and storyboarding are more advanced tools, and they require practice to develop proficiency. Start by applying webbing to one of your goals. Put a goal or wish into the middle of a webbing worksheet and ask yourself why and why else—in order to branch out and to look at it on a more global, abstract level. Then, return and ask yourself what's stopping you, and what else is stopping you, to get a more concrete view of that challenge.

- With storyboards, put one of your goals into the sixth panel. Create an image for what that future will look like if you accomplished it, and then complete the storyboard.

- These tools can be applied formally, but they can also be applied informally. They can be applied in discussions. For example, a coworker comes to you and says, "I'm having a really difficult time with project X." You can facilitate that coworker's thinking by asking what's stopping them and what else is stopping them, and in this way, you can give him or her some insight into the challenges that he or she needs to specifically address in order to move forward.

Suggested Reading

Forsha, *Show Me.*

Fritz, *Creating.*

Runco, *Problem Finding, Problem Solving, and Creativity.*

Activities

Activity 1: Webbing

Practice the webbing tool. Start by choosing a goal, wish, or challenge statement and writing it in the center of the webbing worksheet (see page 61). After applying the webbing tool, look over the range of challenge statements you generated and converge on the ones that you think, if solved, would help you most in attaining your goal.

Activity 2: Storyboarding

Practice storyboarding using the template on page 64. Instructions: Start by choosing a goal, wish, or challenge statement and drawing or writing about it in the last square. Then, draw or write about your current state in the first square. Finally, use pictures to illustrate four steps, in chronological order, that will take you from your current state to your desired future state.

Clarify Even More—Webbing and Storyboarding

Lecture 9—Transcript

My cousin, an ironing board, and his Italian mother, this is a story about clarifying. You see, my cousin, he's a busy professional, and occasionally his mother comes to visit him. And being the good, loving Italian mother, she likes to help out doing chores. So she came along one day to do some chores for him and do some ironing. He had gone off to work. When he returned home at the end of the day, she had shown him the shirts that she had ironed that day, and they all had stains on them. And she said to him, "Your iron is old. It must be creating the stains. Please go buy a new iron." So he went off to buy a new iron. He returned that evening and gave it to her. The next day, he goes off to work. She continues with the chores, doing the ironing. He comes home from work and she complains again that, "Look, the shirts, they still have stains on them. You must not have bought a good iron. Go out and buy a better iron."

So, my cousin, he goes out and he looks for the best iron possible. He finds a Black & Decker iron. Who knew Black & Decker made irons? I thought they only made power tools. So, he comes home, proudly shows his mother the new iron. He goes off to work the next day, returns home. His mother is extremely frustrated. Still, there are stains in the shirts. And now he decides to investigate, and he says, "Mom, show me what you're doing." So, she takes him over to the laundry room and she begins to iron. This time, when she takes the shirt off the ironing board, there's no stain. And my cousin asked, "Well, has anything changed?" And she said, "Well, yeah, I did a load of whites in the afternoon, and I did wash the ironing board cover." And suddenly they realized that it wasn't the iron at all. It was the ironing board cover that was causing the problems. You see, they realized there was a stain in the ironing board cover, and when the hot heat hit that board, it transferred the stain from the ironing board cover to the shirts.

What's the point of this story? The point of the story is that sometimes the problem as it's presented to us, the problem as it's given, isn't the real problem. And if we leap to action too quickly, the solution won't work, because it's not fitting the correct problem. So it's important to move from the problem, as given, to the problem, as understood, which is one of the goals in the clarify step of the creative problem solving process.

The ironing board story is actually a pretty humorous story, but here's a more serious example of the problem as given being confused with the real problem. The inability to reframe approach to warfare had serious consequences during Vietnam. You see, the U.S. Army had a checklist of pre-approved solutions. Soldiers memorized these solutions so that they could respond quickly. The problem was designed for conventional-style warfare, a problem as given, for situations that were predictable; less effective, however, in unpredictable situations, unpredictable situations such as insurgency, as in Iraq and in Afghanistan. This was a problem-as-given approach to war.

In his book, *Little Bets: How Breakthrough Ideas Emerge from Small Discoveries*, this is what Sims said about the situation. Systems and approved solutions had become too much of a substitute for moment-to-moment creative problem solving. To effectively confront the insurgent enemies of today and the future, soldiers must be able to identify and solve unfamiliar problems, rapidly adapting to the circumstances unfolding on the ground.

How did the Army arrive at this pre-approved set of solutions, this problem-as-given approach to warfare, assuming that all the problems could be predicted in advance, and therefore, solutions could be identified in advance? Well, it goes back to the cold war. You see, the Soviet Union had a powerful ground force, formidable and predictable. The U.S. military created doctrine, pre-approved solutions, to manage large operations against such a foe. The approved solutions described precisely how to solve problems that could be predicted, that could be anticipated if such a war should occur. Sounds crazy? No. It's called management. Management is wonderful in predictable situations where you're going for efficiency and attempting to be methodical. But when situations change, when they're unpredictable, then it becomes risky to stick to management practices. So it does have advantages in certain situations, but in other situations, it presents disadvantages, especially in those situations where there's novelty, as was the case in Vietnam.

Robert McNamara was the Secretary of Defense during Vietnam. He was very much influenced by his past experiences, for example, as a corporate leader, as President of Ford. And during World War II, when he worked on statistical models to maximize bombing runs. He approached the Viet Cong in the same way. The problem was, there weren't givens. This was true in terms of the situation in Iraq and Afghanistan. It was similarly unpredictable.

So why is insurgency unpredictable? In insurgent situations, there's no central coordination. Combatants are not trained from military academies, so they're less predictable, and variables are constantly changing. Given this, Colonel Casey Haskins, Head of the Department of Military Instruction at West Point, said, "Not only can we not teach approved solutions—pre-approved solutions—anymore, which take," get this, "roughly two years to approve. The truth is, we don't even know all the problems."

So the military has moved away from the problem-as-given approach, assuming that the full array of problems that will be addressed in the field could be predicted in advance, and they've moved more to a problem-as-understood approach. So what does the counter-insurgency approach look like? What is this new process that soldiers go through? Well, when soldiers arrive to a new city, they meet with the local tribe elders to learn about the nature of the insurgent enemy. They live inside of the city, immersing themselves in the population. This helps to understand the local power structure, and they experiment with different ways of gaining information. Sounds to me like they spend a lot of time in clarifying. This example underscores the importance of clarify as a creative process, and it underscores the necessity to move from an assumption that all problems are given to require a diagnostic approach to problems as understood in the 21st century, because in the 21st century, there are few givens.

In the last lecture, we introduced the concept of clarify, and in this step of the creative problem-solving process, we identified three areas of activity that we go through to clarify. First, we set our goal, we identify the direction we want to move in, the desired future state we wish to create. Then we gather data to examine the current situation, the current reality, and we use that data, then, to lead into the third aspect of the clarify step of the process, and that is to identify the challenges that have to be addressed in order to move to our desired goal.

In this lecture, we look at advanced tools for clarifying. These are more structured approaches to problem clarification. They're helpful in moving us from the problem as given to really understanding the true nature of the problem that needs to be addressed. They will take more practice, but once learned, they're powerful. The two tools that we'll use in this lecture are called webbing and storyboarding. I'll describe the tools to you, and then I'll ask you to apply them after this lecture on two of your wishes or goals.

So let's look at webbing. The way that webbing works is to leverage two fundamental questions. The first question is why. When we ask why, it forces us to think in more abstract terms, to broaden our perspective. The second basic question in webbing is what's stopping you. When you ask the question what's stopping you, it forces you to take a more concrete view, so we use these two questions to fully scope out the problem space. We ask why to broaden our view. We ask what's stopping you to force us to look more specifically at our challenge and our problems.

Let me give you an example, a very simple example. Many years ago, I was driving my youngest son to daycare, and my son asked me, "Dad, why do I have to go to daycare?" My response was, "Well, because Mom and Dad have to work." "Well, why do you have to work?" "Well, Mom and Dad need to make money." He continued to ask why. "Why do you need to make money?" "Well, we need to pay for things in our lives." "Why do you want that?" "It improves the quality of our lives." "Why do you want that?" "It makes us happy." In a very short span of time, because he asked the question why five times, we went from driving him to daycare to suddenly talking about happiness. This is how asking the question why forces us to broaden our view.

Let's look at the question what's stopping you and what happens when we pose this question. So let's say our initial challenge is the fact that someone is not getting to work consistently on time. They're arriving late on a regular basis. So we ask, what's stopping you from being able to arrive on time? The response might be not leaving the house on time. Well, what's stopping you from being able to leave your house on time? Well, too many responsibilities in the morning. I'm running around. Well, what's stopping you from finding ways to reduce those responsibilities? A response might be, well, I do everything. I'm not able to delegate. Well, what stops you from being able to delegate, to have others assist you in the morning? Well, I need to assign appropriate tasks to others. And what's stopping you from doing that? Well, I just haven't made a checklist. Maybe I need to make a checklist for my family, and to review it, and see who might be able to do which chore.

By asking the question what's stopping you, we moved from our initial problem, which is not getting to work on time, to something very concrete, making a checklist. As we ask the question what's stopping you consecutively, we drive the response to a more concrete, action-oriented frame. So what we've done is we've used the why question and the what's stopping you, but we've moved, in a way, vertically.

Edward de Bono talks about lateral thinking and the ability to move sideways. So in the webbing tool, we simply don't move up with why once only, without exploring in a lateral fashion, nor do we do the same with what's stopping you, simply taking one line of thought and drilling down.

The way to move sideways, the way to move laterally, is to tag the word else onto these two basic questions. So, why, why else is this important to you? Why else is this a problem? We can do the same thing with what's stopping you? We can say what else is stopping you. And in this fashion, we begin to spread out, fully scoping out the problem space. Remember, the goal here is to move from the problem as given, assuming that that is the issue that needs to be resolved, and to move to a problem as understood. In the webbing tool, we engage in divergent thinking. The questions help us to respond, but we need to use that mindset of divergent thinking to fully explore all the alternative ways of looking at the problem, all of the alternative challenge statements that help us to better understand our situation.

Let's look at an example. This is an example from my own professional life, but I'm sure many of you can relate to this. The challenge was promotion, advancing inside of my organization, advancing to the level of full professor. So, my initial problem statement, the problem as given, as it initially presented itself to me, was, how might I get promoted to full professor? Now, I'm going to talk us through in a fairly methodical way, because this is a structured tool. I'm going to talk us through the why and what's stopping questions, and we'll see the webbing tool unfold.

So, how might I get promoted to full professor? Let's begin by asking why. Why am I interested? Why am I interested in promotion? Well, one reason, one response may be how to enhance my reputation. I'm interested in enhancing my reputation. Now, notice, because we're in the clarify step of the process, we're writing our responses in the form of a challenge. It's sort of like playing *Jeopardy*. When you provide a response in *Jeopardy*, you have to phrase it as a question. So, how might I get promoted to full professor? Well, I want to enhance my reputation. The challenge statement becomes, how to enhance my reputation. Let's ask why of that challenge statement. So, why might I be interested in enhancing my reputation? Well, I know if I enhance my reputation, it'll create more opportunities for me, and the greater my reputation, the more the likelihood of creating new products, more invitations to do books and so forth, to get involved in interesting and exciting projects. So, with that answer, perhaps my new challenge statement is how to create more products.

Let's return to the initial challenge statement. How might I get promoted to full professor? Now, let's move laterally. Let's tag the question else onto why, because there are probably other reasons for my desire to get promoted to full professor. So let's ask the question, why else might I be interested in getting promoted to full professor? So, a new response, moving laterally, might be, gosh, you know, with promotion comes an increase in salary. So we take that response, again, we always phrase these eventually as a challenge statement, so my response was, well, it'll increase my income. My new challenge statement becomes, how might I make more money? Well, why are you interested in that? Well, the response might be, I'm concerned about being able to afford retirement. That becomes a new challenge statement, how to afford retirement.

Let's return to the initial challenge statement. How might I get promoted to full professor? Let's ask why else again. Why else might I be interested in getting promoted? Well, perhaps I want to attract more graduate students.

I want to get into mentoring relationships, and by being promoted to full professor, it will give me a greater opportunity as a senior faculty member to work more with graduate students. So, my new challenge statement becomes how to engage in mentorships. Why might I be interested in that? Well, I want to leave a legacy. The new challenge statement becomes, in what ways might I leave a legacy?

Now, let's return. We've explored briefly, and that was only a brief example, but hopefully you get the sense for how to ask why, branching out, moving up and laterally. Let's ask the question what's stopping you. Now, remember, when we ask the question what's stopping you, it's going to force us to think in more concrete ways about this challenge, this problem area.

So, what's stopping me from getting promoted to full professor? Well, it may be I'm not able to secure really good letters of support. So, perhaps my challenge is how to secure letters of support. Now we can ask what's stopping you in relationship to this new challenge statement. So, what's stopping you from getting letters of support? Well, gosh, maybe I'm not very good at networking. I'm too introverted. So our new challenge statement becomes how to network more. What else might be stopping me? Now, we can go back to securing letters of support and ask, what else to this challenge statement. Well, I haven't participated in many conferences. So the new challenge statement becomes how to participate in more conferences.

Let's go back to the initial challenge statement. Let's ask, what else is stopping you to branch out from the initial challenge statement. So, the initial challenge statement was how might I get promoted to full professor? What else is stopping you? Well, I haven't kept my resume, my curriculum vitae, up to date. I've fallen way behind. Okay, the challenge statement becomes how to keep your resume, your curriculum vitae, up to date. Is there anything else that's stopping you? Well, sure. Gosh, I haven't published enough. So now a new challenge statement becomes how to publish more. Well, what's stopping you from publishing more? No time, new challenge statement, how to find time to write.

This is a very quick example. We start with an initial problem statement, the problem as it's initially given to us, as it is initially presented to us. And our goal is to branch out, to fully scope out the problem space by asking the question why, why else? What's stopping you? and What else is stopping you? In your guidebook, you've been provided with a worksheet. This will help you as you move through this tool in a methodical way. As you become more proficient with this tool, don't let the worksheet limit you. It's there only initially to give you a hand.

I had a funny reaction one time doing a training program with a group of teachers in which I had taught them this webbing tool. I had walked them through an example. We started with an initial challenge statement, and when we were done, we had a large set of challenge statements, and immediately, when I had completed the exercise, one teacher called out, oh my god, I would never do this. I would never use this tool, and I asked why, and she said, "Well, I started with one challenge, and now I have 30."

How would you respond to that? Well, here's how I responded. I began to call out some of the benefits of this tool. First of all, the challenges are there. By using this tool, we're illuminating, we're revealing the full breadth of challenges related to the problem. Another benefit is it forces you to look at the problem from different angles and different perspectives. It may uncover the true problem. In my example of getting promoted, if I had gone after the promotion, maybe that really wasn't the problem I was trying to solve. Remember, when we were doing the webbing, a different challenge statement came up. When I asked why, the challenge statement came up well, how might I increase my income, or how might I make more money? Now, if we accepted that as the challenge statement, that opens up different possibilities and different solutions.

It also gives us an order of attack. Sometimes in order to resolve a complex problem, there are multiple challenges that need to be addressed, and by looking at the web, you can begin to identify, perhaps a sequence. It also shows the relationships among the challenges, so that if you tackle one challenge and you resolve that challenge, it may have a positive, knock-on effect and solve other challenges. Remember, when we're doing the webbing tool, in order for the webbing tool to work, we have to look at all the options. So when we first begin using the webbing tool, we're putting evaluation off to the side. We're suspending our judgment. We're striving for quantity, trying to generate many challenge statements. We're seeking novelty, so we're looking for unusual perspectives. Then, we shift to convergent thinking, so, our first phase in terms of using the webbing tool is to engage in divergent thinking. Then, when we think we've fully fleshed out the problem space, then we shift to convergent thinking. And hopefully, by fully exploring this, you'll move from the problem as initially given to a better understanding of the problem.

Let's look at another tool that helps us to do this. It's called storyboarding. It's a visual tool designed to tell a story, a story in a visual sequence. Many credit Walt Disney with creating this tool, and certainly Disney used this tool, but he credits an animator, Webb Smith, who sketched scenes on separate pieces of paper and posted them on a bulletin board in a sequence, and that's how it became known as storyboard. Others say it started with silent movies, and soon became the industry standard for pre-visualization to help create the scene in our minds before going to actual filming. *Gone with the Wind* was the first live-action film to be completely storyboarded. When you think of a storyboard, think of a cartoon strip with panels. That's essentially what a storyboard looks like.

It's still in use today. In fact, it's very popular. Pixar uses, literally, tens of thousands of story boards when they create their films, in order to be deliberately creative, to create wonderful animated films, and they've had a terrific track record in producing these films, like *A Bug's Life*, *Finding Nemo*, *Ratatouille*, and *Wall-E*. They use storyboard to explore the possibilities, the characters, the plots, the scenes, and to identify unforeseen problems. For *A Bug's Life*, Pixar worked with nearly 28,000 storyboards; *Finding Nemo*, about 44,000; *Ratatouille*, almost 70,000; and with *Wall-E*, approximately 98,000 storyboards.

So we can use storyboard to help us to clarify in the creative problem-solving step. To do storyboard, you need at least six panels. You can have more, but usually we start with six panels, and your course guidebook provides you a worksheet for storyboarding. The way that storyboarding works is, in the last panel, you begin by telling the end of the story. In the last panel, you draw. And this is a visual tool; I'll encourage you not to use words, but use images. We're trying to see that which we wish to create, so we start with the sixth panel. This is our desired future. This is our goal. This is our wish. In a previous lecture, I had you generate goals and wishes. Your image for what that would look like if you accomplished that goal goes into the sixth panel.

Then we jump back to the first panel, and in the first panel we draw a picture of our current reality. Relative to this goal, where are we now? What does the current situation look like? So now we have our desired future, where we wish to go, and our current reality, where we are. In a way, this is like the Robert Fritz Creative Tension model. How do we resolve that tension? This is the desired future, our destiny. This is our current reality. We fill in the panels in between. We resolve the tension by identifying the challenges that we have to address in order to get to our goal. So, in the four panels in between the desired future and the current reality, in sequence, we draw images of the milestones we have to hit. And in this way, we start to tell the story from the beginning, the middle, and the end. This mirrors the clarify step of the process, because our desired future is our goal. The current reality exemplifies the data related to the current situation, and the four panels in between give us insight into the challenges that we have to address in order to get to our desired future.

Let me share an example with you. This is an example of a graduate student of mine. She had completed all of her course work, and then hit the wall when it came to completing her project, which she needed to do in order to graduate with her Master's degree. So she decided to use storyboarding. She drew a picture in the desired future state—that sixth and last panel—of what she wanted her future to look like, her graduation day. She drew an image of herself in her cap and gown, and then an image moving forward into the future; had a sense of celebration to it. So that set the goal, her desired future.

Next step in storyboard, go back to the current reality, the current situation. Here, she felt a great deal of frustration. She felt incredible pressure by time. She had a writer's block. She was frustrated with the space in her home in terms of being able to write. So, her image reflected all of this frustration. Next step in storyboarding, if we recall, is to then fill in the panels in between the direction you want to move in—the goal you want to attain—and where you are today. So, her four panels were, the first, to create space in her home for dedicated writing. So she took over a room. She identified that room, and she drew a picture of what that would look like, a place where she would be uninterrupted. Then, in the next panel, she had an image of her first submission of her draft Master's project. In the next panel, she drew an image of herself being able to be patient, because that was one of her issues, was that she was rushing to go forward, and she was uncomfortable with feedback and was a little uncertain with feedback, and so she wanted to practice patience while going through this revision process, because she recognized that it wouldn't be just one draft, but there would probably be multiple drafts, so she drew an image of herself being patient through this process. And then, in the fourth panel, that fourth milestone, she drew a picture of the committee congratulating her, her Master's project being approved by her Master's project committee.

So this is an example of storyboarding. What are some ways I've used storyboarding? Well, I've used it for personal goal setting. I use it quite often with strategic planning with teams, and the way I use it with teams is I have individuals draw their desired future in terms of the organization or the unit that they're in. I have them draw their current reality and the milestones that they have to hit in order to move from their current reality to the goals that they have for the team or their organization. And then we compare our storyboards, and we create one master storyboard by synthesizing the team members into one organizational storyboard. We then convert this into a strategic plan.

I've used it with my kids. Before they entered high school, I used storyboard with them so that they could picture for themselves what they wanted to get out of their high school experience. Other applications include planning a presentation, writing a book. In fact, it's becoming increasingly more popular among novelists to storyboard before they write a book. It can be used for planning a trip or laying out a project.

So let's look at how we might apply these tools—webbing and storyboarding. And what I'd like you to do is I'd like you to practice. These are more advanced tools, and they do require practice to develop proficiency. I'd like you to apply webbing to one of your goals; we've identified goals and wishes in an earlier lecture. Put that goal or wish into the middle of the webbing worksheet, and ask yourself why and why else and to branch out and to look at it for a more global, abstract level. Then return and ask yourself what's stopping you; what else is stopping you, to get a more concrete view of that challenge.

With storyboards, take one of your goals. Put it into the sixth panel, like Diane did. Create an image for what that future will look like if you accomplished it, and then complete the storyboard. Now, these tools can be applied formally, as I'm suggesting that you do, but they can also be applied informally. They can be applied in discussions. For example, a coworker comes to you and says, "Gosh, I'm having a really difficult time with Project X." Well, you can facilitate that coworker's thinking by asking well, what's stopping you, and what else is stopping you. And in this way you can give them some insight into the challenges that they need to specifically address in order to move forward. Someone comes to you and says, "I need to do X." "I need to get a new boyfriend." "I need a new job." "I need to move." "I need to make more money." Well, you can ask the question why to get them to think about different issues that they might want to solve before they leap to a solution, such as getting a new job, new boyfriend, or finding ways to make money in other ways.

So the storyboard doesn't need to be so formal. Before a recent trip, I used storyboard to map out my movements over the day to make sure that I didn't miss anything that was important that I needed to do to prepare for this trip. Perhaps Charles Darwin was the ultimate clarifier. While sailing on the HMS Beagle, he diligently stuffed his mind full of facts, poring over books—books on geology—and maintaining meticulous notes. It took him years to form his ideas about evolution. In fact, he said, "After five years of work, I allowed myself to speculate on the subject." After the voyage, he continued to work some 20 years on his theory of evolution. Recall, high clarifiers may suffer from analysis paralysis and may delay moving forward. Perhaps Darwin would have not gone forward if it hadn't been for a letter he had received from Alfred Russell Wallace in which he had mentioned that he was about to go public with a theory that was very similar to Darwin's theory. This prompted Darwin to move to action. The risk of over clarifying is analysis paralysis. Darwin was forced to eventually move forward.

Eventually, we have to stop clarifying. Eventually, we move further into the creative process. And from clarify, once we identify the challenge or the challenges that need to be addressed, we move into the ideate step. In our next lecture, we begin to do exactly this. We move from clarify into idea generation. And I'll see you next time.

Classic Brainstorming and Brainwriting

Lecture 10

In the creative problem solving process, we've gone through the clarify step, where we've identified a goal or wish. We've gone through some data, and as a result, we've identified a challenge or challenges to work on. We're now in the ideate step. We need some tentative solutions to address the challenge. In ideate, we think about lots of options, we explore new combinations, and we build on ideas. We're using the thinking skill of ideational thinking—the ability to produce a variety of original options, images, and thoughts that address our challenges. This lecture focuses on brainstorming and brainwriting.

Brainstorming

- In his book *Applied Imagination*, Alex Osborn introduced the tool known as brainstorming, as well as creative problem solving. The first organized ideation sessions using brainstorming took place in 1938. This tool has been well diffused, but often it's poorly understood.

- Some people believe that brainstorming is just a session where you're just going to have chitchat and idle discussion. In some cases, the group runs with and begins to implement the first good idea that's struck upon in brainstorming sessions. Many individuals don't know that there are rules to a brainstorming session.

- Others see brainstorming as a panacea. It's often talked about as if it were the full creative process instead of one tool within the creative process, and often people neglect the fact that a brainstorming session needs to be facilitated.

- There's a heavy emphasis on divergent thinking in the ideate step of the creative process. The four guidelines for divergent thinking are to suspend judgment, then strive for quantity, then make

The process of brainstorming benefits groups by helping members' divergent thinking transform into convergent thinking.

connections, and finally push for novelty. You can use divergent thinking individually or you can use it in groups.

- The benefit of group divergent thinking is that we can stimulate each other's thinking. We discover new perspectives, and there's lots of energy as we listen to others share their ideas.

- In a conventional meeting, where we're looking for ideas, an idea is suggested and is often immediately evaluated. If it's acceptable, we run off and implement it. If it's rejected, we wait for another idea to come out.

- There are some consequences with this kind of a meeting. First of all, we suggest an idea only if it's good. It's risky unless we believe it's a good idea, so there's a lot of evaluation that happens in our minds before we share the idea.

- Another consequence of this kind of meeting is we attack or defend. Ideas are under attack, or we defend our ideas. We're looking to get that home run, to score big, and if we don't, if an idea is not accepted, we might withdraw.

- A brainstorming meeting looks and feels quite different from a traditional meeting. In a brainstorming meeting, we apply the divergent thinking guidelines as a group. Multiple ideas are suggested, and they're recorded in public view, which makes it easier to build off of those ideas. We ensure that evaluation is suspended temporarily. Then, when we've generated many alternatives and we're satisfied that we've got a sufficient array of options to play with, we converge and use evaluation.

- In a classic brainstorming session, there are three roles. The facilitator is there to guide the process, not to give input in terms of the content. The client brings the challenge to the group and is also responsible for evaluating the ideas afterward and deciding which ones to take forward. The resource group members are there to bring diversity in thought, to engage in divergent thinking, and to help provide the client with many ideas and many options.

- In addition to classic brainstorming, you can also use a tool called brainstorming with Post-its. Each member of a discussion has a large Post-it pad and a large marker to record his or her own ideas, consisting of maybe four to eight words. Call out your ideas to the group so that others can hear and build off of your idea. Then, hand your pad to the group leader, who will put the ideas on a flip chart.

Brainwriting

- Brainwriting is a silent form of idea generation in which each member of the team gets a sheet of paper—a brainwriting form. On the sheet of paper are three columns and three rows. There's a blank sheet in the center of the table. Each person silently writes three ideas across the first row. When he or she is done, to encourage cross-fertilization, each person swaps his or her sheet with the sheet that's in the center.

- Team members continue to do this. As they take the sheet out of the center, they look at ideas that have already been written on that sheet and see if they can build on those ideas, or if they can't, then they continue to add new ideas. The goal is that every time, there are three more ideas—that either build on another idea or are new ideas.

- The advantage of the brainwriting tool is that sometimes you may have a vocal person who dominates a discussion, and brainwriting allows for reflection—silent idea generation. In a way, if you have a dominant person, it sort of neutralizes that effect.

- Also, because people are working independently, brainwriting tends to generate more ideas. When you're using brainstorming with Post-its, or classic brainstorming, you have to wait and listen to each other speak. Sometimes while you're waiting, you're shutting down your thinking because you're listening to someone else.

- One of the other advantages of brainwriting is that people tend to have more elaborate ideas, because they have time to reflect. Of course, we have the benefit of the fact that as they take a sheet and read it, they still are able to connect to other people's ideas. They're still able to use other people's ideas as stimulants—as springboards to their thinking.

Identifying Promising Ideas

- After we've completed the divergent part of the ideate step of the process, the ideas would go to the client, who would review them and begin to move through the converging part, identifying the ideas that look most promising.

- In the ideate step of the creative process, there's a heavy emphasis on divergent thinking. When you follow the guidelines for divergent thinking, you're going to generate many ideas, among which there will be unusual ideas—especially if you're following the principle of seeking novelty—ideas that are bizarre or may seem to be off-the-wall, deviant ideas. These have a value.

- It's important to allow these ideas to come out in an ideation session. Sometimes we can use them as springboards; they spur other ideas. They help to create a more relaxed atmosphere, because when people hear these ideas, sometimes they laugh. There's joking that occurs often after a deviant idea or an unusual idea is shared.

- It's important that we're open to all ideas, mainly because it reinforces the guideline of suspending judgment. Sometimes those really novel ideas lead to a practical, workable solution. Wild ideas can also spur something that can work.

- Tom and David Kelley, founders of IDEO, a well-known design company, wrote an article in the *Harvard Business Review* in which they explored what stops people from being more creative. In this article, they suggest that the main obstacle to creativity is the fear of judgment. They use brainstorming in their sessions with their clients to address this obstacle, and they use the main principle in brainstorming, deferred judgment, to overcome this fear of evaluation.

- IDEO was recently working with Air New Zealand, who was trying to solve the problem of making long-haul flights more comfortable for passengers, so they ran an ideation session with the executives, and they pushed on the crazy ideas that came up—ideas like harnessing people while they're standing, putting hammocks inside the airplane, having bunk beds, etc. This kind of thinking eventually led to the idea of Skycouch, which is a heavily padded section that swings up, and then a couple can lie down comfortably together.

The Nominal Group Technique

- There's a derivation of brainstorming called the nominal group technique in which individuals brainstorm alone, and then the ideas are pooled together. Nominal brainstorming will often generate more ideas than group brainstorming because individuals are working separately, and then, rather than having to wait for each other to talk, they're free to generate as many ideas as they wish without being restrained by having to listen to others.

- When deciding between classic brainstorming and this nominal approach to brainstorming, use what fits the situation. One of the benefits of classic brainstorming is that it encourages team building and allows for cross-fertilization of ideas because we begin to bounce off of other people's ideas. We can use them as springboards to jog our own thoughts.

- When you're done brainstorming, remember that you have to converge. We've demonstrated only the divergent thinking phase of the ideate step. Remember to generally split your time roughly 50/50, or if you're working in a group environment, 40/60, spending about 60 percent of your time on the convergent thinking parts of the ideate step and 40 percent on divergent thinking.

Suggested Reading

Kelley and Kelley, "Reclaim Your Creative Confidence."

Osborn, *Applied Imagination.*

Parnes and Meadow, "Evaluation of Training in Creative Problem Solving."

Ness, *Innovation Generation.*

Activities

Activity 1: Generating Ideas
Look for opportunities to practice using brainstorming or brainwriting in everyday situations, initially with people you are comfortable around.

Activity 2: Raise the Stakes
Work toward increasing the level of challenge when using brainstorming and brainwriting. Work with groups of people you are less familiar with or on problems that are more complex. Be open to opportunities with higher stakes that stretch your level of skill. Try leading brainstorming and brainwriting sessions with these groups.

Classic Brainstorming and Brainwriting
Lecture 10—Transcript

Is the name Alex Osborn familiar to you? How about the book *Applied Imagination*? Do you know the term "brainstorming"? Let me connect the dots here. Alex Osborn was one of the founding partners of an advertising firm, Batten, Barton, Durstine, & Osborn. You can imagine, in advertising, there's a great need for creative thinking, and Alex Osborn developed methods to bring about creative thinking in a deliberate way. You see, he didn't want to leave creativity to chance, and he was sometimes disappointed by the inability to apply imagination on the part of his employees, so he experimented with different methods. One of those methods was brainstorming.

In his book, *Applied Imagination*, he introduced this tool, brainstorming, as well as creative problem solving. You see, he was the originator of creative problem solving, the process we're learning in this course. So brainstorming has literally gone all around the world. Many people have heard of brainstorming. When I ask audiences how many have heard of brainstorming or participating in brainstorming sessions, most hands go up. The first organized ideation sessions using brainstorming took place back in 1938. So this tool has been well diffused, but often it's poorly understood.

Here are some misnomers about brainstorming. Some people believe it's just a BS session, where you're just going to have chit-chat and idle discussion. In some cases, in brainstorming sessions, the first good idea that's struck upon the group runs with and begins to implement. Many individuals don't know that there are rules to a brainstorming session. Others see brainstorming as a panacea. It's often talked about as if it were the full creative process, instead of one tool within the creative process, and often people neglect the fact that a brainstorming session needs to be facilitated.

In this lecture, we examine brainstorming. We examine brainstorming being done well. Let's remember where we are in the creative problem-solving process. We've gone through the clarify step, where we've identified a goal, a wish. We've gone through some data, and as a result of that, we've identified a challenge or challenges to work on. We're now in the ideate step. So we have a challenge. Now we need some tentative solutions to address that challenge. In ideate, we think up lots of options. We explore new combinations, and we build on ideas. We're using the thinking skill of ideational thinking, the ability to produce a variety of original options, images, and thoughts that address our challenges.

There's a heavy emphasis on divergent thinking in the ideate step of the creative process, and as a quick reminder, the four guidelines for divergent thinking are, first, to suspend judgment—that's the principal guideline; to, next, strive for quantity, try to generate many, many alternatives; to make connections, cross-fertilize ideas; and then to push for novelty. You can use divergent thinking individually, or you can use it in groups. The benefit of group divergent thinking is that we can stimulate each other's thinking. We discover new perspectives, and there's lots of energy as we listen to others share their ideas.

Let's compare a conventional meeting to a brainstorming meeting. In a conventional meeting, where we're looking for ideas, an idea is suggested, and it's often immediately evaluated. If it's acceptable, we run off and implement. If it's rejected, we wait for another idea to come out. Now, there are some consequences with this kind of a meeting. First of all, we suggest an idea only if it's good. It's risky unless we believe it's a good idea, so there's a lot of evaluation that happens in our minds before we share the idea. Another consequence of this kind of a meeting is we attack or defend. Ideas are under attack, or we defend our ideas. And we're looking to get that home run, to score big, and if we don't, if an idea is not accepted, we might withdraw.

In a brainstorming meeting, it looks and feels quite different from that traditional meeting that I just described. In a brainstorming meeting, we follow the rules to divergent thinking. We're applying the divergent thinking guidelines as a group. So ideas are suggested—multiple ideas. Many alternatives, and they're recorded in public view, which makes it easier to build off of those ideas. We ensure evaluation is deferred, that it's suspended temporarily. And then, when we've generated many alternatives and we're satisfied that we've gotten a sufficient array of options to play with, then when we converge, then we use evaluation.

Let me share an example of a brainstorming session with you. Pacific Power & Light faced a problem. In fact, the linemen who worked for Pacific Power & Light faced a very dangerous problem. In the fall and the spring, ice storms would come through the northwest, and the power lines would end up having freezing rain. Over time, as the weight built up, these power lines ran the risk of collapsing. Linemen would have to go out, and they would have to climb the poles and knock the ice off of these power lines. As you can see, this would be very dangerous. So, they began to run brainstorming sessions to address this problem.

A couple of hours into the session, the participants took a break, and while they were on break, there were a couple linemen who were talking about some of their experiences, and one retold an experience of running into a bear. Now, it so happened that the individual that was facilitating that meeting heard the linemen tell this story, and so when the facilitator restarted the brainstorming session, the facilitator asked that individual to tell the story about the bear, just to get the creative juices flowing.

Well, it did lead to some interesting ideas. Thoughts that occurred after the linemen shared the story were, "Well, let's train bears to climb the poles, and because of their weight, as they're climbing the pole, it'll shake the pole and the wires and the ice will fall off." Well, that, of course, was met with laughter, and some had suggested, "Well, maybe if we can't train bears, we could use a helicopter to set a honey pot on top of the pole, and the bears will be interested in the honey and will climb up the poles and, again, they'll shake the power lines and the ice will break off." Well, there was an administrative assistant sitting in that meeting, and she was a nurse for a MASH unit, and she recalled running out to the heliport to take injured soldiers into the hospital, and she remembered the downwash from helicopters, and when she heard the idea of putting honey pots on top of the pole using helicopters, she thought, "Why not fly helicopters over the power lines, have the downwash vibrate the power lines, and that would probably break up the ice." In fact, this was the solution they pursued and this was used for many years. This is an example of how brainstorming should be run. Let me be clear about the classic brainstorming session and the components of a classic brainstorming session.

So, in a classic brainstorming session, we have three roles. We have the facilitator, who's there to guide the process, not to give input in terms of the content. We have the client, who brings the challenge to the group, and who is also responsible for evaluating the ideas afterwards and deciding which ones to take forward, and then we have the resource group members who are there to bring diversity in thought, to engage in divergent thinking, and to help provide the client with many ideas and many options.

So, let's bring our team together. I'll be facilitating the meeting from San Francisco, but we're going to bring in great thinkers from all around the world to help us with this challenge. Our first resource group member is Andrew from Siberia.

Gerard: Our first resource group member is Andrew, who's coming in from Siberia.

Andrew: Hi, Gerard. I'm the centrifugal flow engineer.

Gerard: Super. We have Michael from Merida in the Yucatan.

Michael: Hi. I'm a senior product designer.

Gerard: And we have Gretchen, all the way from Melbourne.

Gretchen: Hello. Vice President of Marketing.

Gerard: And Derek, who's in Alaska.

Derek: Hi, Gerard. I'm a materials acquisition specialist.

Gerard: Trish, from London.

Trish: Hi. I'm the director of sales.

Gerard: And, finally, some of you know Scott. He's our client. He's coming in from Rome.

Scott: Executive Vice President.

Gerard: Great. Now, Scott, we've gathered a wonderful resource group here for you, individuals who are extremely good at divergent thinking, and our goal is to help you to get a lot of ideas for how to improve the bathtub.

Now, guys, when we go through this process, we're generating ideas. And we want to give Scott as many ideas as possible. In order to do that, I'm going to give you some rules to follow. The first rule is we're going to suspend evaluation. We're not going to judge our own thinking. If you have an idea, go ahead and say it. Don't block it. And we're also going to defer judgment on other people's ideas as they're generating and sharing their ideas. We're going to strive for quantity to make sure that Scott walks away with plenty of options. Third, we're going to make connections, listen to each other, and see if we can build off of each other's ideas. And then, finally, we really want to open up new thinking. Where might we go? What are our blue sky ideas around what we can do with the bathtub?

Now, before we do physical exercise, we stretch. We're going to be doing some mental work, so let's do some mental stretching. I'm going to give you a fun problem to work on. Imagine we had a huge overrun of paper clips. Let's just take a minute. What are all the other uses you can think of for this overrun of paper clips? What do you have? What might we do?

Gretchen: You could string them together and hang your child's art work off of them.

Gerard: Mm-hmm.

Derek: Or turn them into jewelry.

Gerard: Mm-hmm. What else?

Andrew: Create modern art work.

Gerard: Mm-hmm.

Michael: You could use them as push-pins.

Gerard: Mm-hmm.

Trish: You could use them as picture holders.

Gerard: Good. Let's keep it going. We're thinking divergently. What else?

Derek: Lanyards, or maybe even eyeglass repair.

Gerard: Mm-hmm.

Trish: If you made them oversized, you could use them for bookmarks.

Gerard: Mm-hmm.

Michael: You could melt them down and use the metal for something else.

Gerard: Nice. Okay. I'll tell you what. You guys look like you've got a sense for how to do divergent thinking. I think we're in a place now where we're ready to help Scott out. You've seen the brief. You've seen the data. Our challenge statement is "How might we improve the bathtub?" We're going to keep the same guidelines in mind now, as we work on this real issue. And I'll just remind you of the most important guideline, which is to suspend evaluation. So let's go ahead. Let's get started. Let's see how many ideas we can come up with for Scott. Let's go.

Andrew: Maybe we could use different types of materials. Granites, quartz, you know, exotic types of rocks.

Gerard: Mm-hmm.

Trish: I like the idea of ready-access to different fragrances, oils, things like that, in the tub.

Gerard: Mm-hmm.

Derek: Customized colors and shapes to match your bathrooms.

Gerard: Mm-hmm.

Michael: I really think if we put our minds to it, we could design a non-clogging drain.

Gerard: What else?

Gretchen: Right, and actually something like that in the Jacuzzi. Some way that you can have some kind of a detergent run through the Jacuzzis to keep them clean.

Gerard: Nice. I like how you built on that idea. Anything else? What else do you have?

Trish: What if we had an automatic shutoff for the water level?

Gerard: Mm-hmm.

Derek: Or maybe we could even have a multimedia station connected to the tub or waterproof Internet access or keyboard.

Gerard: Mm-hmm. Let's keep it going, guys. What else?

Michael: Yeah. We could have video screens even built into the walls.

Gerard: Mm-hmm. The ideas are being transcribed. If you need some springboards, just glance at your screen. There's a small screen that's capturing the ideas as they're coming up. What else do you have?

Andrew: Well, I mean, on that note, why not have, like, a small TV tray or someplace to put food, drink, or books without them getting wet?

Gerard: Good. I like how you made a connection there. What else?

Gretchen: Some way that the surface that you're resting on in the tub could be conformed to whatever body position you're in?

Gerard: Mm-hmm.

Gretchen: And something that would keep the water warm while you're taking a bath.

Gerard: Mm-hmm. Good. Let's push forward some more, guys. What else do you have?

Michael: Adjustable height, so it would make it easier for people to get into the bathtub.

Gerard: Mm-hmm.

Michael: We could even have elevated versions where you could have storage underneath.

Gerard: Mm-hmm.

Trish: You could actually, if you could adjust the height, maybe also adjust the width so that you make it smaller for children and wider if you wanted to have more than one person in it.

Gerard: Mm-hmm.

Andrew: Built-in security system so the water doesn't overflow.

Gerard: Okay. Let's push for a few more.

Michael: What if we even thought about different types of water? Salt water, like being in the ocean.

Gerard: Mm-hmm.

Gretchen: And the ability to tuck the tub away in some fashion when you aren't using it.

Gerard: Well, we're going to continue to work on this, but let me just check with Scott. We will have future sessions. Scott, how's this going for you? How do you feel about these initial ideas that we've generated?

Scott: It's a fantastic first start. I'm really looking forward to getting the team together again to help flesh out some more of these ideas.

Gerard: Super. Thanks, Scott. We appreciate that feedback. We're going to continue to generate ideas on this challenge of how to improve the bathtub, but before we had virtual conferencing, we had to actually get together. So let's do that. Let's bring the team together. Great. Wonderful to see you guys. We're going to continue to work on this problem, because it's a serious issue, and we've got some ideas, but we're going to push for even more, because the more ideas you have, the greater chance you have of really having a breakthrough, finding a solution, and that's really what we're looking for.

Now, this time we're not going to do the brainstorming as we did it before, classic brainstorming. Instead, we're going to use a tool called brainstorming with Post-its. Now, the way that works is that each of you has a large Post-it pad and a large marker to work with. You're going to record your own ideas. You're going to jot your idea on that Post-it. After you've written your idea and you've said it out loud you can go ahead and hand it to me, and I'll place it on a flip chart. So, let's go ahead. Let's get started. What ideas do you have to improve the bathtub?

Trish: You could have a massage unit in it besides the Jacuzzis.

Gerard: Mm-hmm. Thank you.

Derek: It could be portable and inflatable.

Gerard: Mm-hmm. Thanks, Derek.

Andrew: What if you had a simulated waterfall in it?

Gerard: Thanks, Andrew.

Gretchen: What if we started a Bubble bath-of-the-Month club to keep people taking more baths?

Gerard: Okay. Thanks, Gretchen.

Michael: An automated, self-cleaning.

Gerard: Mm-hmm. Alright. Let's keep going. What else can we do? We're striving for quantity.

Andrew: Integrated lights into the tub?

Gerard: Mm-hmm.

Trish: Along those lines, something set up so that you could have candles, candle holders actually a part of that set-up of the tub.

Gerard: Alright.

Michael: Maybe you could have cushions at the bottom of the tub or something to keep you from slipping?

Gerard: Mm-hmm.

Andrew: How about a bubble dispenser that's built-in?

Gerard: Nice. You guys are doing great. Let's keep going. What else can we do?

Derek: Adjustable shapes and size.

Gerard: Mm-hmm. Remember, we're not worried about physical constraints or budgets. What else do you have?

Trish: Retractable containers, like, can keep your washcloths and soap and scents.

Gerard: Mm-hmm.

Gretchen: How about a longer tub so you don't have to have your knees out of the water.

Gerard: Okay.

Michael: What if you could get custom art on the surface of the tub?

Gerard: Okay. Good. Let's keep going. We're deferring judgment. Don't judge your own thinking. Whatever you think of, let's go ahead and get it out.

Andrew: What if we had springs at the bottom of the bathtubs?

Gerard: Okay. Springs.

Derek: Could you come up with some sort of washable marker design that you could put on the walls of the tub that washes off?

Gerard: Okay. Washable marker design and springs on the tub. If you run out of ideas, we've got some toys on the table you can play with, manipulatives. I see Michael's doing that already. That might help us to generate some further ideas if you start to run dry. What else do you have?

Gretchen: How about just, you know, toys? Tub toys. Some that come with it when you purchase the tub. Something like that.

Gerard: Mm-hmm. Sure. Tub toys that come with the tub.

Gretchen: Mm-hmm. And somehow they're integrated into the design of it.

Gerard: Mm-hmm.

Michael: If you had a way to have it, almost like you're in a moving stream of water, like it kept cycling through.

Gerard: Mm-hmm. Moving stream of water.

Andrew: Maybe use suction cups to make it easier to store things or put them on the walls?

Gerard: Suction cups. Did you get that from that toy in front of you?

Andrew: Yeah.

Gerard: Yeah? Nice. Yeah. You can make connections like that. What else?

Derek: I'm thinking about a built-in pillow. Some softer areas within the bathtub.

Gerard: Okay. Built-in pillows, softer areas.

Gretchen: And, actually, if you had older folks using the tub, emergency buttons in case they needed help?

Gerard: Mm-hmm. Okay.

Trish: How about a built-in aquarium?

Gerard: Built-in aquarium. Yeah. Andrew.

Andrew: Well, on the note of the elderly emergency button, why not have a baby monitor installed for the kids?

Gerard: Baby monitor. I like how you're making connections. Let's keep stretching.

Gretchen: How about a wine cooler?

Gerard: Wine cooler. Nice.

Derek: What if the surface of the tub would change colors depending on the temperature?

Gerard: Okay. Let's keep going. What else do you have?

Michael: Colors, lights. How about tanning lights inside the bathtub?

Gerard: Tanning lights. Good divergent thinking. Remember, we're allowing for real novelty as well. Original. Out-of-the-box. What else?

Derek: Can we market outdoor bathtubs?

Gerard: We're holding off evaluation, so anything goes.

Michael: Could you have, like, some sort of air blow dryer system after, so you wouldn't have to use towels?

Gerard: Mm-hmm. Air blow-dryer system. And this is the one you said earlier? Yep? Okay. Good. What else? Let's stretch for some more.

Andrew: How about a built-in fan that would provide an aroma and a nice ambience?

Gerard: Okay. Built-in fan for aroma and ambience.

Trish: And also to tag on that is the kind of sounds, like Caribbean sort of beachy sounds, bird sounds, something like that.

Gerard: Sure. You can change the sounds on the kind of mood you want to have.

Trish: Yeah. Mood sounds. Yeah.

Gerard: Mm-hmm. What else could we do? We're not restricting ourselves to budget or what's physically possible. We're trying to break the old paradigm. Remember, we're trying to get a real range here so that we have more options to choose from.

Gretchen: If you could have the jets, you could adjust them to different places. Maybe they're on a track or something like that, so you could have them, adjustable jets.

Gerard: Yes. Think about times you've been frustrated in the bathtub. What did you wish you had, or what do you wish was different?

Derek: A built-in fountain within the bathtub.

Gerard: A built-in fountain within the bathtub.

Trish: Maybe there could be a back that you could adjust so you could, so when you're shaving you could be up but when you're relaxing you could lean back.

Gerard: Okay. Yep. What else could we do? What can we make bigger, larger, smaller, get rid of, combine?

Andrew: Is there any way we could come with, maybe, an aquatic office chair that you could put in your bathtub in case you want to get business done while you're in the shower?

Gerard: Yeah, aquatic chair in the tub.

Trish: Right, and actually something along the same lines. Some desk-like format that you could do over the tub for reading and for if you wanted to work and relax in the tub.

Gerard: Nice. Good. Good. You guys are on a roll. Again, think in terms of what we could eliminate, take away, what we might combine to it. What technologies might we adapt into a tub?

Gretchen: The faucet. Sometimes that gets in the way. If there was some other way, like below the surface that the water could just shoot in instead of having to have that big faucet banging your head or your knees on.

Gerard: Mm-hmm.

Trish: Or maybe the faucet could retract after you're done with it.

Gerard: Good. Good. I like how you did a build.

Michael: Also an improved draining system that would drain the tub almost instantly.

Gerard: Mm-hmm. Thanks, Michael.

Andrew: Maybe more of a fancy, artistic take. We could have designer legs for the tub.

Gerard: Mm-hmm.

Andrew: Lion's feet.

Gerard: Mm-hmm. Is there any way to continue to build off of that? How might we bring artistic, aesthetic features in?

Gretchen: Yeah. It could get very ornate. They could be, you know, have, like, a gothic kind of curl to the edges. I mean, have a Victorian look to them or something very futuristic so the outside could be really imaginative.

Gerard: Good. Good. Let's go ahead and capture that. Any… continue along that line. Any other builds on aesthetics. Aesthetics. Arts. What does that make you think of?

Andrew: This might be kind of weird, but could you put wheels on the bottom of the tub? Make it mobile?

Gerard: We're suspending evaluation, so go ahead and get it down. Yeah. We're not judging these. We're just trying to get them out.

Gretchen: Actually, viewing the materials, I know we talked about materials before, but, you know, mosaic designs on the outside of the tub instead of just the porcelain outside?

Trish: Or maybe we could have, like, magnetic panels that could be decorative, it could be art, or different colors.

Gerard: Mm-hmm. Good. Why don't you go ahead and capture that.

Derek: Or even one that's just pure glass.

Gerard: Mm-hmm. Well, let's play with that. How might we substitute materials? What other materials might we think of that we could replace, besides the current materials we're using? Any other materials you can think of?

Michael: A material that would adjust to the shape of your body.

Gerard: Yeah. Go ahead. Jot that down. Yeah. Mm-hmm. Mm-hmm.

Gretchen: Memory foam?

Derek: Yeah. Waterproof memory foam.

Gerard: Waterproof memory foam. Let's make sure we capture that. Okay. Tell you what, let's do this. Let's switch to another tool. This tool is called brainwriting. It's a silent form of idea generation. The way that brainwriting works is that each participant in the team gets a sheet of paper—a brainwriting form. And on this sheet of paper there are three columns and three rows. There's a blank sheet in the center of the table. Each person silently writes three ideas across the first row. When they're done, to encourage cross-fertilization, they then take their sheet, his or her sheet, and they swap it with the sheet that's in the center, and they continue to do this. Now, as they move along, as they take the sheet out of the center, they look at ideas that have already been written on that sheet, and they see if they can build on those ideas. Or, if they can't, then they continue to add new ideas. But the goal is, every time three more ideas. either builds or new ideas.

So, guys, let's try this out. Everyone needs a copy of this brainwriting form. So, one copy each. I'm going to place one extra copy in the center. If you would just write it across the top, so remember what we're working on, the challenge is,

"How might we improve the bathtub?" And again, the way this works is you'll write your ideas, it's silent, but we do want to have some form of exchange, so you'll take your sheet when you've filled them in with three ideas, and you'll swap it with a sheet in the center. And again, we're following the guidelines for divergent thinking. So why don't we go ahead and get started?

The advantage of the brainwriting tool is that sometimes you may have a vocal person who dominates a discussion, and brainwriting allows for reflection, silent idea generation. In a way, if you have that dominant person, it sort of neutralizes that effect. Brainwriting, also, because people are working independently, tends to generate more ideas. When you're using brainstorming with Post-its, or you're doing classic brainstorming, you have to wait and listen to each other speak. Sometimes while you're waiting, you're shutting down your thinking because you're listening to someone else.

As we look at brainwriting, one of the other advantages of brainwriting is that people tend to have more elaborate ideas, because they do have time to reflect. And of course, we have the benefit of the fact that, as they take a sheet and they read it, they still are able to connect to other people's ideas. They're still able to use other people's ideas as stimulants, as springboards to their thinking.

So, guys, how are we doing? You have some ideas, some more ideas for improving the bathtub?

Trish: Right.

Gerard: Yeah. Good. I'll tell you what. I'll collect these. I'll also take the ideas that we generated using the Post-its. We're going to have all of this transcribed. We're going to give them to Scott. Scott is then going to go through the converging phase of the process, where he's going to go through and do hits and cluster, and see which ideas seem most promising to carry forward into the process. So, thanks a lot. I really appreciate you coming along and helping us out, acting as resource group members, but, for now, you're done. Thanks so much.

So, what would happen next after we've completed the divergent part of the ideate step of the process. The ideas would go to the client, who would review them and begin to move through the converging part, identifying the ideas that look most promising.

In the ideate step of the creative process, there's a heavy emphasis on divergent thinking. When you follow the guidelines for divergent thinking, you're going to generate many ideas, among which there will be unusual ideas, especially if you're following the principle of seeking novelty, ideas that are bizarre, or may seem to be off the wall, deviant ideas. These have a value. It's important to allow these ideas to come out in an ideation session. Sometimes we can use them as springboards. They spur other ideas. They help to create a more relaxed atmosphere, because when people hear these ideas, sometimes they laugh. There's joking that occurs often after a deviant idea or an unusual idea is shared. So it's important that we're open to all ideas, mainly because it reinforces that guideline of suspending judgment.

This also helps to free us up. It creates a more relaxed environment. Often, when an unusual idea is shared, there is laughter, and when the laughter occurs, people begin to relax. Also, sometimes those really novel ideas lead to a practical, workable solution. Wild ideas can also spur something that can work. Remember the honey pot story, how the idea of trained bears led, eventually, to the notion of using the helicopter.

Here's a real example. Tom and David Kelley, founders of IDEO, a well-known design company, wrote a recent article in *The Harvard Business Review*, and in this article they explored what stops people from being more creative. And in this article they suggest the main obstacle to creativity is the fear of judgment. They use brainstorming in their sessions with their clients to address this obstacle, and they use the main principle in brainstorming, deferred judgment, to overcome this fear of evaluation.

Here's an example. They were recently working with Air New Zealand, and they were trying to solve the problem of making long-haul flights more comfortable for passengers, so they ran an ideation session with the executives, and they pushed on, as they say, the crazy ideas, ideas that came up like harnessing people while they're standing, putting hammocks inside the airplane, having bunk beds, etcetera. This kind of thinking, as I mentioned before, creates a more relaxed atmosphere. This led, eventually, to the idea of a Skycouch in economy. This is a heavily padded section that swings up, and then a couple can lie down comfortably together.

Here are some final thoughts about brainstorming. There's a derivation of brainstorming called the Nominal Group Technique, in which individuals brainstorm alone, and then the ideas are pooled together. Now, often, nominal brainstorming will generate more ideas than group brainstorming, because individuals are working separately, and then, rather than having to wait for each other to talk, they're free to generate as many ideas as they wish without being restrained by having to listen to others.

So we have our classic brainstorming, and we have this nominal approach to brainstorming. Use what fits the situation. One of the benefits of classic brainstorming is that it encourages team-building and allows for cross-fertilization of ideas, because we begin to bounce off of other people's ideas. We can use them as springboards to jog our own thoughts. And when you're done brainstorming, remember, you have to converge. We've demonstrated only the divergent thinking phase of the ideate step. Remember to generally split your time roughly 50/50, or, if you're working in a group environment, 40/60, spending about 60 percent of your time on the convergent thinking parts of the ideate step.

I want you to try out these tools while they're fresh. Identify a challenge statement that needs imagination. Construct a really good challenge statement using a statement starter like "how to" or "what might." Make sure that you have a clear owner and it's free from criteria. Since the tools are new, I encourage you to begin with challenges that are less daunting.

Remember, the roles in a classic ideation session, that we have a facilitator, a client, and a resource group member. If you're working on a problem of your own, you might want to have someone else act as the facilitator, provide background before the group begins in ideation. Do some kind of warm-up to get the mental muscles going.

Now that you know how to conduct a real brainstorming session, in our next lecture we'll look at more advanced tools for ideation. And I'll see you next time.

Tools for Enhanced Brainstorming

Lecture 11

Brainstorming is well diffused; it's familiar to many people. In this lecture, you will learn about more advanced tools for ideation. They can be thought of as brainstorming enhancers. In brainstorming and brainwriting, ideas come from your head and the heads of others. These advanced tools use deliberate springboards that boost your imagination. They feed you stimuli from which you can springboard off of to generate ideas. They're typically used after brainstorming, when you want to reenergize your ideation.

Reverse Brainstorming

- Reverse brainstorming is good to use when you've used brainstorming and you're looking for a different kind of ideation tool. It's a fun variation, and it's particularly useful when there are groups who have judgmental participants.

- We take the same initial approach as we did with brainstorming. We begin by identifying a specific challenge statement and making sure that it's well constructed. For example, we'll use the following statement: how to ensure customer loyalty for a new Internet business.

- Next, we take our challenge statement and reverse it into a negative form. For example: how to decrease customer loyalty or how to increase mistrust between our business and our customers. We've taken our initial challenge, our goal of ensuring customer loyalty, and reversed it into what we don't want to happen.

- Once we've diverged on various reversed challenge statements, we then converge on one that comes the closest to capturing the exact opposite of what we wish to do. Then, we generate ideas on that reversed challenge statement, following the guidelines for divergent thinking. We're deferring judgment, striving for quantity, making connections, and remaining open to novelty.

- After the ideas have been generated for this negative statement, we then reverse them, turning the negative ideas into positive ideas and, thus, hopefully responding to our real challenge. Because you are diverging, one negative idea can stimulate multiple positive ideas.

- Starting with the challenge statement—how to ensure customer loyalty for a new Internet business—let's say that we've selected the following reverse challenge statement: In what ways might we frustrate our customers?

- Perhaps one idea that is generated on that negative statement is to ensure that there are many layers to the purchasing process. That's the negative idea. How do we now reverse that to address our original challenge, our goal of ensuring customer loyalty?

- Having many layers to a purchasing process might lead to make the process fun. Use a story as a backdrop to the ordering process. Use a visual dashboard to show progress as the customer moves through the system. Have access to a live person during the ordering process, either via phone or computer camera.

- Let's say that another reversed negative idea was to deliver the product late. Again, we take the negative idea and use that as a springboard to reverse it and generate positive potential solutions. "Deliver product late" might lead to "create a simple tracking system," "give future discounts if an item's not received on time," or perhaps "make all deliveries special—use gift wrap, add a balloon, include a cookie."

- Reverse brainstorming takes a bit more time than classic brainstorming because of the reversals—reversing our initial challenge statement into a negative statement, and then reversing the negative ideas back to positive ideas—so plan on a bit more time.

© Noel Hendrickson/Photodisc/Thinkstock.

Reverse brainstorming involves reversing challenge statements into their negative forms so that you view them differently.

- One advantage of reverse brainstorming is that it can be humorous and playful and often generates lots of laughter when you hear these negative ideas come up. It's also beneficial because it can get individuals who always view the problem from a pessimistic perspective on board.

- When using reverse brainstorming, you may not generate highly novel ideas. This can be avoided by simply doing straightforward reversals. The negative idea comes up—deliver a product late to the customer—and we reverse that in a straightforward manner to the statement "make sure the product is delivered on time," and then you move on to the next idea.

- Instead of doing this, you should take one negative idea and spend a little time with it. Don't just reverse it into the obvious positive idea. Play with it a little bit. See what lateral ideas come up from that one negative idea.

- Some people find this tool easier to use, especially when there's a need to be more playful or a need to shut down some of the pessimistic negative thinking. Also, because you have the negative ideas to build off of, you've got a built-in springboard. We don't have that as much in classic brainstorming, and by having that springboard, you allow ideas to bounce.

Associative Thinking

- Our mind naturally makes connections. You see something, and it jogs a memory or stimulates an idea. Thoughts don't occur in a vacuum. They line up in a chain, one idea linked to another. We call this associative thinking, which refers to how ideas, feelings, and movements are connected in such a way to determine their succession in the mind.

- Sarnoff Mednick believed that the creative process happened as a result of associative thinking. He suggested that the creative process is an ability to form new associative elements that are recognized as being useful. There are a few main tenets to his theory.

- First, he says that when we create, the larger the set of associations, the greater the probability of developing creative solutions. He also suggests that the more remote the association—the more novel the association—the more creative the outcome.

- Mednick created a measure to test his associative thinking theory. The name of this measure is called the remote associates test (RAT).

- The respondent is presented with three words, and they are to make a connection among those three words. For example, what connects these three words? *Rat*, *blue*, and *cottage*. The answer is *cheese*: cottage cheese, blue cheese, and we often associate cheese with rats.

- There are two forms of associative thinking. There are free associations, which are unguided—without purpose or design—and, as a result, are unpredictable. There are also facilitated associations, which is thinking that's regulated by some desire, design, intention, or strategy. It's more predictable.

- In deliberate creativity, we link to the second form of associative thinking, creating facilitated associations. But, of course, this naturally leverages the free associations we make.

Forced Relationships

- The forced relationships tool is a way of facilitating associative thoughts, and it's often used after a group has initially done some brainstorming or ideation. It's used to recharge their thinking. The tool works by selecting an object and asking yourself, what ideas do I get for my challenge by looking at this object?

- We're going to return to the following statement: how to ensure customer loyalty for a new Internet business. We use a magic marker to generate new ideas. We look at the marker to consider attributes. The marker has nothing to do with customer loyalty, so we're forcing associations. We're following the guidelines for divergent thinking, and we're exploring all possibilities.

- What suggestions might we get by looking at a marker, by forcing it into this challenge? We might be able to make it easier for customers to provide feedback. We could have a hidden prize somewhere along in the ordering process that's stimulated by the fact that the marker top hides the top of the marker itself. We might have a wall in the website for customers to leave their graffiti. When you run out of ideas using one object, you select another object.

- You can use the forced connections tool individually or as a group. You can use objects immediately available to you, or you can collect thought-provoking pieces. However, be sure that the object is not related to the challenge. We're going after remote associations, and if the object is too close to the problem that you're working on, it doesn't force you to think in new pathways. We use it after brainstorming. It serves as a springboard, a brainstorming enhancer.

Visually Identifying Relationships (VIR)

- In forced connections, we use objects. In a tool called visually identifying relationships (VIR), we use images, photographs, and pictures to stimulate ideas. We also add to it an excursion. We take a mental break; we distance ourselves from the challenge. Neuroscience research shows that distancing yourself allows your mind to wander. As a result, your thoughts can travel down new neural pathways. It can create new connections.

- In VIR, we take a break. We move away from our challenge, and then we present images to our mind, and we use those images to create, first, random associations, and then, later, we use those images to facilitate direct associations.

- To use VIR, you'll need four pictures. The first picture is designed to take you away, to relax you, to allow your mind to decompress, to take a short vacation. Then, the next three photographs are used as stimulants. We look at the first picture. We relax. We gain some distance. We slow our thinking down, and then we look at the next three and record our observations. We still are distant from the challenge. We're not intentionally thinking about the challenge. We write down our observations, free associations, memories, feelings, and facts related to the photographs. Then, we reintroduce the challenge. We generate ideas using facilitated associations.

- One of the benefits of VIR is that it slows our thinking down. In a brainstorming session, it's often fast paced, and we're throwing out many ideas quickly. When we go to VIR, it changes that pace. It forces us to be more reflective. It forces our mind to take detours, and as a result, we may use new neural pathways.

- VIR works as well individually as it does for a group. In fact, for an individual, the benefit is when you don't have a group, you have these photographs to be a stimulant, a springboard, for you. You don't hear others' ideas, but you use the photographs to create associations.

- It can also be used as a group. In a group application, participants work individually at first, through the entire tool. Then, when they begin to share their observations and new connections—these new associations—they listen to one another and continue to engage in divergent thinking to see if they can now cross-fertilize the ideas that they each had generated.

- If you're going to use VIR, it would be helpful to build up an inventory of photographs. When you select photographs, much like when using the forced connections tool, make sure that the images that you use aren't related to the task that you're working on.

- Use images only. Avoid words, and stay away from well-known brands because we already have associations with well-known brands. We want to force some new thinking.

- Forced connections in VIR are advanced tools. They take practice. We don't spring them on people the first time they're engaging in an ideation session. It's important to warm them up before using these advanced tools.

Suggested Reading

King and Schlicksupp, *The Idea Edge*.

Michalko, *Thinkertoys*.

Activities

Activity 1: Visually Identifying Relationships (VIR)

Find a personal or professional challenge that requires some imagination to resolve. Locate at least four photos, and go through them in a quiet, relaxing atmosphere. The first one should allow you to relax. The rest should be stimulating. For these, record at least three observations for each photo. Finally, generate new ideas by making associations with your observations.

Activity 2: VIR Scenario

Imagine that you parked your car in a deserted parking lot and accidently locked your keys, wallet, and cell phone in your car. You also notice that there is a large advertisement nearby with the following picture.

© Zoonar/Thinkstock.

Use the visually identifying relationships (VIR) tool to generate ideas to get inside your car. Record your observations about the picture in the advertisement, including free associations, memories, feelings, or facts. Then, connect these observations to the challenge of getting inside your car.

Tools for Enhanced Brainstorming

Lecture 11—Transcript

Brainstorming, brainstorming is well diffused. It's familiar to many people. Let's look at more advanced tools for ideation. They can be thought of as brainstorming enhancers. In brainstorming and brainwriting, ideas come from your head and the heads of others. These advanced tools use deliberate springboards. They boost your imagination. They feed at stimuli from which you can springboard off of to generate ideas. Imagine yourself standing on the edge of a pool, and you're on a hard surface, about to dive into the pool. Now compare that to standing on a diving board with a springboard, in which case you can bounce and use that to spring you into the water. The tools that we'll learn in this lecture act like a springboard. They enhance brainstorming sessions. They're typically used after brainstorming, when we want to re-energize our ideation.

Our first tool is called reverse brainstorming. It's good to use when people are familiar with brainstorming, where you've used brainstorming, and you're looking for a different kind of ideation tool. You want to shake things up a little bit. It's a fun variation, and it's particularly useful when there are groups who have judgmental participants. We take the same initial approach as we did with brainstorming. We begin by identifying a specific challenge statement, and making sure that it's well-constructed. By way of example, we'll use the following statement: How to ensure customer loyalty for a new Internet business.

So imagine, you're about to launch a new business. It's going to be primarily through the Internet, and you want to ensure that customers quickly develop loyalty and remain loyal to your new business.

Next, we take our challenge statement and we reverse it. We reverse into a negative form. For example, we might say, "How to decrease customer loyalty," "How to increase mistrust between our business and our customers," "In what ways might we frustrate our customers?" "What might be all the things we could do to drive our customers away?" So we've taken our initial challenge, our goal of ensuring customer loyalty, and reversed those into what we don't want to have happen.

Once we've diverged on various reversed challenge statements, we then converge on one that comes the closest to capturing the exact opposite of what we wish to do, and then we generate ideas on that reverse challenge statement, and of course, we're following the guidelines for divergent thinking. We're deferring judgment. We're striving for quantity. We're making connections, and we're remaining open to novelty.

After the ideas have been generated for this negative statement, we then reverse them back, turning the negative ideas into positive ideas, and thus, hopefully, responding to our real challenge. Because you are diverging, one negative idea can stimulate multiple positive ideas.

So let's return to our example., how to ensure customer loyalty for a new Internet business. Let's say we've selected the negative statement, the reverse challenge statement, in what ways might we frustrate our customers? And let's imagine we've generated ideas on that negative statement. Perhaps one idea was to ensure that there are lots of layers to the purchasing process. That's the negative idea. How do we now reverse that to address our original challenge, our goal of ensuring customer loyalty? Well, having lots of layers to a purchasing process might lead to make the process fun. Use a story as a backdrop to the ordering process. Use a visual dashboard to show progress as the customer moves through the system. Have access to a live person during the ordering process, either via phone or by computer camera.

Let's say another reversed negative idea was to deliver the product late. So, again, we take the negative idea and we use that as a springboard to reverse it and generate positive potential solutions. So, "deliver product late" might lead to "create a simple tracking system;" "give future discounts if an item's not received on time;" perhaps "make all delivery special, gift wrap, add a balloon, include a cookie."

Let's talk about reverse brainstorming. It takes a bit more time than classic brainstorming, because we have these reversals, reversing our initial challenge statement into a negative statement, and then reversing the negative ideas back to positive ideas, so plan on a bit more time. But it has a nice advantage, in that it can be humorous and playful and often generates lots of laughter when you hear these negative ideas come up. It's also beneficial in that it can get negative people on board, those individuals who always view the problem from a pessimistic perspective.

There are some watch-outs. One watch-out when using reverse brainstorming is that you may not generate highly novel ideas. Now, this can be avoided by not simply doing straightforward reversals. So, the negative idea comes up: produce a product or deliver a product that arrives late to the customer. Well, we reverse that back in a straightforward manner to make sure the product is delivered on time, and then you move on to the next idea. Rather, I encourage you to take one negative idea and spend a little time with it. Don't just reverse it into the obvious positive idea. Play with it a little bit. See what lateral ideas come up from that one negative idea.

Again, I've found that some people find this tool easier to use, especially when there's a need to be more playful or a need to shut down some of the pessimistic negative thinking. And also, because you have the negative ideas to build off of, you've got a built-in springboard. We don't have that so much so in classic brainstorming, and by having that springboard you allow for some bounce to ideas.

Speaking of springboards, our mind naturally makes connections. You see something, and it jogs a memory, or it stimulates an idea. Thoughts don't occur in a vacuum. They line up in a chain, one idea linked to another. We call this associative thinking. Associative thinking refers to how ideas, feelings, and movements are connected in such a way to determine their succession in the mind.

Sarnoff Mednick believed that this was the basis to the creative process, that the creative process happened as a result of associative thinking. He suggested that the creative process is an ability to form new associative elements that are recognized as being useful. There are a couple of main tenets to his theory. First he says, when we create, the larger the set of associations, the greater the probability of developing creative solutions. He also suggests that the more remote the association, the more novel the association, the more creative the outcome. For example, if I said salt, the word that might come to your mind first is pepper. That's a pretty predictable association to make. But, if I said salt, and the thought that came to your mind was Angelina Jolie, that's a remote association. By the way, Angelina Jolie starred in a movie called *Salt*.

Mednick created a measure to test his associative thinking theory. The name of this measure is called the Remote Associates Test, for short, the RAT. Here are some examples of the kinds of items on the Remote Associates Test. The respondent is presented with three words, and they're to make a connection among those three words. Think along with me as I give you two examples. Here's example number one. What connects these three words? Rat, blue, and cottage, again, rat, blue, and cottage. Well, the answer is cheese. Cottage cheese, blue cheese, and we often associate cheese with rats. Let's try another one. Here are the three words. Again, think along with me, shot, cleaner, and stained. That's shot, cleaner, and stained. The answer is glass. Shot glass, glass cleaner, stained glass.

Now, in theory, the more right answers, the more associations you can make, and hypothetically, we suggest that, if you can make more associations, the more creative you'll be. But, does that truly work? Does the hypothesis hold? The Remote Associates Test is interesting, but does it work in terms of practical, real creativity? Can associative thinking be leveraged to improve creative thinking? Well, there are two forms of associative thinking. There are free associations, which are unguided, without purpose or design, and as a result, are unpredictable. There are also facilitated associations. This is thinking that's regulated by some desire, design, intention, strategy. It's more predictable. In deliberate creativity, we link to the second form of associative thinking, creating facilitated associations. But, of course, this naturally leverages the free associations we make.

Here's a story that tested whether facilitated associations really work. Does it make a difference? The question the researchers wanted to answer was, "Can you improve creative thinking by deliberately facilitating associative thinking?" They used a tool called *The Fisher Dictionary*, which contains word association lists. For example crimson, flamingo, caboose, and stoplight all relate to the word red. In this dictionary, there are 360 lists that are used to stimulate idea generation. Now, the task the participants worked on, was to generate catchy phrases to print under a picture on a T-shirt. The experimental group was given the Fisher list, remember, which is designed to engage in facilitated association. The control group received no such list.

The results, the groups were not timed. Individuals could take as much time as they wished. The experimental group worked longer—on average, 78 minutes—generating ideas, versus the control group, which worked for about 55 minutes; this is 42 percent longer for the experimental group, and the experimental group generated, on average, many more ideas than the control group—87 versus 64.

Now, this is interesting. When the control group had finished generating ideas, they were presented with the Fisher list, and on average, they worked for 51 more minutes, producing, on average, 50 more ideas. So, this Fisher list, a deliberate associative tool, did serve as an effective springboard, even after the participants were fatigued. We're going to follow this experiment, and we're going to look at a tool that takes advantage of associative thinking.

Our next tool is called forced relationships. This is a way of facilitating associative thoughts, and it's often used in a way like the Fisher list in the study that I just cited, after a group has initially done some brainstorming or some ideation. It's used to recharge their thinking. The tool works by selecting an object and asking yourself, "What ideas do I get for my challenge by looking at this object?"

We're going to return to "How to ensure customer loyalty for a new Internet business?" We have a marker, a magic marker. We use this marker to generate new ideas. We look at the marker to consider attributes. Now, the marker has nothing to do with customer loyalty, so we're forcing associations. We're following the guidelines for divergent thinking, and we're exploring all possibilities. So, what suggestions might we get by looking at a marker, by forcing it into this challenge? Well, we might be able to make it easier for customers to provide feedback. We could have a hidden prize somewhere along in the ordering process that's stimulated by the fact that the marker top hides the top of the marker itself. We might have a wall in the website for customers to leave their graffiti.

When you run out of ideas using one object, you select another object, for example, a pair of glasses. To help build the association, it's often useful to look at the qualities, or the attributes, of the object that you're using to make connections. So I'm looking at this pair of glasses. We have a frame. We have the lenses. We have nose pieces. Again, we ask the question, "What ideas do we get from 'for ensuring customer loyalty' by looking at a pair of glasses?" Well, we could make the ordering process transparent. We could let customers see the fulfillment process while it happens. We could let the customer see any mistakes they make in completing the ordering process before they move to the next screen.

Again, when you run out of ideas, you move to another object. This is even more remote. I have a dinosaur, a T-Rex. So, we begin by looking at the properties of the T-Rex. It's powerful, has short arms. It's extinct. We can only see them in museums. So, what ideas do we get for ensuring customer loyalty from a T-Rex? I'll pause for a moment, and you think about it. What ideas do you get for improving customer loyalty from a T-Rex? Remember, we're following the guidelines for divergent thinking. If you need more time, go ahead and pause the lecture.

So, how did you do? What ideas did you get for ensuring customer loyalty from this dinosaur, the T-Rex? Here are some thoughts that occurred to me. You could create a museum or a "hall of fame" of best customers. You could include a ticket to local cultural experiences with every purchase. You can collect customer feedback and evolve your process, communicating back to the customer how their feedback improved the customer experience.

Let's talk about the forced connections tool. You can use it individually or you can use it as a group. You can use objects immediately available to you, or you can collect thought-provoking pieces. However, be sure that the object is not related to the challenge. Remember, we're going after remote associations, and if the object is too close to the problem that you're working on, it doesn't force us to think in new pathways. We use it after brainstorming. It serves as a springboard, a brainstorming enhancer.

Here's a real-life example of how an ordinary object led to a breakthrough in aerospace engineering. Many dream of commercial space travel, but there are serious engineering challenges. One big challenge is re-entry into earth's atmosphere, moving from the vacuum in space to Earth's dense atmosphere is dangerous and technically challenging. Burt Rutan, a famous aerospace engineer, is on a quest for a failsafe solution. Eventually, the solution was inspired by the humble shuttlecock—that's right, the badminton birdie.

The design of the badminton birdie suggested what is called a feathery re-entry. Rutan's spaceships use light and flexible tail systems that deploy during re-entry. There are many benefits to this. The feathery design means a highly stable re-entry, and it's a thousand times safer than other designs. After the re-entry, the tail lowers to its original configuration, and the spaceship glides to a landing. Virgin Galactic adopted Rutan's design and is in the process of building the first commercial spaceport in New Mexico.

In forced connections, we use objects. In this next tool, Visually Identifying Relationships, or VIR for short, we use images, photographs, and pictures to stimulate ideas. We also add to it an excursion. We take a mental break. We go away. We distance ourselves from the challenge. Neuroscience research shows that distancing yourself allows your mind to wander. And as a result, your thoughts can travel down new neural pathways. It can create new connections.

The ubiquitous bar code. Where did that idea come from? Let me tell you the story. In 1948, a grocery store executive approached Drexel Institute of Technology and challenged the students there to develop a way to inventory the products in the grocery store using technology, a way to encode the products. N. Joseph Woodland accepted the challenge, and in fact, he got so absorbed in this challenge, he quit his graduate student teaching position, and he moved in with his grandfather in Florida. Later that year, he needed to take a break. He was sitting on a beach in Miami. He was dragging his fingers through the sand, just thinking idle thoughts. And he looked at the track that his fingers created, and that pattern sparked an idea. What if a series of lines, or bars, of different widths, could function like the dots and dashes of Morse code?

VIR, Visually Identifying Relationships, works much like the strategy, although unintentional, that Woodland used. We take a break. We move away from our challenge, just like he took a break and went to the beach. And then we present images to our mind, and we use those images to create, first of all, random associations, and then later, we use those images to facilitate direct associations.

So, here's how VIR works. You'll need four photographs, four pictures. The first picture is designed to take you away, to relax you, to allow your mind to decompress, to take a short vacation. Then, the next three photographs are used as stimulants. We look at the first picture. We relax. We gain some distance. We slow our thinking down, and then we look at the next three and record our observations. We still are distant from the challenge. We're not intentionally thinking about the challenge. We write down our observations, our free associations, memories, and feelings, facts related to the photographs. Then, we re-introduce the challenge. We generate ideas using facilitated associations.

Let's walk through an example. We'll go back to the same challenge of customer loyalty. I'm going to share an image with you, and I'll describe it. This first photograph is a stream. It's flowing over some rocks, sort of making a small waterfall. It appears as though it's fall because there are leaves that have changed colors that we see in the water. We use this photograph to distance ourselves from the challenge that we're working on, the challenge of enhancing customer loyalty. We're forgetting about that challenge. We're moving away from it.

Then we go to our next photograph, and at this point we're going to record our observations, now that we're in a relaxed state. This next photograph is a photograph of two boys. They look like they could be brothers. They're running off of a platform, and they're jumping into a large pond or a lake. The free associations that you might have to this photograph might be things like brothers, cold mountain lake, danger, or can't swim.

We move to our next photograph. Again, we're going to capture our free associations with this next photograph, our observations. The next photograph is a photo of a clock. It's inside of a Paris museum, a museum that was once a railway station that's been converted into a museum dedicated to impressionist art. So our observations might be Paris, time, and railway station.

And then we move to our next photograph. Again, we begin by looking at those free associations. This photograph is a photograph of a butterfly sitting on a flower. Our observations might be butterfly, migration, childhood memories.

Now, we re-introduce our challenge. Now that we've taken this mental excursion, we've allowed our mind to go somewhere else, we bring those observations, those free associations, back to the challenge, and now we deliberately facilitate associations. So we return to our first photograph of the two boys jumping into the lake and remind ourselves of the challenge. The challenge that we're working on is how to ensure customer loyalty for a new Internet business. Our observations were brothers, cold mountain lake, danger, can't swim. So, what new ideas might those observations give us? We're following the guidelines for divergent thinking as we make these facilitated associations. From brothers, we might think, oh, let's link customers with other customers. Let's offer a service in which customers support one another, such as a mentoring program. Treat customers like family. Host regional reunion parties for loyal customers, and so forth.

From the observation, danger, can't swim, we might get such ideas as include a navigation map within the website; have a life saver available; phone-a-friend option if you get stuck; make easy-to-follow tutorials; create a system that detects when someone is having trouble and then offers help.

What about the image of the clock inside the museum in the former railroad station? Again, we're looking at the challenge of how to ensure customer loyalty for a new Internet business. Our observations were Paris, time, and railway station. What new ideas might we get from the observation of Paris? Well, we might say free trips awarded randomly, customer loyalty program with rewards for visiting website and making a purchase.

Next, we go our third photograph. This was the photograph of the butterfly on the flower. Our observations might have been butterfly, migration, pollination. What new ideas might we get when we consider the word migration? Well, we might suggest following a butterfly as it's migrating through the web pages as someone visits the web site and makes an order.

From pollination we might say reward customers for sharing the web site with others.

So let's talk about the VIR tool, Visually Identifying Relationships. One of the benefits of VIR is that it slows our thinking down. In a brainstorming session, it's often fast paced, and we're throwing out many ideas quickly. When we go to VIR, it changes that pace. It forces us to be more reflective. It forces our mind to take detours, and as a result, we may use new neural pathways. VIR works as well individually as it does for a group. In fact, for an individual, the benefit is, when you don't have a group, you have got these photographs to be a stimulant, a springboard for you. You don't hear others' ideas, but you use the photographs to create associations.

And it can be used as a group. In a group application, participants work individually at first, through the entire tool, as I just walked you through it. And then, when they begin to share their observations and share their new connections, these new associations, they listen to one another, and they continue to engage in divergent thinking to see if they can now cross fertilize the ideas that they each had generated.

If you're going to use VIR, I recommend building up an inventory of photographs. I've collected well over 100. This is a tool I regularly use when I'm facilitating groups, and groups enjoy it, and it's highly effective. Some tips, though, when you create this photograph montage to share with others, when you select photographs, much like when we did forced connections, make sure that the images that you use aren't related to the task that you're working on. If you're working on something technical, don't show an example of a computer or the internal parts of a computer. and use images only; avoid words, and stay away from well-known brands, because we already have associations with well-known brands. We want to force some new thinking.

Forced connections in VIR are advanced tools. They take practice. We don't spring them on people the first time they're engaging in an ideation session. It's important to warm them up before using these advanced tools. I'd like you to try out Visually Identifying Relationships, VIR, before our next lecture. Find a challenge that requires some imagination. Apply VIR to that challenge. Locate four photographs. Find a quiet space. Go through the photographs, first using the first image for relaxation, and then the next three to record your free associations for each of those photos. Then generate new ideas by making associations with your observations, and after you've gotten comfortable with it in terms of its individual use, then try it out with a group. In this way, when you go to a group, you can share how you used it. You can use yourself and your own personal experience by way of example.

In the next lecture, you'll learn additional ideation tools that use a different kind of springboard—analogies. And I'll see you next time.

Borrowing and Modifying Ideas
Lecture 12

Great creators don't work in isolation. Instead, they borrow and build on others' thinking. In this lecture, you will learn how to incorporate other people's solutions, as well as solutions from nature, into your situation. Specifically, you will learn about two Synectics tools: direct analogy and personal analogy. Analogical thinking is a complex form of thinking, and it takes practice. Once perfected, it will open up a rich range of ideas and solutions. It's important to keep in mind that borrowing and modifying is not stealing; it's just good creative thinking. Perhaps the best muse for future ideas is past ideas.

Synectics

- Synectics is a process in the field of creativity that is based on the notion of borrowing ideas. Synectics was originated by W. J. J. Gordon and George Prince and, later, colleague Tony Poze.

- Gordon got partial inspiration for Synectics from his experiences in World War II, where he worked with an emergency group charged with removing a sunken ship blocking the Tripoli Harbor. The colonel in this group imagined his mother raking the dirt in the garden, and this metaphor led to a solution. The solution was to blow up the ship, and then to rake it flat so that other ships could safely pass over this ship.

- The Synectics process is based on the use of metaphors. It also grew out of hours of analysis of audiotapes of business meetings, where they found that a nonjudgmental climate paired with the use of analogies and metaphors ensured the most creative outcomes.

- There are four operating principles behind the Synectics process. First, according to Synectics, creativity is important to problem solving. We use creativity in problem solving when we're unsure what strategy or solution can help us move from where we are now to where we wish to be. We refer to these as heuristic problems, meaning that they're open ended, versus algorithmic problems, which have a known process and a single solution.

- We don't use creative problem solving on algorithmic problems. Creative problem solving is designed for those more complex, open-ended problems—heuristic problems.

- The second principle of Synectics is that creativity is not mysterious. Rather, creativity is understandable. It's something that we can deliberately provoke.

- Third, creative invention is similar across all fields. In fact, creative problem solving can be used in many, many disciplines.

- Finally, individual and group invention are similar. The processes that individuals use to invent are identical to the processes that groups use.

Synectics Tools: Direct Analogy

- When using direct analogy with groups, there are five steps to take them through. According to the developers of Synectics, Pringles potato chips were invented as a result of the Synectics process. The following is a hypothetical walk-through of how it might have happened.

- In the first step, we identify the challenge; we come up with a description of the issue that needs to be resolved. The problem they were working on dealt with packaging chips in bags that ended up breaking the chips. The chips got destroyed, for example, in shipping.

- In the second step, we diverge on direct analogies; we generate situations that are similar to the challenge we're working on. How do we pack potato chips in such a way that they don't break? What are some other areas that are analogous to this? Perhaps packing a suitcase, eggs in a carton, golf balls in sleeves, bagging leaves, etc.

© iStockphoto/Thinkstock.

Using analogies, such as comparing the process of packing leaves in a bag to packing potato chips in a container, can help you consider new possibilities.

- Once we've identified a list of direct analogies, we then have to choose an analogy to work with—this is the third step. In the Pringles potato chips example, they chose packing leaves in a bag. They thought that was similar to packaging chips in a bag.

- In step four, you then explore ideas that are suggested by the analogy that's been selected. Imagine that it's fall and you've raked the leaves, and you're putting the leaves into a bag. As you think about that situation as they did when they were working on this problem, they recognized that dry leaves take up more space, and when leaves are wet, they conform to one another and sort of mold together. They take up much less space in the bag.

- In step five, we apply the ideas that came to our mind through this analogy. We apply it to our original challenge, and we examine what solutions might occur to us in terms of our challenge. If our challenge is packing potato chips in a way that they don't break, what the wet leaves might suggest is a process in which the chips form to one another as they're being produced—like the leaves when they're wet. In this way, they take up less space and are harder to break.

- In step 5, you use those ideas as springboards to go back to your original challenge to see what solutions might come to mind. How do you find a good analogy? In order for this tool to work, we have to be effective at coming up with analogies.

- In Synectics, they talk about a compressed conflict, which involves using a pair of words to capture a contradiction—two words that get at the essence of the challenge that you're working on.

- Being able to generate a compressed conflict gets at the heart of what many theorists and scholars believe is a trait that highly creative people possess: an ability to hold opposing thoughts in their mind at the same time.

- Let's return to the challenge that we used in a previous lecture: how to ensure customer loyalty for a new Internet business. Perhaps one compressed conflict might be viewed as building relationships via distance. Boiling that down to two words, some possibilities include "distant intimacy," "loose bonds," and "unrestricted commitment." The compressed conflict summarizes the essence of the challenge.

- If "distant intimacy" is a direct analogy we use, we then think about other places where this compressed conflict may have been resolved successfully. Perhaps online dating services might help us. That might be analogous to our challenge of enhancing customer loyalty. So we take this direct analogy, which was based on our compressed conflict, and we ask ourselves, what does online dating suggest for ensuring customer loyalty?

Synectics Tools: Personal Analogy

- With the Synectics tool known as personal analogy, you imagine that you are the challenge—you use empathy to place yourself in the situation.

- For example, imagine that your challenge is to increase sales of a candy bar. When we use personal analogy, we imagine that we're the candy bar. Look around you. What do you notice? What's in your surroundings? How do you feel as people pass you by? How do different people react to you? We record our thoughts and feelings, and then we use those thoughts and feelings to generate ideas that go after our challenge of increasing sales.

- Personal analogy works on a range of challenges, from selling, to improving a patient's experience in a hospital, to erecting a new building in a historical district.

Biomimicry

- David Kord Murray has recast the spotlight on the value of borrowing ideas. In 2009, he released a book called *Borrowing Brilliance* in which he provides a range of places that we can go to borrow ideas: We can borrow from competitors; we can borrow from a similar place; we can borrow from an opposite place; we can borrow from other people.

- Like Sarnoff Mednick, who created the remote associates test, David Kord Murray recommends going to a distant place to borrow. An example of a distant place is nature. Nature has been used as an analogy to solve many problems.

- For example, Qualcomm is creating rich color displays that use less energy by mimicking the photonic microstructures found in butterfly wings. Nature is an expert designer and problem solver. Humans are not the first to figure out how to build homes, make paper, resist water, or insulate.

- Biomimicry is a disciplined creative process that intentionally draws inspiration from nature. The concept is old, but biomimicry was popularized in the 1997 book *Biomimicry: Innovation Inspired by Nature*. The key focus with biomimicry is to create environmentally sensitive solutions, just as nature does.

- When using biomimicry, the first question you ask yourself when you begin a creative problem solving effort is, what would nature do? How would nature solve this problem? For assistance, go to www.asknature.org, and once you've defined your problem, you can search for analogies in nature. This Web site is mainly based on engineering problems.

- Many challenges require only a single metaphor. If you're working on a complex product, however, you may need multiple metaphors.

Suggested Reading

Benyus, *Biomimicry*.

Gordon, *Synectics*.

Martin, *The Opposable Mind*.

Murray, *Borrowing Brilliance*.

Activities

Activity 1: Direct Analogy
Identify a challenge you want to solve. Then, record your thoughts about the compressed conflict inherent in this challenge; generate a number of different forms of compressed conflicts (i.e., which two words capture the essence of the challenge inherent in your situation). Choose the compressed conflict that does the best job of capturing the essence of the challenge you face. Finally, in considering this compressed conflict, ask yourself which other situations share the same compressed conflict. What new ideas for your challenge do you get from thinking about these analogous situations?

Activity 2: Biomimicry

Identify a challenge you want to solve. Next, look to nature for an analogous situation. Examine how nature solved the problem, and make connections to your own challenge. See what new ideas this helps you to generate.

Borrowing and Modifying Ideas
Lecture 12—Transcript

Great creators work in isolation. They can generate ideas entirely on their own. Superstar creators are lone geniuses, right? Wrong. Great creators don't work in isolation. Instead, they borrow and the build on others' thinking. Albert Einstein once said, "The secret to creativity is knowing how to hide your sources."

Let me reveal some sources to well-known creative ideas. The printing press. Gutenberg was frustrated by the tedious process of hand engraving an entire page on a single slab of wood. He borrowed ideas from two sources, coin making, which suggested a stamping process that used separate metal letters, and the wine press, which suggested the printing press mechanism.

Paul McCartney's song "Blackbird" was based on the plight of African-American women during the civil rights movement. And George Lucas, now, he was a master at borrowing ideas. *Star Wars* is rife with borrowed ideas. The story itself is based on mythology. This led to the hero's journey, the mentors, the prophecies, and animals with human-like features. And the dress—modern space suits combined with ancient-looking capes and robes. And the weapons, the light saber is a combination of a sword and a laser beam. Nazi Germany provided further ideas. Stormtroopers, Darth Vader's helmet, and the final scene in the original movie is similar to the last scene in a 1938 documentary of Hitler victoriously taking the stage at Nuremburg.

Here's a more recent example, the iPhone, truly an innovation marvel, inspirational to many of us. Here's a story of one person who was inspired by the iPhone. Her name is Julie Corbett. She was a Canadian native living in Oakland, California. She worked in investment management, and in 2007, she received her first iPhone. It was inspirational for her, but not the phone. What impressed her was the packaging. The iPhone was nestled in a smooth, fiber tray, biodegradable, but sturdy and elegant. Despite not having a design background, she began toying with bottle designs inspired by the iPhone packaging. The design was also inspired by milk bags she used growing up in Montreal, Canada. In 2008, she filed a patent and started a company, Ecologic Brands. The bottles have a sturdy outer shell made of old cardboard boxes and newspaper. The inner pouch is made of thin plastic and holds the liquid. There are many benefits to this design. It uses 70 percent less plastic than conventional bottles and can be broken up easily for recycling. Ecologic has made more than two million bottles, and a new factory is expected to turn out nine million bottles a year.

In the last lecture, we learned brainstorming-enhancing tools that provided a springboard to our thinking. In this lecture, we learn how to incorporate other people solutions, as well as nature solutions, into our situation. Well, it may sound like stealing, but T.S. Eliot said, "Immature poets imitate. Mature poets steal." And Wilson Mizner, a screenwriter, said "If you steal from one author, it's plagiarism. If you steal from many, it's research."

Borrowing ideas and building off of past ideas is not cheating. In fact, it's natural. Research at the Institute of Personality Assessment and Research demonstrates this, IPAR, for short. IPAR was located at the University of California at Berkeley. The Director of IPAR was Donald MacKinnon, a psychologist who worked during World War II developing personnel selection procedures, and he carried on with these procedures, investigating research into highly creative individuals and what made them highly creative, after World War II.

The high creatives in these research studies were the best in their field, from fields like writing and science and from architecture. They were invited to Berkeley for two and three days at a time, and they were closely evaluated. A rich data set was created, personality measures. The psychologist conducted observations and biographical information was collected.

I'll tell you about one classic study, a study of architects, in which they compared three groups of architect. They had the high-creative architects, who were identified as being award-winning, highly innovative for their designs; moderately-creative architects; and low-creatives. And again, they used stringent criteria, including nominations, to identify the individuals in these groups.

When they assessed the data, to be sure, there were personality differences when you compared the high creatives to the moderate to the low creatives, but they found out some other interesting insights. One relates to a common developmental event that was found among the high creatives, but not among the other two groups. You see, as children, the high creatives tended to relocate geographically many times across the U.S, and some of them outside of the U.S. The IPAR team reasoned that this allowed these highly creative architects to borrow ideas from their memories, from the broad range of styles and ideas that they had been exposed to across the country and in other countries. What they had experienced as children influenced what they created as adults.

Only recently have we placed such a high value on originality. In Shakespeare's time, creativity was understood to be improvement. And, boy, could Shakespeare borrow ideas. *Romeo and Juliet* was based on a poem by Arthur Brooke. *Merchant of Venice* was based on a short story by Giovanni Fiorentino. *Measure by Measure* came from a play by George Whetstone. We're going to look at a process in the field of creativity that is based on this notion of borrowing ideas. The name of this process is called synectics. Syn, S-Y-N, comes from the Greek, meaning to bring together. Synectics was originated by W.J.J. Gordon and George Prince, and later, colleague Tony Poze. Gordon gave partial inspiration to synectics from his experiences in World War II, where he worked with an emergency group charged with removing a sunken ship blocking the Tripoli harbor. The colonel in this group imagined his mother raking the dirt in the garden, and this metaphor led to a solution. The solution was to blow up the ship, and then to rake it flat so that other ships could safely pass over this ship.

The synectics process is based on the use of metaphors. It also grew out of hours of analysis of audio tapes of business meetings, where they found that a non-judgmental climate, paired with the use of analogies and metaphors, ensured the most creative outcomes.

There are four operating principles behind the synectics process. I think it's useful to examine these four principles, because these four principles are very much related to this course. First of all, according to synectics, creativity is important to problem solving. We use creativity in problem solving when we're unsure how to move from where we are now to where we wish to be, when we're not clear on what strategy or solution can help us to close that gap. We refer to these as heuristic problems, meaning they're open-ended, versus algorithmic problems. With algorithmic problems, there's a known process and a single solution. You simply follow the formula, and you get to the right answer. We don't use creative problem solving on algorithmic problems. Creative problem solving and the creative process we're learning in this course is designed for those more complex, open-ended problems.

The second principle of synectics is that creativity is not mysterious. Rather, creativity is understandable. It's something that we can deliberately provoke. Third, creative invention is similar across all fields. In fact, we began this lecture by looking at creative process and creative problem solving and suggesting that the process that we learn in this course can be used in many, many disciplines. And finally, individual and group invention are similar. The processes that individuals use to invent is identical to the process that groups use.

So let's look more closely at synectics. Synectics is a process with steps to it. We're going to focus specifically on two tools in synectics. These tools use analogies. One tool is called direct analogy. The second one we'll learn and apply is called personal analogy. Let's look at the steps to direct analogy. When I use direct analogy with groups, these are the five steps I take them through. I'm going to walk you through direct analogy, and I'm going to use an example. Pringles potato chips. According to the developers of synectics, Pringles potato chips were invented as a result of the synectics process. Now, I've not come across a description of how that process, step-by-step, was done, so this is a hypothetical walk-through, how it might have happened.

Step one, we identify the challenge. We come up with a description of the issue that needs to be resolved. So, let's go back in time. Perhaps the problem they were working on, indeed, the problem they were working on dealt with packaging chips in bags that ended up breaking the chips. The chips got destroyed, for example, in shipping. In the second step, we diverge on direct analogies. We generate situations that are similar to the challenge we're working on. So, how do we pack potato chips in such a way that they don't break? Well, what are other areas, things that are similar to this, that are analogous? Well, perhaps packing a suitcase, eggs in a carton, golf balls in sleeves, bagging leaves, etcetera.

Once we've identified a list of direct analogies, we then have to choose an analogy to work with. In the synectics example with Pringles potato chips, they chose packing leaves in a bag. They thought that was similar to packaging chips in a bag. In step four, you then explore ideas that are suggested by the analogy that's been selected. So let's play with, imagine, it's fall time and you've raked the leaves, and you're putting the leaves into a bag. And as you explore that and think about that situation, as they did when they were really working on this, they recognized that dry leaves take up more space, and when leaves are wet they conform to one another. They mold together. They take up much less space in the bag.

In step five, we apply the ideas that came to our mind through this analogy. We apply it to our original challenge, and we examine what solutions might occur to us in terms of our challenge. So, if our challenge is packing potato chips in a way that they don't break, what the wet leaves might suggest is a process in which the chips form to one another as they're being produced, like the leaves when they're wet. In this way, they take up less space and they're harder to break.

Let's review these steps. Step one, you identify the challenge that you need ideas. Step two, diverge on direct analogies. In step three, you then choose a direct analogy that comes closest to your original challenge. In step four, you explore ideas that are suggested by that direct analogy. How is that direct analogy dealt with? How is that situation resolved? What occurred in that circumstance? And then, in step five, you take those ideas. You use them as springboards to go back to your original challenge to see what solutions might come to mind.

Now, how do you find a good analogy? In order for this tool to work, we have to be effective at coming up with analogies. In synectics, they talk about a compressed conflict. That's using a pair of words to capture a contradiction. Two words that get at the essence of the challenge that you're working on. For example, and this comes from Gary Davis' work; he wrote a book called *Creativity is Forever*, for example, let's imagine we have senior citizens who are concerned about their safety. As we look at that situation, the compressed conflict could be fragile strength. We use that compressed conflict because it helps us to understand the essence of the challenge, to think about analogies that also involve fragile strength.

So, what's fragile, yet strong? What analogies come to mind? Well, glass, butterflies, plants, for example. Let's take butterflies. What ideas might we get from examining butterflies that might help seniors in terms of their concern about their safety? Well, perhaps deception, butterflies are often camouflaged; they look stronger than they are. Blending into the environment, into the surroundings, like the butterflies and camouflage, again, perhaps the seniors can blend into their environment. Butterflies migrate. That might suggest that seniors travel together. In this way, they may feel more secure.

I don't want to pass over this too quickly, because being able to generate a compressed conflict gets at the heart of what many theorists and scholars believe is a trait that highly creative people possess. That's an ability to hold opposing thoughts in their mind at the same time. Philosopher Albert Rothenberg called this Janusian thinking after the Greek god Janus, who could look in two directions at the same time.

Let's take a moment. Let's practice this skill of generating compressed conflicts. Let's return to the challenge that we used in a previous lecture, how to ensure customer loyalty for a new internet business. Think along with me. What compressed conflict is inherent in this challenge? Can you generate some compressed conflicts that help to get at the essence of the heart of this challenge? Perhaps one compressed conflict might be viewed as building relationships via distance. How do we boil that down to two words? Well, here are some possibilities. Distant intimacy, loose bonds, unrestricted commitment. The compressed conflict summarizes the essence of the challenge. Let's take distant intimacy. If that's a direct analogy we use, we then think about other places where this compressed conflict may have been resolved successfully. Perhaps online dating services might help us. That might be analogous to our challenge of enhancing customer loyalty. So we take this direct analogy, which was based on our compressed conflict, and we ask ourselves, "What does online dating suggest for ensuring customer loyalty?"

We're going to move on to the next tool in synectics, personal analogy. In personal analogy, you imagine that you are the challenge. We're using empathy to place ourselves in the situation. For example, imagine your challenge is to increase sales of a candy bar. When we use personal analogy, we imagine that we're the candy bar. Look around you. What do you notice? What's in your surroundings? How do you feel as people pass you by? How do different people react to you? We record our thoughts and feelings, and then we use those thoughts and feelings to generate ideas that go after our challenge of increasing sales. Personal analogy works on a range of challenges, from selling to improving a patient's experience in a hospital, to erecting a new building in historical district. Personal analogy is about putting yourself into the challenge.

I'll tell you what. Let's try it out. Let's use the two examples I just shared with you. Let's imagine that our challenge is to improve patient experience in the hospital. Can you empathize with what this is like? Have you had this experience? Can you put yourself into that person and feel what they're feeling and think what they're thinking? And when you do this, what ideas does it give you for improving a patient's experience?

Let's move away from people. This is even more of a challenge. Can you empathize with an object? Imagine an architect is going to erect a new building in a historic district. You're that new building. What would it feel like to be erected in a historic district? Look around you. What do you notice? How do you see yourself in relationship to this historic district? And as you reflect on that, as you empathize, as you put yourself into that scene, what ideas does that suggest to you? We then use those ideas to help us with the design of that building.

David Kord Murray has recast the spotlight on the value of borrowing ideas. In 2009, he released a book, *Borrowing Brilliance*. It's a good book, I recommend it. And in that book he provides a range of places that we can go to to borrow ideas. We can borrow from competitors; we can borrow from a similar place; we can borrow from an opposite place; we can borrow from other people. Let's look at examples of each one of these.

Borrow from your competitors. In 1975, BIC, a disposable pen company, introduced a disposable plastic razor blade. Gillette copied and improved the razor blade, adding a second blade. They called it "the good news razor." Because of this kind of thinking today, Gillette still maintains about 80 percent of the marketplace.

Next example, borrow from a similar place. Google borrowed ideas from library sciences to help build their search engines. Finding a page in the World Wide Web they likened to finding a single page in a library. Another example, while sailing on the HMS Beagle, young Charles Darwin read *The Principles of Geology*. Charles Lyell, the author, argued that geological formations slowly formed over time. The minute changes added up to what we see today, the shape of rivers, mountains, canyons, and such. These thoughts served as the foundation for Darwin's thoughts about change in the biological world.

You can borrow from other people. Surround yourself with other creative people. Edison built a lab to do this. Edison said, "I readily absorb ideas from every source, frequently starting where the last person left off." We can borrow ideas from the opposite place. Imagine you're working on women's fashion, so you might borrow ideas from men's fashion. In fact, this is what Coco Chanel did. In the 1920s, Coco Chanel did exactly this, looking at men's fashion to inspire new women's fashion. The famous Chanel suit was fashioned after men's suits, resulting in an aesthetic combination of a knee-length skirt and a trim, masculine jacket.

Like Sarnoff Mednick, who created the Remote Associates Test, David Kord Murray says, "The further afield one goes to borrow, the more creative," to go to a distant place to borrow. An example of a distant place is nature. Nature has been used as an analogy to solve many problems. Here are a few examples. George de Mestral went for a walk in the Alps with his Saint Bernard dog, and when they returned home, they were both covered in burs. After close examination, he saw that the way the burs fastened themselves to him and his dog could also be used to fasten clothing, like buttons and zippers do. This led to the insight of Velcro.

Analysis of termite mounds, which maintain a constant temperature in extreme heat, led to the design and construction of a building in Zimbabwe that stays cool without use of air conditioning. Qualcomm is creating rich color displays that use less energy by mimicking the photonic microstructures found in butterfly wings.

Nature is an expert designer and problem solver. Humans are not the first to figure out how to build homes, make paper, resist water, or insulate. Biomimicry is a disciplined process, a disciplined creative process that intentionally draws inspiration from nature. The concept is old, but biomimicry was popularized in the 1997 book *Biomimicry: Innovation Inspired by Nature*. The key focus with biomimicry is to create environmentally sensitive solutions, as nature does, as nature creates sustainable solutions.

Let's look at some examples. Buildings that capture water from fog is based on an insect found in the desert that does the same. A tree structure was used to design the internal skeleton of the Opel car, mixing minimal material to gain maximum strength. When using biomimicry, the first question you ask yourself when you begin a creative problem-solving effort is "What would nature do?" How would nature solve this problem? To assist you, there's a web site that you can go to called AskNature.org, and in this web site, once you've defined your problem, you can search for analogies in nature. Now, this website's mainly based on engineering problems.

Many of the examples I've shared with you, with the exception of Star Wars and the printing press, focus on a single metaphor. If you're working on a complex product, you may need multiple metaphors, like the creation of an amusement park, like Disneyland. In fact, the over-arching metaphor for Walt Disney when creating Disneyland was a movie. He wanted families to feel as though they were starring in their own movie.

Let's explore some of the ideas spawned by the movie metaphor. Buildings are referred to as sets. Landscaping is referred to as props, and the employees are cast members. The architectural design of the buildings in Disneyland follow a Hollywood set. The first floors are three-quarter size, the second floor five-eighths scale, and the third floor one-half scale. This makes movie stars feel larger than normal and give the appearance of them being larger than normal.

Let's look at the other metaphors that helped form Disneyland. Nightly fireworks and cleanliness was borrowed from Tivoli Gardens in Denmark. The idea of the Matterhorn roller coaster came from a personal trip. The steam engine that circles the park was reminiscent of one that circled Electric Park in Kansas City, where Walt Disney grew up. The point, don't get wedded to just one metaphor, but borrow from many places.

I'd like you to use analogy to solve a problem before our next lecture. Find a challenge. Since nature is a wonderful teacher, go to nature and find an analogy that helps you with your situation. Examine how nature solved a similar problem, and see what new ideas it gives you in terms of working with your challenge. Analogical thinking is a complex form of thinking, and it takes practice. Once perfected, it will open up a rich range of ideas and solutions. Remember, borrowing and modifying is not stealing; it's just good thinking. It's good, creative thinking. With this in mind, find another challenge and practice borrowing ideas, following David Kord Murray's suggestion. Systematically examine and make a list of ideas that you can borrow from other places. Look at your competitors or a rival. How did they solve a similar challenge? Look to similar places and see how similar solutions, or solutions that were generated for a problem that's similar to yours. How challenges have been solved in an opposite place, much like Coco Chanel, coming up with a new design for women's fashion, but based on men's fashion. And finally, create a list of ideas of how other people solved this challenge. Once you have your list of borrowed ideas, examine the ones that are most promising and explore how you might modify those for your purposes. Remember, perhaps the best muse for future ideas is past ideas.

Let's look at how this process works. I'm going to share with you a metaphor that I borrowed from David Kord Murray, who borrowed it from Sigmund Freud. Imagine your mind has two rooms, between which stands a watchman. One room is the drawing room. Here, the guests—our ideas—are polite and civil. They're well mannered. This is our conscious mind. The other room is a large banquet hall in which there's chaos. The guests here—our ideas and thoughts—are unrestrained. They're free to interact and connect. There's a great deal of energy, and the more guests in the banquet hall, the greater the possible combinations. This is our subconscious mind, our primary source of inspiration. The more guests in the banquet hall, the greater chance of an unusual combination coming together.

The watchman stands in between the two rooms. The watchman is judgment. The watchman vets who can move from the banquet hall, from our subconscious, into the drawing room, our conscious mind. If the watchman is too strict, that is, our judgment is too strong, the drawing room will no longer have access to inspiration, and eventually, the guests in the banquet hall, because they can't get into the drawing room, will leave or no longer interact with one another. To make the most of borrowing ideas, you should be sure your banquet hall is full of guests by giving it lots of input and ensure judgment is not so strict, therefore allowing for novel combinations of thoughts to occur so they can eventually make it into the drawing room.

As Martha Graham said, "I am a thief—and I am not ashamed of it. I steal from the best where it happens to be—Plato, Picasso, Bertram Ross. I am a thief-and I glory in it. … I think I know the value of what I steal and treasure it for all time—not as a possession, but as a heritage and a legacy." And I'll see you next time.

Systematic Tools to Generate New Ideas

Lecture 13

Different tools do different things: They appeal to different people, and they generate different kinds of ideas. You can choose a tool to help you reach the kinds of ideas you desire. For example, brainstorming helps to generate both adaptive and innovative ideas while brainwriting is more adaptive. If you want more innovative responses, you can use a tool like visually identifying relationships. The three tools that you will learn about in the lecture—attribute listing, morphological matrix, and SCAMPER—are more systematic and more structured, and they will tend to generate more adaptive solutions.

Attribute Listing

- Attribute listing is a systematic tool designed to make variations. It was conceived at the University of Nebraska by Robert Crawford, who may have taught the first university course on creativity in the United States in 1931. He saw creativity as taking steps to modify the present conditions.

- In attribute listing, there are a number of steps. The first step is to list the attributes, or components, of the challenge, breaking it down into elements. In the second step, you generate ideas to improve each attribute, and then, you select the best ideas.

- Attribute listing can be used on any challenge that has attributes or components. When those are identifiable, you can use attribute listing.

When you list attributes, you break down your challenge into its elements.

- For example, let's say that our challenge is to reduce employee turnover in an organization. In step one, we list the attributes associated with employee turnover. We've identified three: the physical work conditions, the psychological work conditions, and employee engagement.

- In step two, we now take each of those attributes and generate ideas to see if we can improve each attribute. Let's start with physical work conditions. What ideas might we have for improving physical work conditions? We can make the space cleaner, brighter. We can add health care. We can have an on-premise coffee shop. We could have child-care facilities or personalized office space. We can remove corporate-wide policies and replace them with unit policies.

- In terms of the psychological work conditions, we could have weekly raffles. We could have counseling services available. We could enhance the leadership skills of the management team to improve the psychological work conditions.

- Finally, what ideas might we have to improve employee engagement? One possibility is job rotation. We could have shadow days where you follow different people around and find out what their job responsibilities are. We could have a bring-your-guest-to-work day and have opportunities to expand responsibilities. We could celebrate employees' anniversaries. We can begin an employee-of-the-month recognition program. We can make senior leadership more visible, including having executive leaders hand-deliver birthday cards.

- At the end, we go into each of these components and choose the ideas that we think will best help to address our challenge—the ones that would be the most viable solutions.

- Attribute listing is a systematic idea-generation tool that is in a way like the other tools that provide springboards. The components become your springboard. They isolate specific areas to generate ideas. So there's a clear structure to the tool.

Morphological Matrix

- Attribute listing works on one dimension at a time, but the tool called morphological matrix works across dimensions. It cross-fertilizes ideas. It is a deliberate creativity tool.

- Morphological matrix is an idea-generation tool that extends attribute listing. We generate ideas for an attribute along one axis of the matrix, and ideas for a second attribute along a second axis, and then we can combine these ideas to create new outcomes.

- For example, let's say that we wish to make a new kind of sandwich. The two dimensions, or two axes, will be the kinds of spread, and the other axis will be meats. We can place the spreads along the top of the matrix. Mayo might be a possible spread, so we create a column for mayo. Then, we create three more columns for guacamole, peanut butter, and brown mustard. We then list meats in the very first column: turkey, chicken, roast beef, and ostrich. With this matrix, we can cross these two dimensions and create interesting combinations.

- For example, we might cross turkey with mayo, or turkey with guacamole, or turkey with peanut butter. We might cross chicken with mayo or chicken with guacamole. We could cross roast beef with peanut butter or roast beef with brown mustard. We could combine ostrich with mayo, peanut butter, or brown mustard. In this way, we're taking our two dimensions and crossing every possible combination.

- One of the benefits of morphological matrix is that it's flexible. It can be used on any challenge with multiple dimensions. This tool generates many combinations. A matrix with four dimensions and 10 ideas listed in each dimension yields 10,000 possible combinations.

SCAMPER

- Alex Osborn created brainstorming. He also created idea-spurring questions to enhance these sessions. He would ask questions, when people would run out of ideas, like, what can we add?

What can we take away? What can we modify? In fact, he had 70 idea-spurring questions.

- Bob Eberle organized these questions into a mnemonic that made it easier to remember these questions: SCAMPER, which stands for Substitute, Combine, Adapt, Modify (which should also be Magnify or Minify), Put to other uses, Eliminate, and Rearrange. Each of these has questions that can be used to spur further ideas.
  - Substitute: Who else instead? What else instead? Are there other ingredients, other materials, other processes?
  - Combine: How about a blend? What can we bring together? Can we combine purposes? Can we combine units? Can we combine appeals?
  - Adapt: What else is like this? What can you adapt for use as a solution? What does the past offer as a parallel? What could I copy?
  - Modify: Can you change the item in some way—its meaning, color, motion, sound, smell, or shape?
    - Magnify: What can you add? Can you have greater frequency of something? Can something be stronger, larger, thicker? How might we duplicate it?
    - Minify: What might be subtracted? What could we make smaller or lighter? How might we streamline it?
  - Put to other uses: What might be a different use, or other uses, if we modified this item?
  - Eliminate: What can you eliminate or remove? Eliminate waste, and reduce effort. Can you cut costs?
  - Rearrange: Can we interchange components? Is there another pattern, another layout? Can we transpose cause and effect?

- This is useful on any challenge. The questions are generic enough that SCAMPER can be flexibly applied, from concrete challenges—such as graphic design and interior design or improving machines—to intangible things—such as improving a service or process, writing a story, or making new music. In fact, this kind of creative thinking has been widely used in the music industry.

- **Substitute**. American singer-songwriter Weird Al Yankovic has made a career out of writing musical parodies that comment on popular culture. This is a kind of way of substituting. For example, he used the melody from "American Pie" to create a song he called "The Saga Begins," which is a parody on *Star Wars*.

- **Combine**. Considered to be one of the greatest stadium rock bands in history, Queen began in 1971 and became massively successful. "Bohemian Rhapsody," one of their biggest hits, combined opera and hard rock. The song stayed at number one in the United Kingdom for nine weeks.

- **Adapt**. Colleen Ann Fitzpatrick, known by her stage name, Vitamin C, provides a good example of this. Her hit song, "Graduation (Friends Forever)," adapts a popular classical piece of music, "Pachelbel's Canon," into a hip-hop song style.

- **Modify**. Jazz legend Dave Brubeck heard an unusual time signature while listening to street performers in Turkey. He modified the traditional 4-4 beat in jazz to the more exotic style he experienced overseas. The result is his well-known album *Take 5*.
    - **Magnify**. The great composer Aaron Copland's "Appalachian Spring" provides a good example of magnification within a single piece of music. In this piece, the basic melody, borrowed from a folk song, "Simple Gifts," grows from a more upbeat, lilting tempo and light orchestration to a more majestic tempo with heavier instrumentation.

    - **Minify**. Overtures provide an excellent example of this. In an overture, the composer cobbles together short pieces drawn from the overall performance.

- **Put to other uses**. In the musical *Mama Mia*, 1970s and 1980s ABBA hits are strung together into an interesting story. When *Mama Mia* was turned into a movie in 2008, it was the top-grossing motion picture in England for the year. Perhaps it shouldn't be a surprise; ABBA has sold more than 370 million albums.

- **Eliminate**. Copland's "Appalachian Spring" was originally written for the ballet. He partnered with famous choreographer Martha Graham. When it was performed, the ballet was removed, as well as about 10 minutes of the music, which created the well-known orchestral suite.

- **Rearrange**. *Glee*, a television show featuring a high school glee club, performs mostly rearrangements of past songs, and many times, they mash up two pieces of music into a new combination. Some critics suggest that some of these rearrangements were even better than the originals.

Suggested Reading

Altshuller, *And Suddenly the Inventor Appeared.*

Goldenberg and Mazursky, *Creativity in Product Innovation.*

Activities

Activity 1: Attribute Listing and SCAMPER
Look around you for an object, process, or system that you use for work. Use attribute listing or SCAMPER to generate new ideas and combinations to improve the object, process, or system.

Activity 2: Morphological Matrix

Invent a new pasta dish by completing the matrix below. Generate options for each of the categories, and then combine items. Feel free to add additional categories or modify an existing category—i.e., switching vegetable 2 for a meat category. (Or, create a new matrix by selecting a different challenge and using your own categories.)

Pasta	Sauce	Vegetable 1	Vegetable 2
ziti	tomato basil	tomato	zucchini

Systematic Tools to Generate New Ideas
Lecture 13—Transcript

At a dinner for Nobel Prize winners, President John F. Kennedy said, "I think this is the most extraordinary collection of talent, of human knowledge, that has ever been gathered at the White House, with the possible exception of when Thomas Jefferson dined alone." In so many ways, Thomas Jefferson has been lauded as a great creator, as a statesman, as an author, in agriculture, as an architect, and did you know he was also a furniture designer?

For example, Thomas Jefferson took a traditional Windsor chair made of wood and added a swivel to the seat, thereby creating the first well-known swivel chair, and he didn't stop there. Later, he added a writing surface to his swivel Windsor chair, and supposedly, it was used for some of his work on the Declaration of Independence. And he designed other types of chairs, too. He commissioned at least three hammock chairs, made with an unusual sloping back that allowed him to use what he called the medium position between sitting and lying down. Jefferson certainly seemed to be a good ideator, creating in so many diverse areas. In this lecture, we continue to learn tools for ideating so that you can think like Thomas Jefferson.

Let's review what we already know. We've learned and practiced brainstorming—two versions of brainstorming. Classic brainstorming with a facilitator capturing the ideas, and Post-it brainstorming, where the participants write on Post-its and hand them to the facilitator, so that they can be displayed publicly. We learned and practiced brainwriting, which is a silent form of idea generation, where participants write their ideas quietly and then swap sheets with one another, so that they can read and build off of each other's ideas.

We've also learned reverse brainstorming, which is taking the challenge statement and putting it into its negative form, generating ideas on that and then reversing them back into positive solutions for the original challenge. We learned forced connections, which is designed to allow us to build off of and use objects as springboards for our ideation. We've learned visually identifying relationships, which uses photographs. We take a break, a mental excursion. We look at photographs to create free associations, and then we take those free associations and we facilitate associations connected back to our original challenge.

We learned a number of tools that help us to borrow ideas from other places, from synectics, direct analogy, personal analogy. And finally, we learned to borrow ideas from nature, called biomimicry. Now, different tools do different things. They appeal to different people, and they generate different kinds of ideas. Stan Gryskiewicz did a research study where he took three ideation tools and he gave them to managers, and he had them all work on the same challenge. The challenge they worked on was other uses for tea bags. He had the managers generate ideas using brainwriting, brainstorming, and visually identifying relationships, three tools that are familiar to you. Then he evaluated the kinds of ideas produced by these three tools.

He used Kirton's Adapter-Innovator scale. If you recall, in the scale, creativity ranges from an adaptive style of creativity, which is looking to make improvements, staying within the box, incremental changes, more evolutionary creative thinking, versus at the other end of the continuum we have more innovatively creative ideas. These are more radical ideas. They're more revolutionary. They're out of the box. What he noticed when he took the ideas generated by these three tools is that they tended to generate different kinds of ideas. The brainwriting tool tended to generate more adaptive ideas, ideas that kept the tea bag essentially as it was. For example, instead of tea, put coffee in the tea bag. The visually identifying relationships tool generated a completely different kind of idea. The VIR tool tended to generate more innovative answers, answers that threatened the existing paradigm or changed the existing paradigm. For example, a manager said, "Take the tea bags and make them into parachutes." The third tool, brainstorming, tended to generate a mix of both adaptive and innovative ideas.

What are the implications of this research study? Well, one clear implication is that you can choose a tool to help you to get to the kinds of ideas you desire, the kinds of ideas that you want. Brainstorming helps to generate both kinds of ideas, brainwriting more adaptive. You want more innovative responses? Use a tool like visually identifying relationships, or use some of the other tools that you've learned, such as forced connection, direct analogy, personal analogy, and biomimicry. They tend to generate more innovative ideas as well. Tools like attribute listing, morphological matrix and scamper, tools that you'll learn in this lecture, are more systematic, are more structured, and will tend to generate more adaptive solutions.

A number of years ago I was in Paris, and I visited the Louvre, and I came across Da Vinci's journals. The journal was opened up to a page with multiple sketches of the same face, and each sketch had a slight alteration to it. In one image, the figure had a longer nose. In the next image, smaller ears. Different hair in the next image. A change to the mouth, and so on. Attribute listing, the first tool we'll learn in this lecture, is a systematic tool designed to make variations, much like I saw in Da Vinci's journal. It was conceived by Robert Crawford at the University of Nebraska, who may have taught the very first university course on creativity in the U.S. in 1931. He saw creativity as taking steps to modify the present conditions.

In attribute listing, there are a number of steps. The first step is to list the attributes, the components of the challenge. You break it down into elements. And then, in the second step, you generate ideas to improve each element, to improve each attribute, and then you select the best ideas. Let's try this tool out. Let's say we wish to improve a chair. Perhaps this is how Thomas Jefferson came up with his chair designs. So let's think like Thomas Jefferson, then. In step one, we list the attributes of the chair. We have the seat, the arms, backrest, and legs. In step two, we now generate ideas to improve each attribute, and because we're ideating, we're in the beginning phase of the ideate step, we recall that we're applying the divergent thinking mindset here, so we're suspending our evaluation. We're striving for quantity. We're making connections and we're seeking novelty.

So let's take each attribute, and let's look at some sample ideas that we might generate for each attribute. Let's take the seat first. Perhaps we could use a cushion. We could change the fabric. We could add a trampoline to it. We could make it out of mesh. We could make it Tempur-Pedic. We could add springs to it. We could make the cushion out of water. We can make it round to encourage balance. The arms, perhaps we can make the arms collapsible, or hide-away, adjustable, or removable. Replace from different kinds of events, and we could, perhaps, add a cup holder.

Let's go to the backrest. We could build in a lower backrest. We can add an attachment for lower back support, make an inflatable lower back support. We can add a headrest to it. We can create an adjustable headrest, a headrest that holds your head, like when you're on an airplane. And then finally, let's think about the legs. Perhaps we could have four different legs from four different design periods. Maybe we can put springs in the legs to allow for movement, make the legs look like human legs. We could have do-it-yourself chairs, where you order legs and other components to create your own chair. At the end, when you've generated, within each of these attributes, now that we've done the divergent phase, you know what follows—the convergent phase.

So you go into each of these attributes, and you select the ideas that may be most effective, or most desirable, in terms of modifying the chair. Well, perhaps attribute listing is alive and well in chair design. There are many different kinds of chairs out there. Here are three examples I'll describe to you. They all use the human body sort of as a springboard for their design. In one example, we have a chair where the arms are, in fact, human arms. They're designed to look like human arms. In another example, we have a chair that's designed like a head, where the face we sit in, and it looks out from behind us. And in the third example, we have the entire human body in a chair position so that you can sit on someone's lap. These are examples of how chairs have been modified, how the attributes of the chairs have been modified.

Attribute listing can be used on any challenge, not just tangible things like the chair that I just took us through. It can be used on any challenge that has attributes or components. When those are identifiable, you can use attribute listing. Here's another example. Let's look into an organization, and let's say our challenge is to reduce employee turnover. So, in step one we list the attributes associated with employee turnover. Let's say we've identified three: the physical work conditions, the psychological work conditions, and employee engagement.

Now, you may recall in step two, we now take each of those attributes and we generate ideas to see if we can improve each attribute. So, let's start with physical work conditions. What ideas might we have for improving physical work conditions? We can make the space cleaner, brighter. We can add healthcare. We can have an on-premise coffee shop. We could have childcare facilities, personalized office space. We can remove corporate-wide policies and replace them with unit policies.

In terms of the psychological work conditions, we could have weekly raffles. We could have counseling services available. We could enhance the leadership skills of the management team to improve the psychological work conditions. And finally, with employee engagement, what ideas might we have to improve employee engagement? Well, one possibility is job rotation. We could have shadow days, where you follow different people around and find out what their job responsibilities are. We could bring your guest to work day, have opportunities to expand responsibilities. We could celebrate employees' anniversaries. We can begin employee-of-the-month recognition program. We can make senior leadership more visible, have executive leaders hand-deliver birthday cards, and etcetera. At the end, as before, with the chair, we go into each of these components, and we choose the ideas that we think will work best, the ideas that will help to address our challenge. The ones that would be the most viable solutions.

Let's take another area, a more personal example now. Let's say we want to improve a relationship with a significant other. We begin, again, as with the chair and employee turnover, by listing the attributes associated with improving a relationship or personal relationships. So, communication might be an attribute we would look at, shared social activities, shared domestic activities, finances, and then a broad category, fun, ways to have more fun.

In step two, we generate ideas to improve each attribute. Again, we're engaging in divergent thinking. We'll begin in this example with communication. What might be some ideas? Well, we could have an electronic shared journal. We could telegraph our daily mood to each other. We could go on a couples' weekend. We could have a compliments board in the kitchen, and so forth.

In terms of shared social activities, we could join a health club; we could do yoga together; we could start a couples' group; we could take a cooking class together. In terms of shared domestic activities, we could rotate chores; we could delegate chores; we could chart our domestic duties. With finances, we could work with a financial planner; we could sort our funds into three categories—ours, mine, and yours; we can create our own board game based on Monopoly; we can set financial goals.

Finally, in the fun category, perhaps we could create a garden together, relive our honeymoon, write a joint memoir, create a picture book of our life together, create a bucket list and pursue these items together. And when you're done, when you're done with the divergent thinking phase, you move through—in this case, probably with your partner—and converge on those ideas and those categories that you think will be most effective.

So, attribute listing. It's a systematic idea-generation tool. In a way, like the earlier tools that we learn that provide springboards, the components become your springboard. They isolate specific areas to generate ideas, so there's a clear structure to the tool.

Maybe one of America's great inventors used this method of thinking. Thomas Edison's biography says he had 40,000 pages of notes on finding the right filament to withstand the 40-hour laboratory test for the light bulb. His assistants tested over 1,600 different materials. They swapped one material in for the next until they struck upon the one that worked. They examined such material as coconut fiber, fishing line, and a hair from a friend's beard. Finally, they hit on carbonized bamboo. Much like attribute listing, they swapped one item in for the next for that component of the filament. Attribute listing works on one dimension at a time. The next tool we'll practice works across dimensions. It cross-fertilizes ideas.

A number of years ago, I was visiting western Massachusetts, and I visited the Normal Rockwell museum there. They had an interesting display that gave some insight into his creative process. In this display, they had the final canvas that he created, and next to it was another canvas, and on that canvas they had small images that had variations in the scene that eventually led to the final canvas. In each scene, he changed some aspect of it. He changed the girl, and perhaps, from a blonde, he put in a brunette. He changed the figures in the scene and their positions. He changed the background in the scene, and so this canvas had a variety of these scenes, and he combined them, combined what he liked best, for the final canvas.

In a way, this is similar to a tool called morphological matrix, a deliberate creativity tool. Morphological matrix is an idea-generation tool that extends attribute listing. We generate ideas for an attribute along one axis of the matrix, then ideas for a second attribute along a second axis, and then we can combine these ideas to create new outcomes.

Here's a very simple example. Let's say we wish to make a new kind of sandwich. The two dimensions, the two axes, will be the kinds of spread, and the other axis will be meats. So, for spreads, we can place those along the top of our matrix. We might say mayo, we create a column for mayo; guacamole, another column for guacamole; peanut butter; and brown mustard. For meats, we list those in the very first column. Turkey, chicken, roast beef, and ostrich. Now with this matrix, we can cross these two dimensions and create interesting combinations. So, for example, we might cross turkey with mayo, or turkey with guacamole, or turkey with peanut butter. We might cross chicken with mayo or chicken with guacamole. We could cross roast beef with peanut butter or roast beef with brown mustard. We could take ostrich, and we can combine that with mayo, peanut butter, or brown mustard. In this way, we're taking our two dimensions and we're crossing every possible combination.

Gary Davis, in his book *Creativity is Forever*, indicates that Fran Striker used morphological matrix to produce storylines for radio and comics. Fran Striker was born in Buffalo. He graduated from Lafayette High School, and he attended the University of Buffalo. He was a co-creator of *The Lone Ranger*, as well as *The Green Hornet* and *Sergeant Preston of the Yukon*. Radio needed content desperately at that time. You see, once it was invented, the radio spread faster than the Internet today. With *The Lone Ranger*, Striker wrote more than 150 scripts a year. The radio series ran for 21 years, from 1933 to 1954, with a total of almost 3,000 original episodes. How on earth could you sustain your creativity? According to Davis, Striker used a systematic process, like morphological matrix. He had four dimensions listing ideas that were combined into stories for *The Lone Ranger*.

Let's look at an example. Along the top, we might list four elements that we would find in the story, such as a dilemma, new characters, a place, and a villain. And then, underneath each one of these, we can list ideas. So, under dilemma, we could say, "The well runs dry." "The mine collapses." "The wagon train is caught in a storm." "There is disease." Under new characters we could have zombies, an orphan boy raised by wolves, Abraham Lincoln, and traveling circus. Under place we could have mountain, desert, a ghost town, the U.S.-Mexico border; under villain, Billy the Kid, escaped convict, a rabid dog, or a hungry mountain lion.

Now, we can go across each of these columns, and we can randomly combine these elements to create a story. So, randomly combining these, let's look at one example. A wagon train that's caught in a storm with zombies at the characters. The place could be a ghost town, and the villain could be an escaped convict. Let's look at another random combination. As far as the dilemma, it could be a mine collapse. The characters could include a traveling circus. The location could be the U.S.-Mexico border. And, finally, the villain could be a rabid dog.

So, what are some of the benefits of morphological matrix? Well, it's flexible. It can be used on any challenge with multiple dimensions. I've used it with students to have them write and perform skits, like our Lone Ranger example. This tool generates many combinations. A matrix with four dimensions and 10 ideas listed in each dimension yields 10,000 possible combinations.

Earlier we learned Osborn created brainstorming. He also created idea-spurring questions to enhance these sessions. He would ask questions when people would run out of ideas. He would ask questions like, "What can we add?" "What can we take away?" "What can we modify?" He used these as idea-spurring questions. In fact, he had 70 idea-spurring questions.

Bob Eberle came along later, and he organized these questions into a mnemonic that made it easier to remember these questions. The mnemonic he used was SCAMPER. SCAMPER stands for substitute, combine, adapt, modify—which should also be magnify or minify—Put to other uses, eliminate, and rearrange. Let's go through each of these and look at the kinds of questions that can be used to spur further ideas.

So, with substitute, who else instead? What else instead? Are there other ingredients, other material, other processes? In combine, how about a blend? What can we bring together? Can we combine purposes? Can we combine units? Can we combine appeals? For adapt, what else is like this? What can you adapt for use as a solution? What does the past offer as a parallel? What could I copy? Modify, can you change the item in some way, its meaning, color, motion, sound, smell, or shape? Now, M also stands for magnify and minify. What can you add? Can you have greater frequency of something, stronger, larger, thicker, duplicate? Minify, what might be subtracted? What could we make smaller, lighter, or how might we streamline it? P stands for put to other uses. What might be a different use, or other uses, if we modified this item? Then we come to E, which stands for eliminate. What can you eliminate, remove? Eliminate waste. Reduce effort. Can you cut costs? And, finally, R is for rearrange. Can we interchange components? Is there another pattern, another layout? Can we transpose cause and effect?

This is useful on any challenge. The questions are generic enough that it can be flexibly applied, from concrete challenges, such as graphic design and interior design or improving machine, to intangible things, such as improving a service, a process, writing a story, or making new music.

Let's take this last one as an example. I believe SCAMPER, perhaps not deliberately, but this kind of creative thinking has been widely used in the music industry. Let's take some examples from music and relate to each of our questions in the SCAMPER tool. Weird Al Yankovic, American singer-songwriter, has made a career out of writing musical parodies that comment on popular culture. I think this is a kind of way of substituting. As of 2007, he had sold in excess of 12 million albums, and he's earned three Grammy awards. Here's an example. He used the melody from "American Pie" to create a song, "The Saga Begins," which is a parody on *Star Wars*.

Let's look at C, which stands for combine. Considered to be one of the greatest stadium rock bands in history, Queen began in 1971 and played through the 1980s. "Bohemian Rhapsody," one of their biggest hits, combined opera and hard rock. The song stayed at number one in the U.K. for nine weeks. Let's look at A, which stands for adapt. Colleen Ann Fitzpatrick, known by her stage name, Vitamin C, provides a good example of adapt. Her hit, "Graduation (Friends Forever)" adapts a popular classical piece of music, Pachelbel's Canon, into a hip-hop song style.

Modify, Jazz legend Dave Brubeck heard an unusual time signature while listening to street performers in Turkey. He modified the traditional 4/4 beat in jazz to the more exotic style he experienced overseas. The result is his well-known album *Take 5*. Let's look at modify. Let's specifically look at magnify. The great composer, Aaron Copland's "Appalachian Spring," provides a good example of magnification within a single piece of music. In this piece, the basic melody, borrowed from a folk song, "Simple Gifts," grows from a more upbeat, lilting tempo and light orchestration to a more majestic tempo with heavier instrumentation. Let's look at minify. Overtures provide an excellent example of the use of minify. In an overture, the composer cobbles together short pieces drawn from the overall performance.

How about Put to other uses? A few years ago, I went to the musical *Mama Mia*. Who would have thought that these old 1970s and 1980s ABBA hits could be strung together into an interesting story? By the way, when *Mama Mia* was turned into a movie in 2008, it was the top-grossing motion picture in England for the year. Perhaps it shouldn't be a surprise. ABBA has sold more than 370 million albums.

Eliminate, "Appalachian Spring," which I mentioned earlier, was originally written for the ballet. Copland partnered with famous choreographer Martha Graham. When it was performed, the ballet was removed, as well as about 10 minutes of the music, which created the well-known orchestral suite. How about rearrange? Rearrange, this very term is used widely in the music industry. *Glee*, a TV show featuring a high school glee club, performs mostly rearrangements of past songs, and many times they mashed up two pieces of music into a new combination. Some critics suggest that some of these rearrangements were even better than the originals.

So, SCAMPER. We showed SCAMPER as it applied to music. But like all ideation tools, it can be applied on a range of challenges, from more tangible to more intangible issues. And it's still very useful as a brainstorming enhancing tool to spur further thoughts. You can use SCAMPER to enhance the idea generation in a brainstorming session when people begin to run out of ideas.

The three tools—attribute listing, morphological matrix, and SCAMPER—are systematic. I'd like you to try them out, and perhaps you could begin with SCAMPER. Let's make idea generation an everyday skill. So, find a room in your home. Use SCAMPER to look around. What might you substitute, combine, adapt, minify, and so forth? Remember, when you're doing this, think in divergent ways. After you make a long list of possibilities, then converge. Select the ideas that you think are best, and see if you can implement them. Then take one of the other systematic idea-generation tools and apply them to a personal or professional challenge. Try attribute listing or morphological matrix.

This is the last lecture on the ideate step. You have many tools now in your toolkit, and you know how you can choose those tools based on the kind of ideas that you might want to generate. If you want more adaptive ideas, you now know the kinds of tools to use. Or if you want more innovative ideas, you know the kinds of tools that you can use to purposely generate those kinds of ideas. It's important to note that any ideation tool can be done in a group. And if you are using these in a group, remember the roles. It's best to have a facilitator, someone who's going to facilitate and guide the process and hold the group accountable to sticking to the divergent thinking rules.

We'll have a client. This is the problem owner. The person who ultimately makes the decisions. Be sure that the client is truly open to novelty. One of the ways to undermine idea generation is to have a client who's judgmental. And to enhance the divergent thinking, have a resource group if possible, individuals who bring ideation and divergent thinking and energy to the group.

Sometimes the resource group members and the clients can be the same, where you work with an entire group who is responsible for making the decisions. In such cases, it's particularly useful to have a facilitator that ensures that the group adheres to the guidelines, and especially the divergent thinking guideline of deferring judgment.

In ideate we've really pushed on divergent thinking, and when we look at our work with groups, in general we find that, when they're using ideation tools, they can generate 5 to 10 ideas per minute. Use this as your benchmark. Can you generate 5 to 10 ideas per minute when using these tools, individually or when working with groups?

In our next lecture, we look at how to take our good ideas and turn them into great solutions. See you next time.

Developing Ideas—Toward Great Solutions

Lecture 14

In this lecture, you will learn how to take good ideas and turn them into great solutions. It's not enough to have a good idea. What really makes great creators stand out is their ability to polish and refine their ideas into gems. In a way, this comes naturally for those who have a developer preference. With tools like POINT, which you will learn about in this lecture, we can make this even more efficient—we can make this kind of thinking easier, even for those who may not have the developer preference.

Convergent Thinking: The Develop Step

- In the develop step of the creative process, we're looking at an ability to evaluate and transform a broad idea into a specific, workable solution—one that resolves the challenge that we intended to address.

- Evaluative thinking isn't simply rejecting the bad ideas. In the ideate step, we're generating novelty. In the develop step, we explore the value of that novelty, trying to retain it into something that's workable.

- Because we are exploring novelty in the develop step, this step of the process has more of a convergent orientation that reminds you of the principles of convergent thinking.

- The principle that's key to convergent thinking, much like suspending judgment is for divergent thinking, is to use affirmative judgment. The first thing we see should be something that's positive.

- The second principle is to keep novelty alive; stay open to original thinking and unexpected outcomes. Don't just reject an idea simply because it doesn't fit the old or existing paradigm.

- The next guideline is to check your objectives. The previous guideline focuses on novelty and that side of the creativity equation, but we have to balance novelty with usefulness, appropriateness, and value. We evaluate and screen our ideas against our success criteria to get at the most promising solution.

- The fourth principle for convergent thinking is to stay focused, which is a willingness to work with the idea, to embrace its imperfections, and to refine the idea over time. We recognize that sometimes it takes hard work to make something that you've fallen in love with really work. The principles are important for both developing our ideas and when reacting to others' ideas.

POINT

- Imagine that you've come up with an idea and you've proposed that idea to someone, and you want him or her to give you feedback—to react to your idea. How would you like the person to react?

- In answer to this question, people ask for constructive feedback. They want to improve their thinking. They want to be given a balanced approach, both the positives and the negatives. They want the other person to be honest with them, but not harsh, and to ask questions.

- A tool that sort of takes this advice and puts it into action is POINT, which is an acronym, and it's important that we follow this acronym in the order suggested. P stands for Pluses, so when evaluating an idea and looking to develop an idea, the first thing we do is look for the strengths, the good points, the positives. We should come up with at least three.

- Then, we move on to the O in POINT, which stands for Opportunities. Often, when we evaluate an idea, we only look at what it delivers here and today. We don't think about the future—future scenarios and future possibilities. Opportunities gets us to think like futurists. If we pursued this solution or change, what might happen? What would be future potentials? What would be some spin-offs? What would be some possibilities?

- To help us think about opportunities, we use the invitational stem *it might*. If we implemented this idea, solution, or change, *it might*—and then we fill in the blank.

- We can't be naïve and ignore any possible shortcomings or limitations, so the I in POINT helps us look at the Issues. These are the concerns, drawbacks, the shortcomings of the idea. To invite a problem-solving form of thinking, we phrase these in the form of a challenge. So, the issue begins with *how to*, *how might*, *what might*.

- When we phrase these as questions, they invoke a response. When someone asks us a question, what's our natural reaction? We look to answer the question. So it's important that you phrase the issues in the form of a *how to* or *how might*.

- The next element within the POINT tool, NT, stands for New Thinking. We use new thinking now to address our issues. We begin by prioritizing them. We start with the biggest issue, and we generate ideas to overcome that issue. Then, we go on to the next biggest issue, and so forth—generating ideas, engaging in divergent thinking, with the hope of coming up with ideas that will address the *how to*, the *how might*, that will overcome that challenge that we identified during the Issue phase of this tool.

- You then evaluate your analysis—what you've generated through the POINT—and you make a decision to keep it as is or to change it or to not go forward with it. If you decide to keep it as is, you're ready to move on to the next step of the creative problem-solving process.

- But you might decide that there are some ideas that you generated when you were applying new thinking that might suggest ways to refine the idea, to develop it into an even stronger solution. Or, on balance after doing this evaluation, you might decide to not go forward with it. But at least you've given it a fair analysis.

- Imagine that schools had no teachers. The only adults in the building with the students are project managers, not teachers. What might be three pluses of this idea? What might be three opportunities? What might be three issues?

- So, if schools had no teachers, if there were only project managers, can you think of three strengths to this idea—three advantages that this might pose? How about opportunities? If schools had no teachers, what might happen? Can you think of three *it mights*, three spin-offs, three potentials?

- Then, apply good critical thinking. Identify some issues. What concerns might you have? What might be some shortcomings with this idea? Can you phrase these issues in the form of a challenge statement (*how to*, *how might*, *what might*)?

- Finally, the next step of this tool is NT—New Thinking. Can you think of one big issue that might really get in the way of this idea being effective? Think of that in your mind or capture it on a piece of paper, and then generate ideas. What new thoughts do you have that will help you address this issue?

- Now, evaluate the proposed idea. Once you've generated these pluses and opportunities, step back and look to see if you can refine the idea or if it's good as it is. Probably this highly novel idea in terms of eliminating teachers and having project managers would require some refinement. On balance, you step back and analyze what you have generated. You might decide not to go forward.

Benefits of POINT

- One of the benefits of POINT is that it takes an idea that's really novel, and it can transform it into something that actually is workable. POINT is a tool that is incredibly flexible and can be used in many ways. It doesn't have to be used in a formal way; it can be used in an informal discussion.

- As a team, you can use POINT when you're reviewing a proposed idea. You can go through POINT together, with each person moving through the each part of the acronym. Even school-age children can use POINT.

- POINT is also a wonderful tool for capturing lessons learned from a project. What are some opportunities for the future? What were some of the issues that we need to address? And, while it's still fresh in our minds, what new thinking can we come up with?

- As part of the review process, people receive feedback through the POINT tool during performance reviews or when coming up for a promotion. In addition, it can be used to develop a product concept that you're toying with and thinking about launching into the marketplace. Before launching it, you can use POINT to develop that idea.

- Before you present an idea to a group, you can use POINT with the idea, and then as you're doing the presentation, you can use POINT as the framework to underscore the pluses; the opportunities if the idea were pursued; and some issues and how some of those issues, through your anticipation, could be addressed.

- Finally, POINT can be used to enhance team effectiveness. Michael West, a business school professor who has tracked teams over time, has observed that those teams that are able to sustain their innovation have a quality that he calls reflexivity—that is, that teams stop occasionally and evaluate their performance.

Suggested Reading

Basadur, *Simplex®*.

LeGault, *Think*.

Activities

Activity 1: POINT

- Work through the POINT tool to develop an idea you generated during one of the previous activities.

- Use POINT to evaluate the product featured in the picture below.

Activity 2:
More Ways to Use POINT

Look for opportunities to use POINT informally while responding to someone else's idea. Don't announce that you are using the tool; simply try it out and see how the other person responds to you.

Developing Ideas—Toward Great Solutions
Lecture 14—Transcript

Have you ever had an idea that you tried to implement before its time? What were the consequences of jumping to action before the idea had been fully considered? In some cases, it means bankruptcy. Let's examine the dot com bubble, which roughly lasted from 1997 to about 2000. During this time, there was unbridled optimism about the Internet business. Any business, it seemed, with a dot, com drew investors. In Super Bowl XXXIV, in the year 2000, there were 17 dot com advertisements. Each 30-second spot cost two million dollars. A year later, Super Bowl XXXV, there were only three dot com commercials. The bubble had burst.

There are some pros and cons to this bubble. The upside, the exuberance helped usher in a new economy. The downside, it led to many spectacular failures. And I think it provides a lesson in the importance of fully vetting an idea. Let's look at two examples. Third Voice, it was founded in the late 1990s. Here was the business idea. Users of Third Voice could plant virtual sticky notes on websites that they visited. Other users could then see these comments. Their goal was to promote free speech on the Internet, but here's what happened. The sticky notes quickly degenerated into sarcastic, cynical, and lewd comments. The result? Third Voice gained enemies faster than users. In 2001, they were shut down.

Let's look at another example, Iam.com. Iam.com was designed to link actors and models directly to casting directors. The goal was to cut out the middle man—that is, the talent agent. How? Models and actors posted their portfolios online, so that casting directors could view and spot talent themselves. They received 48 million dollars in financing. Here's the problem. It turns out that casting directors like talent agents. You see, talent agents act as a screen; they save time for the casting directors. This out-of-business dot com employed over 60 people at one time.

Let's look at where we are in the creative problem-solving process. It's not enough to have a good idea. What really makes great creators stand out is their ability to polish and refine their ideas into gems. Now, in a way, this comes naturally for those who have a developer preference. With tools, we can make this even more efficient; we can make this kind of thinking easier, even for those who may not have the developer preference.

So what happens in the develop step of this creative process? We're looking at an ability to evaluate and transform a broad idea into a specific, workable solution, one that resolves the challenge that we intended to address. Let me tell you a story. Do you know about the origins of the Egg McMuffin? Herb Peterson was a franchise owner of several McDonalds out in California. Now, it turns out Herb Peterson really liked Eggs Benedict. Now, you may not know this, but at the time, McDonalds, from its inception until in the 1970s, only served lunches and dinners. Now, remember, Herb Peterson really liked Eggs Benedict, and he felt that, perhaps, he could better utilize his store operations if he began to offer breakfast, and so he tinkered with this idea of an Eggs Benedict and turning it into a sandwich, which eventually led to the Egg McMuffin, and he began to sell these in the morning time.

Now, when McDonalds, the corporation, had heard about this, he was scolded, and in fact, reprimanded for doing this. Later on, Ray Kroc came out to visit Herb Peterson, and Herb insisted that Ray Kroc try this sandwich. If you look at Ray Kroc's biography, you can see his reaction. At first, he said, "It was a crazy idea—that is, until I took a bite," and then he could see the potential. Three years later—it took three years—three years later, McDonalds was serving Egg McMuffins across the entire U.S.. And today, 30 percent of McDonalds' revenue comes from breakfast, and it was all started by this one sandwich.

Evaluative thinking isn't simply rejecting the bad ideas. Remember, in ideate we're generating novelty, kind of like the Egg McMuffin, a very novel idea. In develop, we explore the value of that novelty, trying to retain it into something that's workable.

Since we are exploring novelty in develop, the develop step of the process has more of a convergent feel to it, or a convergent orientation, that remind you of the principles of convergent thinking. The principle that's key to convergent thinking, much like suspend judgment is for divergent thinking, is to use affirmative judgment. When converging, we apply affirmative judgment. The first thing we see should be something that's positive; we go positive first. The second principle is to keep novelty alive. Stay open to original thinking and unexpected outcomes. After all, you have decided to use creative thinking. Don't just reject an idea simply because it doesn't fit the old or existing paradigm.

The next guideline is to check your objectives. The previous guideline focuses on novelty and that side of the creativity equation, but remember, we have to balance novelty off with usefulness, appropriateness, and value. We evaluate and screen our ideas against our success criteria to get at the most promising solution.

And then, our fourth principle for convergent thinking is to stay focused, which is a willingness to work with the idea, to embrace its imperfections, and to refine the idea over time. We recognize that sometimes it takes hard work to make something that you've fallen in love with really work. The principles are important for both developing our ideas and when reacting to others' ideas.

When I do creativity training programs, I like to ask participants a question. Imagine you've come up with an idea, and you've proposed that idea to someone. And you want them to give you feedback; you want them to react to your idea. How would you like them to react? Describe to me the best-case example of good feedback. Here are some of the typical responses that I get. People ask for constructive feedback. Help me to improve my thinking. Give me a balanced approach, both the positives and the negatives. Be honest with me, but not harsh. Ask questions.

Now, here's a tool that sort of takes this advice and puts it into action. It operates the very advice that people give me when I ask them how they would like to receive feedback. The name of this tool is POINT. POINT is an acronym. P stands for pluses, and it's important that we follow this acronym in the order suggested. So, when evaluating an idea and looking to develop an idea, the first thing we do is we look for the strengths, the good points, the positives. We suggest that you should come up with at least three.

Then we move on to the O in POINT, which stands for opportunities. Often, when we evaluate an idea, we only look at what it delivers here and today.

We don't think about the future, future scenarios, and future possibilities. So opportunities gets us to think like futurists. If we pursued this solution, if we pursued this change, what might happen? What would be future potentials? What would be some spin-offs? What would be some possibilities? To help us to think about opportunities, we use the invitational stem, it might. If we implemented this idea, if we implemented this solution, or we implemented this change, it might—and then we fill in the blank.

Now, we can't be naive and ignore any possible shortcomings or limitations, so the I in point has us look at the issues. These are the concerns, the drawbacks, the shortcomings of the idea, and we phrase these in language that we used earlier to invite a problem-solving form of thinking, we phrase these in the form of a challenge. So the issue begins with how to, how might, what might. When we phrase these as questions, they invoke a response. When someone asks us a question, what's our natural reaction? We look to answer the question. So it's important that you phrase the issues in the form of a how to or how might.

This sets us up for the next element within the POINT tool, NT. NT stands for new thinking, and we use new thinking now to address our issues. We begin by prioritizing them. We start with the biggest issue first, and we generate ideas to overcome that issue. And then we go on to the next biggest issue, and so forth, generating ideas, engaging in divergent thinking, with the hope of coming up with ideas that will address the how to, the how might, that will overcome that challenge that we identified during the issue phase of this tool.

You then evaluate your analysis—what you've generated through the POINT, and you make a decision. "Gosh, it's perfect. Nothing is really fundamentally wrong with it. Let's keep it as it is." Now you're ready to move on to the next step of the CPS process.

But you might decide that there are some ideas that you generated when you were applying new thinking, and this might suggest ways to refine the idea, to develop it into an even stronger solution. Or, on balance, after doing this evaluation, you might decide to kill it, not to go forward with it. But at least you've given it a fair shot, a fair analysis.

Let's practice this tool. I'm going to walk you through an example. Here's an example of an idea. I share this with audiences when I work with them; it's a novel design for a wheelbarrow, and in this design, rather than the wheels being on the front of the wheelbarrow, or the wheel being on the front, this wheelbarrow has two wheels, and they're in the back. It has a fairly large hopper. It has two handles that are connected by a bar, and it has two pegs in the front of the wheelbarrow. When I share this with most audiences and I ask them to give me comments, their initial reaction is, "It's crazy. It's backwards. It won't ever work. Those pegs in the front will dig in. It'll be hard to dump the material out." If that's how I'm evaluated, if I receive that kind of evaluation, that kind of criticism, it's likely that I wouldn't go forward with the idea, but let's see what happens when we apply POINT to this unusual wheelbarrow.

So in the first step, we look at pluses, and we might say in considering this wheelbarrow that the hopper has a lot of space. The handle seems reinforced because it's connected. The wheelbarrow won't tip over. The wheels give it more stability, and it might be easier to dump material. Now we move to the O in the POINT tool. We go to opportunities. Remember, opportunities start with it might. It might make gardening easier. It might reduce the number of accidents. It might replace the traditional wheelbarrow. It might cost less to produce. It might be easier to store. Now, notice, these are possibilities. We're not sure they're advantages. They're things that might happen if we pursued this idea.

Now we go to issues. We engage in effective critical thinking at this point. But remember, we phrase the issues in the form of a challenge statement. So our issues that we identify might look like the following: how to make the wheelbarrow easier to maneuver; how to make it more attractive; what might be ways to make the grip more comfortable?; how to improve the traction; how to identify buyers; how to strengthen the center of gravity.

Now, when people first begin applying POINT, a common mistake I see is that they don't phrase the issues in a question. They simply list the issue as if it were an obstacle, and when it's identified as an obstacle, it doesn't compel us to think about ways to get over that issue. So again, it's important that it's phrased in the form of a question, because this sets us up for the next step in this tool, the new thinking, which we use to overcome our issues, again, beginning with the biggest issue first. So, imagine, we've looked over the issues, and we've ranked them, but we've decided that the biggest issue is how to make the wheelbarrow easier to maneuver. Now, remember, at this point, we're flipping into divergent thinking, because we want to mount as many ideas as possible against this issue. So we might say things like, make the handle longer, push down on the wheelbarrow instead of lifting up, attach and extend braces on the sides of the barrow, attach Segway technology to it, make it heavier near the handles. And we would continue piling ideas on the issue, with the goal of coming up with at least some ways in which we could overcome this issue, or at least to give it a fair chance.

A common mistake I see here is that groups, or individuals, instead of selecting one issue to address, after they've gone through identifying the issues and they move to the new thinking, they'll start just generating ideas without really targeting, one-by-one, the issues. They sort of take a shotgun approach. This isn't as effective as it is to move sequentially, beginning with the biggest issue and moving in order. Now, this wheelbarrow that I shared with you, the one that I've described, actually does exist. It's called the LoadDumper, and it does have pluses. It is easier to haul heavy loads, and it has a tighter turning radius because you push down on it instead of lifting up, and it has better balance.

Let's take an idea that's pretty novel. Something that doesn't exist. When I do POINT with teams in training, to help demonstrate the value of POINT, and especially to drive home that concept of staying open to novelty, I'll have them practice POINT on an idea that's pretty outside-the-box. Here's an idea. I'm going to pace you through this, and I'd like you to think through the POINT tool with me. So, try it out. Here's the idea. Imagine schools had no teachers. No teachers. The only adults in the building with the students are project managers, not teachers. What might be three pluses of this idea? What might be three opportunities? What might be three issues? So, if schools had no teachers, if there were only project managers, can you think of three strengths to this idea, three advantages that this might pose? How about opportunities? If schools had no teachers, what might happen? Can you think of three it mights, three spin offs, three potentials?

Then we have to apply good critical thinking. Let's identify some issues. What concerns might you have? What might be some shortcomings with this idea? And again, we phrase them in a challenge statement form—how to, how might, what might. Can you think of, and can you phrase these issues in the form of a challenge statement?

And then, finally, in the next step of this tool, NT—new thinking. Can you think of one of one big issue that might really get in the way of this idea being effective? Think of that in your mind, or capture it in a computer or on a piece of paper, and then generate ideas. What new thoughts do you have that will help you to address this issue? You can pause the lecture if you need to.

Now we evaluate the proposed idea. Once we've generated these pluses and opportunities, we step back, and we look to see if we can refine the idea, or if it's good as it is. Probably this highly novel idea in terms of eliminating teachers and having project managers would require some refinement. Or, again, on balance, we step back and we analyze what we've generated. We might decide not to go forward. Often what people say to me is that one of the benefits of POINT is that it takes an idea that's really novel, and it can transform it into something that actually is workable.

Here are some uses for POINT. This is a tool that is incredibly flexible and can be used in lots of ways, and it doesn't have to be used in a formal way. It can be used in an informal discussion. For example, many years ago when I first began teaching, I was working with at-risk students, freshmen, who were in the Educational Opportunity Program. And I had one young man come to me, and he was kind of bashful, and he came up to me with his head down, and he wanted to talk to me about his major paper in the course, and he had an idea he wanted to share with me. You see, each student had to write a paper on a subject of their own choosing, but they had to relate it to the study of creativity. And this young man came up to me kind of sheepishly, and he said, "Dr. P., can I talk to you about my paper?" "Sure." "Well, I'd like to do my paper on woodworking." And so, my first reaction was, "Well, you know what I like about your idea? I happen to know from things that you've shared in class that this is a hobby of yours, that you're very interested in woodworking." And he kind of lifted his head up and he started to stand straight. "Well, yeah. That's right, Dr. P." "Well, I think that's wonderful, and I do have some concerns. One issue might be I'm not very familiar with this area, and I'm not sure there's a lot of literature out there, so how might you be sure that you can connect this to creativity and the study of creativity?"

So what did I do? I went from a plus into an issue. I was using a shortened version of POINT, and it was interesting. As soon as I phrased my issue in the form of a question, he immediately began to answer it. He said, "Well, you know, Dr. P., I'm pretty sure that the technology department has a furniture-making unit. Maybe I can go speak to some of the professors there and they can help me out." You see, he started to think of ways around the issue that I presented him. By the time our conversation was over with, he had some specific ideas he could follow up on in order to make sure that he was in the best place to write that paper.

As a team, you can use POINT when you're reviewing a proposed idea. You can go through POINT together, with each person moving through the tools, starting with the pluses, looking at the opportunities, the issues, working together to overcome the issues with new thinking.

Even school-age children can use POINT. I remember one of the graduates of our program, who was a middle school teacher working with 5th graders on the New York state geography assignment, had students working in groups, creating a brochure for a different region of the state, as assigned by her. The students created these draft brochures, and then they had to go to another group and present their draft brochure to that group. And the other group had to provide that group with feedback using POINT. And then, before they could submit their final assignment, the final brochure, they had to go through the feedback that they received and had to demonstrate how they responded to that feedback.

POINT is also a wonderful tool for capturing lessons learned from a project. We run a conference every year, an annual conference, and the conference committee, as soon as the conference is over, gets together and does an analysis, a debrief meeting, using POINT to evaluate how the conference went, what worked well, what are some opportunities for the future, what were some of the issues that we need to address, and, while it's still fresh in our minds, what new thinking can we come up with.

When we do performance reviews in our department, and a faculty member is coming up for promotion, as part of the review process, the faculty member receives feedback using the POINT tool. It can be used to develop a product concept, so you have a product concept that you're toying with, and you're thinking about launching it into the marketplace. Before launching it, you can use POINT to develop that idea.

Before you present an idea to a group, you can do POINT on the idea, and then as you're doing the presentation, you can use POINT as the framework to underscore the pluses, the opportunities if the idea was pursued, some issues and how some of those issues, through your anticipation, could be addressed.

And finally, another example. POINT can be used to enhance team effectiveness. Michael West, a business school professor who has tracked teams over time, has observed that those teams that are able to sustain their innovation have a quality that he calls reflexivity. That is, that teams stop occasionally and evaluate their performance. What a wonderful tool. What a balanced, affirmative tool to use that will help to develop a team's effectiveness. You can use POINT to encourage that kind of reflexivity.

So, let's talk about POINT and some of the benefits. Well, it fits the way in which people wish to receive feedback. It's easy to use. Even a 5th grader can use it. It clearly targets us towards development. It gives us, in fact, actions that we can take to enhance the original concept. Yet, it also begins to point towards gaining acceptance and buy-in, because as we start to think about the issues, they often relate to other groups and people, and how they'll respond. And in this way, we not only improve the idea, but we're improving it in such a way that it'll be easier to sell and move it towards action.

We recently conducted a research study where we looked at the transfer of training after taking managers through creative problem solving, and we found that one of the tools most often used after training was POINT. One of the benefits is that when we use POINT to give feedback, we move from what's referred to as controlling feedback, which is more directive, where we point to issues as if they were fixed external demands and requirements, and we move more towards what's referred to as informational feedback, that's providing ways for people to learn and to develop.

So, let's look at taking POINT forward. I'd like you to try it out. Before the next lecture, let's try two applications, and let's try two very different applications. Let's try one that's more formal. Let's take POINT and evaluate an idea that you've generated; maybe it's an idea that you generated previously for one of the challenges that you've selected as we've gone through this course. Work through it in a very deliberate fashion, completely, from beginning to end, and in the examples that I've provided, I limited the number of elements, the number of pluses and opportunities. Don't limit yourself because of those examples, and I mentioned earlier, at least three in each category, but that's a minimum. Go until you run out of thoughts in terms of what the pluses are, what the opportunities are, what the issues are, and then, especially with the new thinking, it's important to engage in divergent thinking, otherwise we may overlook or not get to an idea that will really address the issue that's been identified.

And then try it out informally. It's a powerful tool to guide a conversation. Someone comes to you and shares an idea, maybe a coworker, or someone in your family, maybe even your child. Maybe your child comes to you and says, "Oh, I'm interested in painting my room," and at first you're a little nervous about that. Try responding to that person, identifying the pluses first, then the opportunities. Then think about the issues and phrase them in the form of a question—how to, how might, and I bet you'll see a very different response from that person, because you're giving them feedback in the way that most of us want feedback. See you next time.

Prototypes—How Designers Test Ideas

Lecture 15

This lecture goes more deeply into the develop step of the process. Designers are very good at refining ideas. To help them, they create prototypes. The process and tools in this course have already addressed most of the principles of the design thinking process, especially reframing, collaboration, and ideation. We're in the develop step of creative problem solving, and as such, we will borrow the principles of prototyping and user understanding for this lecture.

The Design Thinking Process

- Design thinking has become very popular. It's a model for the creative process, a deliberate way of engaging in creative thinking. Many companies now have design thinking incorporated into their work. Many universities and their business schools now teach design thinking. The strength of design thinking is that it takes what's called a user-centered approach.

- The first principle of the design thinking process is reframing, which is all about stepping back and looking at the situation differently. Are there assumptions that stop you from identifying the real business challenge? What are the hidden opportunities? We're moving from the problem as initially given to a deeper understanding.

- Collaborating is all about appreciating diversity, working in cross-disciplinary teams, drawing inspiration from many settings to gain different perspectives.

- User understanding is the next principle. Really get to know your user, his or her real behaviors and real needs, digging deeply into both the needs that you see as well as the unarticulated needs.

- Ideation is the belief that no idea is too wild. In design thinking, we generate many human-centered solutions. We create many choices, and then we work from there.

- Finally, prototyping is all about testing it out. We use simple and inexpensive materials to quickly test the idea. Role-plays and other methods can be used to get into the user's mindset and also to share with users and to get their feedback on what we've created. This involves the user early on in the development process.

- Like creative problem solving, design thinking has a process, and it has tools. The first step of design thinking is to understand—it's observation, problem identification. Sometimes designers go out and engage in ethnographic research, where they closely observe the users, trying to understand their real frustrations and needs, sometimes uncovering needs that the user is not even aware of but that the designer can see.

- The next step of this process is to ideate. This information is then taken, and brainstorming occurs—the third step of design thinking. Many alternatives are generated in terms of concepts for products and services that might meet the user's needs.

- The fourth step is prototyping, which involves quickly testing ideas, trying to create working models. In the next step, the testing step, we get feedback from the users and we iterate, working until our solution really works—getting feedback, making modifications, testing again.

Solution Prototyping

- Solution prototyping involves creating a working model of the solution. It generally goes beyond a sketch. If possible, it's an actual working model that can then be given to users. We observe the users interacting with the prototype so that we can improve our concept.

- Actual working models vary from field to field. Solution prototyping can be done in any field, but it'll vary in terms of what an actual working model means. For example, television programs run pilots. These are prototypes. Architects make 3-D models. These are prototypes. Biologists Watson and Crick built enormous stick models to refine their understanding of DNA.

- A physical creation significantly enhances the development. You get to interact with the idea. Many businesses now have rooms for design thinking where they can do rapid prototyping.

- Even at the prototype stage, beware of premature convergence. Automakers use prototypes all the time, but a study found that if engineers focus only on the prototype, it can shut down their creative development of the product. They begin to merely defend and attack the prototype, and this is a risk for high developers.

Having a prototype for a product is useful, but focusing only on the prototype can constrict creativity.

- Some developers get stuck in developing the perfect solution. They might not want to move away from the prototype because they've already put so much energy into developing it. Instead, use prototypes to focus on asking questions and developing solutions.

Foresight Scenario

- Foresight scenario is another design thinking tool. This tool uses trends to generate future solutions to a situation.

- Foresight scenario has six steps to it. First, you list the trends and select the most important. You're trying to see where trends will take you into the future.

- You then identify two trends that you think are most likely to occur. You use these two trends to create a two-by-two box, and then for each box, you write a scenario. What would this look like? You're projecting yourself into the future, looking around to see if these trends were to come true. What would that look and feel like?

- Then, you create a label for each quadrant. You take your ideas from the ideate step, and you then place them into these scenarios. The idea is that you identify, maybe from doing hits, the ones that you've culled down—the ones that seem most promising—and you place them into one of the boxes or scenarios that best fits that idea.

- Then, you look across the ideas, and you combine the ideas within quadrants—and sometimes across quadrants. Then, you write a brief summary for each solution.

Solution Storyboard

- The next tool is called solution storyboard. You already learned about storyboarding in the clarify step, clarifying the challenges that must be addressed to move from the current reality to your desired future. We use the storyboard tool like a cartoon strip, with six panels, to capture the story that looked at how we might overcome the challenges to get to our desired future.

- Now we're going to look at storyboarding in a slightly different way—as a way of refining solutions. We're going to look at storyboard as a way of prototyping. With solution storyboard, you are storyboarding the user's experience as he or she interacts with your proposed solution.

- The story is told from the perspective of the individual who is using this proposed change—what you want to bring into the world—

and the panels in the story show the user's experience of the intended solution.

- The solution storyboard tool helps us create empathy. It gets us out of our own heads and into the user's experience. For example, Walt Disney used storyboarding to understand how families would experience Disneyland. The insights gained from the storyboard helped Disney to understand better how he wanted guests to enter and move through the park.

Solution Enactment

- Another tool is called solution enactment, which is a kind of dress rehearsal: We act out our proposed solution to see how we might improve it. Before going fully live, we want to see the solution in action. Solution enactment is a kind of storytelling that allows developers to communicate abstract ideas to potential users, whereas storyboarding puts the users into the whole context.

- Solution enactment takes the audience through specific scenes. This has five steps, including a number of preparatory steps before we actually get into the enactment.

- We envision the user's journey. We visualize the user's experience. We identify key areas in which the user is benefiting from the proposed solution, and we sketch this out.

- Then, we explore a range of possible encounters. We explore different experiences that might occur. We record a range of possibilities, and we decide which ones we want to focus on in the enactment. We select those, and then we highlight them. We highlight the solution's value relative to those, and we display engaging interactions.

- Then, it's important to rehearse the dramatization. We conduct practice sessions. We videotape them, and we improve upon them. We then present the enactment to the stakeholders. We carry out a brief presentation to an audience. If there's time, we solicit feedback, and we insert suggestions immediately.

- Even novelists have used this kind of approach, from Charles Dickens to Franz Kafka. Writers have gathered with a group of friends to read drafts of their work out loud, and then they solicit feedback. We capture this feedback and discuss the next step. We gather formal and informal feedback from our audience, and we revise our solution, and if we have enough time, we present it again and make adjustments.

- Solution enactment allows us to go for a test drive, and it helps to broaden design thinking beyond tangible products. It can be easily used for proposed new services. Another benefit is that it helps us to build empathy with our user. How often do we assume that something is clear, and then we're surprised when others don't get it? Finally, it gets our stakeholders involved in the development process early.

Suggested Reading

Brown, *Change by Design.*

Kumar, *101 Design Methods.*

Activities

Activity 1: Design Thinking Tools
Apply any of the tools discussed in this lecture (solution prototype, foresight scenarios, solution storyboard, or solution enactment) to a real solution you are considering.

Alternatively, practice on this imagined scenario: Project into the future 20 years from now. Think about current forms of energy or emerging forms of energy. Identify important themes related to energy, and put the current and emerging options through the foresight scenario tool to see how these forms of energy might be combined and refined into future solutions.

Activity 2: Prototyping

Look around your home and identify a product that might be improved. Think about what frustrates you about that product and consider ways you might modify it to reduce these areas of frustration. Construct a physical prototype and share it with others. Ask for their feedback. How did constructing a prototype help to refine and develop the idea?

Prototypes—How Designers Test Ideas
Lecture 15—Transcript

A letter attributed to Mozart has reinforced an image of his legendary creative thinking prowess, and as a consequence, highlights how different his creative genius is from you and me. In this famous letter, Mozart begins by saying that when he is relaxed and in good cheer, say, walking after a good meal, ideas begin to form, as if from nowhere. As he said, "whence and how they come, I know not, nor can I force them. Those ideas that please me I retain in memory."

So, it would seem that ideas occurred to him as if by magic. Later in the letter, it says, "When I proceed to write down my ideas, I take them out of the bag of my memory—if I may use that phrase, what has been previously collected into it in a way I have mentioned. For this reason, the committing to paper is done quickly enough, for everything is, as I said before, already finished."

Unfortunately, this letter perpetuates some of the myths about the creative process, especially the creative process skills possessed by creative geniuses. First, it purports that ideas come to us—well, to Mozart—as if from out of the blue. Second, it makes it sound as if great works emerge whole and complete, requiring no revision. Poof, there it is. The reality is, this rarely happens.

The authenticity of the letter is in doubt, and some scholars now conclude that it is, indeed, a forgery. And the truth is, it doesn't represent Mozart's actual creative process. Instead, a review of Mozart's manuscripts shows that he was constantly revising his music. He edited his thinking, crossing out sections, rewriting whole sections, jotting down vague ideas and setting them aside for later use, sometimes months and years later. Despite the legend supported by the forged letter, the truth is he created like us ordinary humans. Mozart worked hard at perfecting his ideas.

Picasso's enigmatic personality, his avant-garde style, along with the fact that he did not reveal his creative process, reinforced his legendary status as a gifted creative genius. However, since his death, it's been revealed that

Picasso, like Mozart, worked very hard at his craft. Between 1894 and 1967, Picasso created 175 notebooks of his draft ideas, concepts, and pre-work. To understand how much effort went into creating a final work, we will discuss one of his most famous pieces.

In 1907, he showed a piece called "Les Demoiselles d'Avignon." This was a radical departure from past work, and the piece that helped launch cubism. The painting features five women in various poses. The images mix soft human flesh with sharp angles. The women's faces are expressionless. Eight full notebooks were prepared before the final work was produced. Modifications over time included changing the number of female figures. The two figures on the right were added later. At first, they had Iberian facial features, which were later changed to look like African masks. Men were included at times in the painting—a sailor and a medical student. And the medical student changed over time, once holding a skull and other times a book. Postures and poses were modified.

Additional preparatory work included a complete oil sketch and a complete pencil sketch found folded and tucked into one of his notebooks. Howard Gardner, Harvard professor and creativity scholar, indicated that the notebooks served a crucial role in Picasso's creative process, allowing Picasso to experiment privately with his own transformation as an artist, moving from his rose period to what would become cubism.

So, why these two stories? Mozart and Picasso, they're the poster boys for innate creative talent. Geniuses to be revered. We assume they possess some special creative talent. Rather, instead of thinking of them as creative legends to be revered, that they had something special, rather, what we can begin to understand is that they worked very hard. By revering them, the consequence becomes that we might underestimate, and sometimes not engage in, the hard work required to be creative.

This lecture goes more deeply into the develop step of the process. Mozart and Picasso show us how to refine ideas. Designers are also very good at refining ideas. To help them, they create prototypes. Design thinking has become very popular. It's a model for creative process, a deliberate way of engaging in creative thinking. Many companies now have design thinking incorporated into their work. Proctor and Gamble is an excellent example of this. Many universities and their business schools now teach design thinking. Even in schools, schools have begun to teach children design thinking. The strength of design thinking is that it takes what's called a user-centered approach.

Let's look at some of the principles of the design thinking process. I think it's good to overview these principles, because they serve as a reminder for some of the foundational principles in this course. Here's the first principle, reframing. Reframing is all about stepping back and looking at the situation differently. Are there assumptions that stop you from identifying the real business challenge? What are the hidden opportunities? We're moving from the problem as initially given to us to a deeper understanding. Collaborate, this is all about appreciating diversity, working in cross-disciplinary teams, drawing inspiration from many settings to gain different perspectives.

User understanding is the next principle. Really get to know your user, his or her real behaviors and real needs, digging deeply into both the needs that you see, as well as the unarticulated needs. Ideation. This is the belief that no idea is too wild. In design thinking, we generate many human-centered solutions. We create many choices, and then we work from there. And then, finally, prototyping, which is all about testing it out. We use simple and inexpensive material to quickly test the idea. Role plays can be used, and other methods to get into the user's mindset, and also to share with users and to get their feedback to what we've created. This involves the user early on in the development process.

The process and tools in this course have already addressed most of these principles, especially reframing, collaborate, and ideation. We're in the develop step of creative problem solving, and as such, we will borrow the principles of prototyping and user feedback for this lecture. Before the tools, let's look at the process of design thinking.

Like creative problem solving, design thinking has a process, and it has tools. Here are the basic steps of design thinking. The first step is to understand. It's observation. It's problem identification. Sometimes designers go out and engage in ethnographic research, where they closely observe the users, trying to understand their real frustrations and their real needs, sometimes uncovering needs that the user is not even aware of, that the observer can see, the designer can see.

Next is ideate. This information is then taken and brainstorming occurs. Many alternatives are generated in terms of concepts for products and services that might meet the user's needs. In the fourth step, it's prototyping. It's quickly testing ideas, trying to create working models. In the next step, in test, we get feedback from the users, and we iterate, working until our solution really works, getting feedback, making modifications, testing again.

To see this in action, there's a terrific video from the old *Nightline* program. It was a late night news broadcast program that was hosted by Ted Koppel. Many years ago, they did a special on design thinking. They worked with IDEO, the design company in California. They presented IDEO with a fun challenge; they challenged IDEO to redesign the shopping cart, and in only one week. It's a great example of the design thinking process at work, the process I just described to you. We're going to look specifically at tools from the prototyping step of this process.

So, solution prototyping, what that is, is creating a working model of the solution. It generally goes beyond a sketch. If possible, it's an actual working model that can then be given to users. We observe the users interacting with the prototype, so that we can improve our concept. Now, the actual working model varies from field to field. It can be done in any field, but it'll vary in terms of what an actual working model means. For example, TV programs run pilots; these are prototypes. Architects make 3D models; these are prototypes. Biologists Watson and Crick built enormous stick models to refine their understanding of DNA.

When I was an assistant professor and teaching undergraduate courses, we had students in our introductory course create an invention. They kept a journal where they did observations, that first phase of the design thinking process, and then that led into concepts. At the end of the semester, they had to present an invention. They had to build a working model; they had to build a prototype. Here are some of the more interesting examples.

So one young man was in his dormitory with some friends, and they had ordered pizza. When the pizza arrived, they had no plates, so it was kind of awkward to eat the pizza. He thought to himself, "Gosh, this is frustrating. Is there a way to solve this? What if plates came along with the pizza box?" So what he presented to the class was a pizza box that had perforated circles, four of them, cut in the top of the pizza box with a little place to stick your finger in and pop out a plate, so every pizza box came with four plates. You had your pizza, and you could serve it to four people on four plates.

One student was a musician, a drummer. And when he was performing, he would perspire and the sticks would slip out of his hands. He wanted to solve this problem, so he put loops on the end of the drumsticks. He brought his drum kit into the classroom, and he demonstrated how this worked. When the drum stick slipped out, he was able to snap it back, because the loop was there to allow him to flick the drumstick back into his hand.

Another student created a bottle with a removable bottom. He was getting ready to go out for the evening, and he went into the bathroom to get to a hair-care product to finish styling his hair, and there was a little bit of the product left in the bottle, but the pump wouldn't get it out, and he thought to himself, "There's enough product there, I just can't get to it. Only if I could take the bottom of the bottle off." And so he came in with a prototype that had a bottle that you could unscrew the bottom, use your finger to get the product that was there, and that solved the problem for him. You see, a physical creation significantly enhances the development. You get to interact with the idea. Many businesses now have rooms for design thinking where they can do rapid prototyping.

But, a word of caution. Even at the prototype stage, beware of premature convergence. Automakers use prototypes all the time, but if engineers focus only on the prototype, a study found that it can shut down their creative development of the product, where they begin to merely defend and attack the prototype. And this is a risk for high developers, remember, high developers get stuck in developing the perfect solution. They might not want to move away from the prototype, because they've already put so much energy into developing it. Instead, use prototype to focus on asking questions and developing solutions, as we've discussed here.

Let's go to another tool, this is called foresight scenario, another design thinking tool. This tool uses trends to generate future solutions to a situation. It's looking to the future. Now, when we say foresight scenario, this is F-O-R-E foresight, not the F-O-U-R foursight that you learned earlier that identifies your preferences within the creative process. Foresight scenario has six steps to it. You list the trends and select the most important. You're trying to predict the future. You're trying to see where trends will take you into the future. You then identify two trends that you think are most likely to occur. You use these two trends to create a 2 x 2 box, and then, for each box, you write a scenario. What would this look like? You're projecting yourself into the future, looking around to see if these trends were to come true, what would that look and feel like? And then you create a label for each quadrant. You take your ideas from the ideate step, and you then place them into these scenarios. The idea is that you identify, maybe, from doing hits, the ones that you've culled down, the ones that seem most promising, and you place them into one of the boxes, one of the scenarios that best fits that idea, best goes along with that idea. Then you look across the ideas, and you combine the ideas within quadrants, and sometimes across quadrants. And then you write a brief summary for each solution.

Let's take an example. Imagine you are a restaurant entrepreneur, and you're looking for new opportunities. Here's how you might go through this tool. You start by thinking about the trends in food, and I would recommend using divergent thinking to not just think of the first few trends that occur to your mind, but multiple trends. So let's say you evaluate these trends and you decide to focus on these two: the speed of food and the nature of food. For each trend, we need to define the end of a continuum, two poles. The speed of food, we might say, one end is fast food and on the other end is slow food. For the nature of food, on one end we might have organic, on the other end we might have non-organic. You now take these and you create your 2 x 2 box. So, following this example, you might place slow food on the top of the vertical axis and fast food on the bottom of that axis, on the bottom of that line. Then you'll create a horizontal axis that cuts through the vertical axis. On the left side, you might have non-organic and on the right side organic.

We now think about the scenarios that occur where these intersect. We write a description, and then we come up with a label to put into each box. So where we have non-organic meeting slow food, in the top left corner, we would call that, perhaps, hurry up and wait. Moving clockwise in the right corner, where we have slow food intersecting with organic, we might call that farm-to-mouth. In the bottom right, where we have organic connecting to fast food. We might call that mobile fresh food. And then finally, in the left, lower quadrant where we have non-organic interfacing with fast food, we might call that meals on the go. We now take the ideas that we ideated earlier, that we've converged on, and we place them into this 2 x 2 matrix, where the idea fits best. What scenario does it connect to? From there, we then connect ideas, linking them, trying to create more robust solutions.

By way of example, let's say in the farm-to-mouth, we have two ideas that we think go together. One idea is to bring people to the farm. Another idea is to prepare food on the farm. And connecting these two might suggest, hey, gosh, maybe we can open up a restaurant on the farm. Let's look at another example. If we go to the lower, left quadrant, meals on the go, one of the ideas there might be food vans for an existing chain. We connect that to another idea in the lower right quadrant that also deals with vans, maybe using vans to distribute fresh produce. Combining these two ideas might suggest this solution: Hey, how about mobile restaurants for existing chains that offer organic options?

In step six, you then evaluate and develop your ideas into the ones that you think are most likely to be successful. You think about which trends are more likely to occur, and then you go with those solutions that align with those trends. But ask yourself, which scenarios may not occur. How might situations change, and how can I then adapt my ideas as we go forward?

In our example, let's say, for example, you sense that people won't come to the farm for restaurants, and mobile food is pretty popular now, so you might decide to go with creating mobile vans for existing fast food restaurants with healthy food choices. You would solicit feedback from others by presenting this idea to them, and then make adjustments if you need to.

The next tool is called solution storyboard. Earlier, you learned about storyboard in the clarify step, clarifying the challenges that must be addressed to move from the current reality to your desired future. We use storyboard like a cartoon strip—remember, six panels—to capture the story that looked at how we might overcome the challenges to get to our desired future.

Now we're going to look at storyboard in a slightly different way, as a way of refining solutions. The tools [I've] presented often can be used flexibly. Brainstorming, for example. We learned brainstorming in the ideate step. But brainstorming can be used in other areas of the process. You can use brainstorming to generate challenges. You can use brainstorming to generate action steps. That happens to be a fairly flexible tool.

We're going to look at storyboard as a way of prototyping. Again, this is specifically called the solution storyboard. With solution storyboard, you're storyboarding the user's experience, the user's journey as he or she interacts with your proposed solution. The story is told from the perspective of the individual who is using this proposed change—what you want to bring into the world—and the panels in the story show the user's experience of the intended solution. What it does is it helps us to create empathy; it gets us out of our own heads and into their experience. Here's an example. Walt Disney used storyboarding to understand how families would experience Disneyland. The insights gained from the storyboard helped Disney to understand better how he wanted guests to enter and move about the park. Maybe this is why, when you're standing in lines at Disney, that you're entertained in ways, to take your attention away from having to stand in line.

Let's try this out. I want you to imagine that you're a designer, and we're going to design a car. Now, we've talked about cars before. Let's imagine you're going to redesign the car. You're good at divergent thinking. You've been exposed to divergent thinking. Think about what you might want to create. How might you redesign some aspect of the car? Get that in your mind. Select a design change or two.

Now I'm going to walk you through the solution storyboard, sort of like a quick thought experiment. Imagine characters using your design. Who's using it? How do you see them interacting with this design? Map out, in your mind, like you're seeing a story unfolding, how they're first responding to that design change, and then, as they're engaging and using that design change, see how they're responding to it from beginning, middle, and end. Change the character. Try a teen driver. Try a senior. Do they respond differently as they react to this design change that you have in mind? We've gone through this quickly. I facilitated you in applying this as a structured tool, but even quickly it can help to advance our thinking. Did you find that, as you pictured that story, that, even using it quickly, it helped you to see ways to improve the design of that particular solution that you had in mind and how you might improve it?

Let's look at another tool. It's called solution enactment. Why do dress rehearsals? Why start off-Broadway first? Solution enactment is a kind of dress rehearsal. We act out our proposed solution to see how we might improve it. Before going fully live, let's see the solution in action. Solution enactment is a kind of storytelling that allows developers to communicate abstract ideas to potential users, where the storyboard that we just went through puts the users into the whole context. Solution enactment takes the audience through specific scenes. This has five steps, including a number of preparatory steps before we actually get into the enactment. We envision the user's journey; we visualize the user's experience; we identify key areas in which the user is benefiting from the proposed solution; and we sketch this out.

Then, we explore a range of possible encounters. We explore different experiences that might occur. We record a range of possibilities, and we decide which ones we want to focus on in the enactment. We select those, and then we highlight them; we highlight the solution's value relative to those, and we display engaging interactions. And then it's important to rehearse the dramatization. We conduct practice sessions. We videotape them, and we improve upon them. We then present the enactment to the stakeholders. We carry out a brief presentation to an audience. If there's time, we solicit feedback, and we insert suggestions immediately.

Even novelists have used this kind of approach, from Charles Dickens to Franz Kafka. Writers have gathered with a group of friends to read drafts of their work out loud, and then they solicit feedback. We capture this feedback and discuss the next step. We gather formal and informal feedback from our audience, and we revise our solution, and if we have enough time, we re-present it and make adjustments.

What are the benefits? It's like a dress rehearsal. Solution enactment allows us to go for a test drive, and it helps to broaden design thinking beyond tangible products. It can be easily used for proposed new services. Another benefit is it helps us to build empathy with our user. How often do we assume that something's clear, then we're surprised when others don't get it. And finally, it gets our stakeholders involved in the development process early.

Charles Darwin said that all species are descended from some past prototype. Ideas are prototypes too. All ideas are evolving into something else. iPad, the space shuttle, or a masterpiece painting don't emerge from a vacuum. Apple's iPad debuted in 2010, but prototypes began eight years earlier, long before the price for touch-screen technology had come down.

Here's a story of someone who seems to naturally use, or maybe he learned to use, design thinking. It's been reported that Frank Gehry, creator of the Walt Disney concert hall in California and the Guggenheim museum in Spain, is one of the most influential architects of our time. In an era of computer technology and design, he still takes a hands-on approach to his creative process. Like a good design thinker, he begins by getting a thorough description of the site and function of the building. In fact, Gehry says, "The more you know, the freer you are." He then ideates, quickly sketching rough ideas. Once happy with the conceptual design, he then moves to prototyping. He works with associates to cut, fold, crease, crush, and glue various materials together into physical models, and of various scales. Learning ways to improve from the models, he then scans it into a sophisticated computer.

Gehry's process seems to follow the design thinking process I described earlier. Observe, ideate, prototype, and iterate, and it would certainly seem that prototypes provide the crucial bridge from initial concept to final design. The four design tools that you've been exposed to help better our solutions through design thinking. The tools that we've reviewed, the tools that we went through, were prototyping. Foresight scenarios, solution storyboard, and solution enactment. Sometimes it's tough for implementers to be patient, but it's valuable. The cost of an error goes up dramatically after the solution is launched. Consider automobile recalls. These are expensive propositions, not just in the cost to repair faulty work, but also potential lawsuits as well, and, in the worst case, the loss of lives. If the faulty design had been caught during the development phase, it would be a much less costly proposition for auto companies.

I want you to take one of these tools and practice prototyping on a real situation. Match the design tool to your needs. For example, if you have a tangible product, perhaps solution prototyping will work best for you. If you're focused on future possibilities, you might want to use foresight scenario. If you want to understand a solution in the context of the user's experience, use solution storyboard. If you're developing a new service or experience for others, use solution enactment. Test whether the prototyping helped you. I'm confident it will. See you next time.

Evaluating Creative Solutions and Making Decisions
Lecture 16

Criteria can help us choose among the creative alternatives we create. It's common practice to use criteria, which are standards for evaluating our choices. Most often, though, they remain implicit. In other words, we're not aware of our criteria, but they're there, influencing us as we look at the choices before us. The tools in this lecture help us move our criteria from implicit to a more explicit state so that we can direct our choice by using and leveraging these criteria.

The Evaluation Matrix

- The evaluation matrix is a tool that makes the natural process of utilizing criteria more formal and systematic and, therefore, helps us to make better choices. It's also useful at developing our solutions.

- In the evaluation matrix, there are seven steps. The first step is to develop your criteria. We diverge on our criteria, and criteria answer the question *will it or does it?* You can include both tangible and intangible criteria, objective and subjective. Then, afterward, you select the most important criteria.

- In step two, we have to check our criteria. We check them in two important ways. First, the criteria need to be distinct. In other words, there's no overlap. The question *will it fit my budget?* is too close to *will it be affordable?* They're too similar. In addition, don't have one criterion be subsumed by another; they need to be independent from one another.

- Second, we need to make sure that they're positive. The criteria should point you in the direction of what you want, not what you don't want. So they should all go in the same direction. The question *will it make my spouse upset?* isn't probably what you want. It would be better to phrase that as *will it make my spouse happy?*

- In the third step, we build our evaluation matrix. We place our criteria into the matrix, adding choices—the ideas or solutions that one wishes to evaluate. The spreadsheet has choices listed down the first column, and then the criteria are listed across the top of the remaining columns.

- We then need to select an evaluation system. We decide on a system for rating these choices as we look at the criteria against each choice. We can use numbers, number of stars, smiley faces, etc. Some people find numbers easier, but others, perhaps more visual learners, like to use symbols.

- In the fifth step, we evaluate our choices. When we evaluate our choices, we work down each criterion, rating each choice against that criterion. In other words, we're holding that one standard against all options as we move through them.

- In step six, we review the matrix. We look across our ratings. We don't total the numbers, even if you may have used numbers. When we do this, we might get locked into just the highest number. After we do this, we look across the evaluation. If we have a total, it draws our eye just to the total and, therefore, we might miss some subtleties, and we might miss the chance to improve because the evaluation matrix is designed to also help us improve.

- Once we look across these ratings, we make a decision to accept that option; to modify it by looking at where it might be improved, where it might have fallen short against a criterion; or, if it doesn't do well against many criteria, we might decide to reject it.

- In the seventh step, we develop the options, and we make our final decision. We see if options that were identified for improvement can indeed be improved. We refine these solutions, and then we make our final decision.

- When we use the evaluation matrix, we want to make sure that we diverge on our criteria before we converge so that we don't miss any important criteria. In addition, we work down the columns rather than across, using a criterion as a constant reference point.

- The evaluation matrix is great for making explicit decisions, whether they are creative solutions or everyday decisions. It's good for when you need to go with one option—when you can't use multiple solutions.

Musts and Wants

- There's a twist on how you might use the evaluation matrix. You can sort your criteria into musts and wants. Musts are those criteria that are absolutely necessary in order for the choice to be acceptable. Then, we have our wants. These are important, and they add value, or they make the option even more attractive.

- It can be awkward if you mix musts and wants in the evaluation matrix. Musts can be tough to rate. They can be either zeroes or fives if you're using a scale of one to five. Plus, why include an option in the matrix if it doesn't meet a must? Musts can serve as an initial screen to choose your short list of ideas that then go into the matrix, and then the matrix can be used to evaluate those choices based on the wants.

- In this tool, we generate our criteria. Next, we converge and sort those criteria into musts and wants. Next, we use the musts to screen the ideas. In the fourth step, we place the converged ideas into the evaluation matrix. Only those ideas that met the musts go into our matrix, where we have our wants, and we use our wants to then evaluate that short list. Then, we evaluate and develop those solutions.

Solution Evaluation and Solution Map

- Design thinking provides us with a variation of the evaluation matrix. In design thinking, one of the principles is a user-centered focus. In the design thinking version of the evaluation matrix, we use products and services to help us generate criteria, because ultimately the product needs to fit the producer's needs as well as the user's needs.

- There are a few differences between the evaluation matrix and the one that's often applied by design thinkers. Thinking like a designer, you have to satisfy two basic stakeholders: You have to be concerned about producing a product that delights the user and producing a product that the producer can create. The second difference is that the one used by design thinkers is more visual.

- There are six steps to this evaluation tool, which is called the solution evaluation and solution map. The solution evaluation piece looks very similar to the evaluation matrix. The solution map brings in the visual component, where we identify those ideas that do the best against those two sets of criteria: producer and user.

- The first step is to create your user value and provider value criteria. We diverge on criteria in these two sets. For the users, we consider information gathered during our user research phase—the observation phase. User value criteria might be things like ease of use, ease of storage, or whether it is aesthetically pleasing. Producer value criteria might involve questions like the following: Will it be profitable? Will it be easy for us to implement? Will it maintain our brand integrity?

- In the second step, we create a solution evaluation matrix and a spreadsheet. The solutions are listed in the left column, and the criteria are listed across the top. However, this time, the criteria are sorted into two areas: the user value criteria and the producer value categories.

- As with the evaluation matrix, we use a spreadsheet to evaluate our options. But this spreadsheet is broken up. We have columns for criteria that are reserved for user value criteria, and we have columns that are reserved for producer value criteria. In this case, we also have total columns, because the total columns allow us to then plot the options in the solution map, which visually communicates to us which solutions are most promising to pursue.

- One of the benefits of this design thinking approach to evaluating options is that it explicitly takes stakeholders into account. You're specifically looking at end users, and you're also thinking about the producers. This is highly valuable, because in order to sell an option, you need to be thinking about what's acceptable to them. It also gives us a visual representation of the evaluation of the solutions. However, be careful not to get locked in to the totals, missing the development of other really good ideas.

© Photodisc/Thinkstock.

Targeting is a tool that helps you see how close your options or solutions come to your goal.

Targeting

- In targeting, the matrices are structured. They sort of feel objective; they're systematic. Targeting was developed with several goals in mind—to be a tool that was more visual, more intuitive, more fun, and more dynamic. It includes movement in it.

- Imagine a large archery target, in which we have the bull's-eye, usually red, that represents our ideal outcome or solution, for example. We want to see how close our options come to that bull's-eye, sort of like firing arrows at the target. The solutions are the arrows, and if the solution is really on target, then it'll end up on the bull's-eye. If it's not so much on target, then it'll end up in one of the outer rings.

- The first step for targeting is to define the bull's-eye. What does that red zone in the center represent?

- Once we've defined the bull's-eye, we then put our options, ideas, or solutions on Post-its, and in a way, we fire them at the target, locating them on the target relative to how close they come to hitting the bull's-eye.

- In step three, we identify the pulls and pushes—those forces that pull the option in the direction of the bull's-eye and those forces that push it away.

- In step four, we turn our pushes into challenges, much like we do using the POINT tool, where we identify issues. We transform the pushes into *how to*, *how might*, or *what might* statements.

- In step five, we overcome the challenges. We generate ideas to address those pushes, and then we ask ourselves: If we can address this push, where does that now move that idea? Then, you're able to relocate that Post-it. If you were able to overcome that push, does it now move the idea all the way onto the bull's-eye, or are there still some pushes that need to be addressed? At the end of this, we identify the key insights as we look at where all the ideas end up. We make our decision, and then we move to the next step.

Suggested Reading

Jones, *The Thinker's Toolkit.*

VanGundy, *Creative Problem Solving.*

Activities

Activity 1: Using Advanced Tools for Solution Development
Practice using one or all of the tools on a challenge: evaluation matrix, solution evaluation and solution map, must and want criteria, or targeting.

Activity 2: Must and Want Criteria
Develop "must and want" criteria to evaluate options associated with a decision you need to make this week. If the situation involves another person, generate and apply musts and wants together.

Evaluating Creative Solutions and Making Decisions
Lecture 16—Transcript

Creative work involves many decisions. What to add or cut, expand or contract, heighten or diminish. Such decisions, in fact, decisions of any kind, whether part of a creative process or not, can be improved by the use of tools—tools that we'll learn in this lecture.

Think back to a major purchase, perhaps a car. How did you make that decision? If a car, can you identify and list the reasons why you bought that particular car? Did you consider price, fuel efficiency, reliability, performance, certain features, passenger capacity, storage space, and so forth? These are criteria. Criteria can help us to choose among the creative alternatives we create. It's common practice to use criteria. Criteria are standards for evaluating our choices. Most often, though, they remain implicit. In other words, we're not aware of our criteria, but they're there, influencing us as we look at the choices before us.

In this lecture, we move our criteria from implicit to a more explicit state, more visible, so that we can direct our choice by using these and leveraging these criteria. The tools in this lecture are advanced. They utilize criteria. The first tool is the evaluation matrix. The tool makes this natural process more formal and systematic, and, therefore, helps us to make better choices. It's also useful at developing our solutions.

What's the benefit? Ever make a choice, and then later discover that you weren't happy about it, That there were things you didn't like about it? In the evaluation matrix, there are seven steps. The first step is to develop your criteria. We diverge on our criteria, and criteria answer the question, will it or does it, and you can include both tangible and intangible criteria, objective and subjective. And then, afterwards, you select the most important criteria.

In step two, we have to check our criteria. We check them in two important ways. First of all, the criteria need to be distinct. In other words, there's no overlap. Will it fit my budget? Is too close to will it be affordable? They're too similar. Don't have one criterion be subsumed by another as well. They need to be independent from one another. We also need to make sure that they're positive. The criteria should point you in the direction of what you want, not what you don't want. So they should all go in the same direction. Will it make my spouse upset? isn't probably what you want. It would be better to phrase that as Will it make my spouse happy?

In the third step, we build our evaluation matrix. We place our criteria into the matrix, adding your choices in, the ideas or solutions that you wish to evaluate. So the spreadsheet has choices listed down the first column, then the criteria are listed across the top of the remaining columns. We then need to select an evaluation system. We decide on a system for rating these choices as we look at the criteria against each choice. We can use numbers, we can use number of stars, sort of like they use to evaluate restaurants. You can use smiley faces, etcetera. Some people find numbers easier; those give them more meaning. Other, perhaps more visual learners, like to use symbols.

In the fifth step, we evaluate our choices. When we evaluate our choices, we work down each criterion, rating each choice against that criterion. So, in other words, we're holding that one standard against all options as we move through them. In step six, we review the matrix. We look across our ratings. We don't total the numbers, even if you may have used numbers. We don't total them or total the numbers of stars. When we do this, we might get locked into just the highest number. After we do this, we look across the evaluation. If we have a total, it draws our eye just to the total, and therefore we might miss some subtleties, and we may miss the chance to improve, because evaluation matrix is designed to also help us to improve. So, once you look across these ratings, we make a decision to accept that option, to give it a green light, to modify it by looking at where it might be improved, where it might have fallen short against a criterion. Or, if it doesn't do well against many criteria, we might decide to reject it.

In the seventh step, we develop the options and we make our final decision. We see if options that were identified for improvement can, indeed, be improved. We refine these solutions, and then we make our final decision.

Here are some important tips when you use the evaluation matrix. First of all, remember to diverge on your criteria. You don't want to miss an important criterion, like a colleague of mine who went to purchase a new home and looked at three new homes, and he had his evaluation matrix, which he completed after every home. When it was all done and he sat down with his wife across from the kitchen table and said, “Look. It looks like home A is our choice; it meets all of my criteria.” Well, there was something significant in what he said; it met his criteria. His wife sat there, shaking her head, no. And when he asked her what was wrong, she said “The house just doesn’t grab me.” You see, he forgot an important criterion, to include his wife’s opinion.

So we want to make sure we diverge on our criteria before we converge, so we don’t miss any important criteria. Again, we need to be careful if you’re using numbers not to add them. A total score may focus you in just on that number, and if one item has a score of 18 and another 17, that’s probably not a significant difference. And gain, we work down the columns, rather than across, using a criterion as a constant reference point.

So, with this in mind, let’s look at an example. Let’s imagine that you’re working for a company, and you’ve decided to offer a new service program, and you need a software system to support this new service program. We’re going to use that scenario to evaluate the different providers of these software systems. Here’s what the matrix looks like with these options loaded in it. So we have the service providers, those who will provide the software system. We’ll just call them ACME, ABC, Alpha, Beta, Omega, New Century, and Brand X. Those are our options there in the first column. Across the top, we fill in the criteria that we deem the most important. Will it fit our budget? Will this software system be user friendly? Will it be compatible with our existing systems? Will it be something that we can customize so that it can fit well with this new service that we’re providing? Will it be accessible to support services if we should run into problems?

Once we’ve loaded our criteria in there, then we move down each column, beginning with the first criterion, “Will it fit our budget?” Now, we’ve decided in this example to use a ratings scale of 0 to 5, 0 being a poor fit, 3 being a good fit, and 5 being an excellent fit. So we assign a number based on how well that criterion fits the option. So, ACME, let’s say it’s fairly expensive, may not really fit our budget; we assign a number of 1; ABC, their software system is particularly expensive, we give that a 0; Alpha, moderately expensive, we give it a 3; Beta, reasonably cost-efficient, we might give it a 4; Omega, very cost-efficient, a 5; and so forth. We complete that column. Once we've completed that column, we then move to user-friendly and work down the column in a similar fashion, assigning the number based on how well that criterion fits with the solution.

When we're all done, we then make a decision. We have three options. We can accept the solution as it is. In other words, it fared very well across the criteria. We can refine it by looking at, perhaps, where it fell short, where it didn't do so well against the criterion. And then, if it didn't do so well against many criteria, again, we might just outright reject that solution.

In our example, Omega did pretty well, so we might decide to say, "Well, that's acceptable to us." When we look at Beta, it fared pretty well also. But we notice that there are a couple criteria for which, if we could improve the solution, if we could improve that option in some way, it would also be acceptable. Beta didn't do so well on customizable; it got a 3, so perhaps we can contact the provider and see if we can negotiate some way to customize that software system. So we place that in the refine category, and we know which criterion we're going to go after in order to examine that solution further.

Let's talk about the evaluation matrix. It's great for making explicit decisions, whether they are creative solutions or everyday decisions. They're good for when you need to go with one option, when you can't make a decision to use multiple solutions. It's simply one. It can be used for everyday decisions, like purchasing a car, or a home, a major appliance. It can be useful to help you choose a retirement community, a vacation spot, or a college. It's also helpful for those more creative options, making sure that those options meet your criteria that really describe your ideal state, like choosing a new career, deciding on what product to bring to the marketplace, or what service to bring to the marketplace.

Let me share with you a personal story, a personal story in which I used the evaluation matrix, where I used criteria, and it fundamentally changed my decision. In fact, it gave me the confidence to pursue a more novel, a riskier decision. When I was looking around for a doctoral program, I had been accepted into three universities. One was a local university; one was a university in the New York City area; and one was the University of Manchester, overseas. I hadn't done a lot of international travel up to that point, so I was a bit nervous about going overseas; that seemed so far away. And truthfully, my first choice was to go to the local university. My second choice was the university in New York City, and then going to the University of Manchester was my third choice.

I gathered a group of friends to help me in this decision-making process, and together we generated criteria to evaluate the ideal university for my doctoral degree. We generated something like 200 criteria; they were a terrific resource group. I then went through these 200 criteria, and I chose the criteria that were most important to me. And then something happened. My mind shifted completely. You see, when I looked across those criteria, many of the criteria I chose, in fact, the most important criteria for me, had to do with continuing my interest in creativity, being able to further my research in the field of creativity. That was a huge shift, and it moved me in a riskier direction. You see, when I had visited the local university, I was told by the department chair that I would have to get over my interest in creativity when I went there to study. When I had met with the professors at the New York City university, they were interested in creativity, but they didn't have much domain knowledge. The only person of those three universities that I would study with, that had expertise in the field of creativity, was at the University of Manchester, which was initially my last choice. But, by looking at my criteria, it made it obvious to me what my true desires were, and it gave me the confidence to pursue that riskier decision.

Here's a twist on how you might use the evaluation matrix. You can sort your criteria into musts and wants. Must criteria are those criteria that are absolutely necessary in order for the choice to be acceptable. These are the deal breakers, the go, no-go criteria. Then we have our wants. These are important, and they add value, or they make the option even more attractive. It can be awkward if you mix musts and wants in the evaluation matrix. Musts can be tough to rate; they can be either zeroes or fives if you're using a scale like that. Plus, why include options in the matrix if it doesn't meet a must? Musts can serve as an initial screen to choose your short list of ideas that then go into the matrix, and then the matrix can be used to evaluate those choices based on the wants.

So here's how this tool works—musts and wants. We generate our criteria. Next, we converge and sort those criteria into musts and wants. Next, we use the musts to screen the ideas. In the fourth step, we place the converged ideas into the evaluation matrix. Only those ideas that met the musts go into our matrix, where we have our wants, and we use our wants to then evaluate that short list. And then we evaluate and develop those solutions.

So, if we go back to our example, where we're going to offer a new service to our customers, and we need a software system to support that, we can apply this tool to that situation, and the net result is we end up with a shorter list of options that make it into our evaluation matrix. So, in this example, let's say we identify our must criteria as follows. Will it be within our budget? Will it be compatible with the existing systems that we have? Will it be associated with a reputable vendor? So we take our ideas, we take our options, all of the vendors that we saw before, and we put them up against these must criteria. As a consequence, three options, three suppliers, three vendors survive. Let's call them Alpha, Beta, and Omega. We then take those three options, and we put them into our evaluation matrix in which we now have our wants Our want criteria are "Will IT, will Information Technology like it?" "Will it be user-friendly?" "Will it be visually appealing?" "Will it be customizable?" "Will there be accessible support services?" We use a rating scale of 0 to 5—0 being poor, 3 being good, 5 being excellent. We now take this much shorter list and we work through the evaluation matrix, again, working down each column one at a time.

So, Alpha, will our information technology department like it? We assign a 4; Beta, will IT like it? Oh, for sure, we give it a 5; Omega, not so much, we give it a 2. We then move to the next column and so forth. And, at the end, just as before, we use this evaluation to help us make a decision. In this example we decide that Alpha doesn't cut muster, and we decide to reject it. Omega, the same. We decide to reject that as well. But, the Beta system seems to stand out in terms of these value-added, "want" criteria.

In the last lecture, we looked at design thinking—design thinking tools, specifically. Design thinking provides us with a slight twist, a variation of the evaluation matrix. In design thinking, remember one of the principles is a user-centered focus. In their version, in the design thinking version of evaluation matrix, we use product and service to help us generate criteria, because ultimately, the product needs to fit the producer's needs as well as the user's needs.

So, here are the differences between the evaluation matrix we learned earlier and the one that's often applied by design thinkers. Thinking like a designer, you have to satisfy two basic stakeholders. You have to be concerned about producing a product that delights the user, and producing a product that the producer can create. The second is it's more visual. There are six steps to this matrix, or this evaluation tool, and it's called the Solution Evaluation and Solution Map. The Solution Evaluation piece looks much similar to the evaluation matrix that we did earlier. The Solution Map brings in the visual component, where we identify those ideas that do the best against those two sets of criteria—producer and user.

So the first step is to create your user value and provider value criteria. We diverge on criteria in these two sets. For the users, we consider information gathered during our user research phase, that observation phase. User value criteria might be things like ease of use, easy to store, aesthetically pleasing. Producer value criteria might be things like Will it be profitable? "Will it be easy for us to implement? Will it maintain our brand integrity?" In the second step, we create a solution evaluation matrix and a spreadsheet. The solutions are listed in the left column, and the criteria across the top. But this time, the criteria is sorted into two areas—the user value criteria and the producer value categories.

So, as with the evaluation matrix we learned earlier, we use a spreadsheet to evaluate our options. But this spreadsheet is broken up. We have columns for criteria that are reserved for user value criteria, and we have columns that are reserved for producer value criteria. And, in this case, we also have total columns, because the total columns allow us, then, to plot the options in the solution map later.

So let's look at possible evaluation criteria in these two categories, and let's see how this would look. So, user value criteria might be ease of use, ease of storage, and aesthetically pleasing. Producer value criteria might be profit, implementation—will it be easy to implement the solution, the product or service, whatever it happens to be—and brand integrity. So now we take those criteria and we load them into the solution evaluation spreadsheet. Like before, we use each column, each criterion, and we work down, rating the solutions against that criterion. In this case, we'll use a scale of 1 to 3, 1 being low, it's a poor fit; 2 being a medium fit; and 3 being a very high, very good fit.

We start with our user value criteria. We begin with the criterion ease of use, and we work down, comparing each solution against that criterion. When we're done with that criterion, we move to the next column. Will it be easy to store? And then we move to aesthetics. We total those three columns, and then we move to the producer value criteria, and we follow the same procedure, beginning with, Will it be profitable? Do we believe that that solution will be profitable to the producer? Ease of implementation will be next, followed by brand integrity, and then we total those three columns. From here, we take these scores, and we now plot them into a map. This is the visual part of this tool, which telegraphs to us which solutions are most promising to pursue. In this example, options 2, 5, and 6 end up above the diagonal line. These options had both high scores for producer value criteria and for user value criteria. All the other options end up below the diagonal line.

So, what are some of the benefits of this tool, this design thinking approach to evaluating options? It explicitly takes stakeholders into account. You're specifically looking at end users, and you're also thinking about the producers. This is highly valuable, because in order to sell the option, you need to be thinking about what's acceptable to them. It also gives us a visual representation of the evaluation of the solutions. But there's a watch out; be careful not to get locked in to the totals, missing the development of other really good ideas.

This next tool is called "targeting." The matrices are structured; they sort of feel objective. They're systematic. Targeting was developed with several goals in mind, to be a tool that was more visual, more intuitive, more fun, and more dynamic. It includes movement in it. Here's how targeting works. In fact, this is a tool I use pretty regularly. Imagine a large archery target. In fact, that's what I use when I go out and use targeting with groups. In this archery target, we have the bull's eye, usually red. That bull's eye represents our ideal outcome, the ideal solution, for example. And what we do is we want to see how close our options come to that bull's eye, sort of like firing arrows at the target. The solutions are the arrows, and if the solution is really on target, then it'll end up on the bull's eye. If it's not so much on target, then it'll end up in one of the outer rings.

So, here are the steps for targeting. We begin by defining the bull's eye. What does that red zone in the center represent? Once we've defined the bull's eye, we then take our options, our ideas or our solutions, we put them on Post-its and, in a way, we fire them at the target, locating them on the target relative to how close they come to hitting the bull's eye. If the idea really comes close to capturing what we see the ideal solution to be, then that idea would end up on the bull's eye. And then, other ideas, if they're not so close to that ideal solution, end up in different location on the target. In step three, we identify the pulls and pushes, those forces that pull the option in the direction of the bull's eye, and those forces that repel it, that push it away.

In step four, we turn our pushes into challenges, much like as we did using the POINT tool, where we identify issues. We transform the pushes into how to, how might statements, what might, because in step five we overcome the challenges. We generate ideas to address those pushes. And then we ask ourselves, "If we can address this push, where does that now move that idea?" Then you're able to relocate that Post-it. If you were able to overcome that push, does it now move the idea all the way into the red zone onto the bull's eye, or are there still some pushes that need to be addressed? At the end of this, we identify the key insights as we look at where all the ideas end up. We make our decision, and then we move to the next step.

This can be used with groups as well. We begin by defining the bull's eye as a group. We come to consensus in terms of what the ideal solution must be in order to truly work for us. Then we take each idea in turn, and rather than putting the idea on the Post-it, we put the names of the group members on the Post-it, and we do individual targets for each idea. So we have solution 1. We put everyone's name on a Post-it, on individual Post-its, and the group members represent by placing their Post-it in space on the target, relative to how close they see that option to being on the bull's eye. And in this way you can quickly look over the cluster of Post-its to see if there's consensus or how close to being ideal that solution is.

You identify the pulls and pushes, and in this way you ask people to reveal publicly for themselves what pulled that idea towards the center, what pushed it away, and we create a chart of pulls and pushes. Then we repeat this for the next idea, using another target, and then another target if we have a third option. After we've charted the pushes and pulls for each of those solutions that's being evaluated, we then look at ways to overcome those challenges, the pushes. Remember, we turn our pushes into challenge statements, and then we ask people to reposition their Post-its based on whether the ideas generated to overcome the pushes help, according to them and according to their opinion, help to move that idea towards the center. We then identify the key insights in the next steps.

This tool can be used to evaluate solutions, and it can be used in other ways as well. How we think about the bull's eye will vary depending on the application. So, if we're using targeting to select one solution or to create a short list of solutions that you want to pursue, as we've just described, the question to help you to define the bull's eye is, for the solution to be on target, it should. You can also use it to create a vision with a group. I've used it many times for this purpose. When you use it to create a vision, the phrase that helps you to define the bull's eye is, "The ideal vision would...," and you fill in the rest of that statement. It can also be used to evaluate performance against a goal. The bull's eye, the center, representing the goal once it's been achieved. The statement that we use here to define the bull's eye is, "We know the goal has been achieved when..." and you describe that end state when you've reached achievement.

Let's think about targeting. What are some advantages to this tool? Well, it's an evaluative tool that's intuitive, visual, and kinesthetic. In terms of kinesthetic, I've seen it used where the target is laid down on the floor and people actually stand on the target relative to their opinions about whatever they're evaluating, and the facilitator guides a conversation. You can physically track progress as a solution is developed. As it's developed into the ideal outcome, you can literally see the solution moving as it's being developed. It tends to uncover deeply rooted barriers, and as a result of the analysis of the pulls and pushes, the pulls and pushes, these forces, as we begin to think about these, tends to really uncover some deep obstacles, and it has multiple applications, from looking at a single option, to competing options, to using as a group, or using individually.

So we have many tools now with developing, but how do you choose which tool to use? Here are a couple ways to think about this. You can look at the number of options that you're evaluating. POINT is good for a few options. You wouldn't want to do POINT on many options. It would be too time-consuming. It's useful for, maybe, 2, 3, 4, 5 options. The evaluation matrix can handle roughly 12, 15 or so options. Hits and clustering, that you learned earlier, is terrific for whittling down a large set. You can combine hits and clustering with these other tools. You can do hits and clustering, and then apply the POINT tool. You can mix and match the tools.

Another way to think about which tool to use is the nature of the tool. POINT tends to be more intuitive and subjective. Evaluation matrix tends to be more objective because we're using criteria. Foresight scenario is good for predicting the future, casting yourself into what possibilities there might be off in the future, and targeting is more visual. So you might want to think about the nature of the tool and how that fits with your needs or the purposes of the group. We added four development tools as a result of this lecture—evaluation matrix, must and want criteria, solution evaluation, and solution map. We also added in targeting. Adults learn best through practice.

Before the next lecture, apply one of these tools. Tools take what is natural—using criteria—and makes them a bit more deliberate. And not just about making decisions; these tools are also useful in terms of developing solutions, so they help us to make decisions and also turn ideas into great solutions, just like the superstar great creators do. They work, and work, and work to refine their solutions. See you next time.

Giving Ideas Legs—Implementation Planning

Lecture 17

Creativity is about pursuing something new; you're like an explorer. To ensure success, it's critical to make a solid plan. If you're going someplace new, you have to be ready. A plan isn't so important if you're going someplace you've already been. When venturing into a new territory, it's helpful to go in with a clear plan in place. In this lecture, you will learn about a number of tools that help you create a plan, and then you go into action, and you monitor yourself as you're rolling out your plan—making adjustments and applying creative thinking as necessary.

The Implement Step

- Following the natural flow of creative problem solving, we move from the develop step to the implement step. Why include implement in a creative process? Is it enough just to have the solution? Where's the creativity in implementation? There are three reasons why we include implement in a creative process, such as creative problem solving.

- First, the develop step helps to yield novel solutions or a new change. We're leaving our comfort zone, so it's useful to have an action step that guides us as we go into this new direction. Second, sometimes we need to get creative and imaginative in creating an action plan.

- The third reason is that selling or pursuing something novel may require imagination to gain buy-in. When we create, we're intentionally introducing a change, and change is not always warmly embraced by others, so we may need to get creative in selling our idea, which requires imagination.

- In the implement step, we're going to do a number of things. We're going to explore acceptance. Up to this point, we've not really thought about the environment in which we're introducing the proposed solution or change. We have to scan this environment and think about what we need to consider in order to have the solution or change accepted. We make a plan.

Action Plan

- At this point in the process, we're using tactical thinking, which is the ability to devise and carry out a plan that includes specific, measurable steps for attaining the desired state.

- The first tool we're going to use is called action plan, and it has five steps. The first step is to describe a solution, change, or destination you wish to reach. You write out the solution or the proposed change so that it's clear in your mind. We use a statement starter, such as "I, or we, are committed to …."

- This part is important because it needs to be taken into consideration as we create our action plan. We need to prepare to overcome any risk by making sure that we've anticipated the risky aspects of the journey.

- In the next step, we diverge on action steps. We use divergent thinking tools like brainstorming or brainwriting—tools that help us generate many action steps that will guide our tactics, the concrete things that need to be done to successfully realize the solution or change. It's very important to diverge here. It's important that you examine all of the action steps.

- In the third step, we converge on the most important action steps. We use hits to identify those action steps that are going to be most important and valuable to us to achieve our desired end.

- In our next step, we determine the time horizon, and we create a timetable. We organize our action steps, and then we apply them and follow those action steps. We begin by identifying an end date—when we need to have the solution or change fully implemented—and then we create four blocks of time: immediate, short term, intermediate, and long term. We suggest that the immediate block of time begins within 24 to 48 hours in order to create momentum.

- Then, finally, we organize our action steps into a timetable, and we follow that timetable. We place our selected action steps in a sequence in the timetable that we've created, organizing the action steps in a sequence over time, moving from immediate to short term to intermediate and long term. It's important to look this over to make sure that there aren't gaps, steps that are crucial but overlooked.

- You can expand the action step if you want to add more detail to it. You can have action steps along a timeline, and that may be sufficient, but there are times when you want more detail. Detail can be added to make this tool even more systematic. Detail is important, especially when you have a group action plan.

- Beyond the action steps, you can add accountability factors. This is especially helpful when you have a group. You can have a specific deadline instead of large blocks of time. You can have someone who is identified as being responsible for that particular action step, and you can identify to whom the completion of that action step will be reported.

How-How Diagram

- Another tool for implementation is called the how-how diagram. The previous approach to create an action plan was more intuitive. It relied on our ability to think in divergent ways of action steps. The how-how diagram is more structured; it drills down into specific action steps, to move our solution forward.

- This is sort of like the webbing tool that we used in the clarify step, where we asked basic questions to shift our perspective: why and what's stopping you. With the how-how diagram, we ask: How do we achieve the solution? How do we achieve this end goal? How do we get to this end state? We repeatedly ask this, and every time we ask it, it forces us to be more concrete.

- We begin by identifying a solution or a proposed change. We write a summary stating, "I, or we, are committed to fulfilling X, Y, or Z." Then, we ask how, and we record our responses. Considering this proposed solution, how will we accomplish this? We record our responses, and we can add on the word *else* to move us laterally.

- We ask how again and record those responses to the initial set of actions that have been written, and we consider each option that's been created and ask how every time, continuing to drill down. We continue to ask and record until we reach the natural end of this thread of thinking.

- This systematic, deliberate tool has a significant advantage in that it really clearly lays out the things that we need to do. By drilling down, you might ensure that no action step is overlooked. This is particularly good for low implementers or people who are high ideators that tend to think in more global and abstract ways. One of the nice things about this tool is that it's visual, and it shows relationships among the action steps.

Performance Dashboard

- Performance dashboard is a creative and visual way that we can monitor an action plan as we're implementing it. Picture your car dashboard. What are the benefits of these visual metrics? What

In the same way that your car's dashboard gives you information about your progress, the performance dashboard can help you along the way to your goal.

do they do for you? Compare your current car dashboard to a past dashboard. What's useful? What do you have now that you didn't have then?

- The purpose of the performance dashboard is to provide a visual monitor for our progress by giving us dynamic feedback mechanisms. It's based on a simple metaphor—the car dashboard.

- Performance dashboard can be employed individually. It can also be designed for team application. You can come up with a common set of measures and a common language that the team agrees to, and you can monitor the success of a team as they roll out some action steps.

- As a team, there are four steps that you can go through when using the performance dashboard. First, you generate a set of indicators that can be effective for monitoring the progress of your plan. This can include soft measures such as motivation, commitment, ownership, and resistance to change. You pick the measures that are most useful for the stakeholders in the scenario, and then you design those.

- You select and combine the most important indicators, and check that all the critical objectives are being tracked. You transform these indicators into a visual dashboard. You create a visual dashboard, and you make it public. Finally, you meet regularly with the team to review the metrics, updating the dashboard. Use the dashboard to spark conversation with the team, to act proactively, and perhaps to make adjustments.

- One of the benefits of the performance dashboard is that it's a deliberate approach for monitoring the action steps as you're executing and pursuing the solution. As a team, it helps to build consensus upon what metrics are most important. It provides dynamic feedback and real-time feedback. It's visible or posted publicly. It helps to keep people focused on moving forward. It improves communication and coordination. Bring the metrics in to meetings for discussion and update progress regularly.

Suggested Reading

Allen, *Getting Things Done.*

Belsky, *Making Ideas Happen.*

Lumsdaine and Lumsdaine, *Creative Problem Solving.*

Activities

Activity 1: How-How Diagram

Create an action plan for a proposed change using a timetable or how-how diagram. Start by writing a statement that begins like this: "I am committed to …". Select an area that requires real action on your part, perhaps something that you need to implement within the next three to six months.

Plan of Action

Time Frame	Action	By Whom?	By When?	Report to Whom?
Immediate				
Short Term				
Intermediate				
Long Term				

How-How Diagram

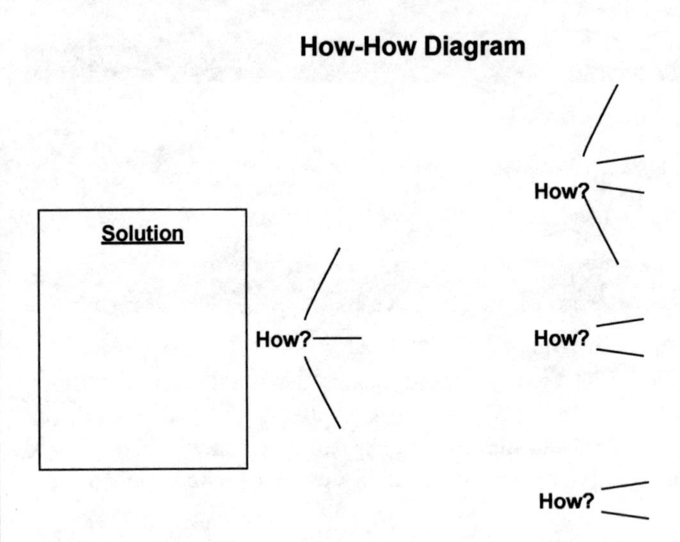

Activity 2: Performance Dashboard

Find an area of your life in which you wish to improve performance (personal, professional, hobby, sport, etc.). Identify specific things that need to be improved and draw visual metrics to track performance. Keep it accessible and use it for a period of time.

Giving Ideas Legs—Implementation Planning
Lecture 17—Transcript

Early in the 20th century, there were few untouched geographical destinations, except for the South Pole. How to get there required great creativity. Creative thinking applied to planning and tactics. Two rival explorers raced to be the first: Robert Falcon Scott of England, and Roald Amundsen of Norway. On January 17, 1912, Robert Scott reached the South Pole to find the Norwegian flag there waiting for him. Amundsen had been there one month earlier, on December 14, 1911. Certainly sad, but coming in second is not a tragedy. The tragedy is that Scott and his party perished on the return trek. Initially celebrated for his heroic efforts, but later analysis by experts showed that the creative planning skills of the two explorers accounted for Amundsen's success and Scott's tragic failure.

Let's examine the different tactics used by these two explorers. Let's look at transportation. Amundsen had a simple plan. He combined skiing for the men and dog sleds to haul the gear. Scott had a complicated plan, combining motorized sledges, ponies, dogs, skiing, and men hauling their own gear. While Scott agreed with the advice from experts to rely mainly on skiing, he provided no training to his team. This inexperience meant that the team did not make good use of the skis. Amundsen's team was composed largely of expert skiers, and in fact, a champion skier was their front runner.

Scott planned to have a majority of hauling work done by the ponies. Ponies are not well suited for the conditions of the South Pole. They have small hooves compared to their weight, which meant they sank into the snow. Dogs are better suited to the cold weather. They have great mobility in the snow, and they need little care. The Norwegian team fed their dogs seal and penguin meat, which are readily available in Antarctica. Scott's team fed their dogs dried fish, which did not agree with the dogs, leading to their deterioration. In fact, all the dogs eventually died and were eaten by Scott's team.

Let's look at diet even a little more. Scott took an insufficient amount of rations, especially to feed men who were hauling equipment, and the rations they had were deficient in Vitamin B and C, and as a result, many in Scott's party developed scurvy. The cooking fuel tins were known to have faulty seals, and, as a consequence, the men in Scott's group had to eat frozen meals and were deprived of water. Amundsen had the fuel tins soldered. They were soldered closed to prevent the leaking fuel problem. Fifty years later, tins from this expedition were found, and they were still full.

In terms of their travel tactics, they varied greatly. Amundsen, learning from the Inuit, recruited experienced dog drivers. To make the most of the dogs, they paced them, deliberately keeping the daily mileages shorter than necessary for 75 percent of the journey. The Norwegian team spent 16 hours per day resting and traveled with their backs to the sun to prevent snow blindness. In contrast, half of Scott's team suffered from snow blindness.

Their approach to route marking and depot laying was vastly different as well. For the last 180 miles of the trip, Amundsen had the route marked like a Norwegian ski route, using marker flags every eight miles. To this, he added a marker every mile by leaving an empty food container that he had painted black before the trip. From 82 miles in, the Norwegians built six-foot cairns every three miles, containing a note recording the cairn's position, the distance to the closest depot, and the direction to the next cairn. Each depot had a line of bamboo flags laid transversely every half-mile for five miles on either side of the depot.

Scott relied on very few depots, and those he established were marked with walls built during lunch to protect the ponies and had a single flag. In his diary, Scott recorded great concern in finding his route and had many close calls. Amundsen used simple navigational sheets that minimized calculations for his team, especially when they were tired and cold. Four of his team were navigators, and they brought along a sexton, which is light and relatively simple for navigation. Scott used heavier navigation equipment that required more mental arithmetic. One final tactical error for Scott was his decision to take a fifth man on the final leg of the journey to the pole, although he had rations for only four.

Why did I share this story with you? I wanted to highlight the importance of tactical thinking when you are going to go into a new area. The arrogance and poor decision making on the part of Scott cost him his life and the lives of his party. Scott and his pole party died 11 miles short of a one-ton depot.

The depot was originally planned to be placed 31 miles closer to the South Pole, but was not, due to the weakness of the ponies.

Creativity is about pursuing something new; you're like an explorer. To ensure success, it's critical to make a solid plan. If you're going someplace new, you have to be ready. A plan isn't so important if you're going someplace you've already been. When venturing into a new territory, it's helpful to go in with a clear plan in place. Following the natural flow of creative problem solving, we move from the develop step to the implement step. So why include implement in a creative process? Is it enough just to have the solution? Where's the creativity in implementation?

There are three reasons why we include implement in a creative process, like creative problem solving. First, the develop step helps to yield novel solutions or a new change. We're leaving our comfort zone, so it's useful to have an action step that guides us as we go into this new direction. Remember, you're like an explorer.

Secondly, sometimes we need to get creative and imaginative in creating an action plan, like how Amundsen painted food cans black and used them as markers after the fuel was spent. And the third reason, selling or pursuing something novel may require imagination to gain buy-in. When we create, we're intentionally introducing a change, and change is not always warmly embraced by others, so we may need to get creative in selling our idea, which requires imagination.

So, in the implement step, we're going to do a number of things. We're going to explore acceptance. Up to this point, we've not really thought about the environment in which we're introducing the proposed solution or the proposed change. We have to scan this environment and think about what we need to consider in order to have the solution or change accepted. We make a plan, and in this lecture, we'll be looking at a number of tools that help us to create a plan. And then we go into action, and we monitor ourselves as we're rolling out our plan, making adjustments and applying creative thinking as necessary.

At this point in the process, we're using tactical thinking, which is the ability to devise and carry out a plan that includes specific, measurable steps for attaining the desired state. The first tool we're going to use is called simply action plan; this has five steps. The first step is to describe a solution, a change, or a destination you wish to meet. You write out the solution, or the proposed change, so it's clear in your mind. We use a statement starter, "I, or we, are committed to…" In the case of our South Pole explorers, they might have said, "We are committed to being the first to get to the South Pole and then returning safely." The returning safely part is important, because this needs to be taken into consideration as we create our action plan so that we are preparing to overcome any risk by making sure that we've anticipated those risky aspects of the trip.

In the next step, we diverge on action steps. We use divergent thinking tools that we've learned before, like brainstorming or brainwriting, tools that help us to generate many action steps that will guide our tactics. The concrete things that need to be done to successfully realize the solution or the change, and note it's very important to diverge here. Remember, you're an explorer. You're going into a new direction, so it's important that you examine all of the action steps.

In the third step, we converge on the most important action steps. We use hits to identify those action steps that are going to be most important and valuable to us to achieve our desired end. Perhaps in some ways, Scott failed here. He had been presented with some diverse opinions about skiing and using dogs, but he ignored these to some degree. He stayed with things that he was comfortable with. As a result of not exploring these more novel action steps, by staying with what was comfortable to him, he threatened his team and the survival of his team.

In our next step, we determine the time horizon, and we create a timetable; we organize our action steps. And then we apply them and we follow those action steps. We begin by identifying an end date—when we need to have the solution or change fully implemented. And then we create four blocks of time: immediate, short-term, intermediate, and long-term, and we suggest that the immediate begin within 24 to 48 hours in order to create momentum. Here again, perhaps Scott failed. He, in fact, deviated from his action plan. One of his critical errors during the last leg of the trip was taking along a fifth member of the team when he only had rations to support four.

And then, finally, we organize our action steps into a timetable, and we follow that timetable. We take our selected action steps and we place them in a sequence in the timetable that you've created, organizing the action steps in a sequence over time, moving from immediate, to short-term, to intermediate, and long-term. And it's important to look this over to make sure that there aren't gaps, things that are overlooked. Scott brought along skis, but he failed to train the members of his team in being able to ski, and therefore wasn't able to use that. That was a gap; that was a step that was crucial and overlooked.

Now, you can expand the action step if you want to add more detail to it. You can have action steps along a timeline, and that may be sufficient, but there are times you want more detail. Detail can be added to make this tool even more systematic. Detail is important, especially when you have a group action plan. Beyond the action steps, you can add accountability factors, and again, this is especially helpful when you have a group. You can have a specific deadline instead of these large blocks of time. You can have someone who's identified as being responsible for that particular action step, and you can identify to whom the completion of that action step will be reported.

Rich Products, a company in Buffalo, New York, a multi-national food producer, ends every meeting with an action register. In this action register, they conclude the meeting by saying, "What actions must we do now that we've brought this meeting to an end, and who is responsible?" Project management literature provides many tools that are useful for following up and tracking actions.

Let's look at another tool for implementation. This tool is called the How-How Diagram. The previous approach to create an action plan was more intuitive; it relied on our ability to think in divergent ways of action steps. The How-How Diagram is more structured; the How-How Diagram drills down into specific action steps, to move our solution forward. It's sort of like the webbing tool that we used in clarify, where we asked basic questions to shift our perspective—why and what's stopping you. With the How-How, we ask, "How do we achieve the solution?" "How do we achieve this end goal?" "How do we get to this end state?" We repeatedly ask this, and every time we ask it, it forces us to be more concrete.

So we begin by identifying a solution or a proposed change. Again, we write a summary stating, "I, or we, are committed to fulfilling X, Y, or Z." And then we ask how, and we record our responses. Considering this proposed solution, how will we accomplish this? We record our responses, and we can add on the word else to move us laterally. We ask how, again, and record those responses to the initial set of actions that have been written, and we consider each option that's been created and ask how every time, continuing to drill down. We continue to ask and record until we reach the natural end of this thread of thinking.

Let's look at an example. Let's imagine that our solution is to improve efficiency and collaboration among employees by rearranging and restructuring the office complex. This is what we're committed to. This is our intended change. So, we ask how; how might we accomplish this? So, we want to improve efficiency and collaboration among employees by rearranging and restructuring the office space. How will we get this done? How can we accomplish this? Well, one response would be, "We need to create a master plan." Well, how else might we accomplish this? "We need to create a project budget." And then we can ask how one more time, and the response might be, "We might need to identify departmental physical space needs with respect to workflow." We can then take this action step, this initial series of responses, and ask how to each one of those. In terms of creating the master plan, we ask how. Well, one response is to consult with a space designer. Well, how else? Well, we could solicit ideas from the section heads. How else? We can examine physical layout of other companies.

And there might be one more action step related to creating a master plan. Conduct a study of the present space utilization. One of the initial action steps with the first question how was to create a project budget. Again, we can drill deeper into this action by asking how; how will we go about creating a project budget? Well, we can identify available financial sources locally. How else? Well, we can speak with senior management at headquarters about the project and identify additional sources of funding.

Let's go back to the original set of responses and try this one more time, drilling down into the response identify departmental physical space needs with respect to workflow. Again, we might ask how to go further into this particular action. One response might be to conduct focus group sessions with employees. Well, how else might we identify departmental physical space needs? Another response might be to capture workflow via a process map.

I encourage you to try this tool. You need a sheet of paper, and you need to follow along using the word how, sort of branching out like a tree. Or you can do it in your mind. I'm going to walk you through this, identifying something that's important for you to accomplish. Think about, perhaps, a goal that you identified earlier, or think about something that you might wish to accomplish within the year or within the next calendar year. Think of a few goals that you have, and then select one, and then write it down, or make sure it's firmly planted in your mind. Now, how will you accomplish this?

Record or think about this. What are two or three things that you need to do to accomplish this? For me, let's say, my goal is to get healthier, to improve my health. Well, three thoughts that might occur to me are change in diet, exercise, find ways to relax more. Now, we take these new action steps, and we ask how again. In your mind, ask how to the initial action steps that you generated. How will you achieve those actions? In terms of a healthier diet, changing my diet, one response might be to take healthy cooking classes. Well, how might I do that? Visit web sites of local cooking classes to examine the programs that they're offering. You see, as we continue to ask how, these become extremely concrete.

You can repeat this and continue to work through this How-How Diagram, and you can, perhaps, do this later after this lecture. Take the time. This systematic, deliberate tool has a significant advantage in that it really clearly lays out the things that we need to do. By drilling down in this way, you might ensure that no action step is overlooked. This is particularly good for low implementers, or people who are high ideators that tend to think in more global and abstract ways. And one of the nice things about this tool is that it's visual, and it shows relationships among the action steps.

Speaking of visual, there's a creative and visual way that we can monitor an action plan as we're implementing it. It's called the performance dashboard. So, picture your car dashboard. If you're driving your car right now, it'll be easy for you to do that, but please don't stare at it. What are the benefits of these visual metrics? What do they do for you? Compare your current car dashboard, perhaps, to a past dashboard. What's useful? What do you have now that you didn't have then?

For example, I like the real-time readout of miles per gallon. That helps me to monitor my driving behavior. The purpose of the performance dashboard is to provide a visual monitor for our progress by giving us dynamic feedback mechanisms. It's based on a simple metaphor, the car dashboard.

Here's an example of a performance dashboard. Maybe you've seen these yourself. At Buffalo State every year, there's a major fundraiser, and when you pull onto the campus, there's a thermometer that you pass by, and the red line on the thermometer indicates how close our organization is to the goal. And every time I pass this, if I haven't contributed yet, it makes me feel guilty. In this way, it compels me to action, and it lets our community know how well we're doing in terms of moving towards our goal.

Performance dashboard can be employed individually. Remember, Hemingway, at the end of every day, charted the number of words that he had written each day. It can also be designed for team application. You can come up with a common set of measures and a common language that the team agrees to, and you can monitor the success of a team as they roll out some action steps.

As a team, here are four steps you can go through when using the performance dashboard. First, you generate a set of indicators that can be effective for monitoring the progress of your plan, and this can include soft measures such as motivation, commitment, ownership, resistance to change. You pick the measures that are most useful for the stakeholders in the scenario, and then you design those. You select and combine the most important indicators, and check that all the critical objectives are being tracked. You transform these indicators into a visual dashboard. You create a visual dashboard, and you make it public. And then finally, you meet regularly with the team to review the metrics, updating the dashboard. Use the dashboard to spark conversation with the team, and to act proactively, to make adjustments perhaps.

Here's an example. A team recently went through a process where the identified cohesion as an issue. The elements of trust and conflict, commitment and accountability were identified as being issues that need to be worked on. After they examined the situation, they decided to create a dashboard, and they defined a couple of metrics that helped them to move towards greater cohesion. One metric might have been what they called a trustometer—like a speedometer—to measure individual willingness to be open with each other. The indicator on this trustometer might have been low, medium, or high. They might have also decided to use an artificial harmony sensor, an alarm that goes off when they are not dealing effectively with conflict.

So, what are some of the benefits of the performance dashboard? Well, first of all, it's a deliberate approach for monitoring the action steps as you're executing and rolling out, pursuing the solution. As a team, it helps to build consensus upon what metrics are most important. It provides dynamic feedback and real-time feedback; it's visible or posted publicly; it helps to keep people focused on moving forward; it improves communication and coordination. Bring the metrics in to meetings for discussion and update progress regularly.

Let's try the performance dashboard. Find an area in your life in which you wish to improve performance. It could be personal, could be professional, could be a hobby, could be a sport that you're pursuing. For me, I'll use golf as an example. Identify the specific things that you need to improve. If I use myself as an example, in golf I might say, "I want to be better at putting," or "I want to get more balls in the fairway," etcetera. After you've identified those areas you wish to improve, create visual metrics to track your performance. Then, if you can, make it visible. Display it. If you can't display it, make it accessible so that you can check this and update it regularly. Use it for some period of time and track your performance. Track your improvement.

In this lecture, we looked at putting creative solutions into action. As Joel Barker said, "Vision without action is nothing more than an idle daydream." In the next lecture, we examine creative ways to sell our novel solutions. See you next time.

Persuasion and the Selling of New Ideas

Lecture 18

In the universal creative process that we call creative problem solving, we're in the implement step. At this point, we're looking out to the context in which we will introduce our idea, solution, or change, and we're exploring it to make sure that what we're proposing will, in fact, be accepted. To help us with that, we create a plan, and then we put that plan into action. In the last lecture, you learned how to create an action plan. Before you leap to action, as this lecture will teach you, you should check your environment for forces that will help or hinder your success.

Assistors and Resistors

- Psychologist Kurt Lewin indicated that proposed change will meet two forces: those forces that will help it be successful and those forces that will hinder success. Wise action plans take these forces into consideration. As you go out to execute the idea, solution, plan, or change that you propose, it's best to anticipate resistance beforehand than to meet it head-on in the field.

- Assistors and resistors is a kind of way of doing a 360-degree force field analysis. It uses contextual thinking. It involves putting ourselves into the future, examining our context, and thinking about how this idea will be received. It uses that kind of projection to influence our plan as we create it now, before we execute it.

- With assistors and resistors, we begin by writing a summary of the proposed solution or change so that it's clear in our mind what we wish to do. Then, we diverge on sources of assistance and resistance. We create two columns, or two areas, to record all of the sources of assistance and resistance that we can think of.

- As always, when you begin with this tool, it's important to engage in divergent thinking. We don't want to overlook a source that might assist us—that can help us to be successful—and we certainly don't want to overlook a potential source of resistance. It's better to anticipate it.

- To help us out, we use the five W's and the H to generate sources of assistance and resistance. As you may recall, the five W's and the H are who, what, when, where, why, and how. Each one of these words jogs our thinking to consider possible sources of assistance and resistance.
    - **Who**: As you think about the plan, what you wish to carry forward, you want to make sure that the world embraces it. We think about individuals or groups that will either help or hinder us.

    - **What**: What are the things that might help or hinder us?

    - **When**: Are there issues related to timing? Are there times where it's, perhaps, best to suggest or advance this idea—to put it into action? Are there times that should be avoided?

    - **Where**: This refers to the physical or process locations that can help or hinder us as we try to advance the solution.

    - **Why**: This refers to reasons that might come up to support this idea or reasons that others might come up with to block the progress of this idea.

    - **How**: This refers to actions that others might take to either help you or hinder or block your success as you move forward.

- In the third step, we select the most important sources of assistance and resistance. We converge. We prioritize. We make sure we zero in on those sources of assistance that we want to make sure that we call in to support us, and we identify the sources of resistance that are likely to resist us.

- In the fourth step of the tool, we generate action steps that take advantage of the assistors. How can we leverage the assistors? We don't overlook the assistors and assume that they're there to support us. Instead, we want to actively engage assistors, and we want to use our divergent thinking to also consider action steps to take to overcome the resistors.

- In some cases, this step involves leveraging our assistors to address some of the resistors. We then select the action steps that we think will be most helpful as we've looked at our assistors and resistors, and then we create an action plan. We build out action steps along a timeline from immediate to short term to intermediate and long term (as you learned in the last lecture), but this time, when we create our action plan, it's fueled with this knowledge of those forces of assistance and sources of resistance.

- It's important not to just address one source of resistance. When you converge on sources of resistance, you prioritize and examine all of the important sources of resistance, and you generate actions steps that will help to address all of the important sources of resistance. You use this information to then create your final action plan.

- People resist even brilliant ideas. Imagination can be used to generate ideas, but we also need to use imagination to convince others to accept our ideas. Sometimes it's not the brilliance in generating the idea that makes a difference in terms of our success; instead, it's the imagination we use to sell the idea that allows us to achieve success.

Stakeholder Analysis

- Stakeholder analysis is a deliberate tool that is designed to identify the key people that will support or hinder the success of any given solution, plan of action, or desired change.

- With this tool, we identify and examine the positions of people or groups that have a stake in the plan. We look at how these people might affect the outcomes, and then we decide where they need to be in order to support the desired change. Then, we devise a set of actions aimed at gaining support from these key players.

Stakeholder analysis is a tool that can help you strengthen your action plan for a particular solution.

- How do you know who the key stakeholders are? The following are some questions that might help you identify these key individuals that you need to take into consideration. Who is affected by the plan or the proposed change? Who has an interest in the plan and its outcomes? Who can affect the plan's adoption or implementation? Who might express discontent to what is being proposed? Who can shape or influence the opinions about the issues involved? Which people have clear roles in the plan?

- Once we've identified our stakeholders, we can move through this tool. We begin by diverging on a list of key stakeholders. We select the key stakeholders, and then we list them in the first column of a six-column chart.

- For each stakeholder, we have to then identify, where are they now? Where do we believe they are now in regard to this proposed plan? Are they strongly opposed? Are they moderately opposed? Are they neutral? Are they moderately supportive, or are they strongly supportive? We mark the position with an X.

- Now we know where they are, but next we need to consider, in order to go forward, do we need to move them along? Where do we need them to be in regard to the proposed plan? We mark this position on our worksheet with an O. We connect these two, the X and the O—where we believe they are now and where we need them to be—with an arrow to represent where they are and how far we have to move them to get to where we need them to be.

- This helps us to then move to the next step in this tool, which is to list the actions required in order to gain support for the implementation of the plan. Then, we include those actions later in our final plan.

- Once we've gone through the stakeholder analysis, we begin to look at how that can enhance our action plan, and in this way, much like assistors and resistors, our action plan is informed by going through this kind of analysis, and it should, as a result, strengthen our action plan.

- It not only takes imagination to create a novel idea, but it also takes imagination to sell it. In fact, it may take more imagination to sell people on the reasons to accept your proposed change. To do this, you may need to use imagination to show others that a better way of doing things has arrived.

Suggested Reading

Lewin, *Field Theory in Social Science.*

Senge, et al., *The Dance Of Change.*

Activities

Activity 1: Assistors and Resistors
Identify something you wish to do in the next six months. Generate assistors and resistors using the five W's and H. Select the most significant resister, and then generate action steps to address this resistor.

Activity 2: Stakeholder Analysis
What initiatives do you need to complete in the next 90 days? Select one initiative that involves others. Generate a list of stakeholders, and use the stakeholder analysis diagram to indicate where they are in relation to the initiative. See how this thinking influences your plan of action.

Persuasion and the Selling of New Ideas

Lecture 18—Transcript

Let's start by talking about radios. A pretty good idea, but having a good idea and selling a good idea are two different matters. When first introduced, and for a very long time, radios were large pieces of furniture, until the transistor was invented, and transistors replaced the vacuum tubes in radios. The transistor radio is still one of the world's most common communication devices. A 2009 study estimated that there were seven billion in existence around the world. The adoption of transistors into radios was a game-changer. Some of the advantages included smaller devices; less energy required; they could operate on standard batteries; instant on, no vacuum tubes to warm up; and shock resistant.

Well, smaller size, light weight, and longer battery life were believed to give the transistor radio a clear market advantage over the old vacuum tube radios. Together, this created an opportunity for the first truly portable radio. Several companies competed to capture this market. In the U.S., we had Texas Instruments, Regency, Zenith, Bulova, and Emerson. In Japan, there was a Tsushin Kogyo Corporation. Working together, Texas Instruments and the Regency Company released the first commercial transistor radio, the Regency TR-1, in 1954. The Tsushin Kogyo Corporation saw an opportunity to enter the American market, and they brought their TR-55 to the United States in 1955.

It was the first commercial success in the U.S. There would be many more, but not under that name. The founders of Tsushin Kogyo Corporation, Ibuka and Morita, saw greater opportunity but recognized the need for some changes. First, they recognized that their company name was difficult for Americans to pronounce, so they came up with the name Sony. They already had a product called the Soni-tape, using the Latin word sonus, which is the root for sonic and sound. It also sounded like sonny, a 1950s American expression, suggesting young boys and youth. Additionally, Ibuka and Morita resisted great pressure from their principal bank to call the company Sony Electronic Industries. They didn't want to be connected to just one industry.

Finally, breaking with a long-held tradition, Ibuka and Morita spelled their company name with Roman letters, instead of Japanese characters. With these changes in place, Sony was almost ready to make its next big push into the transistor radio market. Next, they realized that they needed to reposition their transistor radio to make it distinctive. They needed to do so by introducing it as the first-ever pocketable radio, or pocket radio.

While true that their new model, the TR-63, was somewhat smaller, you still needed a very large shirt pocket to carry it. So, make it a bigger pocket, and this is exactly what several sources allege Sony did. Competitors at that time claim that Sony salesmen were outfitted with oversize shirt pockets that fitted the new pocket radio. Sony claimed, "We sell the smallest transistor radio in the world—and look—it's so small, it will fit in your pocket." By 1959, more than six million transistor radios were sold by Japanese manufacturers, representing $62 million in revenue, helping to launch Sony as one of the world's most successful small electronics manufacturers.

So Sony was creative, to be sure, but their creative genius did not come with the ideation part of the creative process; they didn't invent the transistor. They bought the rights from Bell Labs. They weren't the first to invent the transistor radio, not the first to make the transistor radios commercially available, even. Sony's creative genius came in selling the idea, creative in name change and their first positioning of the pocket radio.

Let's remember where we are in the creative process. This universal creative process that we call creative problem solving. We're in the implement step of the creative process. At this point, we're doing three things. We're looking out to the context in which we will introduce our idea, our solution, or our change, and we're exploring it to make sure that what we're proposing will, in fact, be accepted. To help us with that, we create a plan, and then we put that plan into action. In the last lecture, we learned to create an action plan. Before you leap to action, you should check your environment for forces that will help or hinder your success. Sony recognized this. They recognized the need to change their name, for example. Psychologist Kurt Lewin indicated that proposed change will meet two forces—those forces that will help it to be successful and those forces that will hinder success. Wise action plans take these forces into consideration. As you go out to execute your idea, your solution, your plan, the change that you propose, it's best to anticipate resistance beforehand than to meet it head-on in the field.

There's a tool that you'll learn in this lecture, called Assistors and Resistors, which is a kind of way of doing a 360-degree force-field analysis. It's using contextual thinking. It's putting ourselves into the future and examining our context, and thinking about how will this idea be received, and it's using that kind of projection to influence our plan as we create it now, before we execute it.

So, let's look at Assistors and Resistors. Let's look at the steps within this tool. We begin by writing a summary of the proposed solution, or the change, so that it's clear in our mind what we wish to do. Then we diverge on sources of assistance and resistance. We create two columns, or two areas, to record all of the sources of assistance and all of the sources of resistance that we can think of. And as always, when you begin with this tool, it's important to engage in divergent thinking. We don't want to overlook a source that might assist us, that can help us to be successful, and we certainly don't want to overlook a potential source of resistance. It's better to anticipate it.

To help us out, we use the five Ws and the H to generate sources of assistance and resistance. As you may recall, the five Ws and the H are who, what, when, where, why, and how. Each one of these words jogs our thinking to consider possible sources of assistance and resistance. Let's go through each one briefly and look at some questions and thoughts to consider as we explore Assistors and Resistors.

So, who? So as you think about the plan, what you wish to carry forward, this great idea that you're in love with. You want to make sure the world embraces it. We think about who—individuals or groups who will either help or hinder us. Then we move to what. What are the things that might help or hinder us? When, are there issues related to timing? Are there times where it's, perhaps, best to suggest or advance this idea, to put it into action? Are there times that should be avoided? Let's take that into consideration now.

How about where? Physical or process locations that can help or hinder us as we try to advance the solution. Why? Why refers to reasons that might come up, reasons to support this idea, or reasons that others might come up with to block the progress of this idea. How, the H, how, refers to actions that others might take to either help you or get in the way, hinder, block your success as you move forward.

In the third step, we select the most important sources of assistance and resistance. We converge. We prioritize. We make sure we zero in on those sources of assistance that we want to make sure that we call in to support us, and we identify the sources of resistance that are likely to resist us.

In the fourth step of the tool, we generate action steps. We generate action steps that take advantage of the assistors. How can we leverage the assistors? We don't overlook the assistors and assume they're there to support us. Instead, we want to actively engage assistors, and we want to use our divergent thinking to also consider action steps to take to overcome the resistors. In some cases, it's using our assistors, perhaps leveraging our assistors, to address some of the resistors. We then select the most important action steps, the action steps that we think will be most helpful as we've looked at our assistors and resistors, and then we create an action plan, much like we learned in the last lecture. We build out action steps along a timeline from immediate to short-term, to intermediate, to long-term, but this time, this time when we create our action plan, it's fueled with this knowledge of those forces of assistance and those sources of resistance.

Let's take a hypothetical situation. Let's take a fun scenario. Imagine suddenly you're appointed the czar of education, and let's take a playful idea. You decide that teachers should be replaced with project managers. It's an extreme idea, but it's being used only to take us through an example of how to apply this tool. So, let's apply assistors and resistors to this idea. As the czar of education, you want to get others to adopt this idea of replacing teachers with project managers. Let's run through our assistors.

So, who might help us with this? Who would be there to support this idea? Well, perhaps the Project Management Institute. This is the professional association for project managers. Maybe the states would be supportive; they might see this as an opportunity to save money. What? What are some things that might assist you? Well, there's this notion of problem-based education, and perhaps those who are proponents of problem-based education might see this as an opportunity to advance their own thinking.

When? What are timing issues to take into consideration in terms of assistance? Well, perhaps it might be best to start this when students are seniors in high school and they, perhaps, have a little more flexibility. They've met the requirements for graduation. Where? Where might we find assistance? Well, perhaps private schools and charter schools might be most open to this idea.

Why? What are some reasons we can connect to? Well, there's an initiative in the U.S. called the P21, Partnership for the 21st Century, which is a group of major organizations and educational thought leaders. And the skills that they talk about that are necessary for success in the 21st century, many of them, connect to project management. So, maybe a reason to support this would be that particular initiative. You can use that as a case to support pushing this idea forward. And then we come to H, the how. What are some actions that might be taken? Well, one how might be to look at well-known personalities. Get a big-name proponent to be a spokesperson or a champion for this idea. Maybe Bill Gates, Bill Clinton, or Lee Iacocca.

Now, we've looked at the sources of assistance. Those are forces that will help us. We also need to take into consideration sources of resistance. We'll run through the five Ws and the H again, but this time we'll look at sources that will get in the way, that might impede our success. So, we'll begin with "who," the first W. Who? Well, obviously teachers might have a concern with this. The schools of education and universities might take issue with this, as this will toss out their curricula. Boards of education might have an issue or concern about this, and the states, again, they might be too vested in their current system.

Now, notice I included this for a specific reason. In some cases, and for different reasons, you can have the same item, the same variable, both as a source of assistance and as a source of resistance, but in this case, as we can see with states, for two different reasons. They might be a source of assistance in terms of they could see this as an opportunity to save with regard to budget, but they also might have a concern in that they're so invested in their current system—it's been built up—that there might be resistance to change.

Let's look at "what." What are actions or attitudes that might get in the way? Well, the entrenched view, perhaps, in the public, let's say, that teachers should remain as a sage in the classroom, dispensing knowledge. When? Well, it might be tough to advance this idea if you're the czar if you have a limited budget, so during tough budgetary times it might be difficult to move on this. Where? Where might it be challenging? Well, public schools have lots of demands on them, lots of responsibilities and regulations. So it may be difficult to implement this with public schools.

Why? Why, again, explores reasons. Well, people might say it's too radical. It's too crazy. It's too far out there. It seriously challenges the current system, and it's too risky. We won't know if it's going to be successful. There's no track record. How? How are actions others might take? Well, perhaps here developers of standardized tests have a real stake in the current educational assessment practices. They might argue that this move would undermine standards and rigor in education. So we've gone through an example of assistors and resistors. I hope that this gives you a sense for how this works.

Let's have you try this out. Let me take you through a very streamlined version of assistors and resistors, but now facilitate your own thinking as I walk you through this tool. Think about it in terms of your life. Begin by identifying something you wish to do in the next six months. Reflect on all your responsibilities, all your initiatives and projects. Think about one that is important to you, one that immediately comes to the forefront of your mind, something that you're committed to doing, and now let's take that through this tool, assistors and resistors. Generate some assistors and resistors in your own mind, quickly going through the five Ws and the H, as I did before. So, who? what? when? where? why? And how? Who might help you? What are some things that might help you? Are there timing issues or location issues? Are there reasons you can use to support? Are there reasons that others might resist? Think about that quickly and allow your mind to now move towards a resistor.

As you go through this framework, and especially as you think about resistors, is there one significant resistor that immediately comes to mind? Gosh, I really need to take this into consideration. This will really pose a challenge for me as I pursue this project or initiative. Focus on that resistor, and now ask yourself, what action steps can I take to address this resistor? Are there any sources of assistance that came to mind that might help you as you address the source of resistance?

This was a very quick application of assistors and resistors, and we didn't spend time diverging on lots of sources of assistance, and we didn't comb through those sources of resistance. I had you immediately go to one immediate source of resistance, but I hope in that quick demonstration you found moving through that, even in a streamlined manner, that you found it helpful, that it gave you some sense for the value of anticipating sources of assistance, and especially, anticipating sources of resistance, as I had you just do as you think about creating your plan, as you think about going forward.

It's important not to just address one source of resistance; let me be clear about that. When you converge on sources of resistance, you prioritize and you examine all of the important sources of resistance, and you generate ways to overcome—actions steps that will help to address all of the important sources of resistance.

So you use this information to then create your final action plan. Let me tell you a story, a story about Charles Kettering. At the beginning of the auto industry, it was dominated by one company and one car, the Ford Model T. That is, until General Motors drove the Model T into retirement. Well, how did that happen? Well, one reason was their Head of Research, Charles Kettering. He had a goal. His goal was to make cars consumers wanted. He believed consumers wanted cars that were efficient, comfortable, powerful, and driver-friendly. Boss Kettering, as he was called, was a prolific inventor, and—this is important to remember—he was a massive practical joker.

When he accepted the position as Head of GM's new research division, he did so on the condition that he could work on three hand-picked problems, and the first problem he tackled was the painting process. You see, at this time, when cars were being produced, as a consumer, you had one choice in terms of the color of your car; that choice was black. There were no options, and Kettering believed that consumers would love to have cars in different colors. He thought they would like to have some degree of choice. Now, here's the other problem with the painting process at that time. You see, at that time, it took 37 days to paint a car. This was a huge bottleneck in the manufacturing process. The process was based on an old paradigm. It was based on how carriages were painted—layer upon layer of paint with lots of time in between to dry.

Kettering wanted to eliminate this bottleneck, so he gathered the painting unit, and he challenged them to reduce the time. They went away; they thought about it for some time; and they came back and they said, "Boss, we've been thinking about this, and after close examination, we believe we could get the painting process down to 30 days." Kettering said, "That's not exactly what I had in mind. I was thinking more of an hour." The painting boys were completely shocked. They went away to give it some more thought, and Kettering went away as well. It's said that he was on a trip to New York City when he had an aha moment. He was walking along in New York City doing some window shopping, when he looked through the window, and a small pill box that was beautifully painted caught his eye. He went into the store and talked to the manager and asked about the production process behind that pill box, and he was told that if he wanted to find out about that process that he should go talk to the developer who lived out in New Jersey. So he went out to visit the craftsman, and the craftsman showed him the kind of paint he was using. He was using lacquer paint, and he described how the lacquer paint had some advantages, like drying quickly. "Aha," Kettering said, "drying quickly."

So he got together with DuPont, and he shared this lacquer paint, and he asked DuPont if they could find a way to thin it out enough so that it could be sprayed on. After some time, they were successful. Now Kettering had his solution. He had his breakthrough. Now, was that enough? He went to the painting unit again, and he shared the idea, and you can imagine their response. Did they warmly embrace it and celebrate Kettering? No, they said, "We've invested too much infrastructure into our current process. It would be too costly to make this change," so they absolutely resisted the idea.

Now, remember, Kettering was a practical joker, so he took the head of the painting unit out to lunch one day, and as they were having lunch, Kettering tried again to convince him of the value of his idea, and sort of idly, as they were having discussion, at one point he happened to ask the head of the painting unit, “What’s your favorite color?” and he told him his favorite color, and they carried on having their conversation. At the end of the lunch, Kettering still had not convinced this man. So, as a gentleman, he got up with him and he said that he would walk him out to his car. So he escorted the head of painting out to his car, whose jaw dropped when he saw his car. Now, remember, during that lunch Kettering had asked him his favorite color. During lunch, Kettering had a team paint the head of the painting unit’s car in his favorite color.

Well, you know the rest of the story. Shortly after that, they established a prototype line, and they tested this idea, and then it became the industry standard. You see, people resist even brilliant ideas. Imagination used to generate ideas, that’s great, but we also need to use imagination to convince others to accept our ideas. Kettering used his imagination to convince a critical stakeholder to accept his idea. Sometimes it’s not the brilliance in generating the idea that makes a difference in terms of our success, it’s the imagination we use to sell the idea that allows us to achieve success.

Here’s a deliberate tool that helps you, in a way, to kind of think like Kettering. It’s called stakeholder analysis. It’s designed to identify the key people that will support or hinder the success of any given solution, plan of action, or a desired change. The way it works is we identify and examine the positions of people or groups who have a stake in the plan. We look at how these people might affect the outcomes, and then we decide where they need to be in order to support the desired change, and then we devise a set of actions aimed at gaining support from these key players.

So here are some questions. How do you know who the key stakeholders are? Here are some questions that might help you to identify these key individuals that you need to take into consideration. Who’s affected by the plan or the proposed change? Who has an interest in the plan and its outcomes? Who can affect the plan’s adoption or implementation? Who might express discontent to what is being proposed? Who can shape or influence the opinions about the issues involved? Who has clear roles in the plan?

Once you've identified your stakeholders, we can move through this tool. So we begin by diverging on a list of key stakeholders; we can use the questions that I just read. We select the key stakeholders, and then we list them in the first column of a six-column chart. For each stakeholder, we have to then identify, where are they now? Where do we believe they are now in regard to this proposed plan? Are they strongly opposed? Are they moderately opposed? Are they neutral? Are they moderately supportive? Or are they strongly supportive? We mark the position with an X. For each stakeholder, we identify where we need them to be as well. Now we know where they are, but we now need to consider, in order to go forward, do we need to move them along? So where do we need them to be in regard to the proposed plan? And we mark this position on our worksheet with an O. We connect these two, the X and the O, where we believe they are now, and where we need them to be. We connect those two points with an arrow to represent the position X, where they are, and how far we have to move them to get to where we need them to be.

This helps us to then move to the next step in this tool, which is to list the actions required in order to gain support for the implementation of your plan, and then we include those actions later in our final plan.

Let's look at an example. Let's imagine you're in a corporation, and you've decided you want to implement this idea. You want to take a team, and you want them to operate as internal facilitators, people who will conduct creativity intervention sessions, sort of like a SWAT team. A creativity SWAT team. They're going to use creative problem solving to run interventions, to tackle business challenges, or challenges within your organization.

So, we identify our stakeholders, and we converge on our stakeholders, and let's say our stakeholders, the ones that we consider to be the most important, are the CEO, the Chief Executive Officer; the Chief Operating Officer, the COO; the Chief Financial Officer; the HR Director; the union president; mid-level managers; and supervisors. We then identify, using an

X, where they are currently relative to this idea of creating an internal team of creativity facilitators.

Let's say the CEO is someone who's familiar with this idea, and he's supportive. Let's say he's moderately supportive, or she is moderately supportive. The COO, through discussions, we know the COO is moderately opposed. The CFO is in the same place. The HR Director, a close colleague of yours, you know that he or she is really on board and strongly supportive. The union president, neutral. Mid-level managers, neutral; they're very busy. It's not something they tend to give a lot of thought to. And supervisors, your sense is that supervisors might be moderately opposed. The X represents where they are now. Now we ask ourselves, where do we need these stakeholders to be in order for this plan to be successful?

Well, we recognize that the CEO really needs to be an outspoken advocate. We really need him or her to be strongly supportive. We also recognize that, with other executives, like the COO or the CFO, that if we don't get them on board, the idea is not likely to be successful, so we need to move those two also forward from moderately opposed to moderately supportive.

The HR Director is already strongly supportive. We don't want to ignore that; we want to keep that in mind. The union president, we know that we need to get him or her on board, and we need that person to be strongly supportive. With mid-level managers, we need to move them from neutral to moderately supportive. Supervisors, we need to move them from moderately opposed to neutral.

Now, we go through, looking at the distance that we need to move these stakeholders, and we generate required actions. So, the CEO, how do we move him or her along? Well, we could show the value of creative problem solving by conducting high level training for executives. The CEO, we could provide examples of operational innovation. The CFO, demonstrate return on investment, and we continue generating action steps for each of these stakeholders. When it comes to the HR director, we might need to leverage his or her support. He or she is already strongly supportive, but we don't ignore this person. How do we take advantage of that as we look at our action steps? So, once we've gone through the stakeholder analysis, we begin to look at how that can enhance our action plan, and in this way, much like assistors and resistors, our action plan is informed by going through this kind of analysis, and it should, as a result, strengthen our action plan.

This lecture focused on ways to get our proposed solutions and change accepted. I encourage you to practice stakeholder analysis. You started on an initiative to consider the things that you need to do. You might try stakeholder analysis or assistors and resistors and complete those tools on that particular project, initiative, or solution you want to take forward. See how this thinking helps to influence your plan. Will it help you to better sell your idea?

Remember, it not only takes imagination to create a novel idea, but also takes imagination to sell it. If Peter Senge is right when he said, “People don’t resist change. They resist being changed,” then it may take more imagination to sell people on the reasons to accept your proposed change. To do this, we can be guided by another quote, this time from Robert Vanderpoel, who said, “The most successful businessman is one who holds on to old ideas as long as it is good and grabs for the new just as it is better.” In such cases, you may need to act like Charles Kettering, using imagination to show others that better has arrived. See you next time.

Tools for Bringing It All Together

Lecture 19

At this point, we've explored each step of the universal creative process, from identifying goals to making plans and implementing. The goal all along the way is to improve your creative thinking by learning and practicing deliberate cognitive strategies, adding a variety of thinking tools to your toolkit. But how do you make decisions about which tools to use? The goal of this lecture is to develop higher-level thinking skills—metacognitive skills. In this lecture, you will learn about a few tools known as searching for success zones and assessing a situation.

Assessing the Situation

- Metacognition is the ability to think about your thinking. By being able to stand above the process and look at it, we can better manage our way through it. In de Bono's six hats, he has a metacognitive hat. It's called the blue hat, which stands above the other hats, and we use it to organize the other hats.

- In this universal creative process—creative problem solving—we use something called diagnostic thinking, which is gathering data and then determining where to begin in the creative problem solving process, and then how to move around in this process.

- There is a meta-step in creative problem solving—a fifth step that stands above the others. It's called assessing the situation. This is where we use diagnostic thinking to be more conscious about how we move around in this process.

- In assessing the situation, we do two things. We first determine whether creative problem solving is a fit; we don't use creative problem solving or creative thinking for every problem.

- Then, if we decide that our problem does require creative thinking, the next element within this step is diagnosing the entry point.

© Fuse/Thinkstock.

Metacognition, which is the ability to think about your thinking, is engaged in the creative problem solving process—specifically in assessing the situation.

We're committed to using creative thinking, but what's the best way to use this process? You have many tools, and it's best to choose the tool that best fits the task.

- To help us choose whether creative problem solving is a good fit for the problem at hand, we can use three criteria, the three I's: Influence, Imagination, and Interest.
    - **Influence**. Do you own the problem? Are you the chief decision maker?
    - **Imagination**. This is the crucial question in terms of creativity. Are you really looking for something new? Is the answer already out there? If it's already out there, you don't need creative thinking. Are you really looking for novelty? That helps us figure out whether you are, indeed, looking for imagination.

- **Interest**. Is it a priority? Do you want to work on this? Are you motivated?

- If you have goals that meet these three I's, an additional sorter can be immediacy: How urgent is it for you?

Searching for Success Zones

- A more advanced tool is called searching for success zones. The purpose of this tool is to identify wishes and goals with the greatest probability of success. It informs us which goal will be most likely to bring success.

- With this tool, we evaluate the options against the degree of importance. On a scale of one to nine—one being not important to nine being extremely important to you. Then, we evaluate the options against the probability of success on the same kind of scale—one to nine, where one means that success will be unlikely and nine means that success is highly likely.

- Then, we plot these results on a grid so that we have a visual map of where they fall. As we plot them, there's information on the grid that helps us determine whether it's a goal we should pursue or not. We can consider the results of this, and then we make a decision.

- The success zones graph is organized along the bottom for probability of success. We take our number, and it fits into one of three areas: low, moderate, or high—meaning low probability of success, moderate probability of success, or high probability of success. Low would be a score of one to three, moderate is four to six, and high is seven to nine.

- We do the same thing for degree of importance, which we place along the vertical axis from low to high—low, moderate, and high. This creates a three-by-three matrix.

- When we have a situation that has a low probability of success and the degree of importance is low as well, we call this kind of a scenario self-abuse. Why do it? Why pursue it? If you put energy into it, it's going to be a waste.

- If we have a scenario, or goal, that has a low probability of success and a moderate degree of importance, this is what we refer to as a difficult endeavor. It's not very likely to be successful, and it's moderately important or valuable to you. It's going to take some energy to do.

- If you have something that's low in terms of probability of success and high in terms of degree of importance, that's a creative challenge. It's something that needs to happen. It's highly important, but it's going to take a lot of imagination to make it happen.

- If the probability of success is moderate and the degree of importance is low, why bother? You might be successful, but why put energy into it? It's really not that important to you.

- If we have a moderate probability of success and a moderate degree of importance, it sort of falls right in between all of the others—into the gray area. That scenario can be pushed in any direction.

- If you have moderate probability of success and a high degree of importance, that's a stretch goal. It's moderately probable that we're going to be successful, and we're really seeing it as something that is important—that moves us out of our comfort zone into a learning zone.

- If the probability of success is really high and the degree of importance is low, you can be successful, but why pursue it? It's a distraction. It's not really that important to you. It's a waste of energy. It takes you away from other more important things that you can be doing.

- If the probability of success is high and the degree of importance is moderate, we call that low-hanging fruit. It's likely to be successful, and it's sort of valuable to you. You can easily pick that off the tree.

- In the last scenario, we have what we call promising opportunities. These are scenarios, goals, or wishes that are both high in probability of success and high in degree of importance.

- Those areas within this success zone that really require the most creative thinking are the creative challenges, the stretch goals, and the promising opportunities.

- This tool helps you set priorities so that you are focusing on what's really important. Sometimes we pursue something only to find out later that it was a waste of our time—that our time would have been better spent elsewhere. This tool helps us to overcome that.

- This tool can be used individually, and it can be used in teams as well. In fact, it's a terrific way to build consensus and commitment toward goals.

Cheat Sheet for Diagnostic Thinking

- There is a tool within assessing the situation called the cheat sheet for diagnostic thinking. The following are four different scenarios, and by looking at those scenarios, you'll be able to determine if that is the place to start in creative problem solving.
  - If the problem is unclear and you need to identify the specific barriers or obstacles that are in the way of achieving a goal, you begin in the clarify step. You start with a goal statement beginning with "Wouldn't it be great if…" or "I, or we, wish …." Then, you move through that step of the process.

  - If you have identified a specific challenge that must be addressed in order to achieve the goal, then you're ready for the ideate step. You start on this step with a challenge statement that begins with "How to …" "How might …" "In what ways might …" or "What might …."

  - If you have an idea and you need to have it transformed into a workable solution, then you can enter this process at the develop step. You start with a summary of the tentative solution: "What I see myself doing is …" or "What we see ourselves doing is …."

- If you have a proposed solution and you wish to carry it forward—you're committed to it, and you're ready to go—you don't need to explore any other options. You're in the implement step. You start with the description of the proposed solution: "I, or we, are committed to …."

- There are some common metacognition mistakes that beginning learners tend to make when they do this kind of diagnosis. They tend to see almost all situations as though they need ideas. They tend to diagnose the situation, or problem, into the ideate step. It's a problem, so we need ideas.

- Beginning learners also make assumptions that the problem as initially presented is the true problem, and they tend not to challenge what others say or how the problem presents itself to them.

- The third mistake is accepting the challenge statement that's too vague or too broad. When you have a very vague problem statement or challenge statement, you have, therefore, vague ideas—your ideas are everywhere.

- The consequence of any of these three mistakes is wasted time, often requiring the need to cycle back into the process, generally going back to clarify.

Suggested Reading

Flavell, "Metacognitive Aspects of Problem Solving."

———, "Speculations about the Nature and Development of Metacognition."

Activities

Activity 1: Success Zones

Generate a list of goals/wishes/challenges and practice using the success zones tool.

Activity 2: Metacognition

Practice metacognition at your next meeting or family conversation when a problem is being described. Ask yourself the following.

- Does this require creative thinking?
- Where would it be in the creative problem solving process?
- What tools might be applied?

Tools for Bringing It All Together

Lecture 19—Transcript

At this point, we've explored each step of the universal creative process, from the beginning, identifying goals, to making plans, and implementing. Our goal all along the way is to improve your creative thinking, and to do so by learning and practicing deliberate strategies, deliberate cognitive strategies, thinking tools, adding a variety of tools to your toolkit, but how do you make decisions about what tools to use? The goal of this lecture is to develop higher level thinking skills—metaprocess skills, if you will. We'll learn searching for success zones and assessing a situation.

Let's start by looking at the framework of our toolkit, the thinking skills that we've been exposed to in the steps that we've learned. So in this universal creative process we refer to as creative problem solving, we went from clarify, which is identifying the challenges that we have to address in order to get to our goals. We then went to the ideate step of the process, where we learned to generate many ideas, and we learned a variety of tools in this area to help us to be more effective ideators. We then went into the develop step, which is all about turning a good idea into a great solution, and then, most recently, we looked at implement, which is giving our solutions legs. It's thinking about what we need to do to successfully bring this proposed change, this solution, to the world, so that it will be embraced.

In each of these steps, we have a different way of thinking. In clarify, we consider this strategic thinking, which is the ability to sense the problem, identify the key issues, and to see the past that will move you towards your desired future. When we go into the ideate step, we're engaging in ideational thinking; it has a sense of, or a focus on, divergent thinking, especially; the ability to produce a variety of original options, images, or thoughts that address the challenges.

In the next step, we have to evaluate our ideas. The skill here is the ability to evaluate and transform a broad idea into a specific, workable solution that resolves the challenge. And then the last skill, the tools that we learned in the implement step help us to think tactically, to be creative when it comes to thinking about the tactics necessary to be successful. This ability is the ability to devise and carry out a plan that includes specific, measurable steps for attaining your desired future.

Tools and skills can be used independently, outside of this creative thinking process, in a way much like we've learned these tools. Or the tools can be woven together. They can be sequenced to help us to move along a project, if you will. Like building a fine piece of furniture, we string the tools together into a process. We begin with drafting tools, then measuring tools, then cutting tools, building tools, and finishing tools. Using this sequence, it helps us to be successful in that project.

The same is true for the creative problem-solving process. We can use the tools independently. We can pull one tool out and use it, or we can sequence the tools in an order, a procedure that follows from the beginning, identifying a goal, all the way through to the end with an action plan, and then monitoring that action plan. But what links these steps of the process? We really haven't looked at how we make the transition from one step to another, so let's look at what bridges these steps within this process.

When we begin in clarify, we're looking at our goal, identifying the data, and then moving to challenges that we recognize, we must address in order to achieve our goal. The output, the bridge from clarify, what sets you up for ideate, is a clear challenge statement. "How to…" "How might…" "In what ways might…" or "What might…" Now, in ideate, we generate lots of possibilities against that challenge. These are possible solutions.

What helps us to move from ideate to develop? How do we know when we can step through that gate? Well, it's when we have a tentative solution. The bridge from ideate to develop is a sense that we're moving towards a solution that will work. We use the invitational stem—what I see myself doing—when we leave the ideate step and we move into develop. In this way, we move into develop with a proposed solution. In develop, we evaluate it. As a result, we hope to refine it and perfect it. The outcome of the develop step is a proposed solution, something that we're really committed to. In fact, we use that language to set ourselves up for the implement. We move to the implement step when we have that statement—what I am committed to do. It's something that you have great energy for and you want to carry forward.

Through the implement step, we create our action steps and we leave implement when we have our action plan together, and then we continue to monitor. But, in a way, we never really leave creative problem solving behind, because as we're implementing, as we're taking action, sometimes things don't go the way we expect and therefore, we may need to go back into our tool kit and use a tool that helps us to resolve an emerging situation.

Now, how do we use this model? You can go in sequence, step-by-step, as I've just described it. You can move back and forth among the steps. We can combine the steps in any way in order to suit our needs. In order to do this, we need to be able to stand above the process and look at it. This is called metacognition. Metacognition is the ability to think about your thinking. By being able to stand above the process, and looking at it, we can better manage our way through it. In de Bono's six hats, he has a metacognitive hat; it's called the blue hat, which stands above the other hats, and we use it to organize the other hats.

In this universal creative process, creative problem solving, we use something called diagnostic thinking, which is gathering data and then determining where to begin in the creative problem solving process, and then how to move around in this process.

Let me give you an analogy. In this course, we've been working on the mechanics of your car, so to speak. In the car, we have the engine, and we've been improving the horsepower by giving you tools that help you to be more effective at divergent thinking, so we've made a more powerful engine. We've also worked on the braking system by giving you tools for convergent thinking. Well, that's wonderful. Now we have a beefed-up car, but how do we maximize the mechanics of our car?

Well, we need to improve the driver skills. To do that, there is a meta step in creative problem solving, a fifth step, if you will, that stands above the others; it's called assessing the situation. This is where we use diagnostic thinking to improve our driving skills, to be more conscious about how we maneuver and move around in this process.

In assessing the situation, we do two things. We first determine, is creative problem solving a fit? We don't use creative problem solving or creative thinking for every problem. So, we begin by diagnosing whether our problem deserves creative thinking or calls for creative thinking, and then, if we decide it does require creative thinking, the next element within this step assessing the situation, we have to diagnose the entry point. Yes, we're committed to use creative thinking, but what's the best way to use this process? You have lots of tools. Do you choose them randomly? No, it's best to choose the tool that best fits the task.

We'll learn and practice several meta-tools, and it's best if you participate with me. So, I encourage you to think along with me as I go through these tools, and at certain points I'll invite you to participate. In fact, let's begin by having you think about some goals or wishes. Quickly make a list, either with pen and paper, or a computer, or, like J.K. Rowling, in your head. And you can even go back to past lists if you have those handy. I'll ask you some questions if you don't have goals immediately in mind, just to jog your thinking. What have you done lately that you wish you could do better? What challenges have been on your mind lately? What would you like to do, to accomplish, within, let's say, the next six months? What would you like to accomplish within a calendar year?

Let's think in bigger terms. What are your dreams? What are your personal aspirations? What are your professional aspirations? What wishes would you like to have come true? Again, if you need time, go ahead and take the time necessary to respond to those questions, and we'll look at a way that we can take our list of goals and we can converge. We're not going to apply this now. There are three criteria, the three I's; you were introduced to these earlier. Influence, do you own the problem? Are you the chief decision maker? Imagination, this is the crucial question in terms of creativity. Are you really looking for something new? Is the answer already out there? If it's already out there, you don't need creative thinking. Are you really looking for novelty? That helps us to figure out whether you are, indeed, looking for imagination.

The third I is interest. Is it a priority? Do you want to work on this? Are you motivated? And let me add a fourth I. If you have goals that meet these three

I's, an additional sorter can be immediacy. How urgent is it for you? Now, these three Is, with the additional I of immediacy, help us to choose whether creative problem solving is a good fit for the problem or not.

Let's look now at a more advanced tool. It's called searching for success zones. Here's the purpose. We identify wishes and goals with the greatest probability of success. That's what we want to have happen as a result of using this tool, searching for success zones. It informs us as which goal will be most likely to bring me success.

Here are the steps. We evaluate the options against the degree of importance. On a 1-to-9 scale, 1 being low, not important; to 9, being highly important, extremely important to you. Then we evaluate the options against probability of success on the same kind of scale, 1 to 9, 1 being low, success will be difficult and unlikely, and 9 being high, success is highly likely. Then we plot these results on a grid so that we have a visual map of where they fall. As we plot them, there's information on the grid that helps us to determine whether it's a goal we should pursue or not. We can consider the results of this, and then we make a decision.

Now, I had asked you to participate, and I had asked you to think about some goals and some wishes. I hope that you did that. I'd like you to choose one. A goal or a wish that just immediately comes to mind, either looking at your list or it pops into your mind as you consider the question. And rate it on degree of importance and on probability. Ask yourself, how important is this goal for me? 1 to 9. What's the probability of success? Again, 1 to 9.

Now, let's take that information, and let's use that information to put it within the success zones graph. The way this graph works is it's organized along the bottom for probability of success, and we take our number, and it fits into one of three areas, either low, moderate, or high—low probability of success, moderate probability of success, or a high probability of success. Low would be a score of 1 to 3. Moderate is 4 to 6, high 7 to 9. We do the same thing for degree of importance, which we place along the vertical axis from low to high, blocked out low, moderate, and high. This creates a three by three matrix. Let me interpret the combination of these two axes.

So, when we have a situation that has a low probability of success, you have ranked it 1 to 3, and the degree of importance is low as well, we call this kind of a scenario self-abuse. Why do it? Why pursue it? If you put energy into it, it's going to be a waste. If we have a scenario, a goal—think about your goal—that has a probability of success that's low, and our degree of importance is moderate, this is what we refer to as a difficult endeavor. It's not very likely to be successful, and it's moderately important or valuable to you. It's going to take some energy to do.

If you have something that's low in terms of probability of success and high in terms of degree of importance, boy, that's a creative challenge. It's something that needs to happen. It's highly important, but it's going to take a lot of imagination to get there, to make it happen.

Let's move to the next area within the success zones. Again, be thinking about your wish, the one that you identified. Where is it in terms of probability of success? Did you rate it as a moderate degree of probability of success? Let's look at the next scenario. So if the probability of success is moderate, and the degree of importance is low, why bother? You might be successful, but why put energy into it? It's really not that important to you. The next, we call this the gray area, it sort of falls right in between all the others, where we have a moderate probability of success, and we have a moderate degree of importance. That can be pushed in any direction.

Moderate probability of success and a high degree of importance—that's a stretch goal. So it's moderately probable that we're going to be successful, and we're really seeing it as something that is important, that moves us out of our comfort zone into a learning zone, into a stretch goal area.

Let's move to probability of success is really high. The degree of importance is low. Yeah, you can be successful, but why pursue it? It's a distraction. It's not really that important to you. It's a waste of energy. It takes you away from other more important things that you can be doing. If the probability of success is high, and the degree of importance is moderate, we call that low-hanging fruit. It's likely to be successful and it's sort of valuable to you. You can easily pick that off the tree.

And then, in our last scenario, we have what we call promising opportunities. These are scenarios, these are goals, these are wishes, that are both high in probability of success and high in degree of importance. Those areas within this success zone that really require the most creative thinking are the creative challenges, the stretch goals, and the promising opportunities. Here's where we might bear the greatest fruit.

So, what's the value in this? Well, it helps you to set priorities, a priority focus on what's really important. Sometimes we pursue something only to find out later that it was a waste of our time. Our time would have been better spent elsewhere. This tool helps us to overcome that. It can be used individually, and it can be used in teams as well. In fact, it's a terrific way to build consensus and commitment towards goals. Let's say we're generating our goals for the year. We've generated our goals. We can then put them into the searching for success zones matrix, and we can see which ones are most promising to pursue, and we can see where the consensus is around that. It helps to ensure resources are invested wisely. So, through this kind of diagnosis, you determine if creative problem solving is necessary, and the kinds of problems you want to bring into creative problem solving.

So now that you've determined this, the next question is, where do I begin in creative problem solving? The process has a natural progression to it. You begin with clarify, and you have to have a challenge before you go to ideas, and you have to have the idea before you develop, and you have to have the solution before you implement. So there is a natural sequence to it. But the process can be used flexibly, and you can start anywhere. If you need the screwdriver, and it's in the bottom drawer of your toolbox, you don't have to go through every drawer before the bottom drawer, using each tool in order to get to the screwdriver. We can jump into this process at whatever point we need, going into, if you will, the tool drawer that's most appropriate for the task that we're working on, and we can move around as necessary. To do this, again, diagnostic thinking helps us.

Here's a tool that will help us to be able to do that. It's within assessing the situation. It's called the cheat sheet for diagnostic thinking. I'm going to describe to you four different scenarios, and by looking at those scenarios, a sort of an if, then graph, you'll be able to determine if that is the place to start in creative problem solving. So, when you come up against a scenario that sounds like this, if the problem is unclear, and you need to identify the specific barriers or obstacles that are in the way of achieving a goal, you begin in the clarify step. You start with a goal statement beginning with "Wouldn't it be great if...," or "I or we wish...," and then you move through that step of the process.

Let's look at another if scenario. If you have an identified a specific challenge that must be addressed in order to achieve the goal, then you're ready for the ideate step. How do you start on this step? Well, you start here with a challenge statement that begins with "How to..." "How might..." "In what ways might..." or "What might..."

In the next scenario, we're setting ourselves up for the develop step. So if you're dealing with a task that sounds like this: you have an idea and you need to have it transformed into a workable solution, then you can enter this process at the develop step. How do you start? You start with a summary of the tentative solution. "What I see myself doing is..." or "What we see ourselves doing is..."

And then the fourth if-scenario statement, if you have a proposed solution, and you wish to carry it forward, you're committed to this, you're ready to go, you don't need to explore any other options, you're in the implement step. Here we start with the description of the proposed solution. "I or we are committed to..."

So, let's try this out. I'm going to ask you to participate. I'm going to ask you to engage in diagnostic thinking, practicing this skill of metacognition, standing above the process, using these five scenarios that I just described to you, and taking situations, examples of problem situations, which I'll describe, and use the information that I just shared with you to see if you can find out if creative problem solving is appropriate and, if so, where you would begin.

This is going to sort of be multiple choice. I'm going to read five options to you. One option is inappropriate to creative problem solving. The other four scenarios I'll read to you are appropriate, and you can decide then which process step you would begin with. I'll give you a little bit of time to reflect between each one, but feel free to pause the lecture if you need more time.

So here's the first scenario, Donna and her team are responsible for professional development. They surveyed various topics and have narrowed the choices for this year's program down to two. Both options are good, but given budget and time constraints, they can only focus on one. There are advantages and disadvantages to both options. How might they decide what's best for their organization? Would you use creative problem solving on this? Could you use creative problem solving? If so, where would you begin in the process?

As I look at this scenario, my reaction to this would be, you could begin in the develop step. Donna and her team have narrowed the options down to two choices. They really don't need to explore other choices. They're committed to these two. They simply have to choose one, one that fits the organization well, that's going to work best for the organization. So perhaps a tool like POINT might be useful—Plus, Opportunities, Issues, and New Thinking.

Let's try another scenario. For unknown reasons, ACME, Inc. is experiencing some morale issues among its employees. It seems that the low morale is contributing to some unproductive behavior. The goal is clear, that is, they wish to increase morale, but they're not sure how to get started. What would you recommend? Is this appropriate for creative problem solving? And, if so, what step would you use? What drawer within the tool kit would you go into?

If I were working on this problem and I was working with ACME, I think I would recommend to them the clarify step. The issue of morale is very vague. They know that that's a goal they want to work on to improve, but where would they start? They need specific challenge statements. They need to gather data first, and then to use the data to help identify those specific challenges.

Here's the next scenario. Jim is going to teach a unit on World War II. It's the first time he has taught this particular material. His Social Studies book provided some information on this subject, but he needs to get some more details. He is especially interested in information on Neville Chamberlain's peace treaty with Adolf Hitler. What would you do? What would you recommend? Is creative problem solving appropriate? If so, where would you begin?

As I look at this scenario, my reaction is, well, gosh. I think Jim can just do the research. I'm not sure that creativity and creative thinking is necessary, so I'm not sure creative problem solving would serve him well in this particular situation.

Let's look at the next example. Pat's department has developed a new service, to be offered to others inside the organization. It's a large organization, and they want to use this new program to grab the attention of colleagues. They will be using standard internal communications systems to announce this new service, but feel strongly that an imaginative name will be necessary to make it stand out. Pat has decided to conduct a meeting during which the team will search for potential names for the new service. What would you recommend? Is creative problem solving useful for Pat? If so, where would you start?

In this case, if I were working with Pat, I would recommend holding an ideation session. The challenge is clear. They have this new service, and they recognize that, in order to get attention, they want to have an imaginative name. So we could hold a brainstorming session or use some other ideation tools for that exact purpose, of generating imaginative names.

Here's our last scenario. Jan's team has identified a new idea that they believe will be a real game-changer for their organization. They have developed the idea and tested it with some customers. The reaction has been very positive. However, they know that some key internal groups will resist the idea.

Is this appropriate for creative problem solving? How might creative problem solving be used? If I were working with Jan, my recommendation would be to go into the implement step. They have a solution; they've begun to test it; they've gotten positive reactions from customers. They think, however, there'll be some resistance to this from inside of the organization, so they could begin to look at how to sell the solution, the product, or new service, whatever it is. How they might gain buy-in in order to successfully take action. They could use a tool like stakeholder analysis, for example.

So, we've gone through five scenarios, sort of testing out our metacognitive skills. There are some common metacognition mistakes that beginning learners tend to make when they do this kind of diagnosis. Beginning learners tend to see almost all situations as though they need ideas. They tend to diagnose the situation, the problem, into the ideate step. It's a problem, so we need ideas. They also make assumptions that the problem, as initially presented, the problem as given, is the true problem, and tend not to challenge what others say or how the problem presents itself to him or her.

The third is accepting the challenge statement that's too vague, too broad. Remember, earlier I talked about this is kind of like trying to boil the ocean. When you have a very vague problem statement, a very vague challenge statement, you have, therefore, vague ideas; your ideas are everywhere. The consequence of any of these three mistakes is wasted time, often requiring the need to cycle back into the process, generally going back to clarify.

I'd like you to take more of your wishes and goals and locate them in the searching for success zones matrix. We tried it out on one. Try it out on a larger set, and then reflect on this. Make some decisions. As you look at these goals and they're laid out in your matrix, what should you do? What should you pursue? What should I not do? What should I stop doing? What's missing that I should be doing? Does it tell you what goals might still need to be generated?

Practice metacognition. Practice diagnosis. Listen to others. When you're in a meeting or in a conversation with the family and a problem is being discussed, ask yourself, does this require creative thinking? If I were to apply creative problem solving to this, where would I begin in creative problem solving? What tools might I use?

As you become more adept, it will indicate greater mastery of this higher-order thinking skill. As you improve your metacognition, you improve the skill of choosing the right tool and the right process step to use. You become a better driver of your own mind, of your own creative thinking, and this is really sharpening your saw, really arranging every tool in your toolkit.

Lifting the Emotional Lid on Creativity

Lecture 20

Creativity is more than thinking. It's also a feeling—an attitude. Much of this course has focused on cognitive skills, especially the tools that are provided to you for your toolkit. They're thinking tools; they're cognitive strategies. Early in this course, a distinction was made between skills, tools, and mindset. Lectures on process focused on tools to improve our skills. This lecture focuses on mindset. The mindset we have serves as a lid for our skills, and it limits our success in using the tools. We need the right mindset to maximize the power of creative thinking.

Emotional Quotient (EQ)

- To improve mindset for creativity, we will explore an increasingly popular topic, emotional intelligence, also referred to as emotional quotient (EQ).

- IQ focuses on an ability to process information. It's fallen short of its promise to predict success. In contrast, emotional intelligence looks at how we relate to ourselves—our inner world—and to others.

- Emotional intelligence was popularized by Daniel Goleman, and it's based on sound psychological study. Put simply, emotional intelligence is about three things: being self-aware, understanding your emotions, and then learning to facilitate and work with those emotions. In other words, it's about self-awareness, self-control, and empathy (being able to connect to others readily, to understand their emotional states).

- Some psychologists have attributed presidential creativity and success to EQ. Case studies of presidents highlight the impact of emotional intelligence on success. Empirical studies provide similar evidence.

Emotional Hijacking

- Looking at the evolution of the brain gives us hints to our emotional intelligence and how it works. The brain evolved over time to add layers to its structure and function, and it evolved in three stages. First was the autonomic brain, responsible for basic physical functions that occur naturally and automatically for us, such as breathing.

- Then came the limbic brain, which is responsible for emotions. It helps us to sense danger and to react quickly—the freeze, flight, or fight response.

- Then came, more recently, the cortex and neocortex, referred to as the rational brain. Learning is recorded here. This area of the brain is responsible for higher thought, such as creativity and problem solving.

- Emotional intelligence is about managing ourselves and our relationships in order to achieve our intentions, or goals. The interplay between our emotions and our thinking, then, translates into behavior.

- Low emotional intelligence allows our emotions—reactions in our limbic brain—to override our rational brain. We become so emotional that we no longer think. Daniel Goleman coined a term that describes when our emotions get in the way of our ability to achieve our goals, when our emotions get in the way of allowing us to be successful at solving problems or being creative. He called it emotional hijacking.

- When discussing emotional intelligence, we're not talking about getting rid of our emotions. When we talk about emotional intelligence, rather, we're trying to minimize the degree to which emotions hijack our thinking and stop us from achieving our goals, such as when we wish to create.

- Certainly, passion and love are indicators of intrinsic motivation, and this is good for creativity. It creates a commitment to what we're working on and persistence. The problem is when emotions overrun our ability to create.

- It's not about shutting down our emotions but, rather, working with them. The suffering artist cliché has a germ of truth. Fierce, lucid resistance to what hurts or disappoints us can be risky. Practice emotional jujitsu.

- Emotional hijacking occurs because our limbic brain responds much faster than our emotional brain. We have an emotional reaction before we're able to fully process it in our rational minds. In fact, the limbic brain responds 80 to 100 times faster than our rational brain.

Practice emotional jujitsu instead of resisting to whatever hurts or disappoints you.

- When threatened, the limbic system takes over; the rational brain is not consulted. This is not necessarily a bad thing; it's part of our evolution. We sense danger quickly before we can even think. Our limbic brain takes over. It reacts much faster through emotion than through thought.

- However, the downside to this is that we become susceptible to emotional hijacking, allowing quick reaction to derail us, and especially in situations where there's no real physical threat.

- This course has focused on giving you cognitive tools. Creativity involves thinking and feeling. Fear, anger, stress, and other emotions can override your emotional brain. It makes it difficult to fulfill your creative potential. Runaway emotion stops our thinking.

Improving Emotional Intelligence

- Recent brain research has shown that a good mood improves creativity. Good mood activates the anterior cingulate. When anxious, it's not activated. As a result, we limit our options. The anterior cingulate is divided into an emotional and a cognitive component. When we're in a good mood, both parts are activated, and this enhances our emotional intelligence.

- We can deliberately improve our emotional intelligence by learning some strategies. We can use metacognition, and we can become more mindful. There are two specific ways that we can use metacognition and become more mindful: We can reflect and redirect.

- Reflection improves our self-awareness. This is mindfulness. We use our rational brain to process our experience, and then we can redirect. Once we become aware of how we're responding and how we're feeling, we can choose to redirect in a purposeful direction.

- Over time, once you become successful at doing this, you can build new patterns. In fact, you can learn to shift from your panic zone quickly back into your learning zone.

- We can use the power of emotional intelligence to set our own mindset for creativity. We begin with self-awareness, becoming aware of our internal climate for creativity—setting our own mood. We begin by becoming aware of the psychological attitudes that affect our creative problem solving abilities, looking at what attitudes we can adopt and control in ourselves that enhance our creative problem solving.

Internal Climate

- Arthur VanGundy refers to our internal world as the internal climate, and he says that we should begin here first, because this is something we can control. Also, when we create a positive internal climate, it helps us to combat a negative external climate. VanGundy talks about several internal attitudes.
    - Openness to new ideas: Do you demonstrate a willingness to hold off judging ideas and judging others?
    - Curiosity: Do you constantly ask questions or express wonder about things in your environment?
    - Independence: Are you willing to express your own opinion, independent of others' views?
    - Perseverance: Do you press on even in the face of resistance?
    - Risk taking: Do you engage in situations for which there is some degree of uncertainty?
    - Discipline: Do you take structured approaches to problems? Do you have a sense of calm about you?
    - Playfulness: Do you toy with possibilities?
- To VanGundy's elements we can add an internal locus of control, which refers to a belief that success is personally determined. This is in opposition to an external locus of control, in which you believe that your fate is controlled by things outside of you—by chance and external factors.
- We can also add tolerance for ambiguity—which is an ability to deal with uncertainty and to avoid leaping to conclusions—to VanGundy's list. When facing novel situations, there's going to be more ambiguity, and in a world that's changing quickly, we will be facing more novel situations and, therefore, more ambiguous situations.

- Low tolerance for ambiguity causes people to become overwhelmed and anxious. People like this want the answer now, prematurely leaping to a solution or conclusion. This is an example of another form of emotional hijacking. For some, tolerance for ambiguity comes a bit more naturally.

Facts, Feelings, and Hunches

- We can learn a tool that will help us improve tolerance for ambiguity. The tool is called facts, feelings, and hunches. Whether tolerance for ambiguity is kind of natural for you or it's an area that you struggle with, this structured tool can help you deal with ambiguity.

- This tool involves a series of clarifying questions designed to organize an ambiguous situation.
  - Facts: What do you know about the situation? What are the facts related to this problem? Who is involved? When did it start? Where is it happening? How have you handled similar situations? Why is this a challenge?

  - Feelings: What are your emotions as they relate to the situation? In a way, we're practicing the self-awareness component of emotional intelligence. What are your feelings about that situation? What excites you? What are you afraid of? What makes you anxious? How does the situation affect your emotions?

  - Hunches: What do you believe is contributing to the situation? What does your gut tell you about the situation? What makes you curious? What questions do you have that you would like to have answered?

- This is a structured way to deal with ambiguity. We organize our thinking along these three areas—facts, feelings, and hunches. We capture our responses to these questions in three categories.

- This tool is useful for team discussion, especially where assumptions are being made. It allows for a 360-degree view of the situation. It helps to clear up assumptions. What is a fact may actually be a hunch or a feeling, and we're able to discuss it and recognize what really is a fact versus a hunch or a feeling.

Suggested Reading

Goleman, *The Brain and Emotional Intelligence.*

Lynn, *The EQ Difference.*

Activities

Activity 1: Facts, Feelings, and Hunches

- Take a difficult, ambiguous situation and apply the facts, feelings, and hunches tool.

- Take a shared situation with a trusted friend, family member, or coworker and together apply facts, feelings, and hunches.

Activity 2: Emotional Intelligence—Reflection and Redirection

- Reflect on your emotional triggers. What situations tend to hijack you? Make a list.

- Practice modifying your response to those triggers.

- Practice shifting from the panic zone to the learning zone.

Lifting the Emotional Lid on Creativity

Lecture 20—Transcript

Creativity is more than thinking. It's also a feeling. An attitude. Much of this course has focused on cognitive skills, especially the tools that we provided to you for your toolkit. They're thinking tools. They're cognitive strategies.

Let's look at an analogy for creativity, the analogy of a car. Thinking is like the systems in your car, the engine and the braking system. Our process lectures have worked on improving the mechanics of these systems. The driver controls the mechanics of the car—when to use the accelerator or when to use the brake, how to shift. In fact, shifting is very much like the metacognition skills that we've learned; moving through the gears, knowing when to be in what gear. Overall, the driver determines how effectively the mechanics are being used. Are they being maximized? So what is it about the driver that helps to maximize the use of these mechanics? Well, often it's the driver's attitude, the driver's emotional state.

Some artists might even say that creativity is about feeling far more than it is about thinking, a complex shifting mixture of feelings. Either way, we want to pay attention to our emotions, how emotions can hinder us or how they can help us. In terms of managing these, kind of like managing a car, paying attention to our attitude will help us to be more effective, both in maximizing our car, as well as maximizing our creativity.

Early on, a distinction was made between skills, tools, and mindset. Lectures on process focused on tools to improve our skills. This lecture focuses on the mindset. The mindset we have serves as a lid for our skills, and it limits our success in using the tools. We need the right mindset to maximize the power of our car. We need the right mindset to maximize the power of creative thinking. To improve mindset for creativity, we will explore an increasingly popular topic, emotional intelligence, also referred to as EQ, or Emotional Quotient.

IQ focuses on an ability to process information. It's fallen short of its promise to predict success. In contrast, emotional intelligence looks at how we relate to ourselves, our inner world, and to others. Emotional intelligence was popularized by Daniel Goleman, and it's based on sound psychological study. Put simply, emotional intelligence is about three things. It's about being self-aware, understanding your emotions, and then, once you understand your emotions, to learn to facilitate and work with those emotions. Self-control, it's referred to, and empathy. Empathy, being able to connect to others readily, to understand their emotional states.

Let's look at some popular examples. Not necessarily creative examples, but popular examples that bring to light how emotional intelligence works. Here are two sets of names. In set A, we have Washington, Lincoln, Franklin, Roosevelt, Kennedy, Reagan, and Obama. In set B, we have Wilson, Hoover, Johnson, and Nixon. You see, some psychologists have attributed presidential creativity and success to EQ—their emotional quotient.

Let's look for the evidence of EQ—self-awareness, self-control, and empathy—among Presidents with high IQ. Lincoln demonstrated self-awareness and self-control when he stated, "Nearly all men can stand adversity, but if you want to test a man's character, give him power." Despite having great power, Washington, who probably could have made himself a king, showed incredible self-control. Obama demonstrated unflappable self-control in the face of a political campaign that featured high levels of mudslinging, including questions about his citizenship. But sometimes he was criticized for being cool, having an apparent lack of empathy. Kennedy showed instant empathy with others in his famous Berlin speech that featured and ended with the statement, "Ich bin ein Berliner."

EQ allows for some Presidents to be successful by building productive relationships with others. Ronald Reagan is a good example of this. Ronald Reagan was described by those he worked with as a kind, humble, and decent person, who was devoid of meanness and pettiness. Soviet leader Mikhail Gorbachev described Reagan in this way: "While adhering to his convictions, Reagan was not dogmatic. He was looking for negotiation and compromise."

Less successful presidents are, perhaps, indicators of low EQ. Let's take Richard Nixon as an example. It is said that he was a demanding boss who often resorted to bullying. He disregarded others' feelings and their rights, especially those who he believed were against him. Lyndon Johnson had a tendency to be manipulative and interpreted criticism of his policies as personal attacks. Herbert Hoover and Woodrow Wilson possessed great intellectual gifts and self-control. However, they found it difficult to connect to others, and they were received by those in the public as being austere and cold. This might highlight an inability to project empathy.

Case analyses of these Presidents highlight the impact of emotional intelligence on success. Empirical studies provide similar evidence. Let's look at emotional intelligence more closely. Let's unpack it. Let's look at the evolution of the brain, because this gives us hints to our emotional intelligence and how it works. The brain evolved over time to add layers to its structure and its function, and it evolved in three stages. First was the autonomic brain, responsible for basic physical functions, like breathing. Things that occur naturally for us, automatically, we don't need to think about how to make that work within our body.

Then came the limbic brain, which is responsible for emotions. It helps us to sense danger and to react quickly. The freeze, flight, or fight response. Then came, more recently, the cortex and neocortex, referred to as the rational brain; learning is recorded here. This area of the brain is responsible for higher thought, like creativity and problem solving. Emotional intelligence is about managing ourselves and our relationships in order to achieve our intentions, or our goals. The interplay between our emotions and our thinking then translates into behavior.

Low emotional intelligence allows our emotions, reactions in our limbic brain, to override our rational brain. We become so emotional, that we no longer think. Daniel Goleman coined a term that describes when our emotions get in the way of our ability to achieve our goals; when our emotions get in the way of allowing us to be successful at solving problems or being creative. He called it emotional hijacking.

Now, before I go into examples of emotional hijacking, I want to be clear. When I speak of emotional intelligence, I'm not referring to getting rid of our emotions. When we talk about emotional intelligence, rather, we're trying to minimize the degree to which emotions hijack our thinking, stop us from achieving our goals, such as when we wish to create. Certainly, passion and love are indicators of intrinsic motivation, and this is good for creativity. It creates a commitment to what we're working on and a persistence.

The problem is when emotions overrun our ability to create. It's not about shutting down our emotions but, rather, working with them. The suffering-artist cliché has a germ of truth. Fierce, lucid resistance to what hurts or disappoints us can be risky. Practice emotional jiu-jitsu. Philosopher Martha Nussbaum said, "Do not despise your inner world. Read a lot of stories. Listen to a lot of music. And think about what the stories you encounter mean for your own life and the lives of those around you." So let's look at some examples of emotional hijacking, when our emotions get in the way of our ability to achieve our goals, and I'll share two examples with you. The first example is a personal example, and the second example is a creativity example.

Let's say it's Sunday evening, and you can't relax, or you wish to focus on a creative project. You're fidgety, and you're stressed, because you know every Monday morning your boss holds a meeting in which the staff are regularly criticized. That's an emotional hijack. Your goal is to enjoy the last night of the weekend or to work on a fun, creative project, but your emotions prevent you from doing that, from allowing that to happen.

Let's look at an example that's squarely on creativity and a creativity experience in an organization and a team. You're in a meeting. You share a novel idea that's immediately met with criticism. You might feel anger and engage in a fight behavior, or you might experience fear, at which point you engage in flight behavior; you withdraw your idea. Over time, regular criticism might create a freeze response, inertia, in which people are emotionally hijacked so often, it becomes a permanent state of inertia in the organization, not just for you, but for others. They live in fear. It inhibits creative thinking. This is a kind of permanent emotional hijacking that clearly puts a lid on our creativity.

So why does this happen? Our limbic brain responds much faster than our rational brain. We can hear this in language that we use. I have a gut reaction. My stomach has butterflies. I have goose bumps. It's a pain in the neck. It makes my stomach turn. Often, we use these expressions after our body has already responded to some situation. This language indicates how fast our bodies work. We have an emotional reaction before we're able to process it in our rational minds fully. In fact, the limbic brain responds 80 to 100 times faster than our rational brain. Notice how fast you pull your hand back when you touch a hot pot. The limbic system pulls you away from danger faster than your rational mind can think about it. Perhaps those with a slow limbic system were eaten, and therefore, this reaction, this fast reaction, was carried on through evolution, passed from one generation to the next. When threatened, the limbic system takes over. The rational brain is not consulted.

This is not necessarily a bad thing, it's part of our evolution. We sense danger quickly before we can even think. Our limbic brain literally takes over. It reacts much faster than our rational brain. However, there is a downside. We become susceptible to emotional hijacking, allowing quick reaction to derail us, and especially in situations where there's no real physical threat.

This course has focused on giving you cognitive tools. Creativity involves thinking and feeling. Fear, anger, stress, and other emotions can override your emotional brain. It makes it difficult to fulfill your creative potential. Runaway emotions literally stop our thinking.

Recent brain research has shown that a good mood improves creativity. Good mood activates the anterior cingulate. When anxious, it's not activated. As a result, we limit our options. The anterior cingulate is divided into an emotional and a cognitive component. When we're in a good mood, both parts are activated, and this enhances our emotional intelligence, and we can deliberately improve our emotional intelligence by learning some strategies.

How might we improve our emotional intelligence? Well, we can use metacognition, and we can become more mindful. And there are two specific ways that we can become more mindful and use metacognition. We can reflect and redirect. Reflection improves our self-awareness. This is that mindfulness. We use our rational brain to process our experience, and then we can redirect. Once we become aware of how we're responding and how we're feeling, we can choose to redirect in a purposeful direction.

Over time, once you become successful at doing this, you can build new patterns. In fact, you can learn to shift from your panic zone quickly back into your learning zone. In fact, this is how psychologists help people deal with residual effects of trauma. They help them to learn to discern danger, to stop and assess, to reflect. Is this really dangerous? Working on becoming more self-aware, self-aware of the reaction that they're having to the situation, and then modifying their reaction accordingly. Again, over time a new pattern emerges, and we become able to more quickly recognize non-dangerous situations, and then this stops emotional hijacking.

We can use the power of emotional intelligence to set our own mindset for creativity. We begin by self-awareness, becoming aware of our internal climate for creativity, setting our own mood, psychological attitudes that affect our creative problem-solving abilities, looking at what attitudes we can adopt and control in ourselves that enhance our creative problem solving. When I do training with people, they often say to me, "This creativity training is wonderful. This is great, but the reason I can't be creative—it's someone else. They're stopping me from being creative." They're referring to the external climate factors that surround them, that hinder their creativity.

In the next lecture, we'll cover the external climate factors, but for now let's stay with the internal world, the internal climate. In fact, Arthur VanGundy refers to this, specifically, as the internal climate. And he says that we should begin here first, because this is something we can control. It also helps when we create a positive internal climate. It helps us to combat a negative external climate.

So, we'll begin by examining the internal mood that we can create for ourselves—our own climate for creativity, and this comes from Arthur VanGundy's work. Think about yourself as I describe these internal attitudes. So, the first one he talks about is openness to new ideas. Do you demonstrate a willingness to hold off judging ideas and judging others? Next is curiosity. Do you constantly ask questions or express wonder about things in your environment? The next is independence. Are you willing to express your own opinion, independent of others' views? How about perseverance? This is the next attitude for internal climate that VanGundy talks about. Do you press on even in the face of resistance? Risk-taking. Do you engage in situations for which there is some degree of uncertainty? How about discipline? Do you take structured approaches to problems? Do you have a sense of calm about you? And playfulness, do you toy with possibilities?

To VanGundy, I would add a few more elements to this internal climate. I would add an internal locus of control. It's an old psychological term. It refers to a belief that success is personally determined, versus an external locus of control, in which you believe that your fate is controlled by things outside of you, by chance and external factors.

I've done some research that has taken Kirton's adaptor-innovator continuum, where people express different preferences for different styles of creativity, and we mapped their preferences for what their jobs demanded of them, the kind of creativity that was demanded by their work. Was it adaptive or innovative? And we looked at the gap in between their personal preferences, their personal comfort zone, if you will, and what their job demanded, and what we found was, where there was a misfit, where there was a gap, someone who preferred to think in adaptive ways but was required by his or her work to be innovative, we found that they reported greater levels of stress, versus those who had a match, a fit between themselves and their environment.

However, for those who had an internal locus of control, those who believed that their own destiny was in their hands, it didn't matter how large this gap was. It was superfluous, and as a result, they reported low levels of stress, even if there was a large gap between where they were and how they perceived their environment.

Next to VanGundy's internal climate, I would add tolerance for ambiguity, which is an ability to deal with uncertainty and to avoid leaping to conclusions. When facing novel situations, there's going to be more ambiguity, and in a world that's changing fast, we will be facing more novel situations, and therefore, more ambiguous situations. Low tolerance for ambiguity causes people to get overwhelmed, anxious. They want the answer now, prematurely leaping to a solution or a conclusion. This is an example of another emotional hijacking.

For some, tolerance for ambiguity comes a bit more naturally. We can learn a tool that will help us to improve this, however. The tool is called Facts, Feelings, and Hunches. So, no matter where you are, this is kind of natural for you, the tolerance for ambiguity, or it's an area that you struggle, this structured tool can assist you, can help you to deal with ambiguity. It's a series of clarifying questions designed to organize an ambiguous situation. In fact, it might be useful for you to think through this tool as I describe it to you. You might want to consider a messy, ambiguous situation that you're currently dealing with.

So, let's think about the facts relative to that situation. What do you know? What are the facts related to this problem? Who's involved? When did it start? Where is it happening? How have you handled similar situations? Why is this a challenge? From facts, we then move to feelings. What are your emotions as they relate to the situation? In a way, we're practicing the self-awareness component of emotional intelligence. What are your feelings about that situation? What excites you? What are you afraid of? What makes you anxious? How does the situation affect your emotions? Let's look at hunches now. These are hypotheses. What do you believe is contributing to the situation? What does your gut tell you about the situation? What makes you curious? What questions do you have that you would like to have answered?

This is a structured way in dealing with ambiguity. We organize our thinking along these three areas—facts, feelings, and hunches. We capture our responses to these questions in three categories. It's useful for team discussion, especially where assumptions are being made. It allows for a 360-degree view of the situation. It helps to clear up assumptions. What is a fact may actually be a hunch or a feeling, and we're able to discuss it and recognize what really is a fact versus a hunch or a feeling.

I want to encourage you to personally apply this tool—Facts, Feelings, and Hunches. Take a difficult, ambiguous situation and apply it. Once you get comfortable using it individually, take a shared situation with a trusted friend, family member, or coworker, and together apply Facts, Feelings and Hunches. Perhaps start by independently generating facts, feelings, and hunches, and then compare your analysis. Discuss the assumptions. Discuss the differences. Work towards some common understanding. This kind of work will help to improve your emotional intelligence, and remember, you can also improve your emotional intelligence through the practice of reflecting and redirecting. Recognize what your triggers are. Practice modifying your response to those triggers. Practice shifting from the panic zone to the learning zone. Recognize when you're in the panic zone.

For example, I gave an earlier example of the Sunday-night hijack. Become aware of how your emotions are undermining your goal to enjoy Sunday night, and redirect your response. As you use creative problem solving, recognize that there are different emotions that help us to be more effective in each area of the process. In clarify, it's helpful to be more tolerant of complexity. Remember the teacher who was overwhelmed by the webbing tool that I used and too many challenge statements. This creates a tunnel vision. We get locked into the problem as given, and we're not able to explore the problem as understood if we're not able to tolerate complexity.

In ideate, playfulness is helpful, playfulness, as VanGundy talked about it. When we're generating ideas, brainstorming, and the use of other ideation tools, it's beneficial to have a playful attitude. Those I see who struggle with ideation often are those who struggle with being playful. There's a difference, you see, between being childish and childlike. High creators are childlike; they use that imagination that they were gifted with as children.

When we develop, here we want to avoid premature closure, resistance to the urge to make a decision and move forward to implementation too quickly. Remember the carpenter's old adage, measure twice, cut once. Developing great solutions takes time. Premature closure—rushing a decision—can get in the way of fully developing a great outcome.

When we implement, here, because we're making a creative decision, we need to tolerate risk. When we're creative, we need to be bold. We're going to be introducing something new to the world. So we have to make sure we allow ourselves to not get shaken, or prevent ourselves from getting shaken or unnerved by the possibility of failure or setbacks.

When pursuing something new versus something that you've done many times, that zone of familiarity, the zone of comfort, the chance of failure is going to be high because it is novel. Great creators use failure as learning opportunities. As the old saying goes, "The person who makes no mistakes usually makes nothing."

Develop awareness of the emotions that help creativity, such as those that I just described, as well as those that get in the way of your creative thinking. When does fear, anxiousness, uncertainty get in the way of your creativity? Develop awareness and redirect. When you uplift your emotional intelligence, you'll find that you'll also be uplifting the lid on your creativity.

The Environment—Physical and Psychological
Lecture 21

This lecture focuses on the environment for creativity. Environment encompasses and affects all the stages and processes you've been learning about so far. When we create, there are three important elements that interact to produce a creative outcome. First, we have the person—the skills, abilities, knowledge, creative thinking, and attitudes that the person might possess. Then, we have the process that he or she goes through to be creative. In addition, we have the surrounding environment—the conditions for creativity. In this lecture, you will learn about the creative environment.

Creativity Research

- The first wave of creativity research focused on the person. The fundamental question was, can you identify creative people? The second wave focused on the process. In this case, we were asking the question, can you develop creative people? You can have creative people, and you can have a creative process—but does that guarantee that creativity will be produced?

- A third wave of research has occurred that recognized that even when you have creative people and a creative process, it's not a guarantee that creativity will occur. You can have people who have the ingredients to be creative inside of them, but if you put them into the conditions that don't support their creativity, it's not likely to emerge.

- When we talk about the environment that supports creativity, we can talk about it in terms of the physical setting that we're in, as well as the psychological setting.

- There's no one right answer for the physical environment that facilitates creativity. Why doesn't a one-size-fits-all solution for physical work space exist? We can turn to a theory about learning styles for the answer.

Learning Styles

- Learning styles, at least how education specialists Rita and Ken Dunn define it, are preferred ways and conditions you need when engaging in a difficult task—processing new and difficult information, such as we have to do when we're engaged in creativity and creative thinking. These educational leaders have a framework for their theory about learning styles. In it, they suggest that there are different components that make up one's learning style.

- One of the components they talk about is time of day. In their theory, they say that people will create at different times of the day. Some people will prefer morning; others will be best in the afternoon and some at night.

- Another dimension is called structure. The theory says that people will prefer different kinds of physical settings in which to work—some will prefer a more formal structure while others prefer an informal structure.

- The next is sound. The theory, according to the Dunns, is that people will vary in preference to sound. Some can work terrifically well when they're surrounded by sound, yet others will need absolute quiet in order to create.

- Another dimension is intake. The theory says that people will vary in terms of the need to ingest—to eat and drink—while creating.

- Another dimension is light, which refers to the level of lighting that you like to work in. Some people prefer to work under bright light. Others prefer to work in dim light.

- The theory seems to hold. There seems to not be one precise formula that fits all creators—one formula that you can follow to ensure your creativity in terms of a physical setting and a physical

© iStockphoto/Thinkstock.

When you are in a group setting, it is important to understand other members' learning styles so that you can more productively communicate with each other.

ritual. It's best to figure out your own learning style and your own creating style.

- Some research recently published looked at the physical work setting and other variables that contributed to creativity with knowledge workers, and they found that when they looked at the creativity that these knowledge workers produced, it was predicted best by their personality, the psychosocial climate, and then the physical work setting—in that order.

- Psychological climate refers to the atmosphere in the workplace, home, or classroom. It relates to the feelings, attitudes, and behaviors that you have in that atmosphere. Just like the physical climate has an impact on our attitudes, feelings, and behaviors, so does the psychological climate.

10 Predictors of Creativity

- Göran Ekvall, a Swedish researcher, was perhaps the first to study climate in relationship to creativity. He noticed that there were 10 dimensions in the psychological climate that predicted high levels of creativity.

- The first dimension is challenge, which refers to meaningfulness. To what degree are you engaged in the work in a particular location? To what degree do you find purpose in what you do? Are you stimulated by what you do?

- The next is freedom, which refers to autonomy—having some discretion. Are you able to determine how you'll carry out procedures and work? Or, in a low-freedom environment, everything is prescribed to you. You do A, B, and C without deviating, and when you're done, you go back to A and start over again.

- The next dimension is idea support, which refers to how ideas are received. When an idea is put forward, is it listened to in a generous way? Is there a sense that there's an openness to receiving ideas, or is there a concern for sharing ideas—concern for how they'll be reacted to because often they're reacted to in a negative way?

- The next dimension looks at relationships. It's called trust. In a high-trust environment, there's a sense that you can open yourself up, that you can share who you are at work rather than hiding yourself. In a low-trust environment, there's a concern for people in the situation talking behind each other's backs—gossiping and backstabbing.

- The next dimension is called dynamism, which refers to eventfulness and energy. In a high-dynamic situation, you gain energy. The day moves quickly. In a low-dynamic situation, the day moves slowly. It feels like drudgery. Rather than gaining energy, you lose energy.

- The next dimension is playfulness, which refers to good-natured joking and humor. Is it okay to be playful, or is it a highly restricted, buttoned-up environment? The advantage of playfulness is that it helps people to relax.

- The next two are debate and conflict. They're both a sort of clash, but they are two very different kinds of clashes. In a debate, it's a clash of opinions or different perspectives. We want this kind of clash, but in this kind of clash, there's still mutual respect. We can disagree. We can have very different views. We can be vehement in those different views, but we're open to being influenced. As we debate, we hopefully get to some greater level of insight through that debate.

- According to Ekvall, conflict is not good for creativity. In fact, of these 10 dimensions, conflict is the only one you want low amounts of. Ekvall describes conflict in a very particular way. He refers to it as personal tension. We're not debating the issue—it becomes more personal. We're not attacking ideas; we are attacking each other. It's an environment in which there isn't respect for one another. In such cases, people tend to withdraw. They sort of work or live or operate in fear.

- The next dimension is risk taking, which refers to how uncertainty is dealt with in this environment. In an environment where there are low levels of risk taking, people are concerned about trying something new, about making a mistake. They tried to be perfect, and as a result, they don't try new things; it's more difficult to engage in novel behavior and thinking. In an environment that supports risk taking, it's OK to experiment. It's an environment in which experimentation is demand and expected, and failure is dealt with as a learning opportunity.

- The next dimension is idea time, which refers to, simply, time to think. Remember, with creativity, we need to slow our thinking down. In an environment that's moving quickly, where there isn't time to think, we tend not to think of new ideas because we tend to go with the old, familiar ideas. In an environment that allows for idea time, people can slow down their thinking. They can think in longer-term ways. They have more time to experiment, reflect, and look for alternatives.

- Through various studies, Ekvall has validated his theory. It clearly predicts innovation—and not just in corporations, but in universities as well.

Myths about the Creative Environment

- Teresa Amabile of the Harvard Business School has also examined climate. Her dimensions are very similar to Göran Ekvall's. As a result of her research, she shattered or challenged some myths about the organizational environment for creativity.

- One of the myths that was challenged was the myth that creativity comes from creative types. Instead, she found that people throughout the organization, not just in research and development, were producing creative ideas.

- The second myth that she challenged was that money is a creativity motivator. The participants that she studied focused on finding passion in the work that they did; they hardly talked about money and reward. They felt most creative when they were making genuine progress on projects, when they were making contributions.

- Another myth is that time pressure helps creativity. She found that deadlines tend to seize people up.

- A final myth is that fear forces breakthrough. She found that people tended to not be creative when they were angry or in fear. In fact, she found that when people expressed happiness, shortly after that they tended to be more creative.

Suggested Reading

Doorley and Witthoft, *Make Space.*

Ekvall, "Organizational Climate for Creativity and Innovation."

Grant, et al., *Who Killed Creativity?*

Activities

Activity 1: Creative Environment
How can you use information on the physical and psychological environment to evaluate current situations and build more creative environments for yourself? How might you change your physical space to facilitate your creative thinking? How do you support or contribute to the creative environments of others?

Activity 2: Creative Rituals
Evaluate your learning style. How might you refine your creative ritual in light of your learning style preferences or initiate a new creative ritual to promote effective creative thinking?

The Environment—Physical and Psychological
Lecture 21—Transcript

What's the right environment for creativity? The author James Joyce liked to play a piano before starting to write. Charles Schulz, creator of the cartoon strip Peanuts, drove his children, and even his neighbor's children, to school each morning before turning to Snoopy, Charlie Brown, and the rest of the gang. He did this 9:00 to 4:00 every day, Monday through Friday. The mathematician Paul Erdos said simply, "A mathematician is a machine for turning coffee into theorems." Coffee, kids, a piano, I recently moved into a new home, and in this home I had a basement office, and the first time I went into my basement office to write, I just couldn't do it. It didn't feel right, so I moved to a space in the foyer, actually a much smaller space, but because I had natural light, that made all the difference.

Today's lecture focuses on the environment for creativity. Environment encompasses and affects all the stages and processes we've been discussing so far. When we create, there are three important elements that interact to produce a creative outcome. We have the person, the skills, abilities, knowledge, the creative thinking, attitudes, that that person might possess. We have the process that he or she goes through to be creative, and then we have the surrounding environment, the conditions for creativity.

The first wave of creativity research focused on the person. And the fundamental question was can you identify creative people? The second wave focused on process. Here, we were asking the question, can you develop creative people? So, you can have creative people, and you can have a creative process; does that guarantee creativity will be produced?

A third wave of research has occurred; a third wave that recognized even when you have creative people and a creative process that it's not a guarantee that creativity will occur. It's like throwing good seed on soil that's not very fertile. It doesn't have a lot of nutrients. The same thing is true for creativity. You can have people who have the ingredients to be creative inside of them, but if you put them into the conditions that don't support their creativity, it's not likely to emerge.

When we talk about these conditions, when we talk about the environment that supports creativity, we can talk about it in a number of ways. We can think of the physical setting that we're in, as well as the psychological setting. We're going to start with the physical setting. Let's look at a couple of examples.

Maya Angelou—we'll begin with her. Dr. Maya Angelou. She's a remarkable renaissance woman, hailed as one of the great voices of contemporary literature. She's a poet, educator, historian, best-selling author, actress, playwright, civil rights activist, producer, and director. She continues to travel the world spreading her legendary wisdom. Her creative routine begins in the morning, rising before the sun comes up, Monday through Friday—but, not on weekends. She rents a hotel room to write. She leaves home at 6:00. In the hotel room, she keeps such items as pens, pads, crossword puzzles, and a deck of cards. She uses these items to get herself into the right mood to write, which generally occurs by 7:00, and then she writes until noon.

Let's look at another writer, Ray Douglas Bradbury, who wrote fantasy, science fiction, horror, and mystery fiction. Best known for his novel *Fahrenheit 451* and for the science fiction and horror series gathered together as *The Martian Chronicles* and *The Illustrated Man*. Let's contrast him to Maya Angelou. Bradbury worked in his basement and worked seven days a week, surrounded by mementos of what seemed like clutter. He kept everything he ever cared about since childhood—memorabilia, souvenirs, photos, all there deliberately. According to Bradbury, a writer's past is very important. For him, an object, even a ticket stub, reminds him of an entire experience and has the potential to give him an idea for a story.

Clutter worked for Bradbury but not for Toucan Design, an award-winning graphic and web design company. They had a strong belief that clutter impeded their creativity. They cleared out years' worth of clutter when they refurbished their office, and they claimed that de-cluttering significantly improved their creativity. In fact, they wrote a blog about this, pronouncing the benefits of a tidy office. They concluded that it presents a better image and a welcoming setting, ensures important files are easily at hand. Usable and practical desk space is available, and less distracting, allowing for focus over longer periods of time.

There's no one right answer for the physical environment that facilitates creativity. Einstein said, "If a cluttered desk signs a cluttered mind, of what, then, is an empty desk a sign?" If no one-size-fits-all solution for physical work space exists, why is this? Well, here we can turn to a theory, a theory about learning styles. Learning styles, at least how education specialists Rita and Ken Dunn define it, are preferred ways and conditions you need when engaging in a difficult task. Processing new and difficult information, such as we have to do when we're engaged in creativity and creative thinking. These educational leaders have a framework for their theory, their theory about learning styles. In it, they suggest that there are different components that make up learning style.

Let's test their theory. Let's try it out. Let's apply it to the rituals found by high creatives. A book was released recently called *Daily Rituals: How Artists Work*. In this, the daily routines, the creative routines, of artists are described in great detail. If the Dunns are right about learning styles, their learning style components should come up in these rituals, and famous creators should show a variety of preferences within these dimensions, with no single winning formula.

Let's start to examine some of their components. One of the components they talk about is time of day. In their theory, they say that people will create at different times of the day. Some people will prefer morning; others will be best in the afternoon, some at night.

Let's start with night. Do we have examples of the night owls? Thomas Wolfe, a novelist, began writing at midnight. Writer Ann Beattie, the same. Her best hours were between midnight and 3:00 am. How about afternoon? Can we find examples of those who created best in the afternoon? F. Scott Fitzgerald worked from 5:00 in the afternoon until 3:30 in the morning. Composer Steve Reich produced 95 percent of his work between noon and midnight. How about early birds? Is there evidence for those whose creative period in the day was best in the morning? Here we can find Hemingway, who started writing at 6:00, Beethoven, who began at dawn, Margaret Mead, a cultural anthropologist who wrote 1,000 words before breakfast. And Frank Lloyd Wright, his design work occurred between 4:00 am and 7:00 am.

Let's try another dimension; they call it structure. The theory says that people will prefer different kinds of physical settings in which to work, some more formal, others less formal, informal structure. An example of formal structure, Charles Dickens. His writing desk had to be precisely arranged in order for him to work. He had to have goose quill pens, blue ink, a small vase with fresh flowers, a large paper knife, a gilt leaf with a rabbit perched on it, and two statuettes—a pair of toads dueling and a gentleman being swarmed by puppies.

How about an informal structure? Voltaire, philosopher, and Truman Capote, a writer, liked to work in bed. Capote, in fact, called himself the horizontal writer. Agatha Christie, she moved around, writing on any surface available, the dining room table, marble-topped washboards. In fact, she moved around so much it frustrated journalists who wanted to capture a picture of her working at a writing desk. You see, she didn't use a writing desk.

The next is sound. The theory, according to the Dunns, is that people will vary in preference to sound. Some can work terrifically well when they're surrounded by sound, yet others will need absolute quiet in order to create. Gustave Flaubert wrote only at night, because the noise associated with the day was too distracting for him, where Maira Kalman, an author and illustrator, gets bored in the studio and goes out to a café for the buzz of conversation in order to be stimulated to create.

Let's look at another dimension, intake. The theory says that people will vary in terms of the need to ingest, to eat and drink while creating. Food as a stimulant, who did this assist? Patricia Highsmith wrote psychological thrillers, got into the right mood by sitting in bed surrounded by coffee, sugar, cigarettes, and donuts. And just for good measure, before she began writing, she would take a stiff drink. Mark Twain, on the other hand, began the day with a heavy breakfast and would not eat again until his writing was done.

Another dimension is light, the level of lighting that you like to work in. Some people prefer to work under bright light; others prefer to work in dim light. Nikola Tesla, a scientist. When he came into the office, he had his secretary draw the blinds so that he could work in darkness. In contrast,

Dickens had his writing desk positioned in front of the window so he could have natural light.

So the theory seems to hold. There seems to not be one precise formula that fits all creators, a formula that you can follow to ensure your creativity in terms of a physical setting and a physical ritual. It's best to figure out your own learning style and your own creating style. Henry Miller, as a young novelist, wrote at midnight. Later he discovered he really was a morning person, and he shifted to writing after breakfast, and he found he was much more creative.

In your guidebook, there are some questions that will help you to determine your learning style. I encourage you to do that activity. What comes through these quirky stories is a larger point about regularity. Find what you prefer, however strange that may seem to anyone else, then stick to that. Do it regularly. As novelist, Stephen King said, the cumulative purpose of doing these things the same way every day seems to be a way of saying to the mind, "you're going to be dreaming soon," and then this helps you to get ready to create.

Some research recently published looked at the physical work setting and other variables that contributed to creativity with knowledge workers, and they found that, in this order, when they looked at the creativity that these knowledge workers produced, it was predicted best by their personality, and we've talked about personality in this course; the psychosocial, that's the psychological climate; and then the physical work setting, we just talked about different physical work settings, they all significantly predicted levels of individual creativity, and in that order.

Let's now examine what we mean by psychosocial. The other two we've dealt with, personality and physical work setting. Let's look at the psychological climate for creativity. Psychological climate refers to the atmosphere in the workplace, the home or the classroom. It relates to the feelings, attitudes, and behaviors that you have in that atmosphere. You see, psychological climate is a metaphor for physical climate. You wake up in the morning, and it's an overcast day. It's chilly. It looks like it's going to rain. Just like the physical climate has an impact on our attitudes, feelings, and behaviors, so does the psychological climate. So there are some organizations, some places, where we go to create that are like that cloudy, overcast, cold day, and there are others that are more like the morning when you wake up, and it's bright and sunny, which has a positive impact on our feelings, attitudes, and behaviors.

Göran Ekvall, a Swedish researcher, was perhaps the first to study climate in relationship to creativity. He didn't start off by studying climate. Instead, he began by working for the car company Volvo. You see, he was charged with assessing the idea management systems within Volvo. These are employee suggestion systems, where employees could put ideas forward into the organization, and they could be evaluated, and the organization could select the ideas that they might implement.

So he traveled around in Volvo from one plant to another, evaluating these idea suggestion systems, and he found vast differences. In some plants, he found a very large percentage of participation, many employees participating, many ideas coming forward, many ideas being accepted and being put into implementation. But by contrast, in the same corporation, he would go into other plant environments, and he'd find that the idea suggestion systems weren't working so well. Very few employees were participating. Few ideas were coming forward, and as a consequence, few ideas were being adopted, and this made him curious. How could this be? They're working in the same physical settings; what's accounting for the difference in terms of their participation in these employee suggestion systems?

That's when he began to notice an atmospheric difference, a psychological atmosphere, and as he called it, a psychological climate. And what he found was that there were 10 dimensions in the psychological climate that predicted high levels of creativity. I'll describe each dimension. Select one of your current environments, and let's try this out. Think about these dimensions relative to your own experiences, a place where you spend time, specially an environment in which you need to apply your imagination in order to get things done. And evaluate that environment by selecting an area, as I describe these 10 dimensions, that you think particularly shines well, and an area that needs some development. So in other words, a strength and a weakness in terms of this environment relative to these 10 dimensions.

So these are the 10 dimensions. The first is challenge. Challenge refers to meaningfulness. To what degree are you engaged in the work in this location? To what degree do you find purpose in what you do? Are you stimulated by what you do?

The next is freedom. Freedom refers to autonomy, having some discretion. Are you able to determine how you'll carry out procedures and work? Or, in a low-freedom environment, everything is prescribed to you. You do A, B, and C. Don't deviate, and when you're done, go back to A and start over again.

The next dimension is idea support. Idea support refers to how are ideas received? When an idea is put forward, is it listened to in a generous way? Is there a sense that there's an openness to receiving ideas, or is there a concern for sharing ideas, concern for how they'll be reacted to, because often they're reacted to in a negative way?

The next dimension looks at relationships. It's called trust. In a high trust environment, there's a sense that you can open yourself up, that you can share who you are at work, rather than hiding yourself. In a low trust environment, there's a concern for people in the situation talking behind each other's back, gossip occurring, backstabbing.

The next dimension is called dynamism. Dynamism refers to eventfulness and energy. In a highly dynamic situation, you gain energy. The day moves quickly. In a low dynamic situation, the day moves slowly; it feels like drudgery. Rather than gaining energy, you lose energy.

So we've gone through five. Again, let me remind you to think about these in terms of a particular place in your own world, a particular situation. The next one is playfulness. Playfulness refers to good-natured joking and humor. Is it okay to be playful, or is a highly restricted, buttoned-up environment? The advantage of playfulness is it helps people to relax.

Now, the next two I'll describe together. I'll sort of contrast them against each other. The next two are debate and conflict. They're both a sort of clash, but two very different kinds of clashes. In a debate, it's a clash of opinion.

It's a clash of different perspectives. Now, this, we want; we want this kind of clash, but in this kind of clash there's still mutual respect. We can disagree. We can have very different views. We can be vehement in those different views, but we're open to being influenced. As we debate, what hopefully happens is that we get to some greater level of insight through that debate. Now, that's very positive.

But sometimes you hear people say, "Well, conflict is good for creativity." Well, not according to Ekvall. In fact, of these 10 dimensions, conflict is the only one you want low amounts of. Now, he describes conflict in a very particular way. He refers to it as personal tension. So we're not debating the issue; it becomes more personal. We're not attacking ideas. We are attacking each other. It's an environment in which there isn't respect for one another. And, in such cases, people tend to withdraw. They sort of work, or live, or operate in fear.

The next dimension is risk taking. Risk taking refers to how is uncertainty dealt with in this environment? In an environment where there are low levels of risk taking, people are concerned about trying something new. They're concerned about making a mistake. They tried to be perfect and as a result, they don't try new things. It's more difficult to engage in novel behavior and thinking. In an environment that supports risk taking, it's okay to experiment. It's an environment in which experimentation is demanded, expected, and failure is dealt with as a learning opportunity.

The next dimension is idea time. Idea time refers to, simply, time to think. Remember, with creativity, we need to slow our thinking down. An environment that's moving quickly, fast-paced, where there isn't time to think, we tend not to think of new ideas, because we tend to go with the old, familiar ideas. Who has the energy to entertain anything new and different? In an environment that allows for idea time, people can slow their thinking down. They can think in longer-term ways. They have more time to experiment. They have more time to reflect. They have more time to look for alternatives.

So, I've gone through these 10 dimensions, and I've asked you to think about a strength in an environment that you're currently in and an area of weakness, an area that you wish could be developed. Let's focus on the area that could be improved, because that's likely to have a positive impact. If you could improve that area, what would you do? Which one of these dimensions is most sorely missing in that environment that you're in, the environment that you thought of? What actions would you take to improve it?

When I work with organizations and I share these dimensions, I do a similar exercise, and almost uniformly, when I ask for areas that they wish they could develop, one comes up almost every time, and that's idea time. It seems to be an issue that's fairly widespread in organizations. The people feel like there's a rush, deadlines to meet, that they have to move quickly, that there's short-term thinking.

Some organizations get this right. In fact, some organizations have creativity practices that build in time for thinking. In the R & D area in 3M, workers in research and development can spend up to 15 percent of their time working on projects of their own choosing. There's a similar practice in Gore and in Google.

Through various studies, Ekvall has validated his theory. It clearly predicts innovation, and not just in corporations, but in universities. There's one interesting study that he conducted that I want to share with you. It's a study where he began by comparing the innovation output of a number of organizations, and he was able to categorize these organizations based on their climate dimensions. He has a measure he uses to quantitatively measure these 10 dimensions. And based on their results, he was able to show that those who have the poorest dimensions, the lowest scores, also came out lowest on his innovation scales, and those who have the best, highest dimensions, quantitatively turned out to be the most innovative.

Now, that's interesting, but the story gets even more interesting. He wanted this to be a longitudinal study. About five years later, he returned to these organizations to administer his measure again, but there was a problem. Three of the four organizations that had the poorest dimensions, the poorest scores on these climate dimensions, had gone bankrupt. They were out of business.

Let's look at a positive example. W. L. Gore and Associates provides us a good example of an organization that has a climate for creativity, an organization that has adopted strategies to build a climate that promotes creative thinking. This company is regularly in the top 100 companies for best places to work, in the U.S. and in other countries where it operates.

They're the makers of Gore-Tex and a wide range of other innovative products, and I think they're a good exemplar of Ekvall's dimensions. They have company rules that they operate by. I'll share some of these rules with you, and I'll connect them to these dimensions.

Here's their first rule. There's power in small teams. This allows for the minimum amount of rules, and it keeps things flexible and personal. I think this is a good example of freedom and trust. Their second rule is ranks, titles, and bosses are not part of Gore's vocabulary or system. Anyone can communicate with anyone else. I think this creates an atmosphere in which debate might be encouraged. Rule number three, long-term thinking is okay. This sounds like this rule is squarely designed to encourage idea time and reflection.

Lead by leading is their next rule. Ten percent of your time at work can be spent on your own projects, projects of your own choosing, and you can launch that project if you can convince others to join in with you. This sounds like it's a combination of idea time and idea support. And the last one I'll share with you is, celebrate failure. They do this, literally. When a project fails, they celebrate with beer and champagne. They throw a party, almost as if it were like a success. In fact, they treat it much in the same way. They want to learn from these failures. I think this rule, celebrate failure, highlights both risk taking and idea support.

Teresa Amabile of the Harvard Business School, has also examined climate. Her dimensions are very similar to Göran Ekvall's. We're going to focus on a recent study of hers, though, that looked at an interesting way of collecting data. She had 238 employees write a daily journal on their experiences at work. This generated 12,000 journal entries. She and her colleagues then analyzed these journals, and as a result of this analysis, they shattered, or challenged, some myths about the organizational environment for creativity.

Here are some of the myths that were challenged. Creativity comes from creative types. That's not what she found. She found that people throughout the organization, not just in research and development, were producing creative ideas. The second myth that she challenged was, money is a creativity motivator. Most in her survey in these journals wrote about finding passion in the work that they did; they hardly talked about money and reward. They felt most creative when they were making genuine progress on projects, when they were making contributions. Time pressure helps creativity. She found that deadlines tend to seize people up. Fear forces breakthrough. She found that people tended to not be creative when they were angry or they were in fear. In fact, she found that when people expressed happiness, shortly after that they tended to be more creative. In fact, Amabile said herself, "One day's happiness often predicts the next day's creativity."

So we've looked at Ekvall, we've looked at Amabile's myth that she's busted. Let me close with this point. Being creative is like a crime. You have to have the motive, the means, and the opportunity. With motive, you have to have that intrinsic drive. The means, you have to have the thinking skills and the tools to be creative. And finally, you have to have the opportunity. You have to have the right environment. Are you in the right environment?

Creative Leadership—Regardless of Title

Lecture 22

In this lecture, you will explore three ideas. The first idea is how the evolving theories of leadership have begun to move in the direction of embracing creativity—merging, in some ways, with creativity. The second idea you will explore is that leadership's role is crucial in promoting creativity. The third idea that you will examine is creativity specifically as a leadership skill, as a leadership competence. Keep in mind that contemporary theories of leadership do not limit leadership to position or power. It's not about the title that you have; it's about what you do.

Transformational Leadership

- Transformational leadership refers to leaders who are able to draw the fullest potential out of others. They transform others that they interact with and work with.

- In transformational leadership theories, there are four factors that are often talked about. Many of these factors tie into creativity. Idealized influence is one of those factors—that's where the transformational leader presents a strong role model for others.

© Image Source/Thinkstock.

Transformational leaders inspire and motivate those they work with.

- The next factor is inspirational motivation, in which the leader inspires a shared vision and gets people to come together and fuse their energy as they advance on some vision.

- The next factor is called intellectual stimulation. When leadership theorists talk about intellectual stimulation, they in fact use the words *creativity*, *innovation*, *creative thinking*, and *problem solving*.

- Intellectual stimulation is about leaders who stimulate their followers to be creative and innovative. It's recognizing that as a leader in a complex world, you can't have all the answers—that you need to draw ideas out of others in order for a team or organization to be successful. It's also about challenging followers' beliefs and assumptions, challenging them to think in new ways.

- This kind of approach promotes followers to think in different ways and to engage in careful problem solving, which is essential in the 21st century. Intellectual stimulation also encourages followers to try approaches and to think of innovative ways to handle issues.

- The fourth factor of transformational leadership, individualized consideration, is all about leadership that creates a supportive environment, an environment that allows individuals to think in creative ways.

- The three facets that predict creativity are person, process, and environment. If we think about these three facets like gears interacting with one another, leadership in a way becomes the lubricant that allows these gears to work—to not stick, to flow.

- When you look at the environment for creativity, research has shown that anywhere from 40 to 70 percent of the psychological environment—the climate for creativity—is directly linked to leadership behavior.

The Three-Legged-Stool Model

- The three-legged-stool model can be referred to as such because if you remove any one of the legs, it collapses. We might think about it as a Venn diagram.

- The three elements, the three legs in this model, are creativity, innovation, and leadership. They all intersect and reinforce one another. What combines all three of them is change. When we decide to be creative, we're intentionally going after change. It's a process that leads to change. Innovation is the successful adoption of change, and we often look to leaders to be a catalyst for change.

- Where does creativity intersect with innovation? In order for innovation to happen, we need creative ideas. In the United States, 88 percent of organizations include innovation in their mission, vision, or values, but innovation just doesn't happen because you put it in your value statement or on your Web site. We first need creativity; it's the stimulant to innovation.

- Where do innovation and leadership overlap? Leaders set the climate for change and for innovation. Leadership can put the cap on an environment for creative thinking and, ultimately, for innovation.

- Where do leadership and creativity overlap? It's being argued that creative problem solving, this universal creative thinking process, is in fact now a core leadership ability—an ability that can be developed and that needs to be deployed in a more complex world.

A Capabilities Model of Leadership

- Michael Mumford from the University of Oklahoma has an eloquent argument for why creative problem solving is now considered a core leadership skill. He has a theory of leadership that he calls a capabilities model of leadership, in which he lays out a solid case for why leaders need to be creative problem solvers.

- Mumford says that as opposed to thinking about specific behaviors, leadership can be framed in terms of capabilities, knowledge, and skills that contribute to effective leadership. If you want to understand what these capabilities are, you have to look at what leaders do.

- Leaders are required to facilitate others toward meaningful goals. As they do this, it doesn't always go smoothly. Mumford says that successful goal attainment depends on an ability to circumvent and resolve issues that impede progress. The selection and implementation of actions to bring goals to fruition involves problem solving.

- As we pursue goals, we can anticipate that we're going to run into challenges, especially goals that are more innovative. Mumford concludes that leadership performance, therefore, is directly related to an individual's capacity to use his or her creative problem solving skills to resolve complex social problems.

- He says that complex social problems are made up of three characteristics: They're ill defined, novel, and ambiguous. He suggests that in a fast-paced world, we are contending with these complex social problems more and more.

- When Mumford says that complex social problems are ill defined, he means that there's no single solution path—no right or wrong answer. The problem can be defined in any number of ways, and solutions have to be invented or discovered.

- In a fast-moving world, we face increasingly more frequent novel challenges, meaning that our past experience and knowledge is not sufficient to resolve the present situation. We simply can't go into our solution bank and find the answer to a problem that we recently solved that was just like the current problem.

- These complex social problems are also ambiguous. There are gaps in information, or there is a plethora of information of which only some of is relevant, that require clarification and diagnosis.

- Mumford has found that the available evidence indicates that creative problem solving may indeed represent an important influence on leader performance. In fact, he has longitudinal research that demonstrates that.

- That's research, but what about the real world? IBM conducted a recent survey of about 1,550 executives around the world. The study asked these CEOs to describe the world that they live in and work in now, and they said that they operate in a world that's substantially more volatile, uncertain, and complex, and they suggest that it will become even more complex.

- Today's complexity is only expected to rise, and more than half of these CEOs in the face of that doubted their ability to manage this kind of complexity. When asked, in the face of this complexity, what leadership skills are going to be most important in the future, they said that creativity is the most important leadership quality.

Developing Creative Leadership

- There is a model that describes our movement toward becoming a creative leader. At the lowest level of development, we have what is called a spectator, which is someone who is unconsciously unskilled about their creativity. They leave it up to chance. They don't know about facilitating their own creativity through deliberate practices like the ones that you've learned.

- Through awareness, recognizing the importance of creativity, we might move to the second level of development. We call this person a student of creativity. This is where we become consciously aware of our deficiencies—consciously unskilled. We know what we don't know. We're at the beginning stages of learning.

- Through deliberate practice in terms of trying out the tools, moving our creativity from chance to being able to deploy it on demand, we move to a third level of development. At the third level, we become consciously skilled. We refer to this person as a skilled practitioner, someone who is able to efficiently and effectively, with some mastery, use the tools and process of creativity.

- At the fourth level, we have the highest level of development. Not everyone reaches this level of development. We call this person the creative leader, because at this level, the individual is unconsciously skilled. Creativity is simply a way of life—a way of being. The spirit and the tools and the skills and the attitudes have become so internalized that it's second nature.

- As we move up in these levels of development, our breadth of impact becomes broader. As a skilled practitioner, using a tool and using the process on a task is terrific. It helps to resolve that task, hopefully reaching a creative breakthrough.

- But the breadth of our impact is even greater as we move up to the highest level of development, as a creative leader. When we're a creative leader, we carry this with us all the time, and we transform the context that we're in. We model creative behavior. We create climates that encourage others to be creative.

Suggested Reading

Abrashoff, *It's Your Ship*.

Northouse, *Leadership*.

Puccio, et al., *Creative Leadership*.

Activities

Activity 1: Self-Evaluation
Evaluate yourself against the four principles of divergent thinking: defer judgment, go for quantity, make connections, seek novelty. To what degree have you internalized these principles? Do some of the principles come easier for you? In what ways do you still need to grow?

Activity 2: Creative Leadership
Evaluate yourself as a creative leader and make a plan for how to improve your internalization of creativity. How might you be a better model for others of creative leadership behaviors? After completing activity 1, honestly ask yourself to what degree you readily support other people's creativity, especially creating a climate for creativity. Generate four or five action steps for what you can do to support others' creativity.

Creative Leadership—Regardless of Title

Lecture 22—Transcript

We've all had experiences with leaders, some good, some bad. I'm going to give you the power to create your own leader. Think about the kind of leader you would want to create who would be successful in the 21st century, in a world in which things are moving much faster. What attributes, skills, attitudes, would this person need to lead a team, either in a professional setting, a community, or in a personal setting, such as in a home?

I've worked a great deal in the area of leadership and do a fair amount of leadership training, and this is an exercise that I do with many groups. Here is an example of the typical kinds of responses that I hear when I give them this activity: Visionary, flexible, takes risks, trustworthy, good communicator, solicits ideas, engages others, someone who's a good listener, calm when facing chaos, someone who's humorous, supportive, manages conflict, someone who can anticipate opportunities, someone who's really good at building a team, someone who's willing to change his or her mind, someone who can see things from multiple perspectives.

Now I want you to think about another question. The question is, from this list, what attributes would you also associate with creativity? When I ask participants to do this in leadership training, they review their list, and they mark off the attributes. Now, thinking about creativity—not leadership, but thinking about creativity—that they associate with the concept of creativity. The typical connections I see are things like, well, visionary, flexible, someone who takes risks, someone who solicits ideas, humorous, someone who can anticipate opportunities, who can forecast things that will happen in the future. Someone who's able to change his or her mind to be influenced by others, and who can see things from multiple perspectives.

Now, why do I do this? Why do I do this exercise? I do this to begin to highlight a connection between creativity and leadership, and I would suggest that these two areas are beginning to merge. When I do this exercise, all groups are able to find connections. Some can find so many connections that their list of leadership attributes is completely circled. They connect everything from their list to creativity.

Today, I believe there's a very strong connection between creativity and leadership. How we view leaders and what leaders need to be successful is contextual. It changes over time. Theories of leadership, therefore, evolve over time. Leadership is sort of defined by the spirit of the time. Let's look at some theories that have stood out over time in chronological order from the field of leadership studies.

Trait theory approach, the trait theory approach to leadership is the assumption that leadership is something that's innate, something that you're born with, something that you come into the world with, and the trick is to find some universal set of traits that can be useful in identifying these people so that you can then put them into positions of leadership. In some ways, the field of creativity started the same way, examining traits that are inside of creative people so that we can identify them and select them. This goes back about a hundred years ago in leadership studies.

Now, this particular approach came up short; they didn't find a universal set of leadership traits. So the theories and the research evolved, and the next wave of research in the field of leadership studies looked at the behaviors of leadership. What did leaders do, not what they were born with, but what did they do in order to be effective? When you look at the behaviors, they found that they sorted into two categories, task-oriented behaviors, the kind of behaviors that helps to get things done, and relationship-oriented behaviors, behaviors that help to build harmony in teams and help to create good interpersonal connections with others.

This, then, went to another approach to leadership, situational theories. In terms of looking at these behaviors, situational theories suggest that understanding the behaviors is fine, but how do you deploy those behaviors? Well, you should deploy them based on the situation. So sometimes, it's best to focus on the task, to engage in task-oriented behaviors when you really need to get things done, when there's a crisis. At other times it's more beneficial to focus on relationships when you need to get things done with people.

More recently, and I'm skipping a number of theories, more recently, the talk is about transformational leadership. Transformational leadership refers to leaders who are able to get the most out of others, who are able to draw the fullest potential out of others. They transform others that they interact with and work with.

In this lecture, we explore three ideas. How the evolving theories of leadership, as I've just described them, have begun to move in the direction of embracing creativity, merging, if you will, in some ways with creativity. The second idea we explore is that leadership's role is crucial in promoting creativity. An then the third idea that we'll examine in this lecture is creativity, specifically, as a leadership skill, as a leadership competence, and I'll make a case that creative problem solving is now considered a core leadership competence. As you listen to these ideas, I hope that you'll reflect on your own leadership development.

Let me describe someone to you, athlete, humanitarian, a cancer research activist. In 1980, after having one leg amputated at age 23, he embarked on a cross-country run. In fact, across Canada, no small country. He ran the equivalent of a marathon every day. After 143 days, he had covered 3,339 miles. Unfortunately, the cancer began to spread to his lungs, and it forced him to stop. His name is Terry Fox. He began his quest with little fanfare, and he died within a year after he stopped. However, by this time, he was known around the world. Today, the annual Terry Fox run is the largest single-day fundraiser for cancer research. Initially, his goal was to raise one dollar for every Canadian—24 million dollars. To date, the Terry Fox foundation has generated over 600 million dollars in his name.

What's the point to this story? The point is leadership isn't about position. No one appointed Terry Fox to a leadership position. No one gave him a title, but he decided to make a difference. He decided to have an influence. And when you look at contemporary theories of leadership, you see that they're not limiting leadership to position or power. It's not about the title that you have, it's about what you do.

Let's examine transformational leadership. In transformational leadership theories, there are four factors that are often talked about. I think many of these factors really begin to tie into creativity. Idealized influence is one of those factors, that's where the transformational leader presents a strong role model for others, which sort of leads to the next factor, inspirational motivation. They inspire a shared vision; they get people to come together and fuse their energy as they advance on some vision.

We know the importance of vision for creativity, so we can start to see a connection to creativity through this theory around leadership. The next two factors make an even stronger connection. In fact, this next factor is called intellectual stimulation, and when leadership theorists talk about intellectual stimulation, they in fact, use the words creativity, innovation, creative thinking, and problem solving. Intellectual stimulation is about leaders who stimulate their followers to be creative and innovative. It's recognizing that, as a leader in a complex world, you can't have all the answers, that you need to draw ideas out of others in order for a team or organization to be successful. It's also about challenging followers' beliefs, challenging their assumptions, challenging them to think in new ways. This kind of approach promotes followers to think in different ways and to engage in careful problem solving, which is essential in the 21st century. Intellectual stimulation also encourages followers to try approaches and to think of innovative ways to handle issues.

The last one, individualized consideration, the fourth factor of transformational leadership, connects to a topic we've gone deeply into. Individualized consideration is all about leadership that creates a supportive environment, an environment that allows individuals to think in creative ways. If we go back to the three facets that predict creativity, those three facets are person, process, and environment. If we think about these three facets, like gears, interacting with one another, leadership, in a way, becomes the lubricant that allows these gears to work, to not stick, to flow.

Often, when I do leadership training, the individuals in that program will say, "You know, this is terrific, but you know who should be here? Our boss should be here." And they're right. When you look at the environment for creativity, what research has shown is that anywhere from 40 to 70 percent of the psychological environment, that climate for creativity, is directly linked to leadership behavior.

Let me give you an example. In my first year of teaching, I was given a GM Quality Educator internship. I worked at a Forge plant for the summer; I worked in the training and development office of this plant. And I was given a project to assess the climate, the environment in this plant. There were 20-some teams that we had complete a survey about the environment. We used Ekvall's 10 dimensions. I was tasked with the responsibility of analyzing that data and giving feedback to the teams. This is a story about two teams who had the exact same job. They were called the extruders. I looked at the results for one group just before they came into the room, and they had, honestly, pretty disastrous results. It was the first shift extruders. When they came into the room, they were quiet, hardly any energy. They plopped themselves down. I began to describe these 10 dimensions of a creative climate, challenge and freedom, risk-taking. And then, the middle of my presentation, the supervisor stopped me and said, "Wait. Challenge, freedom, playfulness, risk-taking. That has nothing to do with what these guys do. They make axles. That's all they do. What's the relevance of this?" And it suddenly occurred to me, as the supervisor talked, I now knew why their climate was so poor. Remember what I said, 40 to 70 percent of the psychological climate can be linked to leadership behavior.

Now, I was a bit confused, because the next group to come in was the third shift extruders, and if you've been around a plant environment, you know that you don't sign up for the third shift. You get banished to the third shift. And what surprised me was that, of all the teams, the third shift extruders had, by far, the most positive results on these 10 dimensions. When they came into the room, they were laughing and joking. A couple of guys were sort of wrestling with each other. When I started, I had to ask them to quiet down so I could begin the presentation. I delivered my presentation on these 10 dimensions. As I was presenting, the supervisor said, "You know, this is fascinating information. How might we use this information, guys? What else can we do? And I notice there are some areas where we have some opportunity for growth." This supervisor was demonstrating a completely different kind of leadership compared to the first shift And again, that explained to me the reasons why, perhaps, that their results were so positive.

Let me share a model with you. I call it the Three-Legged Stool Model, because if you remove any one of these legs, it collapses. We might think about it as a Venn diagram. The three elements, the three legs in this model are creativity, innovation, and leadership; they all intersect and reinforce one another. What combines all three of them is change. When we decide to be creative, we're intentionally going after change; it's a process that leads to change. Innovation is the successful adoption of change. Leadership, we often look to leaders to be a catalyst for change, to bring about change, so change unifies all three.

Let's look at how these elements interact. So, where does creativity intersect with innovation? Well, in order for innovation to happen, we need creative ideas; 88 percent of organizations in the U.S. have innovation or innovate in their mission, vision, or values, but innovation just doesn't happen because you put it in your value statement or in your website. We first need creativity; it's the stimulant to innovation.

Let's look at the overlap between innovation and leadership. As we were just discussing, leaders set the climate for change; they set the climate for innovation. Leadership can put the cap on an environment for creative thinking, and ultimately, for innovation.

Let's look at the third area of overlap, the overlap between leadership and creativity. Now here, it's being argued that creative problem solving, the process that you've learned, this universal creative-thinking process, in fact is now a core leadership trait. Well, better said, a core leadership ability, an ability that can be developed, an ability that needs to be deployed in a more complex world.

Michael Mumford, University of Oklahoma, has an eloquent argument for why creative problem solving is now considered a core leadership skill. He has a theory of leadership that he calls a capabilities model of leadership. He lays out a solid case for why leaders need to be creative problem solvers. Let's examine his line of thinking. He says that opposed to thinking about specific behaviors, leadership can be framed in terms of capabilities, knowledge, and skills that contribute to effective leadership. Now, if you want to understand what these capabilities are, you have to look at what leaders do. So Michael Mumford says, "The development of a capability model of leadership should begin by identifying the performance requirements placed on leaders."

Let's continue with his line of thinking. So what are leaders required to do? He says, "A leader's performance within an organizational context is based on the degree to which he or she can successfully facilitate others towards meaningful goals. That's what they're required to do." Now, as we're facilitating others towards goals, it doesn't always go smoothly. So Mumford says that successful goal attainment depends on an ability to circumvent and resolve issues that impede progress. The selection and implementation of actions to bring goals to fruition involves problem solving. So, as we pursue goals, we can anticipate that we're going to run into challenges, especially goals that are more innovative. Mumford concludes that leadership performance, therefore, is directly related to an individual's capacity to use his or her creative problem solving skills to resolve complex social problems.

Now, what are complex social problems? He says complex social problems are made up of three characteristics; they're ill-defined, they're novel, and they're ambiguous. And he suggests that more and more in a fast-paced world we are contending with these complex social problems. Ill-defined, meaning there's no single solution path, no right or wrong answer. The problem can be defined in any number of ways, and solutions have to be invented or discovered. They're novel. In a fast-moving world, we face increasingly more novel, more frequent novel challenges, meaning our past experience and knowledge is not sufficient to resolve the present situation. We simply can't go into our solution bank and say, gosh, I solved a problem just like this two months ago. Let me go back and use the exact same solution. And they're ambiguous; they're sort of gray, fuzzy. There are gaps in information, or there is a plethora of information of which only some of it is relevant, which requires clarification and diagnosis. Now, what he's found in his research is that the available evidence indicates that creative problem solving may, indeed, represent an important influence on leader performance. In fact, he has longitudinal research that demonstrates that.

So that's research, but what about the real world? IBM conducted a recent survey of 1,550-some executives around the world. The study asked these CEOs to describe the world that they live and work in now, and they said that they operate in a world that's substantially more volatile, uncertain, and complex, and they suggest that it will become even more complex. Today's complexity is only expected to rise, and more than half of these CEOs, in the face of that, doubted their ability to manage this kind of complexity. And when asked, well, in the face of this complexity, what leadership skills are going to be most important going forward into the future, they spoke with one voice. They said that creativity is the most important leadership quality. Now, I'm not saying all creators are leaders. They're not leaders, not necessarily. But leaders today may need to be, probably have to be creative, given the environments that they work in.

Let's look at how we develop creative leadership. Here's a model that describes our movement towards becoming a creative leader. It's a model I want you to think about in terms of your own development, especially now that we're nearing the end of this course. At the lowest level of development, we have what we call a spectator. This is someone who's unconsciously unskilled about their creativity. They leave it up to chance. They don't know about facilitating their own creativity through deliberate practices, like the ones that you've learned.

Through awareness, recognizing the importance of creativity, we might move to the second level of development. We call this person a student of creativity. This is where we become consciously aware of our deficiencies, consciously unskilled. We know what we don't know. We're at the beginning stages of learning. Through practice, deliberate practice in terms of trying out the tools, moving our creativity from chance to being able to deploy it on demand, we move to a third level of development. At the third level, we become consciously skilled. We refer to this person as a skilled practitioner, someone who's able to efficiently and effectively, with some mastery, use the tools, use the process of creativity.

And at the fourth level, we have the highest level of development. Not everyone reaches this level of development. We call this person the creative leader, because at this level, the individual is unconsciously skilled. Creativity is simply a way of life. It's a way of being. The spirit, and the tools, and the skills, and the attitudes have become so internalized, it's second nature.

Many years ago, when my children were young, I was having dinner with the boys, and my oldest son announced to me, in the middle of dinner—

his name is Gabriel—he said, "Dad, you know, you're not like other dads." "Well, that's curious. What do you mean, Gabe, I'm not like other dads?" And he said "Well, what you just did just now. You just asked me a question. You do that a lot." I said, "Well, in what other ways am I not like other dads?" And he said, "Well, you know when I'm fighting with Anthony, you say things like, 'Well, how else might you solve this problem?'" And it suddenly dawned on me, especially when he used that invitational stem, that my training in creativity had bled into my parenting skills, my role as a parent, really unbeknownst to me until he reflected that back to me. That's what it looks like at this level of development, the creative leader. These things become automatic. It's a way of living.

As we move up in these levels of development, our breadth of impact gets broader. As a skilled practitioner, using a tool and using the process on a task is terrific. That's great. It helps to resolve that task, hopefully get to a creative breakthrough. But the breadth of our impact is even greater as we move up to the highest level of development, as a creative leader. Because when we're a creative leader, we carry this with us all the time, and we transform the context that we're in. We model creative behavior. We create climates that encourage others to be creative. This is the difference between doing and being.

I'll give you an example. We have mentors in our lives who help us to grow and develop. We learn from mentors, and we can also learn from people we might struggle with, people who we might consider tormentors. When I was pursuing my Ph.D., I worked in a consultancy to help support my graduate studies, and I worked with someone who was established in the field of creativity, was a really good, skilled practitioner, who was excellent at delivering creativity training and was very effective at facilitating others.

He could do creativity, but he had a difficult time being creative. I remember after we had finished a training event and we sat down to debrief the training event, and he turned to his team and he said, "Right, okay, well, we're done now. Let's think about the participants. Who was your least favorite participant?" I was shocked. Didn't we just teach deferring judgment and affirmative judgment? Now, this kind of behavior spilled over into his leadership behavior.

So, this is what I mean between doing and being. It's one thing to do creativity, but it's a completely different matter to make it part of your own being. Evaluate yourself. Think about yourself as a creative leader. Where are you? Some people naturally, by nature, sort of slot in higher along this plan, this model for leadership development. Where are you in terms of internalizing these skills?

Let's think about an area that we've focused a lot of time talking about, divergent thinking; the ability to defer judgment; the ability to strive for quantity; the ability to make connections, to look at random things and see a new insight or have a new idea. Seeking novelty, do you live those principles? Are you starting to make them a part of your natural behavior? Ask yourself, to what degree do I really support other people's creativity? To what degree do I create a climate for creativity for others? Think about what you can do to advance your own development. Generate four or five action steps of what you can do to support others' creativity.

Let's look at how we might take this forward. I'm sure the skills that you've learned in this course not only make you personally more creative, but they can also help to make you a better leader, and thus a better contributor to creative solutions by others as well. And if you're not sure you're a creative leader, let me tell you a story by Joel Barker.

The story goes like this. A man is walking along a beach, an older man, and he looks off into the distance, and he sees a figure running back and forth on the beach, and he's kind of confused. He's curious. This person is out there on his own. It almost looks like he's dancing. As he gets closer, he sees that this is a young man, and he's running between the shoreline and starfish that are spread all over the beach, and he's picking up one starfish at a time, and he's running to the edge, and he's throwing them into the water. The older man looks at this young man and thought, what a crazy act. There's no way he can help all these starfish. So he goes up to the young man, and he points out to him that this is ridiculous. There's no way you can help all of these starfish. "What are you doing?" he says to him. The young man doesn't respond; he turns his back to the older man. He walks over, picks up a starfish, jogs down to the shoreline, and he tosses the starfish into the water. He turns, and he walks back to the older man, and he says “I may not be able to help all of them, but I just helped that one.”

So if you’re ever in doubt about your leadership, think about that story. It’s about what you do, not the title you hold. And if you use your creativity, if you internalize it, you’ll find that you’ll pass it forward to others, that you’ll be in a better position to enable others to be more creative. See you next time.

Overcoming Blocks and Barriers
Lecture 23

Creativity is the ability to modify self-imposed constraints. In this lecture, you will explore the factors that get in the way of creativity, beginning with those that are internal and moving to the external. Tools for deliberate creativity move creativity beyond chance to creativity on demand. There are many deliberate tools that will likely be useful for you in the future to overcome potential barriers and blocks. In this lecture, you will learn some strategies for overcoming blocks. Information from neuroscience, the study of how the brain works, gives us insights into how these strategies help us overcome these blocks.

Internal Blocks

- Internal blocks happen in our minds. We're going to look at three particular blocks to creative thinking. One is perceptual. This is rigidity in terms of how we see things. The next is habitual blocks, which are fixed patterns that we might get into. The third block is mental blocks. This is when the idea is elusive to us. Our creativity just doesn't seem to come.

- Perceptual blocks are getting locked into viewing things in a familiar way, making it difficult to see something in a new or different way.

- There are three consequences to this block. One is jumping to premature solutions, not seeing other possibilities. The next is limited flexibility in seeing alternative solutions, which is also known as functional fixity—seeing something as if it could only be used for one purpose and not seeing other potential in terms of how it might be used.

- When we get caught in a perceptual block, we fail to get an accurate picture of our environment. We might miss opportunities. The schoolteacher or parent who has a restricted view of a child might

© iStockphoto/Thinkstock.

In addition to external blocks to creativity, there are many internal blocks that prevent people from thinking creatively.

miss his or her talents. A salesperson might successfully sell a product to someone but might not recognize other needs that could have led to more sales.

- Great creators use simple habits, even very strange habits, to get themselves going. But a habitual way of thinking can interfere with our creativity.

- As a consequence of this block, getting into habitual ways of thinking, we may not change. We go down the same pattern again and again, and when conditions in our environment change, we run the risk of becoming extinct. We see this happen with organizations.

- The next block, the mental block, is that moment when the idea, or aha moment, simply just doesn't come. Think of the classic writer's block, where you struggle to find the solution. You can't break through. The idea that you want so desperately just isn't coming. The consequence of this block is frustration, emotional hijacking, derailing yourself even further from your goal of creating. We lose confidence as another consequence of this kind of mental block.

Defer Judgment, Defocus, Distance

- Neuroscience shows us that we can engage in activities that alter our brain function. This improves the probability of coming up with a breakthrough. The strategies aren't new. In fact, humans have experimented with and developed these over centuries, but neuroscience now gives us some sense for why they work.

- The successful strategies follow the three D's: defer judgment, defocus, and distance. We can use these three strategies to help combat internal blocks.

- When we defer our judgment, we're opening up our minds. People who are good divergent thinkers are turning down their self-monitoring brain, the prefrontal cortex, which serves as a gatekeeper between our rational and irrational thinking. Therefore, by deferring judgment, we open up new thoughts, new ideas, and new possibilities.

- The next strategy is defocus. When we slow our brain down, we allow the mind to wander. Your thinking occurs along different neural networks. This allows for new pathways to be explored and new combinations of ideas.

- As a neural strategy, distancing involves stepping away, shifting from vertical to lateral thinking, forcing connections, deliberately introducing a new stimulus into our thinking. That stimulus can then act as a springboard.

- There are five specific strategies that you can employ that are based on the three D's. The first is to vary your routine. Research shows that even slight changes from what you typically do can improve divergent thinking by 10 to 15 percent. When we vary our routine, it creates new connections for us. But you do need to be cautious: Varying your routine during work can also be distracting.

- The next strategy is to take an incubation break, which is when you go away from the problem. Where are you, and what are you doing, when you get your best ideas? Familiar responses include when running, when shaving, just before falling asleep, and while driving. When you're working hard on trying to get to that breakthrough, and then you move away from the problem, it's during this time of incubation that the idea presents itself.

- Research shows that the best kind of incubation break to take is to take a break that involves a nondemanding task. The kinds of incubation time that work best seem to be times when our body is occupied but our mind is able to wander. In this way, our prefrontal cortex is less active. Our minds are wandering and finding new neural pathways, and in this way, we create new connections.

- The third strategy for overcoming internal blocks is forced connections. You've learned some tools that help you make forced connections—for example, visually identifying relationships, where we look at photographs to stimulate our thinking, and random word entry, where we choose a word randomly and force it into our thinking.

- These kinds of tools shake up our thinking; they require our minds to take a new route. You can use deliberate distancing tools such as this that shift your focus, and you can use springboards such as objects and photographs. This allows your mind to travel along new neural pathways, and it reinforces deferral of judgment.

- The fourth strategy for overcoming internal blocks is called in-and-out note taking. Have you ever noticed that when you're in a meeting, your mind wanders? You might start to think about something that you have to do or something that you forgot to do. It is natural for our minds to wander.

- With in-and-out note taking, we take advantage of what our minds naturally do. When you're in a meeting, draw a line down the center of your piece of paper that you're taking notes on, or on your computer, create a Word document that has two columns in it.

- The left column should be labeled "in thoughts," which are the notes that you take that are directly related to the content—the things that you want to remember. The right column should be labeled "out thoughts," which is where you capture the connections you're making—those random thoughts that get spurred, perhaps, by what's being said in the meeting.

- One of the biggest benefits of in-and-out note taking is it helps us tune in to what's happening in our minds, this natural mind wandering that happens, and it helps us keep track of those new ideas that present themselves to us. It's a way of keeping track of your creativity.

- The fifth solution for overcoming internal blocks can be referred to as the Hemingway system. Hemingway would work through his writer's blocks, and he would only stop when he knew where he would start when he began next to write. He never walked away when he had a writing block. Instead, he would push through it, and when he got to a point where he was picking up momentum again, when he knew where he would start next, that's when he would stop.

External Killers of Creativity

- Teresa Amabile has looked at more external killers to creativity. She has more than a decade of research that highlights a range of creativity obstacles. The following are a few examples of her creativity blocks, or killers. They can be referred to as being external because they are situational; however, they then influence us internally, especially in that they undermine our intrinsic motivation.

- First, expected evaluation is when you know that your ideas or products will be judged by others. The creator then becomes preoccupied by future evaluation. Rather than doing his or her most creative work, the focus is on pleasing others. This moves the focus from doing the task for pure pleasure to doing it for external reasons.

- Next, she talks about competition, which is not a good thing when it comes to creative work. When we compete, we start to focus on others versus the work that we're doing. It makes us do things quickly; thus, we are less likely to pursue other options and explore. It focuses us on winning, and as a result, we are less likely to try something original when the outcome is unknown. If we're concerned with winning, we know that trying something new is risky—that there's a chance of failure while we're less likely to try the original idea.

- B. F. Skinner and other behaviorists showed how rewards reinforce behavior, but do rewards promote creative behavior? Amabile has demonstrated that external rewards and the promise of a reward undermine creative thinking. A reward moves our focus to something that is external to the creator. Time and time again, great creators say that they create out of their own interest and pleasure.

- Expected evaluation, competition, and rewards kill creativity. They erode our intrinsic motivation. Extrinsic motivation is fine for many tasks, but not for creativity. It is recommended that you avoid or downplay these situational factors and try not to impose them on others.

Suggested Reading

Adams, *Conceptual Blockbusting.*

Currey, *Daily Rituals*.

Activities

Activity 1: In-and-Out Note Taking

Over the course of a week, while you attend meetings or participate in presentations, practice in-and-out note taking. Afterward, look over your notes to see what you generated. In particular, when looking at your "out" notes, do you see new ideas, new insights, and new possibilities?

Activity 2: Overcoming Blocks

Pick another one of the four strategies for overcoming blocks: vary your routine, incubation break, forced connection, Hemingway system. Make this strategy a regular practice, just like the great creators.

Overcoming Blocks and Barriers

Lecture 23—Transcript

Creativity is the ability to modify self-imposed constraints. In this lecture, we will explore the factors that get in the way of our creativity, beginning with those that are internal and moving to the external. Let's look at a classic example of self-imposed constraints. It's called The Nine Dot Problem. So we have nine dots, three rows of three dots in each row. The challenge is to connect all nine dots with four straight lines, four continuous lines. Once you begin writing your answer, you're not to pick your pen up and move it; It's four continuous lines. Now, if this isn't familiar to you, I suggest that you try it, and then, when you're ready, come back.

Let's look at the answer to the nine-dot problem. In order to solve this problem, we have to move outside of a perceptual block we create for ourselves. So, we start in the top right corner, and we draw a line across through the first three dots, extending outside of the box that we often create for ourselves, this imaginary box. Then we create a diagonal line, again, extending outside of the box. Then the fourth line goes straight up, meeting the dot where we originally started, and then another diagonal line to the last dot.

That's the four-line solution, and that's the standard solution, and it's very familiar to many of us. But there are other solutions the nine-dot problem. In fact, there's a three-line solution. Think about that. How can you connect these nine dots with three straight lines? If you want to pause and try it out for yourself, go ahead. Here's the answer to the three-line solution. You have to imagine that the dots are circles, and that the lines can pass through these circles at different points. Again, we start from outside of the nine dots. We draw a line that touches the top portion of the first circle, passes through the middle of the next circle, and then the bottom of the third circle, continuing on, and then eventually coming back and following the same pattern for the next three dots, touching the top, the middle, and the bottom of those circles, and then returning once more, passing through the three dots, the three circles, in the same way—touching the top, passing through the middle, and then the bottom of the third circle.

Now, there is even a one-line solution. How might you connect all nine dots with one line? Think about that. What self-imposed constraint might you be placing on yourself? Well, the answer to the riddle with one line is to think about the width of the line. We can connect all nine dots with one very wide line.

As we do this nine-dots problem, it begins to reveal to us self-imposed constraints. In order to solve the problem with the four lines, we have to be able to go outside of the box. With three lines, we have to think about the dots more as circles, in passing through the center, and with the one-line solution, we have to challenge the self-imposed constraint of forgetting about the thickness of the line. We tend to think about lines as narrow.

Tools for deliberate creativity move creativity beyond chance to creativity on demand. This will likely be useful for you in the future to overcome blocks, to be sure. There are many deliberate tools that you've learned already that will help to overcome potential barriers and blocks in the future.

In this lecture, we look at other strategies for overcoming blocks. Information from neuroscience, how the brain works, gives us insights into how these strategies help to overcome these blocks. Internal blocks happen in our minds. We're going to start with these blocks. We're going to look at three particular blocks to creative thinking. One is perceptual; this is rigidity in terms of how we see things. The next is habitual blocks; these are fixed patterns that we might get into. And then the third block we'll look at is mental blocks; that's when the idea is elusive to us; our creativity just doesn't seem to come; the wellspring has dried up. Then we'll present strategies for overcoming each of these blocks.

Let's look at perceptual blocks. Perceptual blocks are getting locked into viewing things in a familiar way. The nine-dot example is perfect in terms of illustrating this, making it difficult to see something in a new or different way. In that example, we get locked into the shape of the box created by the nine dots.

There are three consequences to this block. One is jumping to premature solutions, not seeing other possibilities. The next is limited flexibility in seeing alternative solutions, which is also known as functional fixity, seeing something as if it could only be used for one purpose, and not seeing other potential in terms of how that might be used.

Here's a classic example; it's called the Dunker candle stick problem. Imagine that you're presented with this material: a box of thumb tacks, a box of matches, and a candlestick. In this case, a small candle. The task is to use these objects to attach the candle to a cork wall, a cork bulletin board, to attach it to the wall in such a way that when you light the candle, it doesn't drip wax onto the floor. Think about that. How would you do that? You have thumb tacks in a box. You have a box of match sticks. You have one candle. Now, the solution pushes on an ability to not get caught in functional fixity, to shift your perspective. You see, in order to solve this problem, you have to look at the box that contains the thumb tacks, not just as a container, but you have to be able to see it as something else, that it can be used for another purpose. You see, it becomes the platform, the platform upon which you set the candle, and then you use the thumb tacks to attach it to the wall. When most people try to solve this problem, they see the container. They see the box only as something to hold thumb tacks; they don't see another purpose, another potential, another possibility.

Perceptual blocks, when we get caught in a perceptual block, we fail to get an accurate picture of our environment. We may miss opportunities; the school teacher or parent who has restricted view of a child and misses his or her talents; a salesperson who successfully sells a product to someone but doesn't recognize other needs, which could have led to more sales.

Let's move to the next example of the kinds of blocks we might run into. Great creators use simple habits, even very strange habits, to get themselves going. But an habitual habit, a habitual way of thinking, can interfere with our creativity. You may know the old saying in terms of a definition of insanity is doing things the same way and expecting different results.

As a consequence of this block, getting into habitual ways of thinking, well, we may not change. We go down the same pattern again and again, and when conditions in our environment change, we run the risk of becoming extinct. We see this with organizations. Kodak, for example, having created digital photography, but failing to see the potential in that; they were wedded to old film photography. When you become wedded to a routine, you reject new opportunities, like Kodak did, or you simply don't see the opportunities.

Here's an example. I'm going to bring up a series of numbers in a column, and I'd like you to add these numbers as you go through this exercise. For those of you listening, I'll give a verbal description afterwards. So, again, here's the exercise. I'm going to bring up a number, and then I'll slowly bring up a series of numbers. As each number appears, you're to think in your mind of the total, the sum. So, the first number is 1,000. I'll bring up a number of numbers now, a series of numbers, and you add them in your mind, thinking of the total. So the total would be, and the total, total, total, total, the total, and the final total.

Now, what happened here? What happened here, if you're like most people, when I bring these numbers up, you come up with an answer of 5,000. But, the real solution is 4,100. Let me explain this. Let's look at what happened here. I presented a series of numbers in an order that creates a pattern. The order is 1,000 is presented first, then 40, then another 1,000, then 30, then 1,000, then 20, then 1,000, then 10. Because of this order, your mind is focused on two-digit places, because these are the numbers that are changing—thousandths and tenths. The pattern of the sums, after the first number 1,000, is 1,040, 2,040, 2,070, 3,070, 3,090, and then 4,090. Now, here is where the pattern changes. With the number 10, when we add that in, we have a new piece of information. We have the hundredths place. Our mind hasn't dealt with that piece of information yet. We've only worked with tens and thousands. We've gotten into a pattern in very short order. So what happens? Well, if you're like most people, 99 percent of us ignore that. They ignore that new piece of information—the hundredths place—and they round up to 1,000, to 5,000, specifically.

Let's look at the next block, moving away from patterns, and to that moment when the aha, the idea, simply just doesn't come. Think of the classic writer's block, where you struggle to find the solution. You can't break through. The idea that you want so desperately just isn't coming. The consequence of this block is frustration, emotional hijack, derailing yourself even further from your goal of creating. The wellspring of creativity dries up, and we lose confidence as another consequence of this kind of mental block.

Neuroscience shows us that we can literally engage in activities that alter our brain function. This improves the probability of coming up with a breakthrough. The strategies aren't new. In fact, humans have experimented and developed these over centuries, but neuroscience now gives us some sense for why they work. The successful strategies I'll share with you follow these three words, or these three Ds, if you will: defer judgment, defocus, and distance. We can use these three strategies to help combat the blocks that I just described.

Let's look at how neuroscience helps us to understand how defer judgment, defocus, and distance work. So, defer, when we defer our judgment, we're opening up our minds. When we improvise, for example, we find that individuals who are good at improvising are turning down their self-monitoring brain. People who are good divergent thinkers are turning down their self-monitoring brain, the prefrontal cortex. You see, that serves as a gatekeeper, a bouncer at the door that stands between our rational and irrational thinking. So by deferring judgment, we open up new thoughts and new ideas and new possibilities.

The next is defocus. When you slow your brain down, we allow it to mind-wander. Your thinking, literally, occurs along different neural networks, which allows for new pathways to be explored and new combinations of ideas. Let's look at distancing as a neural strategy, if you will. Distancing is stepping away, shifting from vertical to lateral thinking, forcing connections, deliberately introducing a new stimulus into our thinking, and that stimulus can then act as a springboard.

Now I'm going to share five specific strategies that you can employ that are based on these three D's, the things that we can borrow from neuroscience. They all tap into one or more of these three D's. The first is to vary your routine. Research shows that even slight changes, how to make a sandwich, if you make a ham sandwich in a different way, a peanut butter and jelly sandwich in a different way from what you typically do, can improve divergent thinking by 10 to 15 percent. This creates new connections for us when we vary our routine. But, you do need to be cautious. Varying your routine during work, hmm, well, such changes can also be distracting. Einstein famously wore the same clothes. Charles Schulz ate the same ham sandwich with a glass of milk.

Let's look at the next strategy. The next strategy is to take an incubation break. One of the first deliberate descriptions of the creative process came out in the 1920s by a gentleman named Graham Wallas. He had a four-step model of the creative process. The four steps in this process were preparation, incubation, illumination, and verification.

Let me describe each step. Preparation is when the problem presents itself to you. You become familiar with your domain, or the problem area. You're preparing your mind to understand the ins and outs of the problem that you're trying to deal with. Incubation is when you go away from the problem. Where do you get your best ideas? Where are you? What are you doing when you get your best ideas? When I ask people in the audiences I work with this question, the responses I generally get are, "Well, when I'm running," "When I'm brushing my teeth," "When I'm shaving," "Just before falling asleep," "While I'm driving my car." These are all examples of taking an incubation break. In preparation, we're working hard on trying to get to that breakthrough; we're understanding what the challenges are. But often we move away from the problem, and it's during this time of incubation that the idea presents itself, which is the third step in the Wallas process, illumination. It's when you're shaving or driving, and suddenly, that light bulb goes on. The idea presents itself to you. But, the process doesn't end there. There's a fourth step to the Wallas model—verification. It's then taking the idea and testing it to see if it works.

When I look at writers and composers as they're described in the book *Daily Rituals*, while they had great variety in the rituals that they created for themselves, there seemed to be one thing that was consistent, and that is, many of the rituals included some kind of incubation break. Here are some examples of the different kinds of incubation breaks that are featured in this book and the work of these superstar creators.

Some enjoy taking a walk. In fact, that seemed to be the most popular way to take an incubation break. Beethoven, Kierkegaard, Freud, Carl Jung, Strauss, Faulkner, John Adams, Tchaikovsky, Henry James, all took daily walks. Swimming was also mentioned. Gustav Mahler and Hemingway swam almost every day.

Here are some other examples. Crossword puzzles, Maya Angelou and W. H. Auden use crossword puzzles to give their minds a break. Here's an interesting one. John Cage and Morton Feldman, when they needed to take a break, would copy work that they created previously, which allowed them to relax, in a way. They weren't continuing to push for creativity, but they were taking a break from that creative idea generation work. Woody Allen provides another example for different activities for taking an incubation break. He would pace on his terrace, change rooms, or take a shower.

Research shows us that the best kind of incubation break to take is to take a break that involves a non-demanding task. A recent research study looked at three kinds of incubation breaks. Participants were given a divergent-thinking task to work on, and part way through that task, they were given a break. In some cases, they went to another cognitive task that was demanding, building something, let's say. Another group went to a non-demanding task, like sorting things, sorting bricks into—Legos, let's say—into different colors, into piles of different colors. Pretty low-demanding task. And then a third group simply rested. Now, at the end of this, they went back to working on the divergent thinking task, and what they found was the individuals who worked on the low cognitive-demanding task did significantly better than the other two groups.

So, the kinds of breaks, the kinds of incubation time that work best, seem to be times when our body is occupied, but our mind is able to wander. In this way, our prefrontal cortex is less active. We're not evaluating. The brakes aren't on our thinking. Instead, the brakes are off. Our minds are wandering and finding new neural pathways, and in this way we create new connections.

Speaking of connections, that's the third strategy for overcoming internal blocks, when the aha doesn't come to you, when you can't get that idea. So the third strategy is forced connections. You can also think about it as the

Spielberg solution. You see, Spielberg, when he runs out of ideas, he has a large canvas, an original painting of Norman Rockwell above his desk, and when he has that writer's block, he reports, he looks at that painting, and he uses that painting, that visual, as stimulation.

Now, you've learned some tools that help you to do this, tools in this course, visually identifying relationships where we take photographs and we look at photographs to stimulate our thinking. Random word entry, where we choose a word randomly, and we force it into our thinking. Again, these kinds of tools, they shake our thinking up; they require our minds to take a new route. So you can use deliberate distancing tools such as this that shift your focus, and you can use springboards, such as objects and photographs. This allows, again, your mind to travel along new neural pathways, and it reinforces deferral of judgment.

Here's the fourth strategy, and one that I use, I must tell you, on a regular basis. It's called In-and-out note taking. Have you ever noticed that when you're in a meeting that your mind wanders, that you might start to think about something that you have to do, or you start recalling the items that you had forgotten about on your to-do list, or something that you forgot to bring to work, or you remember suddenly, gosh, I have to pick up eggs on the way home. This is natural, for our minds to wander.

In this tool, in-and-out note taking, we take advantage of what our minds naturally do. It's a simple tool. The way it works is, when you're in a meeting, you draw a line down the center of your piece of paper that you're taking notes on, or if you're using a computer, you create a Word document that has two columns in it. The left column we label our In Thoughts. The in thoughts are the notes that we take that are directly related to the content, the things that we want to remember.

In the right column, we label this Out Thoughts. Here's where we capture the connections we're making, those random thoughts, those thoughts that get spurred, perhaps, by what's being said in the meeting. Have you ever had that experience where you're lying in bed at night, or just before you're falling asleep, and you have this idea, and it's so brilliant, you think you'll remember it, and you don't write it down? Or you're doing some activity, and you have this breakthrough idea; the light bulb turns on, and you don't take the time to capture it, and then, later, when you're trying to recall it, it's gone? Well, in-and-out note taking is designed to overcome that challenge, overcome that problem. One of the biggest benefits of in-and-out note taking is it helps us to tune in to what's happening in our minds, this natural mind wandering that happens, and it helps us to keep track of those new ideas that present themselves to us. It's a way of keeping track of your creativity.

Let's look at the fifth solution. I refer to it as the Hemingway solution, because what Hemingway would do is he would work through his writer blocks, and he would only stop when he knew where he would start when he began next to write. He never finished with the writing block. He didn't walk away when he had a writing block. He would, again, push through it, and when he got to a point where he was picking up momentum again, where he knew where he would start next, as he would say, when he still had some "juice" left in him, that's when he would stop.

Let's now look at some work out of the Harvard Business School, work by Teresa Amabile, who's looked at more external killers to creativity. She has more than a decade-plus of research that highlights a range of creativity obstacles. Here are a few examples of her creativity blocks, or killers, and I will refer to these as external, because they are situational, but then they influence us internally, especially in that they undermine our intrinsic motivation.

Now, all of these examples that I share with you are supported by solid, rigorous, empirical research. Expected evaluation, this is when you know your ideas or products will be judged by others. The creator, then, becomes preoccupied by future evaluation. Rather than doing his or her most creative work, they focus on pleasing others. This moves the focus from doing the task for pure pleasure, to doing it for external reasons.

Next, she talks about competition. Competition is good, right? Wrong. Not when it comes to creative work. When we compete, we start to focus on others, versus the work that we're doing. It makes us do things quickly, thus less likely to pursue other options and explore. It focuses us on winning, less likely, as a result, to try something original when the outcome is unknown. If we're concerned with winning, and we know trying something new is risky, that there's a chance of failure, well, we're less likely to try the original idea.

Think of many Hollywood sequels and movies based on stories that have been successful books or comics; they're less risky. Novelty means uncertainty. Also, when we compete with others inside of our organization, we hold back knowledge, and we hold back information, and therefore, it's kind of a creativity block for an entire group. The group suffers.

B. F. Skinner and behaviorists showed how rewards reinforce behavior. But do rewards promote creative behavior? Amabile has demonstrated that external rewards and the promise of a reward undermine creative thinking. Again, a reward moves our focus to something that is external to the creator. Picture two mice racing through a maze. The one that gets out gets the reward, gets the cheese. Well, what if one mouse wants to explore, wants to find a different pathway, is curious about new, different corners, places that haven't been experienced yet, wants to take a more creative path? Well, this poor mouse won't ever get the reward. Time and time again, great creators say they create out of their own interest and pleasure.

So, let's review. Expected evaluation, competition, rewards kill creativity; they erode our intrinsic motivation. Extrinsic motivation is fine for many tasks, but not for creativity. So what I recommend is that you avoid, or downplay, these situational factors, and try not to impose them on others.

At the beginning of this lecture, I defined creativity as the ability to overcome self-imposed constraints. Here's a story of one of the most prolific architects in American history, and he suffered from his own self-imposed constraints. In 1991, the American Institute of Architects recognized Frank Lloyd Wright as the greatest American architect of all time. Over his career, he created more than a thousand designs, with approximately half of them being built. However, he was not always so productive. You see, during a nine-year period, from 1924 to 1933, his production was akin to a slow dripping faucet. During this time, he completed two projects. Why the sudden change in his creative productivity when compared to the decades before? Author Adam Grant suggests it was due to the fact that he withdrew himself from exposure to other architects and craftsmen and sculptors, exposure he had enjoyed when he worked in Chicago and Oak Park, Illinois, very creative, productive decades.

Apparently, during his middle period, he isolated himself, assuming he could excel alone. It would seem Frank Lloyd Wright didn't understand the value others brought to his creative process, stimulating his thinking, completing his concepts for him, making his designs work. So, it would seem Frank Lloyd Wright found a way to impose constraints on himself. Thank goodness for his wife, who insisted that he begin a program for apprentices. Once he began this, his creative productivity soared again.

What can we learn from Frank Lloyd Wright? Even superstar creators suffer from self-imposed constraints. Don't buy into your own creativity so much that you discount or neglect sources of inspiration and creative collaboration. Be aware of the conditions that promote your creativity. Blocks are serious matters, so I want to encourage you to do three things. Practice in-and-out thinking; learn to leverage incubation breaks; break up your creativity by injecting low-demand tasks. This can be done as a group as well. When running ideation sessions, it's useful to build in excursions, trips to museums, exercises, and some shopping. Pick another one of the four strategies for overcoming blocks. Make it a regular practice; make it a routine, just like the great creators.

Living a Creative Life

Lecture 24

Creative thinking skills can help anyone, whether making contributions to a larger field or overcoming daily challenges and living in a more creative way. This concluding lecture examines principles for living a creative life. You are encouraged to apply these themes in your life and to examine ways that you can internalize them. This lecture will also expose you to things that undermine our creativity, that stop us from being more effective—things that we, perhaps, should pay attention to that may rob our creativity.

Losing Creative Power

- There are some things that people do that undermine their creative power. The first is letting others' approval be more important than their own—sort of checking to see how others are reacting to them before they dive into the work, being overly cautious about how others will react to them.

- This tends to take us away from our own intrinsic drive or internal interests. As we become less concerned about others, we can focus more on what's important to us.

- The next way in which we can lose our creative power is by running ourselves down, always putting other people first. By nurturing and actualizing our own creativity, enhancing our creative power, we're in a better position to then enhance others and to share that power with others.

- The next way in which we can give up our power is asking for permission inappropriately, looking to make sure that before we do something we have the permission of someone else. In this way, we're trying to avoid making mistakes.

- The next is credentializing. This involves looking at a field you wish to get into or something that you wish to embark on and talking yourself down by thinking that you don't have the right things on your resume, the right credentials, to prove your validity in the field.

- The next is demanding guarantees. Looking for 100 percent guarantees of success will always stop us from pursuing something, especially something that's new to us.

- The final way in which we give up our power is being unwilling to say no, stretching ourselves too far—saying yes to everything, not taking control of decisions in our lives. As a result, we are running our energy down.

Gaining Creative Power

- In contrast to the principles that cause us to lose creative power, there are principles that give us creative power. These are habits to continue to grow or to initiate anew in your life.

- The first principle is to live your life. As Amabile has shown in her research, intrinsic motivation is a strong predictor of those who will ultimately show high levels of creativity. It doesn't matter what intrinsically motivates you; what really matters is finding what intrinsically motivates you. Pursue what you love, and this is where you'll find your greatest creativity—your flow, your peak psychological experiences.

- The next principle is to reclaim your creativity. Creativity is natural; we're born to create. Evolution has wired us to be creative. In order to be creative, we have to recognize, though, how we get in the way of our own creativity—those self-imposed constraints. Sure, we can blame others, but we need to first reclaim what is a natural gift that we all have.

- When you create, you actualize your potential. You expand yourself. You discover yourself. When you create an idea, it's like seeing part of yourself grow. It helps you to become a larger self.

- There are some legends and myths about how creativity comes along with mental illness. In fact, research by many psychologists show the opposite. Research shows that when we reclaim our creativity, we have greater coping skills and resiliency—resiliency to deal with life's challenges, because creativity just doesn't happen in our professional lives between 9 and 5. We're required to be creative in other aspects of our lives as well, so it's important that wherever we go, we bring our imagination along.

- The next principle is to go big or go home. Remember, creativity is made up of knowledge, imagination, and evaluation. Children have lots of imagination. Adults, however, seem to stop dreaming. They limit their imagination. This is crucial, as Fritz says in his creative tension model.

- In order to create change in our lives, we have to begin by first looking at what we want. What's our desired future state? The more the goal is a stretch, the more it takes us out of our comfort zone, the more compelling it becomes. It's important to be clear and unapologetic about what you want, just like children. It's how children get their way.

- In their book, which looked at the habits that make corporations successful over time, Collins and Porras identified a number of things that organizations did that were habitual. One of the important habits was what they called a BHAG—a big hairy audacious goal.

- Here's a description of a BHAG: 46-year-old businessman Henry Ford's big hairy audacious goal was to democratize the automobile. He was very clear in describing what this desired future state would be. He wanted to build a motorcar for the great multitude. It would be so low in price that no man making a good salary would be unable to own one. The horse will have disappeared from our highways, and the automobile will be taken for granted.

- In order to dream big, we have to be able to engage in the next principle, which is called suspend disbelief. When we hold on to an idea or make a conclusion and are not willing to be flexible—not willing to suspend our disbelief—even when an opportunity comes knocking on our door, we just might miss it. So it's crucial for us to see opportunities, to be able to suspend our disbelief and to be able to play with possibilities. We need to manage our judgment, to not edit our thinking prematurely.

© iStockphoto/Thinkstock.

In order to dream, you must suspend your disbelief.

- Principle five is to create options. In order to achieve the goal you are pursuing, it's helpful to have multiple options. When solving a problem, it's helpful to have multiple options. Great creators do this. They don't create just one option for themselves. Picasso, for example, generated 20,000 works over his lifetime.

- When we have a problem to solve and we have one option, it really doesn't give us a choice—it's either succeed or fail. When you create two options, then you're in a better place, but that forces choices into a black-and-white scenario. When we create more choices for ourselves, we maximize our power. It allows for greater flexibility, and it increases the probability of getting to our end goal.

- The sixth and final principle is to do it again and again. Creating is hard work. It takes practice and persistence. It takes 10 years, on average, before great creators have their breakthrough. Franklin Delano Roosevelt called this "a time of persistent experimentation." Be willing to learn from your mistakes. Failure is just another way of learning.

Practice, Practice, Practice

- As you practice, as you do it again and again, find a teacher to guide you—someone who will grow with you. Tennis players and golfers, even at the highest level, have coaches. Today, many executives even have coaches. Find a paragon that you can emulate, someone you can look to who has a similar approach in terms of creativity, and look at what they've done. Learn from them as well.

- It is important to keep in mind that learning without application achieves the same end as ignorance. Practice what you've learned in this course, applying the tools to your everyday life.

- If we wish to see change, we have to be the change we wish to see. We have to model the way for others to see. Embrace your creativity as you go forward. Model it for others. For yourself and for others, be a creative force in your work and all that you do, and live a more creative life.

Suggested Reading

Amabile and Kramer, *The Progress Principle.*

Csikszentmihalyi, *Creativity.*

Robinson, *Out of Our Minds.*

Activities

Activity 1: Identifying a Vision
Take some time to read and reflect on the following questions.

- What are your goals?

- What are your passions?

- What is something you would like to accomplish by the end of the year?

- What is something you would like to accomplish by this time next year?

- What are some of your long-term wishes?

- What's on your bucket list?
- What have you not done that you would like to do?
- What opportunities have been on your mind?

Select one question, phrase it into a wish statement starting with "It would be great if …", and then complete a cartoon storyboard.

Activity 2: Taking It Forward

Look back over your notes and at the list of activities above. What did you find interesting? What tools and concepts do you want to use and retain? Place these items in the first column below. Then, in the second column, diverge on a list of potential uses for each of those items.

Interesting Content (Tools and Concepts)	Potential Uses

Living a Creative Life

Lecture 24—Transcript

Creativity is a state of doing, not a state of being. I heard this definition in a presentation by someone who played a very important role at the McArthur Foundation; in fact, an important role in giving out their Genius Awards. When I first heard this definition, I thought, yes, that's it. It's about producing. Creativity is not just about reflecting and thinking; it's about doing something. Then I ran into people who did creativity very well in one area, but who didn't live creativity as a way of being.

So in this lecture, we'll look at the rest of the story—creativity as a way of being. We talked last time about Frank Lloyd Wright, who was recognized as the greatest American architect. He designed such famous buildings as Falling Water near Pittsburgh, the Guggenheim museum in New York City, and the Darwin Martin House in Buffalo. In a career that lasted about seven decades, he generated an average of more than 140 designs, and 70 structures per year. So obviously, he was a prolific creator.

My question is, to what degree did he also live creativity? The ability to suspend judgment or to use affirmative judgment, as you've learned in this course. To what degree did his eminent ability to do creativity translate into creativity in everyday life? Csíkszentmihályi says, "This is a common divide: A creative attitude in a specialized area may not be apparent elsewhere."

Although he gained much from surrounding himself with apprentices, as we discussed last time, he did not pay his apprentices. In fact, he expected them to do cooking, cleaning, and field work, and he continued to overlook ways he benefited from their efforts. As one apprentice who worked with him on Falling Water said, "He needed people like myself to make his designs work, although you couldn't tell him that." Although Wright promised his own son, John, a salary for working on several projects with him, when John requested payment, Frank Lloyd Wright instead gave John a bill for the money John owed him starting from birth.

Let me remind you of a model for the development of creative leaders and the steps in this model as we move from a spectator—someone who may not be consciously aware of the importance of creativity. We refer to a spectator as someone standing on the sideline, kind of watching creativity going by, as someone who's unconsciously unskilled. Then, through awareness we begin to recognize that we can put the lightning in the bottle. We don't have to wait for creativity to strike us, and we become consciously unskilled, recognizing that it's important and beginning to develop some motivation in deliberately provoking our own creativity. Then, through practice, over time, being more deliberate, we can move to a level where we become consciously skilled at our creativity. We refer to this level as the skilled practitioner, someone who can do creativity.

But at the fourth level, the highest level of development, we have the creative leader, the individual who's unconsciously creative in everyday modeling creative behavior to others, someone who creates a context, a climate, within the home, in organizations, in the community, that promotes creative thinking among others. In this way, they serve as a transformational leader.

While Frank Lloyd Wright was a super-skilled creativity practitioner, someone who mastered creativity, maybe this didn't translate into his lifestyle. Maybe he didn't have a creative lifestyle, or didn't operate as a creative leader, at least not in how he may have interacted with others. Skills that might have given Frank Lloyd Wright, in effect, another decade or more to do even more of the creative work he loved so much.

Creative thinking skills can help anyone, whether making contributions to a larger field or overcoming daily challenges and living in a more creative way. So, this concluding lecture we examine principles for living a creative life. The principles I'll share with you were generated by a colleague and I, David Gonzalez. We generated these principles by reviewing classic and popular books on the topic of creativity and examining them for common themes. These six principles represent some of the most common themes you find in these popular books.

I want to explore these themes, and I will encourage you to live these themes in your life and to examine ways that you can internalize them. We'll also look at things that undermine our creativity, that stop us from being more effective, things that we, perhaps, should pay attention to that may rob our creativity. In fact, let's start there.

Here are some things that we recognize that people do that take their creativity away, that undermines their creative power. Here's the first, letting others' approval be more important than your own. Sort of checking to see how others are reacting to you before you dive into the work, being overly cautious about how others will react to you. What this tends to do, it takes us away from our own intrinsic drive, our own internal interests. I remember when my son Anthony was young and was in gymnastics, and he was practicing routines, and in the gymnasium there was a large foyer with large glass windows, and we could look at see how the kids were engaging in their routines. And when he would try something new, immediately when he was done he would look to me to see how I was responding, and I told him at one point, I said, "Anthony, don't worry about me. Focus on what you're doing. Focus on what the coach is trying to teach you." So, as we become less concerned about others, we can focus more on what's important to us.

The next way in which we can lose our creative power is by running ourselves down; always putting other people first. When we get on the airplane and the airline attendant goes through the emergency procedures, what do they tell you should the cabin lose pressure? An oxygen mask will suspend from the ceiling, and you're to apply that to whom first? Well, they always recommend that you apply it to yourself first. The reason why is, by taking care of ourselves, nurturing our own creativity, actualizing our own creativity, enhancing our creative power, we're in a better position to then enhance others and to share that power with others.

The next way in which we can give up our power is asking for permission inappropriately, looking to make sure that before we do something we have the permission by someone else. In this way, we're trying to avoid making mistakes. There's an old saying that sometimes it's better to ask for forgiveness than to ask for permission.

The next is credentializing. This is sort of looking at the field that you're going into, or something that you wish to embark on, and you talk yourself down by saying, "I don't have the right things on my resume yet. I don't have the right credentials. I don't have the right degree. I haven't yet had the right experiences that make me, that prove my validity in terms of this field." In that way, we're talking ourselves down.

The next is demanding guarantees, saying in your mind, "I will pursue this only if I know I'll be successful." Looking for 100 percent guarantees of success will always stop us from pursuing something, especially something that's new to us. And then the final way in which we give up our power is being unwilling to say no, stretching ourselves too far, saying yes to everything, not taking control of decisions in our lives and, as a result, running our energy down.

So now let's turn to those principles that give us creative power. The things that I just reviewed are aspects that we need to turn down the volume on in our lives. Let's now examine where we need to turn the volume up. These are habits to continue to grow or to initiate anew in your life. The first principle is to live your life. As we've talked before, intrinsic motivation is a strong predictor of those who will ultimately show high levels of creativity. Amabile has seen this in her research. Paul Torrance, in his work with inventors, found that the main reason why inventors invent is for the love of it, not because of fame and fortune. Martha Graham took up dance at age 22, which was fairly late for a dancer, but when she started, she said she had found her destiny.

When I was studying for my Ph.D. at the University of Manchester, every Monday I would go to play tennis with my doctoral supervisor's wife. She would take me to her tennis club, and I thoroughly enjoyed the courts at this tennis club. They were very different from the concrete, hard surfaces that I had played on before. I especially liked the clay surfaces. And one day, when we had finished playing, I commented to Liz about how much I enjoyed the surface, and she said, "You should speak to Ron. He's the groundskeeper." And I hadn't met him yet, so she introduced me to Ron.

When I first met Ron, he was sort of disheveled-looking, and as we began to talk I could see he wasn't terribly well-educated, but he made a profound impact on me. As I started to talk to him about the clay courts and expressed my appreciation, I could see him lighting up, and he began to tell me about all the work that he did to ensure that these courts were in perfect playing condition. And he asked me, "Have you seen the grass courts yet?" And I said "No." He said, "Well, let me take you over there," and he took me over to the grass courts, and he walked me onto the grass courts, and he spent a long time telling me about all the things he had to do to make sure that the courts were just right. In a way, I thought, this is like talking to an artist. He's telling me about his artwork. The courts are his canvas.

Some time later, after I had moved back to the U.S. and I had returned to England on a visit, I went to play tennis with Liz, and, as I always do, I went to find Ron, and we started chatting, and we were both happy to see each other, and I asked him about how things were going. We had played that day on the grass courts, and I had asked him what had happened to the clay courts. You see, they had removed the clay courts and had put in an all-weather pitch for playing hockey. And as he began to tell me about this, it was almost as if he had lost a cherished possession, and it struck me from hearing Ron talk about his courts and having lost his clay courts, it struck me, here's a great example of intrinsic motivation. And it doesn't matter what intrinsically motivates you. What really matters is *finding* what intrinsically motivates you. Pursue what you love, and this is where you'll find your greatest creativity. This is where you'll find your flow, your peak psychological experiences.

Here's the next principle. Reclaim your creativity. Early on, when I took undergraduate courses, I would pose questions at the end of every class, and students would have to journal about those questions. And at the end of one class, I put out the question, write to me, tell me about why you think it's important to study creativity. And I remember reading one young man's journal. He wrote a simple, short answer. He said, "The reason why I believe it's important to study creativity is that when we study creativity we study ourselves."

You see, creativity is natural. We're born to create. As we've talked, evolution has wired us to be creative. In order to be creative, we have to recognize, though, how we get in the way of our own creativity, those self-imposed constraints. Sure, we can blame others, but we need to first reclaim what is a natural gift that we all have. When you create, you actualize your potential. You expand yourself. You discover yourself. When you create an idea, it's like seeing part of yourself grow. It helps you to become a larger self. And although there are some legends and myths about how, in order to be creative, it comes along with mental illness, in fact, research by many psychologists, like Donald McKinnon, in fact, show the opposite. It shows that when we reclaim our creativity, in fact, we have greater coping skills and resiliency. Resiliency to deal with life's challenges, because creativity just doesn't happen in our professional lives between 9 to 5. We're required to be creative in other aspects of our lives as well, so it's important that wherever we go, we bring our imagination along. Remember what Guilford said, "To live is to have challenges, and to solve challenges creatively is to live a creative life."

Let's go to the next principle. The next principle is go big or go home, just as the X-Gamers say. Remember, creativity is made up of knowledge, imagination, and evaluation. Children have lots of imagination. Adults, however, seem to stop dreaming; they limit their imagination. This is crucial, as Fritz says in his Creative Tension model. In order to create change in our lives, we have to begin by first looking at what we want. What's our desired future state? And the more the stretch goal, the more it takes us out of our comfort zone, the more compelling it becomes.

It's important to be clear and unapologetic about what you want, just like children. It's how children get their way. Picture the scene, the child in the grocery store who asks his or her parent, "I want that candy bar," and the parent at first says "No." And then, the child says "I really want that candy bar." And the parent says, "No." And then, the child again, more insistently says, "I really want that candy bar." And eventually the parent gives in. That's what makes the child powerful. The child is clear and unapologetic about what he or she wants, whether it's a toy, or attention of that parent.

We need to do the same thing, just like John F. Kennedy, who, despite what advisors had told him at the beginning of the 1960s, said "By the end of the decade we'll take a man to the moon and return him safely." Or Gandhi, who had a dream for home rule in India. And Walt Disney, who wanted to create a clean, well-organized amusement park.

In their book, looking at the habits that make corporations successful over time, Collins and Porras identified a number of things that organizations did that were habitual. One of the important habits was what they called a BHAG—a Big Hairy Audacious Goal.

Here's a description of a BHAG. Forty-six-year-old businessman Henry Ford, his big hairy audacious goal was to democratize the automobile. He was very clear in describing what this desired future state would be. He wanted to build a motor car for the great multitude. It would be so low in price that no man making a good salary would be unable to own one. The horse will have disappeared from our highways, and the automobile will be taken for granted.

So, in order to go big, in order to dream big, we have to be able to engage in this next principle. The next principle is called suspend disbelief. Let me tell you a story; this is a Buddhist story. In this story, there's a wealthy merchant. He's a widower, and after his wife passed away, he poured all of his love into his son. His son was the center of his world. And one day came, and he had to leave his village to go conduct business elsewhere, and while he was away, some bandits came to the village, and they caused great havoc. And they came to this merchant's street, and they looked to the end of the street and they could see a grand home. They knew the home must have belonged to someone wealthy. So they went to the home and they broke in, and they stole items, and they found this merchant's son there, and they kidnapped the boy and took him away, and just out of spite, as they left they burnt the house down.

Later that day, in the evening, the merchant returned home, and he looked to the end of his street, and he could see the smoldering ashes of his house, and he ran to his home, and he looked down, and lying there near the home was an unrecognizable figure of a small child, a small boy. He assumed that this was his son, and he began to mourn. And time went by, and he rebuilt his home. Now, he did not know that his son had been kidnapped. To him, his son was dead and gone.

But over time, eventually, the small boy was able to escape from the bandits, and he returned one evening to his father's home. He went to the street and he saw the house, and he ran to the house, which had been rebuilt, and he knocked on the door, and he called out, “Father, I’m home. Let me in.” And the father said, “No. Go away. Leave me alone.” And the boy knocked louder. “Father, I’m home. Let me in.” And the father called back, “No. Stop taunting me. Don’t make fun of my sorrow.” You see, he thought it was the neighborhood children who were making fun of him. And the boy knocked again, and the father refused to let him in, and eventually the boy gave up and went away.

Now, the Buddhists tell this story because they’re trying to drive home the point that when we hold on to an idea, when we make a conclusion and we’re not willing to be flexible, when we’re not willing to suspend our disbelief, even when an opportunity comes knocking on our door, loudly calling to us, we just might miss it. So it’s crucial for us to see opportunities, to be able to suspend our disbelief, to be able to play with possibilities. There’s an old saying, “Those who believe the sky is the limit have a limited imagination.” We need to manage our judgment, to not edit our thinking prematurely. As Hemingway said, “Too much scrutiny early in the creative process kills creative ideas. Enough people will judge your ideas. Don’t be your own worst enemy.”

Principle five is to create options. Pursuing a goal in order to achieve it, it’s helpful to have multiple options. When solving a problem, it’s helpful to have multiple options. Great creators do this. Recall, they don’t create just one option for themselves. Picasso—great example of this—generated 20,000 works over his lifetime. When we have a problem to solve and we have one option, it really doesn’t give us a choice—it’s either succeed or fail. When you create two options, well, you’re in a better place, but that forces choices into a black-and-white scenario. When we create more choices for ourselves, we maximize our power, as it allows for greater flexibility, and it increases the probability of getting to our end goal.

Here’s a business example. A colleague of mine was working with a group. They were generating names for a new product, and very early in the brainstorming session they struck on an idea that they absolutely loved, and my colleague said, “Well, let’s keep going.” And they said “No, no. This is great. We’ve got what we want.” And he said, “No. Maybe we should stretch for some more." And upon his insistence, they did, and they eventually had several hundred ideas that they generated, and they created a short list of options for themselves. Well, it's a good thing my colleague insisted that they continue to generate, because the idea that they struck on earlier, that they absolutely fell in love with, they found out soon afterwards that that name had already been trademarked, so they ended up going with one of the other alternatives.

Principle six, our last principle. We call it Don't just do it. Do it again and again. Creating is hard work; it takes practice and persistence. Remember the 10-year rule, that it takes 10 years, on average, before great creators have their breakthrough. Franklin Delano Roosevelt called this "a time of persistent experimentation." Be willing to learn from your mistakes. Failure is just another way of learning. Let me share two thoughts on failure from two very different sources. Here's one. "Far better it is to dare mighty things, to win glorious triumphs even though checkered by failure, than to rank with those poor spirits who neither enjoy nor suffer much because they live in a gray twilight that knows not victory nor defeat." That was Theodore Roosevelt.

And this one. "I can accept failure. Everyone fails at something. But I can't accept not trying." That was Michael Jordan. Edison, one of the greatest inventors in U.S. history, in his search for the filament for the light bulb, he and his team had tried 1,600 different materials. One of his colleagues during this process complained that they had too many failures, and Edison said to him, "What? We haven't failed. We've learned every time, and we're now that much closer to the solution."

As we practice, as we do it again and again, find a teacher to guide you, someone who will grow with you. Tennis players and golfers, even at the highest level, have coaches. Many executives have coaches today. Find a paragon that you can emulate, someone that you can look to who has a similar approach in terms of creativity, and look at what they've done. Learn from them as well.

Learning without application achieves the same end as ignorance. I'd like you to look at this course and reflect on what you've taken from this course, and I'm going to take you through a quick exercise, and I'm going to encourage you to do this, to pause the video if it's helpful. I want to look at what we've learned and how you might be able to apply it.

Let's begin by looking at what stood out as interesting for you. To do this exercise, you'll need a piece of paper or a computer, and if that's not handy, then picture this in your mind. It won't be terribly difficult. So we're going to begin by looking at what you found interesting and intriguing. On this piece of paper, or in the computer, or in your mind, draw a line down the center. And on the left side, this column is for all those things you found interesting and intriguing. So think back across the lectures that you listened to or viewed. What were the tools, the principles, the attitudes that stood out for you? What intrigued you? And make a list as long as you can of those things that caught your attention.

Now let's look at the right column on that piece of paper, or your computer, or in your mind. And I'd like to challenge you. For those items that you've listed in the left column, the things that you found interesting, intriguing, the things that stood out for you, the tools, the principles, the content, the attitudes that we talked about. I'd like to challenge you to think about ways that you might apply each of those items, both in your professional life and your personal life. You may need time for this, so feel free to pause.

I'm going to close this lecture, this course, with a manifesto written by Paul Torrance, one of the true pioneers in the field of creativity. I think it provides a good summary for what we've learned in this course. It begins with,

> "Don't be afraid to fall in love with something and pursue it with intensity. Know, understand, take pride in, practice, develop, exploit, and enjoy your greatest strengths. Learn to free yourself from the expectations of others and to walk away from the games they impose on you. Free yourself to play your own game. Find a great teacher, a mentor who will help you. Learn the skills of interdependence. Don't waste your time trying to be well-rounded. Do what you love and can do well. Embrace your creativity. Use it every day. Share this great gift with others, and soon others will view you as a creative leader."

Several years ago, I had the opportunity to visit India, and when I was there I had the chance to go see the location where Gandhi had been assassinated, and it made quite an impression upon me. My hosts were terrific. They shared many stories with me, and I asked them for many stories about Gandhi. And one of the stories that they shared with me was this story, and I want to leave you with this.

There were two parents who had a son who was often very sickly, and the mother and father were at their wit's end in terms of what to do with their son. So they thought, "We need to speak to someone wise. Well, who's the wisest man in our land? Gandhi." So they went to visit with Gandhi. When they went in to meet with Gandhi, Gandhi asked what he could do, and they said, "Well, it's our boy. You see, he has a very poor diet, and he's often very sickly, and in particular, he eats way too much sugar." Gandhi looked at them and said "I can't help you today. Please go away and come back in three days." They were confused. Why? But they left, and they came back three days later, and they met with Gandhi again. And Gandhi began by saying, "How can I help you?" and they started to re-tell the story, and he said "Oh. Oh. I remember. I remember. That's right. Your son has a poor diet. He eats too much sugar." "Well, can you help us?" And Gandhi says "Yes. I can. And he leans over and he looks at the small boy and he says "Stop eating sugar." The parents were aghast. They were confused. "Why couldn't you say this three days ago?" And Gandhi looked at them and said, "I couldn't say this three days ago, because three days ago I was eating too much sugar."

So the point of the story is that if we wish to see change, we have to be the change we wish to see. We have to model the way for others to see. I encourage you to embrace your creativity as you go forward. Model it for others.

I'm very much tempted to say "And th-, th-, th-, that's all, folks." But that's not all, folks. Now, go, for yourself and for others, and be a creative force in your work and all that you do, and live a more creative life.

Bibliography

Abrashoff, D. M. *It's Your Ship: Management Techniques from the Best Damn Ship in the Navy*. New York: Warner Brothers, Inc., 2002. An in-depth description of how distributed leadership was successfully used to turn around a poor-performing naval ship.

Adams, J. *Conceptual Blockbusting.* 4th ed. New York: Basic Books, 2001. A true classic book in the field of creativity, this book provides a description of how such blocks as perceptual, emotional, cultural, environmental, intellectual, and expressive get in the way of individual creativity.

Allen, D. *Getting Things Done: The Art of Stress-Free Productivity*. New York: Penguin Books, 2001. Allen provides readers with methods aimed at reducing stress and clearing their minds so that they can be more productive.

Altshuller, G. *And Suddenly the Inventor Appeared: TRIZ, the Theory of Inventive Problem Solving*. Worcester, Massachusetts: Technical Innovation Center, Inc., 1996. Altshuller's analysis of patent filings in the former Soviet Union led to the creation of systematic tools useful for invention and innovation; this is the book that introduced TRIZ, the Russian inventive thinking process, to the world.

Amabile, T. M. *Growing Up Creative: Nurturing a Lifetime of Creativity*. Buffalo, NY: Creative Education Foundation, Inc., 1992. Written by one of the preeminent scholars in the field of creativity, this book explores factors shown to enhance individual creativity and provides practical advice for parents and teachers.

Amabile, T. M., and S. J. Kramer. *The Progress Principle: Using Small Wins to Ignite Joy, Engagement, and Creativity at Work*. Boston: Harvard Business School Publishing, 2011. Based on analysis of more than 12,000 diary entries of workers, the authors describe what managers can do to enhance employees' inner work lives.

Arnold, J. D. *The Art of Decision Making*. New York: AMACOM, 1978. The author describes a seven-step process for making better decisions.

Basadur, M. *Simplex®: A Flight to Creativity*. Buffalo, NY: The Creative Education Foundation, Inc., 1994. Basadur provides a detailed description of how to apply his creative problem solving process, called *Simplex*, in organizational contexts.

Belsky, S. *Making Ideas Happen: Overcoming the Obstacles between Vision & Reality*. New York: Penguin, 2010. The author uses his studies of highly productive individuals and teams to provide the reader with practical principles and techniques to move ideas from the drawing board to reality.

Benyus, J. *Biomimicry: Innovation Inspired by Nature.* New York: HarperCollins Publishers, Inc., 1997. Detailed description of a creative process based on ways to borrow ideas from nature to solve human problems.

Brown, S. *Play: How It Shapes the Brain, Opens the Imagination, and Invigorates the Soul.* New York: Penguin Group, Inc., 2009. Brown uses the science of play to make the case that play is crucial to happiness, sustained social relationships, and higher levels of creativity.

Brown, T. *Change by Design: How Design Thinking Transforms Organizations and Inspires Innovation.* New York: HarperCollins, 2009. Brown provides a description of design thinking, a collaborative systematic process through which designers' ideas are matched to people's needs.

Carruthers, P. "Human Creativity: Its Cognitive Basis, Its Evolution, and Its Connections with Childhood Pretence." *British Journal for the Philosophy of Science* 53, no. 2 (June 2002): 225–249. A fascinating journal article written by a philosopher who offers an eloquent argument that the attitude of "suspended disbelief" was a necessary partner to creative cognition that, together, brought about the creative explosion in human civilization approximately 50,000 years ago.

Collins, J. C., and J. I. Porras. *Built to Last: Successful Habits of Visionary Companies*. New York: HarperCollins, 1994. The authors report on their detailed analysis of the factors that distinguish companies that have been able to sustain themselves over time, compared to those that have been much less successful; a number of these habits are excellent organizational examples of principles described in the field of creativity.

Colvin, G. *Talent Is Overrated: What Really Separates World-Class Performers from Everybody Else.* New York: Penguin Group, Inc., 2008. An engaging book, based on the science of expertise, that describes how deliberate practice can be used to achieve high levels of accomplishment in any skill area, including examples of creativity.

Cropley, A. "In Praise of Convergent Thinking." *Creativity Research Journal* 18 (2006): 391–404. The author makes a strong case for the role of convergent thinking in the creative process; a useful schema is shared in which the consequences of right and wrong combinations of divergent and convergent thinking are explored.

Csikszentmihalyi, M. *Creativity: Flow and the Psychology of Discovery and Invention.* New York: HarperCollins Publishers, Inc., 1996. Drawn from interviews with creative people, the author describes the factors that lead to a peak creative experience; moreover, Csikszentmihalyi provides an eloquent case for why creativity needs to be cultivated in today's complex world.

Currey, J. *Daily Rituals: How Artists Work.* New York: Alfred A. Knopf, 2013. Detailed descriptions of the daily practices and habits adopted by well-known artists, scientists, writers, and other great creators.

de Bono, E. *Serious Creativity: Using the Power of Lateral Thinking to Create New Ideas.* Toronto, Canada: Harper Perennial, 1992. Articulate description of creativity that replaces popular misconceptions of creativity with an argument that creativity is a skill that is crucial for success in life, a skill that can be developed principally by learning to shift from vertical modes of thinking to lateral ways of thinking.

———. *Six Thinking Hats*. Revised and updated. Boston: Little, Brown and Company, 1999. Author Edward de Bono, perhaps one of the most well-known global experts on deliberate creativity, explains how to apply one of his most popular methods, called the six thinking hats, for both individual and group use.

Doorley, S., and S. Witthoft. *Make Space: How to Set the Stage for Creative Collaboration.* Hoboken, NY: Wiley, 2012. This book highlights how to design physical workspace that promotes collaboration and creativity and draws the best out of people.

Dunbar, R., et al. *Evolutionary Psychology: A Beginner's Guide to Human Behaviour, Evolution and the Mind.* Oxford, England: Oneworld Publications, 2007. Introduction to evolutionary psychology; of particular relevance to individual creativity is the description of humans' built-in conformity bias and how this interfaces with our innate ability to engage in creative thinking.

Ekvall, G. "Organizational Climate for Creativity and Innovation." *European Journal of Work and Organizational Psychology* 5 (1996): 105–123. Journal article by a leading researcher on the climate for creativity; in this paper, Ekvall provides a detailed description of his theory, the dimensions of creative climate, and the research that highlights the relationship between climate and innovation.

Flavell, J. H. "Metacognitive Aspects of Problem Solving." In *The Nature of Intelligence,* edited by L. B. Resnick, 231–296. Hillside, NJ: Lawrence Erlbaum Associates, 1987. In this chapter, written by one of the leading experts on metacognition, the author explores how effective problem solving and metacognition intersect.

———. "Speculations about the Nature and Development of Metacognition." In *Metacognition, Motivation, and Understanding,* edited by F. E. Weinert and R. H. Kluwe, 21–29. Hillside, NJ: Lawrence Erlbaum Associates, 1987. In this chapter, Flavell updates his model of metacognition, originally described in his class article published in 1979; included in the more current piece is a series of speculative thoughts about the development of metacognition.

Forsha, H. I. *Show Me: The Complete Guide to Storyboarding and Problem Solving*. Milwaukee, WI: ASQC Quality Press, 1995. Historical review of the development of the storyboarding tool and examples of how to use storyboarding in a variety of ways.

Fritz, R. *Creating: A Guide to the Creative Process*. New York: Fawcett Columbine, 1991. Writer, composer, and entrepreneur Robert Fritz focuses the reader on "creating," the ability to bring into existence that which you desire; the purpose of the book is to help people create what they want in their lives, which begins by recognizing what you love.

Gabora, L., and S. B. Kaufman. "Evolutionary Approaches to Creativity." In *The Cambridge Handbook of Creativity*, edited by James C. Kaufman and Robert J. Sternberg, 279–300. Cambridge: Cambridge University Press, 2010. This chapter, which is included in a collection of works authored by some of the most esteemed contemporary creativity researchers, explores how humans, and especially their brains, evolved to be creative.

Goldenberg, J., and D. Mazursky. *Creativity in Product Innovation*. Cambridge: Cambridge University Press, 2002. Complete with many examples from industry, this book provides creativity templates useful in creating a systematic approach to product improvement and creation.

Goleman, D. *The Brain and Emotional Intelligence: New Insights*. Northampton, MA: More Than Sound LLC, 2011. This popular book made the concept of emotional intelligence clear and accessible to all; Goleman makes a strong argument for the predictive value of emotional intelligence along with ways to boost emotional intelligence.

Gordon, W. J. J. *Synectics*. New York: Harper & Row, 1961. A classic book in which one of the original developers of the Synectics process provides strategies for using analogies to creatively solve problems.

Grant, A., et al. *Who Killed Creativity? And How Can We Get It Back?: Seven Essential Strategies to Make Yourself, Your Team and Your Organisation More Innovative*. Melbourne, Australia: John Wiley & Sons Australia, Ltd., 2012. This book playfully examines the death of creativity as if it were set in a crime scene; particular focus is given to the factors in the setting that undermine creative thinking.

Grivas, C., and G. J. Puccio. *The Innovative Team: Unleashing Creative Potential for Breakthrough Results*. San Francisco: Jossey-Bass, 2012. A two-part book whose first section features a fable of a team that used their understanding of FourSight preferences and creative problem solving to overcome dysfunctional team behaviors to achieve creative results; the second section explains how to use creative problem solving.

Jones, M. D. *The Thinker's Toolkit: 14 Powerful Techniques For Problem Solving*. New York: Three Rivers Press, 1995. Former CIA analyst presents detailed descriptions of creativity tools and decision-making tools, such as divergent-convergent thinking, the probability tree, devil's advocacy, hypothesis testing, and advanced utility analysis.

Kanji, G. K., and M. Asher. *100 Methods for Total Quality Management.* London: Sage Publications, 1996. A tool book filled with 100 examples, complete with detailed steps, for applying total quality methods individually and in teams.

Kelley, T., and D. Kelley. "Reclaim Your Creative Confidence: How to Get Over the Fears That Block Your Best Ideas." *Harvard Business Review,* December 2012. Accessed February 18, 2013. http://hbr.org/2012/12/reclaim-your-creative-confidence. Creativity experts from the design firm IDEO describe how fear and judgment undermine creative thinking among organizational members; Kelley and Kelley provide business examples of how creative methods have been used successfully to overcome these barriers to creativity.

King, B., and H. Schlicksupp. *The Idea Edge: Transforming Creative Thought into Organizational Excellence.* Methuen, MA: Goal/QPC, 1998. A tool book filled with step-by-step how-to instructions for using a wide range of creative thinking methods.

Kirton, M. *Adaptors and Innovators: Styles of Creativity and Problem Solving.* New York: Routledge, 1989. A detailed description of Kirton's theory of adaptive and innovative styles of creativity, with examples and implications aimed at promoting deeper insight into individual and organizational creativity.

Kumar, V. *101 Design Methods: A Structured Approach for Driving Innovation in Your Organization.* Hoboken, NJ: Wiley & Sons, 2013. A tool book that contains short, but detailed, descriptions, along with visual examples, of how to use 101 different design tools.

LeGault, M. R. *Think: Why Crucial Decisions Can't Be Made in the Blink of an Eye.* New York: Threshold Editions, 2006. The author makes the case that, despite the position taken in the book *Blink*, our best decisions are made after careful analysis and incisive reasoning.

Lewin, K. *Field Theory in Social Science.* New York: Harper & Row, 1951. A classic book in which psychologist Kurt Lewin describes the forces that interact to either undermine or promote change.

Lumsdaine, E., and M. Lumsdaine. *Creative Problem Solving: Thinking Skills for a Changing World.* New York: McGraw-Hill. 1995. The author introduces a whole-brain approach to greater success at work and life in general; the book includes case studies, team activities, and assignments.

Lynn, A. *The EQ Difference: A Powerful Plan for Putting Emotional Intelligence to Work.* New York: The American Management Association, 2005. A hands-on book that presents a practical model for developing emotional intelligence, mainly aimed at those who wish to employ greater levels of emotional intelligence in their professional lives.

Martin, R. *The Opposable Mind: Winning through Integrative Thinking.* Boston, MA: Harvard Business School Press, 2009. The author, Roger Martin, argues that to be an effective leader, people should learn to emulate how great leaders think (not how they are); with this in mind, Martin suggests that leaders are able to integrate what appear to be opposing data, models, and perspectives.

Michalko, M. *Thinkertoys: A Handbook of Business Creativity for the 90's*. Berkeley, CA: Ten Speed Press, 1991. An engaging book focused on the practical application of creativity tools, from those tools that are more linear to those that are much more intuitive; the book includes useful instructions for a variety of idea-generation techniques.

Mithen, S. *The Singing Neanderthals: The Origins of Music, Language, Mind, and Body*. Cambridge, MA: Harvard University Press, 2006. The author uses cognitive archeology to examine developments in brain function that led to the creative explosion; special attention is given to humans' ability to combine thoughts across domains and to the fact that such intersections of thought promote higher levels of creative thinking.

Murray, D. K. *Borrowing Brilliance: The Six Steps to Business Innovation by Building on the Ideas of Others.* New York: Penguin Group, Inc., 2009. Murray, corporate innovation officer, presents a strong case, along with an easy-to-follow process model, for how borrowing ideas can be used to drive creative breakthroughs.

Ness, R. *Innovation Generation: How to Produce Creative and Useful Scientific Ideas*. New York: Oxford University Press, 2012. The author provides readers with ways to escape habitual approaches to everyday life and to learn to apply proven methods for enhancing the generation of original ideas.

Northouse, P. G. *Leadership: Theory and Practice.* 6th ed. Los Angeles, CA: Sage, 2013. A comprehensive review of a wide-ranging set of theories and models of leadership, from historical to contemporary.

Osborn, A. *Applied Imagination: Principles and Procedures of Creative Problem-Solving.* 3rd ed. New York: Scribner, 1963. A pioneering book that is credited with being a catalyst to practices aimed at promoting creativity, and to the field of creativity at large; in this book, Osborn introduces creative problem solving and describes how to use the creativity tool he invented called brainstorming.

Parnes, S. J. *Source Book for Creative Problem Solving*. Buffalo, NY: Creative Education Foundation, 1992. A collection of papers, written by historically recognized creativity experts, that explore a variety of issues and applications relative to the use of creative problem solving.

Parnes, S. J., and A. Meadow. "Evaluation of Training in Creative Problem Solving." *Journal of Applied Psychology* 43 (1959): 189–194. One of the early classic studies that demonstrated that creative thinking, particularly idea generation, could be taught.

Proctor, T. *Creative Problem Solving for Managers: Developing Skills for Decision Making and Innovation*. New York: Routledge, 2010. A wide-ranging survey of various creative processes and tools, including creative problem solving, Synectics, decision-making models, and computer-aided creativity.

Puccio, G., et al. *Creative Leadership: Skills That Drive Change*. 2nd ed. Thousand Oaks, CA: Sage, 2011. This book positions creativity and creative problem solving as core leadership skills; it is filled with practical creativity tools aimed at helping leaders be more effective creative thinkers.

———. *Creativity Rising: Creative Thinking and Creative Problem Solving in the 21st Century*. Buffalo, NY: ICSC Press, 2012. This book places creative thinking into the context of the 21st century by highlighting current trends that render creativity an essential life skill, followed by a detailed review of creative problem solving, both the process and some of its tools.

Rickards, T. *Creativity and Problem Solving at Work*. Aldershot, UK: Gower Publishing, 1990. An introduction to creativity and to a range of creative problem solving tools that are easily applied in organizational settings.

Robinson, K. *Out of Our Minds: Learning to Be Creative*. Chichester, UK: Capstone Publishing, Ltd., 2011. A highly accessible book that makes a strong case for the importance of creativity in business, yet emphasizes how our educational practices undermine individual creativity; the core point of the book is that tapping into one's creativity is essential for anyone who wants to reach his or her fullest potential and that creativity is a teachable skill.

Runco, M. A. *Problem Finding, Problem Solving, and Creativity*. Norwood, NJ: Ablex, 1994. A scholarly book aimed at sorting out the distinctions and relationships among the concepts of problem finding, problem solving, and creativity.

Sawyer, K. *Zig Zag: The Surprising Path to Greater Creativity.* San Francisco, CA: Jossey-Bass, 2013. A research-based book that outlines an eight-step process to increase creative potential, from how to ask better questions to strategies for manifesting your ideas.

Senge, P., et al. *The Dance Of Change: The Challenge of Sustaining Momentum in Learning Organizations*. New York: Doubleday, 1999. Senge uses his vast experience with organizations to help business leaders recognize how to develop personal and organizational capabilities that will sustain change.

VanGundy, A. B. *Creative Problem Solving: A Guide for Trainers and Management.* Westport, CN: Quorum Books, 1987. A detailed description of how to employ creative problem solving in a business environment.

———. *Idea Power: Techniques & Resources to Unleash the Creativity in Your Organization.* New York: AMACOM, 1992. Creativity expert Arthur VanGundy provides practical approaches to business creativity, highlighting tools that can range in application from group use to use across the entire organization.

Wagner, T. *Creating Innovators: The Making of Young People Who Will Change the World.* New York: Simon & Schuster, Inc., 2012. A Harvard professor of education makes the case that creativity and innovation are essential 21st-century skills; the book includes stories and recommendations aimed at enhancing innovation skills in young people.

———. *The Global Achievement Gap*. New York: Basic Books, 2008. An in-depth examination and description of the skills young people need to get a good job in a global knowledge economy.

Weisberg, R. W. *Creativity: Understanding Innovation in Problem Solving, Science, Invention, and the Arts*. Hoboken, NY: Wiley, 2006. A broad review of the field of creativity that covers a diverse range of creativity topics, including psychometric, personality, and cognitive approaches to creativity; there is a strong focus on creative processes that include case studies, research, reviews, and models.

FourSight® Thinking Profile

Discover your preferences as a creative thinker

The FourSight® Thinking Profile is an in-depth problem-solving assessment, based on 10 years of research. It reveals what parts of the creative process naturally align with your thinking style.

A universal process

Humans are naturally creative. Every day we solve new problems, meet new challenges, and pursue new opportunities. We do it, whether we know it or not, by following the universal steps of the creative process.

Discover your profile

The FourSight® Thinking Profile reveals your preference for each of the four distinct steps of the creative problem-solving process. Knowing your preference(s) unlocks your ability to solve problems, collaborate, and lead with better results.

Directions:

The 36 statements on the following pages describe various activities associated with solving problems or dealing with challenging situations. **For each statement indicate the extent to which you feel the statement describes you.** Do not worry about how effective you are in regard to that activity; instead, simply consider the extent to which it sounds like you. Respond to each statement by indicating how descriptive that statement is of you. **Indicate your response by placing an "X" through one of the dots that follow each statement.** The response scale ranges from "Not like me at all" to "Very much like me." Remember, there are no right or wrong answers, just opinions about yourself—not the way you wish you were, but the way you honestly are.

Examples:

	Not like me at all		*Like me*		*Very much like me*
29 I am a tall person.	OO	XO	OO	OO	OO
30 I enjoy eating salad.	OO	OO	OO	OO	XO

Please complete the whole four-page survey (on pages 445, 447, 449, and 451) before you begin scoring your results. You'll find scoring directions on pages 453-455.

Name:__________	Not like me at all		Like me		Very much like me	Scoring Only ↓
1 I like testing and revising my ideas before coming up with the final solution or product.	○○	○○	○○	○○	○○	1___
2 I like taking the time to clarify the exact nature of the problem.	○○	○○	○○	○○	○○	2___
3 I enjoy taking the necessary steps to put my ideas into action.	○○	○○	○○	○○	○○	3___
4 I like to break a broad problem apart and examine it from all angles.	○○	○○	○○	○○	○○	4___
5 I find it difficult to come up with unusual ideas for solving a problem.	○○	○○	○○	○○	○○	(5___)
6 I like identifying the most relevant facts pertaining to a problem.	○○	○○	○○	○○	○○	6___
7 I don't have the temperament to sit back and isolate the specific causes of a problem.	○○	○○	○○	○○	○○	(7___)
8 I enjoy coming up with unique ways of looking at a problem.	○○	○○	○○	○○	○○	8___
9 I like to generate all the pluses and minuses of a potential solution.	○○	○○	○○	○○	○○	9___
Scoring key for ___ :	1	2	3	4	5	
Scoring key for ⬭:	5	4	3	2	1	

Don't score yet. Turn to page 447 and continue the assessment.

FOR SCORING USE ONLY:
Transfer the score for each item
to the white box on the corresponding line

	A	B	C	D
1				
2				
3				
4				
5				
6				
7				
8				
9				
Total each column				

then transfer column totals to page 455

	Not like me at all		Like me		Very much like me	Scoring Only ↓
10 Before implementing a solution I like to break it down into steps.	OO	OO	OO	OO	OO	10____
11 Transforming ideas into action is not what I enjoy most.	OO	OO	OO	OO	OO	(11____)
12 I like to generate criteria that can be used to identify the best option(s).	OO	OO	OO	OO	OO	12____
13 I enjoy spending time looking beyond the initial view of the problem.	OO	OO	OO	OO	OO	13____
14 I don't naturally spend much time focusing on defining the exact problem to be solved.	OO	OO	OO	OO	OO	(14____)
15 I like to take in a situation by looking at the big picture.	OO	OO	OO	OO	OO	15____
16 I enjoy working on ill-defined, novel problems.	OO	OO	OO	OO	OO	16____
17 When working on a problem I like to come up with the best way of stating it.	OO	OO	OO	OO	OO	17____
18 I enjoy making things happen.	OO	OO	OO	OO	OO	18____
Scoring key for ___ :	1	2	3	4	5	
Scoring key for ◯:	5	4	3	2	1	

Don't score yet. Turn to page 449 and continue the assessment.

FOR SCORING USE ONLY:
Transfer the score for each item
to the white box on the corresponding line

Item	A	B	C	D
10				
11				
12				
13				
14				
15				
16				
17				
18				
Total each column then transfer column totals to page 455				
	A	B	C	D

	Not like me at all		Like me		Very much like me	Scoring Only ↓
19 I like to focus on creating a precisely stated problem.	OO	OO	OO	OO	OO	19____
20 I enjoy stretching my imagination to produce many ideas.	OO	OO	OO	OO	OO	20____
21 I like to focus on the key information within a challenging situation.	OO	OO	OO	OO	OO	21____
22 I enjoy taking the time to perfect an idea.	OO	OO	OO	OO	OO	22____
23 I find it difficult to bring my ideas to fruition.	OO	OO	OO	OO	OO	(23____)
24 I enjoy turning rough ideas into concrete solutions.	OO	OO	OO	OO	OO	24____
25 I like to think about all the things I need to do to implement an idea.	OO	OO	OO	OO	OO	25____
26 I really enjoy implementing an idea.	OO	OO	OO	OO	OO	26____
27 Before moving forward I like to have a clear understanding of the problem.	OO	OO	OO	OO	OO	27____
Scoring key for ___ :	1	2	3	4	5	
Scoring key for ⬭:	5	4	3	2	1	

Don't score yet. Turn to page 451 and continue the assessment.

FOR SCORING USE ONLY:
Transfer the score for each item to the white box on the corresponding line

Item	A	B	C	D
19				
20				
21				
22				
23				
24				
25				
26				
27				
Total each column then transfer column totals to page 455				
	A	B	C	D

	Not like me at all		Like me		Very much like me	Scoring Only ↓
28 I like to work with unique ideas.	OO	OO	OO	OO	OO	28____
29 I enjoy putting my ideas into action.	OO	OO	OO	OO	OO	29____
30 I like to explore the strengths and weaknesses of a potential solution.	OO	OO	OO	OO	OO	30____
31 I enjoy gathering information to identify the root causes of a particular problem.	OO	OO	OO	OO	OO	31____
32 I enjoy the analysis and effort it takes to transform a rough concept into a workable idea.	OO	OO	OO	OO	OO	32____
33 My natural tendency is not to generate lots and lots of ideas for problems.	OO	OO	OO	OO	OO	(33____)
34 I enjoy using metaphors and analogies to come up with new ideas for problems.	OO	OO	OO	OO	OO	34____
35 I have little patience for the effort it takes to refine or polish an idea.	OO	OO	OO	OO	OO	(35____)
36 I tend to look for a quick solution and then fly with it.	OO	OO	OO	OO	OO	36____
Scoring key for ___ :	1	2	3	4	5	
Scoring key for ◯:	5	4	3	2	1	

Finished! Turn to page 453 for scoring instructions.

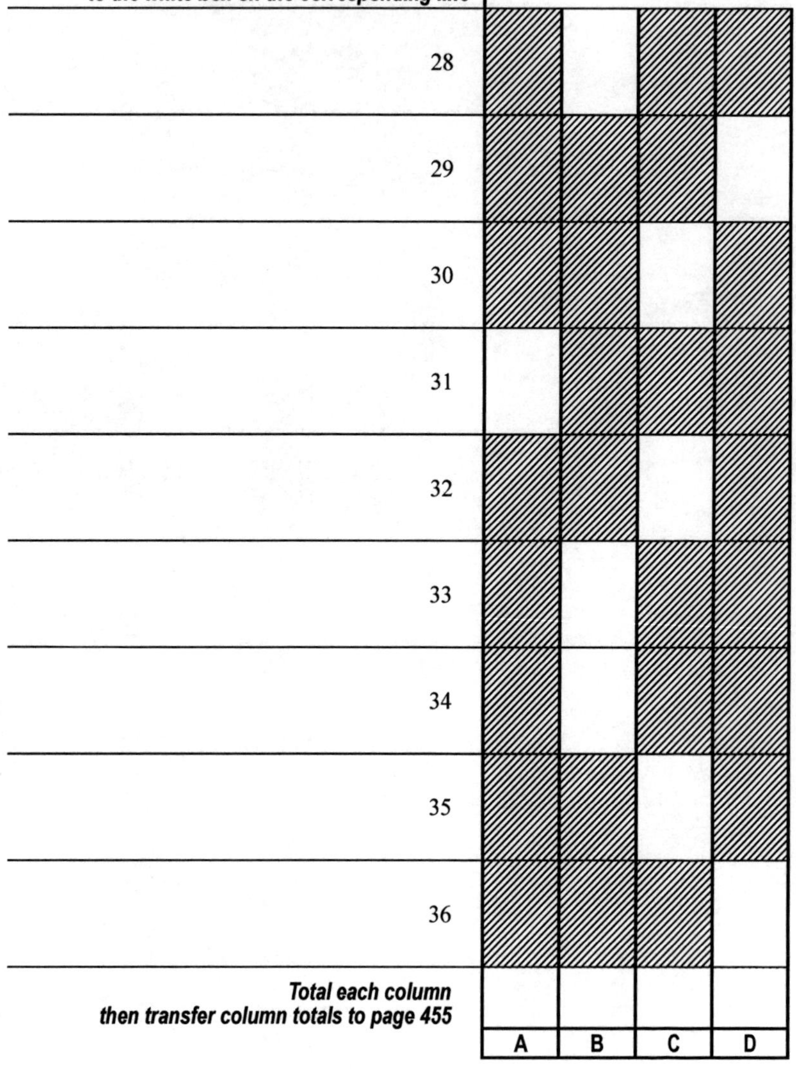

FOR SCORING USE ONLY:
Transfer the score for each item to the white box on the corresponding line

Item	A	B	C	D
28				
29				
30				
31				
32				
33				
34				
35				
36				
Total each column then transfer column totals to page 455				

Directions for graphing your score

Now that you have completed the FourSight® Thinking Profile, it's time to calculate your score. You can do this in 12 steps:

1. Use the two scoring keys at the bottom of pages 445, 447, 449, and 451 to score each of your responses. (*Note that the circled items use a different scoring key.*)

34 I enjoy using metaphors and analogies to come up with new ideas for problems.	OO	OO	OO	OO	OX	34 5
35 I have little patience for the effort it takes to refine or polish an idea.	XO	OO	OO	OO	OO	(35 5)
36 I tend to look for a quick solution and then fly with it.	OO	OO	OO	OX	OO	36 4
Scoring key for ___ :	1	2	3	4	5	
Scoring key for ◯:	5	4	3	2	1	

2. Fold page at the dotted line and transfer each score to the corresponding white box on that row of the scoring grid.

3. At the bottom of each scoring grid on pages 446, 448, 450, and 452, total the scores for each column.

Scoring Only ↓	R SCORING USE ONLY: the corresponding line				
28 5	28		5		
29 3	29				3
30 3	30			3	
31 4	31	4			
32 2	32			2	
(33 4)	33		4		
34 5	34		5		
(35 5)	35			5	
36 4	36				4
	Total each column / umn totals to page 455	4	14	10	7
		A	B	C	D

(*continued*)

4. Transfer your totals to the graph on page 455.

5. Add each column for a cumulative total for each preference.

6. Graph each of your four results in the appropriate column.

7. Draw a connector line between the dots.

8. Find your highest score and count down 5 — draw a horizontal line.

9. Find your lowest score and count up 5 — draw a horizontal line.*

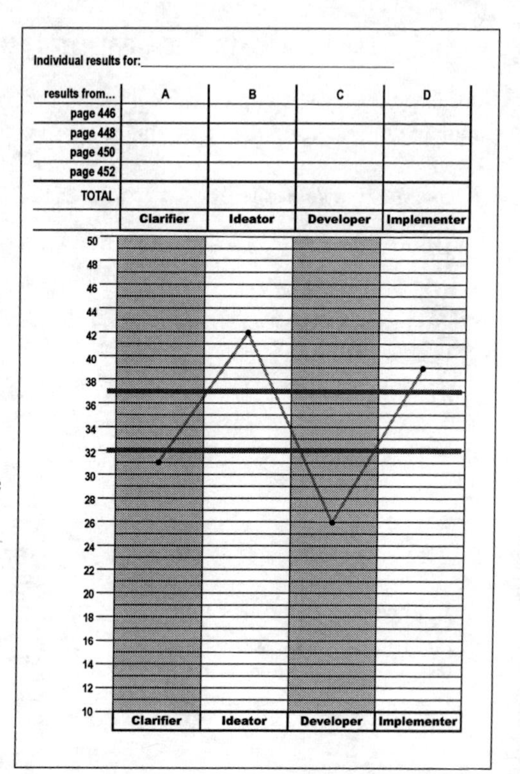

What are your preferences?

10. Anything above the highest line is a high preference for you.

11. Anything below the lowest line is a low preference for you.

12. Anything between the lines is a non-preference.

*If these lines end up on the same value, count up 3 and down 3 and redraw the lines.

Individual results for:______________________________

results from...	A	B	C	D
page 446				
page 448				
page 450				
page 452				
TOTAL				
	Clarifier	Ideator	Developer	Implementer

50				
48				
46				
44				
42				
40				
38				
36				
34				
32				
30				
28				
26				
24				
22				
20				
18				
16				
14				
12				
10	Clarifier	Ideator	Developer	Implementer

There are no “good” or “bad” scores

Each of these four preferences has its own strengths and potential weaknesses. The high points on your graph reflect the types of thinking you most prefer.

Preference is not ability

Preference does not guarantee ability, nor does lack of preference suggest lack of ability. Creative thinking skills can be learned. The brain, like a muscle, can be developed. Growing more aware of your own preferences may help you anticipate where you'll need additional tools or more practice and where you might be of assistance to others.

What are your preferences?

For each preference, write whether you scored HIGH, LOW, or have NP (no preference)

Clarify: ______________________________

Ideate: ______________________________

Develop: ______________________________

Implement: ______________________________

Learn more about it

Now read the descriptions about each preference on the following pages and learn how to improve your skills at every stage of the creative process.

The preferences at a glance

Clarifier-at-a-glance

Enjoys exploring challenges and opportunities

Likes to examine the details

Wants a clear understanding of the issue

Prefers a methodical approach to solving problems

May suffer from "analysis paralysis"

Ideator-at-a-glance

Likes to look at the big picture

Enjoys toying with ideas and possibilities

Likes to stretch his or her imagination

Enjoys thinking in more global and abstract terms

Takes an intuitive approach to innovation

May overlook details

Developer-at-a-glance

Enjoys putting together workable solutions

Likes to examine the pluses and minuses of an idea

Likes to compare competing solutions

Enjoys analyzing potential solutions

Enjoys planning the steps to implement an idea

May get stuck in developing the perfect solution

Implementer-at-a-glance

Likes to see things happen

Enjoys giving structure to ideas so they become a reality

Enjoys seeing ideas come to fruition

Likes to focus on "workable" ideas and solutions

Takes the Nike approach to innovation (i.e., "Just Do It")

May leap to action too quickly

The Integrator

While most people have high and low preferences, roughly 20 percent of FourSight® respondents take a very even approach to the breakthrough thinking process. These so-called integrators show no particular peaks or valleys. Integrators' energies stay rather steady as they work through the breakthrough thinking process. They can be very flexible team players, easily accommodating whatever the task requires. They may lose their voice in a group.

The four preferences

Clarifier

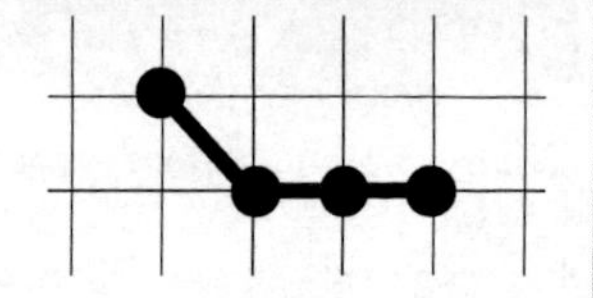

Clarifiers are...

Focused Methodical
Orderly Deliberate
Serious Organized

Give Clarifiers...

Order
The facts
An understanding of history
Access to information
Permission to ask questions

Clarifiers annoy others by...

Asking too many questions
Pointing out obstacles
Identifying areas that haven't been well thought out
Overloading people with information
Being too realistic

Clarifier in action

Albert Einstein was once asked, if some imminent disaster threatened the world and he had one hour to address the crisis, how would he spend his time. Einstein thought for a minute and then replied, "I would spend the first 55 minutes identifying the problem and the last five minutes solving it. For the formulation of a problem is often far more essential than its solution, which may be merely a matter of mathematical or experimental skill."

Ideator

Ideators are...

Playful
Social
Flexible
Independent
Imaginative
Adaptable
Adventurous

Give Ideators...

Room to be playful
Constant stimulation
Variety and change
The big picture

Ideators annoy others by...

Drawing attention to themselves
Being impatient when others don't get their ideas
Offering ideas that are too off-the-wall
Being too abstract
Not sticking to one idea

Ideator in action

Edwin Land was an ideator. Like all ideators, he had the big picture. In fact, he made a fortune off the big picture, because Edwin Land was the inventor of the Polaroid camera. The story goes that after taking photographs for a full day in 1943, Land's three-year-old daughter asked why she had to wait for the film to be processed. Land considered her question, and, after much experimentation, he came up with the Polaroid camera, which made photographs that developed almost instantly.

The four preferences

Developer

Developers are...

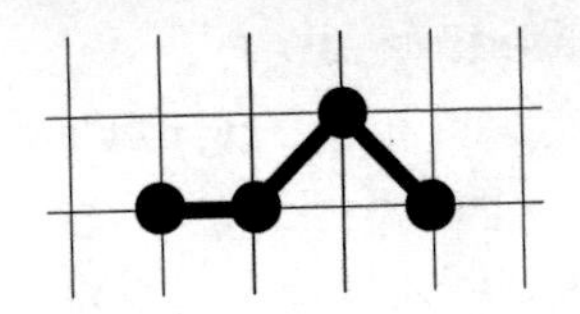

Reflective Cautious
Pragmatic Structured
Planful

Give Developers...

Time to consider the options
Time to evaluate
Time to develop ideas

Developers annoy others by...

Being too nit-picky
Finding flaws in others' ideas
Getting locked into one approach

Developer in action

Thomas Edison was not actually the first to invent the light bulb, but he routinely gets the credit. That's because Edison did all the testing and retesting necessary to discover the materials for making the optimal light bulb. Then he purchased all the patents related to its development. Edison and his team tested literally thousands of different materials to find the ones that would burn brightest and longest. In fact one story goes that after 1,000 attempts to discover the perfect light bulb, Edison was asked, "What does it feel like to be a failure so late in your career?" And Edison replied, "Young man, you know little of how the world works. Where you see failure after 1,000 trials, I see that we're that much closer to a solution."

Implementer

Implementers are...

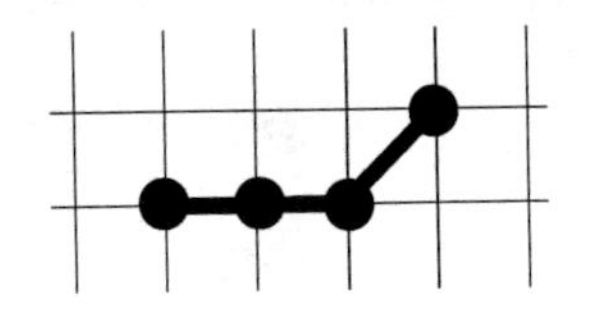

Persistent Decisive

Determined Assertive

Action-oriented

Give Implementers...

The sense that others are moving just as quickly

Control

Timely responses to their ideas

Implementers annoy others by...

Being too pushy

Readily expressing their frustration when others do not move as quickly

Overselling their ideas

Implementer in action

Alexander the Great, who brought nearly the entire known world under his rule before he died at age 32, may have been among history's greatest implementers. Like every other global aspirant in the 4th century BC, he knew the prophecy of the Gordion knot—that the person who could untangle it was fated to conquer the world. When one of his conquests actually brought him face to face with the cryptic knot, Alexander simply hefted his sword and cut it in two. You can almost imagine him looking up and saying, "Can we get on with the business of conquering the world now?"

Creating with others

FourSight has given you a look at your own strengths and potential pitfalls as a creative thinker. Now consider how you might collaborate more effectively with others. Then answer the questions on the following page to devise your individual plan.

Remember, when working with other preferences:

Give Clarifiers...

- Order
- The facts
- An understanding of history
- Access to information
- Permission to ask questions

Give Ideators...

- Room to be playful
- Constant stimulation
- Variety and change
- The big picture

Give Developers...

- Time to consider the options
- Time to evaluate
- Time to develop ideas

Give Implementers...

- The sense that others are moving just as quickly
- Control
- Timely responses to their ideas

Devise your individual plan

1 Who are the people you work with? What are their preferences?

2 Who do you find it easiest to collaborate with? Who do you find it most difficult to collaborate with? What factors are operating there?

3 What steps might you take to shore up your weakest preferences to become a more creative thinker? How might you better exploit your strongest preferences?

4 What do you need to keep in mind to make it easier for others to collaborate with you?

5 Who would be good to collaborate with on a project that called on your strengths? Who would be good to collaborate with on a project that leaned on your weak points?

6 With whom do you find it easiest to share your ideas? With whom do you have difficulty communicating? What strategies can you use to overcome that?

7 What do you need to keep in mind when managing others?

8 What are the preferences of the people you admire? What can you learn from them?

To learn more about creativity and FourSight, visit: foursightonline.com

Notes